Family Reunification in Europe

This book provides a multi-disciplinary investigation of family reunification laws, policies and practices across the European Union.

Family reunification – the possibility for family members to (re)unite in a country where one of them is residing – has been high on the political agenda. Building on original empirical research with families and practitioners as well as in-depth doctrinal analyses, the book explores the fragmentation of legal rules, the gaps between formal regulations and practices, and their consequences for families across borders. Different contributions in the volume point to the growing inequalities among and within applicant families, based on residence status, gender, location, citizenship and socio-economic resources, due to the family reunification regimes currently in place.The book enhances interdisciplinary dialogue by providing clear insights into the specific contribution of migration law, private international law and social scientific analyses to the study of family reunification.

The book is aimed at researchers working on the topic of family reunification, as well as students of law and socio-legal studies and practitioners in the field of migration.

Ellen Desmet is Associate Professor of Migration Law at the Faculty of Law and Criminology of Ghent University, where she founded the Migration Law Research Group (MigrLaw). Her research is situated at the intersection of migration law, human rights and legal anthropology, with a focus on asylum and family reunification. She serves as co-chair of the Human Rights Research Network, chair of the Belgian Refugee Council – NANSEN and board member of the Centre for the Social Study of Migration and Refugees (CESSMIR).

Milena Belloni is Assistant Professor in Migration and Global Mobility in the Department of Sociology at the University of Antwerp. Her research concerns migration dynamics in contexts of crisis, protracted displacement in Europe and in the Global South, refugee families and ethnographic methods. Her monographic study on the migration of Eritreans to Europe, *The Big Gamble*, is published (open access) by the University of California Press (2019).

Dirk Vanheule is full Professor of Law with the Government and Law Research Group at the University of Antwerp, where he is also a member of the MIGLOBA network on migration studies. His teaching and research interests include constitutional law and migration and asylum law. He is also advocate, called to the Ghent Bar, working in the field of administrative and constitutional litigation. He is editor of *Tijdschrift voor Vreemdelingenrecht* (Belgian Journal for Migration Law).

Jinske Verhellen is Professor of Private International Law at the Faculty of Law and Criminology of Ghent University. Her research focuses on international family law and its interaction with migration law. She is a member of the Ghent University Interfaculty Research Group CESSMIR (Centre for the Social Study of Migration and Refugees), the Ghent University Human Rights Research Network and the coordination team/editorial board of the CUREDI project (Cultural and Religious Diversity under State Law across Europe), coordinated by the Max Planck Institute for Social Anthropology.

Ayse Güdük is a doctoral candidate at the Migration Law Research Group (MigrLaw) at Ghent University. Her research interests concern family reunification, marriage migration and transnational families from a socio-legal perspective. She is currently finalising her doctorate on family reunification of Turkish migrants in Belgium, a study of lived experiences and legal consciousness.

Routledge Research in Asylum, Migration and Refugee Law

Available titles in this series include:

Unaccompanied Children in European Migration and Asylum Practices
In Whose Best Interests?
Edited by Mateja Sedmak, Birgit Sauer & Barbara Gornik

European Asylum Law and the Rights of the Child
Ciara Smyth

Asylum Law in the European Union
Francesco Cherubini

The Socio-Economic Rights of Asylum Seekers
Liam Thornton

Serious International Crimes, Human Rights, and Forced Migration
Edited by James C. Simeon

Migration Law, Policy and Human Rights
The Impact of Crisis in Europe
Rachael Dickson

Reconceptualizing Unaccompanied Child Asylum Seekers and the Law
Jennifer L. Whelan

Family Reunification in Europe
Exposing Inequalities
Edited by Ellen Desmet, Milena Belloni, Dirk Vanheule, Jinske Verhellen and Ayse Güdük

For more information about this series, please visit: www.routledge.com/Routledge-Research-in-Asylum-Migration-and-Refugee-Law/book-series/MIGRATION

Family Reunification in Europe

Exposing Inequalities

Edited by Ellen Desmet, Milena Belloni, Dirk Vanheule, Jinske Verhellen and Ayse Güdük

Routledge
Taylor & Francis Group
LONDON AND NEW YORK

First published 2025
by Routledge
4 Park Square, Milton Park, Abingdon, Oxon OX14 4RN

and by Routledge
605 Third Avenue, New York, NY 10158

Routledge is an imprint of the Taylor & Francis Group, an informa business

British Library Cataloguing-in-Publication Data
A catalogue record for this book is available from the British Library

Library of Congress Cataloging-in-Publication Data
Names: Desmet, Ellen, editor. | Belloni, Milena, 1985– editor. | Vanheule, Dirk, editor. | Verhellen, Jinske, editor. | Güdük, Ayse, editor.
Title: Family reunification in Europe : exposing inequalities / edited by Ellen Desmet, Milena Belloni, Dirk Vanheule, Jinske Verhellen, and Ayse Güdük.
Description: Abingdon, Oxon [UK] ; New York, NY : Routledge, 2025. | Series: Routledge research in asylum, migration, and refugee law | Includes bibliographical references and index.
Identifiers: LCCN 2024016970 (print) | LCCN 2024016971 (ebook) | ISBN 9781032614540 (hardback) | ISBN 9781032836447 (paperback) | ISBN 9781003503217 (ebook)
Subjects: LCSH: Family reunification—Law and legislation—European Union countries. | Emigration and immigration law—European Union countries. | Noncitizens—Family relationships—European Union countries.
Classification: LCC KJE6044 .F36 2024 (print) | LCC KJE6044 (ebook) | DDC 342.408/3—dc23/eng/20240416
LC record available at https://lccn.loc.gov/2024016970
LC ebook record available at https://lccn.loc.gov/2024016971

ISBN: 978-1-032-61454-0 (hbk)
ISBN: 978-1-032-83644-7 (pbk)
ISBN: 978-1-003-50321-7 (ebk)

DOI: 10.4324/9781003503217

For Product Safety Concerns and Information please contact our EU representative: GPSR@taylorandfrancis.com
Taylor & Francis Verlag GmbH,
Kaufingerstraße 24,
80331 München, Germany.

Contents

Contributors

Aleksandra Ancite-Jepifánova is an interdisciplinary scholar working in the field of European and comparative migration, asylum and nationality law and policies. She received her doctorate in law from Queen Mary University of London and has held fellowships, teaching positions and visiting appointments at various institutions, including LSE, Cardiff University, Forum Transregionale Studien, and VU Amsterdam. She is also a research affiliate with the Refugee Law Initiative, University of London. Her doctoral thesis examined the concept of marriages of convenience in EU and UK law in so far as it relates to the exercise of EU citizens' right to family reunion.

Sara Arapiles is a postdoctoral researcher at Lund University, where she works on the interdisciplinary project 'Refugee Finance: Histories, Frameworks and Practices (REF-FIN)'. Arapiles completed her doctorate at the University of Nottingham, which provides a normative and methodological sound framework for determining refugee status in slavery cases. She is also a research affiliate of the Refugee Law Initiative of the University of London and an associate tutor on their MA in Refugee Protection and Forced Migration Studies. She also serves as a member of the coordinating committee of the ESIL Interest Group on Migration and Refugee Law.

Leontine Bruijnen is a doctoral researcher and teaching assistant in private international law at the University of Antwerp under the supervision of Prof. Dr. Thalia Kruger and Prof. Dr. Marta Pertegás Sender. Her doctoral subject is the role of private international law in the recognition of kafala and child marriage for family and migration law purposes. Leontine also works for Ghent University on the FAMIMOVE project, which is co-funded by the European Commission. This project aims to contribute to the coordination between international family law and migration law.

Simone Christ is a social anthropologist. She is a senior researcher and head of the postgraduate programme at the German Institute of Development and Sustainability (IDOS). Her research interests focus on displacement, transnationalism and labour migration. She holds a doctorate in Southeast Asian Studies from the University of Bonn. Before joining IDOS, she worked at the Bonn International

Centre for Conflict Studies (BICC) and was responsible for the Germany case study in the TRAFIG project.

Laura Cleton is a postdoctoral researcher at Erasmus University Rotterdam, where she studies legitimacy deficits in the implementation of deportation policy across Europe. She has a keen interest in 'the politics of the family' in migration governance and has studied these both in the domains of deportation governance and family migration governance by relying on feminist theory. She acts as an associate editor of the *Journal of Ethnic and Migration Studies*, secretary of the Dutch Association for Migration Research, and is a board member of the IMISCOE Standing Committee on Gender and Sexuality in Migration Research.

Giselle Corradi is a legal anthropologist specialised in human rights. Her areas of expertise include legal pluralism, the relationship between law and culture, international cooperation and gender. In her work she adopts a 'law in action' perspective that enquires how differently situated actors' experiences with multiple registers of law relate to normative and social change. Since 2020, Giselle Corradi coordinates the Human Rights Research Network of Ghent University, an interdisciplinary research consortium aimed at societal impact.

Pascal Debruyne finished his doctoral thesis at the Department of Conflict and Development of Ghent University in 2013, where he focused on the spatial rearticulations of statehood, examining Jordan's geographies of power under globalization. He worked as a postdoctoral researcher at Ghent University, focusing on such themes as 'solidarity in superdiversity' and intra-European migration. Since 2019 he has worked at Odisee University for Applied Sciences, teaching courses on migration and superdiversity for social professionals. Debruyne's most recent research is on family reunification of refugee families, undocumented migrant families and (migrant) beggary in Brussels.

Betty de Hart is a Professor of Transnational Families and migration law at Vrije Universiteit Amsterdam. She conducts legal, empirical and historical research on the national, European and international rules that transnational families encounter, the views behind these rules as well as the impact on the everyday lives of transnational families. Family migration, citizenship, gender, racialisation and belonging are central issues in her research.

Francesco Della Puppa is a Professor in Sociology at the Department of Philosophy and Cultural Heritage of the Ca' Foscari University of Venice and a member of the master's programme on 'Immigration: Migratory Phenomena and Social Transformations' at the same university. He carries out research and teaching activities in the field of international migration and asylum, migrant family and family reunification, the social construction of gender and the transformations of masculinity in the migratory experience, the transformations of work, digital work and daily life and the Bangladeshi diaspora in Europe.

Sarah Den Haese obtained a bachelor's degree in social work and studied law at Ghent University. After her studies, she became a doctoral researcher under the supervision of Prof. Dr. Jinske Verhellen at the Institute for Private International Law at Ghent University. She successfully defended her doctoral research 'Crossing borders: proving your personal status. Interactions between private international law and human rights law' in 2021. She currently works as a legal expert in migration law and private international law for the Flemish Integration Agency (*Agentschap Integratie en Inburgering*).

Benjamin Etzold is a social geographer with more than 16 years of experience in studying people's vulnerability and livelihoods, trajectories of migration and displacement, as well as informal labour relations and patterns of food security. He holds a doctorate in geography from the University of Bonn. Benjamin works at the Bonn International Centre for Conflict Studies (BICC) in Germany and led the international and interdisciplinary EU-funded research project 'Transnational Figurations of Displacement' (TRAFIG) as scientific coordinator. The TRAFIG project looked into the role of mobility and trans-local connectivity for people in protracted displacement situations.

Kees Groenendijk is Emeritus Professor of Sociology of Law at Radboud University Nijmegen, founder and research fellow of its Centre for Migration Law and member of the Standing Committee of Experts on international immigration, refugee and criminal law (Meijers Committee). He publishes on the social and legal status of immigrants, EU migration law, anti-discrimination law, integration of immigrants and nationality law.

Ifigeneia Intzipeoglou is a lawyer, researcher and human rights defender. A member of the Athens Bar Association, she holds an LLB from Aristotle's University in Thessaloniki and an LLM from the London School of Economics and Political Science with a focus on International Law and Human Rights. She has six years of working experience in refugee law on a national and supranational level.

Hester Kroeze completed the Utrecht Law College Program and the Legal Research Master at Utrecht University. After her studies she obtained her doctoral degree at the Ghent European Law Institute at Ghent University, under the supervision of Prof. Dr. Peter Van Elsuwege. Following the completion of her dissertation, she moved back to the Netherlands, where she is currently working as an EU specialist at the Council of State in The Hague. She also continues to be an affiliated scholar to the Ghent European Law Institute.

Daniel Mekonnen is a Geneva-based independent consultant and a non-resident fellow of the African Studies Centre Leiden. Formerly, and among other things, he was a senior legal advisor and research professor at the International Law and Policy Institute (ILPI) in Norway. He serves as a member of the International Team of Legal Advisors for Cartoonists Rights Network International (CRNI), a project supported by UNESCO's Global Media Defence Fund. His most recent research projects focus on the developing norm of 'meaningful refugee participation', as introduced by the 2018 Global Compact on Refugees.

Laura Merla is a sociologist with a background in political science and a professor at the Catholic University of Louvain (Belgium), where she is the director of the Cirfase, an interdisciplinary research centre on families and sexualities. She is also a member of the Belgian Royal Academy of Sciences, Fine Arts and Humanities. Her research is currently focused on the transformation of family relationships in a context of mobility and geographical distance. Her work has been published in renowned journals and publishing houses in English, French, Spanish and Japanese.

Irene Olivero (doctorate in philosophy) is a post-doc at the University of Genoa. She has worked as a visiting researcher and instructor of ethics and bioethics courses at the University of Miami, as a lecturer of philosophy of language at the University of Padua, as a researcher at the University of Bonn and in Rio de Janeiro and as a post-doc at the Polytechnic University of Milan. She has published articles in philosophy of language, in the interconnection between semantics and metaphysics and in semantics and ethics for international blind-reviewed journals. Her research interest is expanding to the ethics of migration and adoption.

Giacomo Orsini concluded his doctoral studies at the Department of Sociology of the University of Essex in 2016. Before joining Ghent University in 2020, he worked as postdoctoral researcher both at Essex and the Université Catholique de Louvain. Since 2015, he also teaches courses on migration, race, ethnicity and the politics of diversity at the Université libre de Bruxelles. Orsini's most recent research is concerned with refugee families' everyday experiences of administrative and legal complexity, and with exploring unaccompanied minors' migration into Europe and the structural violence they face along their trajectories.

Maria Nefeli Skotori is a researcher in international law and arbitration. She holds a Bachelor of Laws from the London School of Economics and Political Science (2020), and an Advanced Master of Laws in International Dispute Settlement and Arbitration from Universiteit Leiden (2023). Her research focuses on interdisciplinary and critical perspectives with an emphasis on oral histories and empirical approaches.

Nicole Štýbnarová is an Assistant Professor of International Law at Leiden University (Faculty of Global Governance and Affairs). Previously she was a lecturer in international law and forced migration at the University of Oxford (Refugee Studies Centre). Her doctorate from the University of Helsinki addressed family reunifications in the analytical frameworks of law and feminist-Marxist social theories. She also published multiple articles addressing migration law and political economy. In her current research, she focuses on international law and women's social movements.

Gert Verschraegen is a Professor of Sociology at the University of Antwerp. He has published widely in the domains of ethnic and migration studies, social theory and sociology. His current research is engaged with the transformations of citizenship and belonging in global society. Recent book publications are *Divercities. Understanding superdiversity in deprived and mixed neighbourhoods* (2019, with Stijn Oosterlynck) and the *Elgar Encyclopedia of Global Social Theory* (2024, with Raf Vanderstraeten).

Acknowledgements

This book partially results from project G048018N of the Research Foundation – Flanders (FWO).

1 Exploring inequalities in family reunification in Europe

Perspectives from legal and social sciences

Ellen Desmet, Milena Belloni, and Jinske Verhellen[1]

1. Introduction

Family reunification can be defined as the regulations concerning entry and residence in a country of the family members of a person who resides lawfully in that state.[2] These rules, which aim to create or preserve the family unit, partially reflect the fundamental right to respect for family life in a migratory context. While this definition highlights that family reunification is primarily a legal issue, it does not convey the complexity of administrative procedures, political discourses, family practices and existential experiences that surround and shape this legal process. All these aspects, however, we argue, are crucial to understand family reunification in today's European Union (EU). Legal requirements to prove family ties are combined with administrative hurdles to certify one's own identity. The decision-making of immigration officers is embedded in dominant discourses on security and borders. Families' attempts to reunite are shaped by their awareness of legal possibilities on the ground. Unequal capabilities to enjoy family life are thus determined not only by the interaction of different bodies of law but also by multiple social and political practices. This book seeks to explore the legal, social and socio-legal entanglements that produce and reproduce inequalities in family reunification policies and practices.

Building on insights mainly from migration law, private international law and social sciences, this book advances the debate on how current family reunification regimes in Europe shape and reinforce inequalities within and across families, based on their residence status, nationality, location, socio-economic resources, age, gender and type of family relationship. Inequalities are an omnipresent subject of our work, but social scientists and legal scholars have, in practice, different

1 We thank Robin Vandevoordt and Dirk Vanheule for their valuable comments on earlier versions of this introduction.

2 In sociological studies, family reunification migration is usually distinguished from family formation migration, the latter referring to the mobility to form a new family, through marriage or a registered partnership. From a legal perspective, however, the Family Reunification Directive explicitly regulates both forms of migration under the umbrella term of 'family reunification'. This is why family reunification in this book comprises the two forms of migration and respective sets of rules.

DOI: 10.4324/9781003503217-1

concerns and definitions when it comes to inequalities. This is why this introduction foregrounds some key notions on inequalities and how they can be combined to study family reunification.

After a brief recognition of the political context and academic debate on family reunification, this introduction analyses the meaning of inequalities, drawing on the most relevant sociological theories and legal debates on the topic. In particular, we focus on how intersectionality theory and the principle of non-discrimination and equality can be combined to analyse three sources of inequalities among and within families: those concerning access to family reunification rights; those related to proving one's personal status and family ties; and those emerging from the implementation of laws and policies on the ground. We then present some cross-cutting themes of the book (documents, refugees and children) as well as its specific structure and content. We conclude by suggesting a threefold strategy for future research: following the laws, following the documents, and following the people. We argue that inequalities inherent and resulting from family reunification legislation should be systematically analysed from a multidisciplinary perspective, and that such research should move towards interdisciplinarity, conceived as real integration of insights.

2. Why a book on family reunification?

The urgent need to analyse regulations and practices of family reunification becomes evident when reading the daily news and following political debates. Who should have the possibility to be joined by their family? Which and how many family members should be allowed to enter? Are migrant families representing a burden to the welfare state? These questions are repeatedly asked by journalists and politicians. Family reunification is thus presented as a problem of 'unwanted migration', which governments should regulate. In the last decade, an increasing number of countries across the European Union have imposed more stringent regulations on families (Ahlén, 2024); governments have even fallen while discussing whether to set more restrictive requirements for reunification.

The dynamics behind this political discourse are multifaceted. First, migration has been systematically framed as a security problem (Karyotis, 2007; Huysmans & Squire, 2009; Buonfino, 2004): states are keen to control their borders and to ensure that persons posing threats to national security, such as terrorists and criminals, are identified and stopped. Not only asylum seekers and irregular migrants but also family migrants are frequently framed, within this securitised discourse, as fraudulent applicants, victims or perpetrators of forced marriages (Bonjour & de Hart, 2013; Heinemann et al., 2016; Vandenbroucke, 2020). Second, concerns about the loss of national cultural and religious and racial identity (Adamson et al., 2011; Burgess & Gutwirth, 2011) have been growing in Europe, fuelled by nationalist politics (Thorleifsson, 2017; Jaskulowski, 2019; Paterson & Karyotis, 2022). This has led to specific political attention to 'ethnic and racially diverse' families who are perceived as a threat to the preservation of the European identity. Third, specifically for family migrants, it is assumed – yet highly debatable – that they contribute less to national economies and that their presence will lead to more problems for the welfare state and educational systems (Bonjour & Duyvendak, 2020). As a consequence of this cocktail of security, cultural and economic considerations, family reunification has increasingly become the target of restrictive state regulations and policies.

These regulations and the challenges they pose to transnational, mixed and religiously and culturally diverse families have been the object of a significant number of studies in the last decade. Many of these studies have at least partially succeeded in addressing 'the absence of law in the study of transnational families' and 'the absence of families in the study of law', as Betty de Hart and colleagues (2013) put it. In the field of migration law, comparative studies have analysed family reunification laws and policies in selected countries (EMN, 2016; Friedery et al., 2018; Strik et al., 2013), with an additional focus on how these rules impact the 'integration' of both the sponsor and their family members in the host country (Strik et al., 2013). From a human rights perspective, Klaassen (2015) investigated whether a human right to family reunification exists in international and European law and in selected national jurisdictions, while Wray (2023) studied UK Supreme Court decisions on family life and immigration in the light of Article 8 of the European Convention on Human Rights (ECHR). Within EU law, Berneri (2017) disentangled the historical development of the rules on family reunification of third-country nationals with EU citizens. From a predominantly sociological perspective, Heinemann and colleagues (2015) have focused on the practice of DNA testing in family reunification procedures and how it affects migrant families. More recently, Tiilikainen and colleagues (2023) have examined the challenges of family reunification in the context of forced migration, reviewing different state legal frameworks as well as the experiences of separated refugee families.

Although these studies have greatly expanded our understanding of the historical, legal and social ramifications of the procedures in place, there have been limited attempts to systematically study, by combining the approaches of different disciplines, how family reunification policies and practices create and reproduce legal and social inequalities between migrants and citizens, among migrants and among citizens. This is precisely the gap that our book aims to address.

This book thus starts from the observation that family reunification is a complex legal and social issue that needs to be investigated in its many dimensions. First of all, family reunification is an intricate legal topic, as relevant rules are 'scattered' across various fields of law. These include migration law on conditions and procedures; private international law on the recognition in the host country of family relationships established abroad; family law on the exercise of family life; human rights law on the fundamental right to respect for family life; and social welfare law on the access to family welfare benefits. From a socio-legal perspective, family reunification is an interesting field when seeking to understand how historical and social norms shape regulations and laws, the role of discretion in the work of street-level bureaucrats and legal officials, and the ways transnational families navigate the law, its opportunities and its constraints (de Hart et al., 2013). Family reunification is also a material and techno-social process made up of paperwork, documentation practices and identification procedures (Geoffrion & Cretton, 2021; Horton & Heyman, 2020).[3]

3 As a consequence, family reunification is studied by scholars with different profiles: scholars of legal doctrine, socio-legal scholars (who may have a primary background in law and/or certain social sciences, such as legal sociologists or legal anthropologists), and social and political scientists more broadly. This 'categorisation' of scholarly profiles may come across as artificial. For many scholars,

To better grasp the legal, practical and social implications of these sets of regulations and practices, this book innovatively combines mainly three perspectives: migration law, private international law – both considering the human rights dimension – and social sciences. This is also where the story of this book began: when three PhD researchers at the law faculty of Ghent University (Belgium) observed that they were all studying family reunification, yet from different angles. From an EU law perspective, Hester Kroeze was unravelling the rules on family reunification with EU citizens (Kroeze, 2021; Kroeze, this volume). From a private international law and human rights perspective, Sarah den Haese was analysing the cross-border recognition of personal status, focusing on the proof of family ties in reunification proceedings as a case study (Den Haese, 2023; Den Haese & Verhellen, this volume). From a socio-legal approach, Ayse Güdük was researching how experiences with and perceptions of family reunification rules shaped the legal consciousness of Turkish migrants (Güdük & Desmet, 2022). They were joined by Milena Belloni, conducting postdoctoral research on refugee families attempting to reunite, based on multi-sited ethnography (Belloni & Verschraegen, this volume). Triggered by their distinct approaches to the same topic, they launched the idea of organising an event in which these different fields could meet on a larger scale.

And so it happened that, on 9 and 10 September 2021, the international conference '(Dis)connecting people? The law and practice of family reunification' took place in Ghent, jointly organised by the universities of Antwerp and Ghent. The main aim of the conference was to create a platform for knowledge exchange on family reunification across the legal and social sciences. The conference targeted not only academics, but also policy makers and practitioners, in order to build bridges between these different professional groups, all engaged with the challenges of reunifying families across borders. This volume aims to represent this plurality of disciplinary perspectives, professional backgrounds and views, to mirror the complexity of family reunification, not only as a legal issue, but also as a family concern, and a topic of political and societal debates. Before presenting the structure and content of the book, the next section reflects on the meaning of studying inequalities across disciplinary borders.

3. The meaning of inequalities: at the crossroads of law and social sciences

Unequal access to opportunities and resources for different social groups, and the way this is reproduced across time and space, is probably the most important and defining theme of the social sciences. From a social science perspective, legal provisions have historically been one of the main sources of inequalities, as individuals

self-identification with one particular (sub)discipline or field has become increasingly uncomfortable and unfeasible, as they draw on concepts and theories from various disciplines – the boundaries of which are also becoming more fluid and grey. On the other hand, distinct approaches are still there, and luckily so, because they all enhance our understanding of the multifaceted phenomenon of family reunification.

have systematically been excluded from specific activities, such as voting, owning property and studying, based on gender, class, race, etc. (cf. Seron & Munger, 1996). Law instead looks at inequalities from a somewhat different angle. On the one hand, it is one of the basic functions of law to devise categorisations and assign different rights and obligations to these categories of people – a function of which migration law is particularly illustrative. On the other, a fundamental principle in law is that of equality and non-discrimination, meaning that persons or groups in a comparable situation should not be treated less favourably because of certain personal characteristics. Studying inequalities at the crossroads between social sciences and legal studies thus means addressing multiple meanings of inequalities and the different factors producing them.

In particular, the notion of intersectionality is key to understanding how class, race, gender, age and legal status interact to reinforce the exclusion of certain individuals. This notion emerged in the 1970s, originally in the legal sciences, to make sense of the experience and the disadvantage of black women in the US context (Crenshaw, 1989). The concept has been widely applied ever since across social sciences to analyse how different systems of inequality – defined as the unequal distribution of resources and life chances, which includes the possibility to live with one's family – overlap to produce advantage and disadvantage for certain individuals and groups based on their position within and across structures. Race, gender and class are defined as 'axes of differences' (Amelina & Horvath, 2020). They are forms of social categorisation interwoven with social inequalities and associated with institutional and legal categorisations that may reduce or reinforce inequality. Studying family reunification across law and social sciences through an intersectional lens thus means to systematically disentangle how different forms of social and legal categorisation produce and reproduce differential access to the possibility of families to be together.

Overall, we identify three sources of differences in treatment and inequalities within family reunification policies and realities that need to be addressed intersectionally. A first source relates to whether a person, according to the law in the books, has a right to family reunification – meaning that family reunification has to be granted when the conditions are fulfilled. An overall constraint is the restricted definition of family members entitled to reunification, which is generally limited to the nuclear family (Saroléa & Merla, 2021). Moreover, the right to family reunification is variably regulated and stratified based on – among others – residence status, nationality, class and gender, creating a stratified form of citizenship that has become the prevalent form of citizenship in Europe (Morris, 2003; Kofman, 2002). In the European courtroom, however, such differences in treatment have until now rarely led to judgements finding a family reunification rule to amount to discrimination.[4] Overall, restraining factors are the importance attached in migration law to

4 For an exception, see ECtHR, 24 May 2016, *Biao v. Denmark* [GC], No. 38590/10 (relating, however, to discrimination between two categories of Danish nationals, depending on when nationality was acquired).

the principle of state sovereignty, and the broad discretion given by the European Court of Human Rights (ECtHR) to states when striking a balance between the interests of states in migration management and the interests of the families concerned (Dembour, 2015). This is evident from the way in which the 'right to respect for family life', as mentioned in various human rights treaties, has been interpreted. Courts, including the ECtHR, have on several occasions established that the right of families to be together does not imply that families can choose their place of residence.[5] This means that there is no general 'human right' to family reunification.

Moreover, not all groups are considered to be in a comparable situation – a prerequisite for identifying a violation of the principle of non-discrimination. Third-country nationals, for instance, are not seen as being in a comparable situation to EU citizens.[6] In addition, family reunification law (and migration law in general) has moved away from differences in treatment based on grounds that are explicitly prohibited in human rights treaties (such as ethnic origin or gender), as such potential 'direct' discrimination leads to a high level of judicial scrutiny. Rather, distinctions in migration law are increasingly based on meritocratic criteria (such as class and education) – which are seemingly 'neutral' and entail lesser scrutiny (Farcy, 2020). Examples include the socio-economic criteria, such as income requirements, imposed in family reunification regimes and the more lenient rules for the highly skilled. Scholars have argued that this use of meritocratic criteria may amount to indirect discrimination, since they in practice link back to prohibited grounds of discrimination such as gender (Farcy, 2020; Spijkerboer, 2018). For instance, due to the gender pay gap, women will have fewer possibilities to comply with resource requirements in family reunification, and consequently will have less easy access to the 'global mobility infrastructure' (Spijkerboer, 2018).

The second source of inequalities identified in this volume relates to proving one's personal status and family ties. The capability to prove identity and kinship with others (e.g., acquisition, translation and legalisation of documents) is highly dependent on the legal and bureaucratic context that transnational families inhabit. Some countries of origin have had no functioning registries for years and are unable to provide certification that will be recognised internationally (Szreter & Beckenridge, 2012). Others are unwilling to register and certify certain segments of the population for political reasons (Lawrance & Stevens, 2017). Similar considerations often apply to transit countries where migrants apply for asylum or reside while waiting to be reunited with their families. The legal framework of countries of destination does not sufficiently acknowledge these issues (Belloni & Verschraegen, this volume). This is why people coming from fragile, war-torn countries or living in exile are structurally exposed to difficulties in meeting the legal requirements for family reunification and often end up being separated for years.

5 See, e.g., ECtHR, 24 April 1985, *Abdulaziz, Cabales and Balkandali v. The United Kingdom*, Nos 9214/80, 9473/81, 9474/81.

6 CJEU, 2 September 2021, C-930/19, *X.*, ECLI:EU:C:2021:657. Similarly, in some European countries, 'mobile' EU citizens, who made use of their freedom of movement, on the one hand, and 'static' citizens, on the other, are not considered comparable groups. See Corradi and Desmet (this volume).

The final source of inequality is related to the implementation of laws and policies on the ground. Families, depending on their nationalities, the different legal status of their members and socio-demographic characteristics, are confronted with multiple practical barriers concerning the costs of certificates to be provided, the accessibility of embassies and the widespread culture of suspicion (Jubany, 2017) among migration officials responsible for processing and assessing applications. In this context, several chapters illustrate *a shift from legal to bureaucratic governance of family reunification.* Even though the main purpose of the EU legal framework on family reunification is to reunite families across borders,[7] in practice, issues that should be rights-based are managed in administrative encounters where families have limited possibilities to appeal against a decision or to contest its fairness. The troublesome paperwork migrant families have to complete in order to be reunited often leads to situations of *de facto* rightlessness. Inequalities enshrined in the law are thus amplified by differences in the functioning of state bureaucracies. In this sense, an *enhanced* intersectional perspective seems important, as inequalities tied to identity characteristics or meritocratic factors may be exacerbated by divergences in the functioning of bureaucratic systems and the discretion applied by street-level bureaucrats. As Farcy (2020) argues, an additional impediment to judicial findings of violations of the principle of non-discrimination in the context of migration law is that courts always assess a particular measure, without taking the broader, restrictive policy environment into account. He singles out the topic of family reunification to illustrate his broader argument:

> For example, in many destination countries family reunification is increasingly under strain, despite being depicted as an individual right. Ever increasing obstacles to the enjoyment of that right include, among others, higher administrative fees, a compulsory (and costly) DNA test in certain cases, higher income requirements, the introduction of a waiting period for certain categories of immigrants and integration requirements before or after arrival. Although each measure could possibly be justified on its own, the same can hardly be said if they are taken all together.
>
> (Farcy, 2020, p. 18)

Within a broader turn in migration studies to analyse migration law from a non-discrimination perspective (see, e.g., Den Heijer, 2018; Spijkerboer, 2018), this book thus contributes to a deeper understanding and critical analysis of inequalities between and within family reunification regimes, leading to pressing questions as to whether these can stand the test of non-discrimination (see, in particular, Groenendijk, this volume; de Hart, this volume).

7 For instance, the CJEU has repeatedly held that the Family Reunification Directive is intended to promote family reunification and to grant protection to third-country nationals, in particular children. See, e.g., CJEU, 4 March 2010, C-578/08, *Chakroun*, ECLI:EU:C:2010:117, § 43; CJEU, 6 December 2012, C-356/11 and C-357/11, *O., S. and L*, EU:C:2012:776, § 69; CJEU, 13 March 2019, C-635/17, *E.*, EU:C:2019:192, § 45.

4. Documents, refugees and children: some cross-cutting themes

By working at the intersection of different fields of law and sociological approaches, the book specifically focuses on three overlooked and/or emerging issues in the debates on family reunification: the importance of documents; the growing attention to refugees and beneficiaries of subsidiary protection in the political and legal debate; and the impact on children.

A first remarkable development is the growing academic focus on *documents*, required in family reunification procedures to prove, for instance, one's identity. Traditionally mainly studied by private international law scholars (Den Haese & Verhellen, this volume; Bruijnen, this volume) and often overlooked or ignored by actors in the field of migration law, this book exemplifies an increased engagement with this topic by social scientists. They analyse the challenges linked to submitting the necessary paperwork and thus the importance of 'administrative citizenship', as defined by Belloni and Verschraegen (this volume, see also Arapiles & Mekonnen, this volume; Debruyne, this volume).

Second, the volume highlights the particular challenges faced by *refugees and beneficiaries of subsidiary protection* seeking to be joined by their family in Europe. Legally, these persons are recognised as unable to develop their family life in their countries of origin, as they have a well-founded fear of persecution or face a real risk of serious harm upon return. However, there is little legal and political recognition of the difficulties that families of these persons may face when attempting to reunite. In fact, many families remain in limbo for years, often waiting in a transit country to be reunited with the sponsor who has managed to reach Europe. Various contributions demonstrate the substantial legal, administrative and practical challenges these persons face in family reunification proceedings, despite the more lenient rules included in the Family Reunification Directive for refugees (Christ & Etzold, this volume; Arapiles & Mekonnen, this volume; Belloni & Verschraegen, this volume; Debruyne, this volume).

Third, the book exposes persisting inequalities for and between *children*. These relate, for instance, to unequal treatment between accompanied and unaccompanied refugee children, and between children of families with DNA connections and children of families with social and legal ties (Olivero, this volume). Moreover, migrants from countries whose documents are considered unreliable are today facing systematic suspicion of fraud in Europe. This has an impact on children as well, for instance in cases where marriages involving children are designated as marriages of convenience and where authorities and judges ignore the principle of the best interests of the child (Ancite-Jepifánova, this volume). From a children's rights perspective, the current family reunification framework is challenged when faced with family institutions unfamiliar to European states, such as the Islamic concept of kafala (Den Haese & Verhellen, this volume) or child marriages concluded abroad (Bruijnen, this volume). Even though the courts in Luxembourg and Strasbourg have increasingly paid attention to the detrimental impact of family reunification rules on children (Desmet, this volume; Den Haese & Verhellen, this volume), it is crucial to keep examining these issues from an integrated perspective that includes legal as well as sociological and social work approaches.

Besides its analysis of these three core themes, the book is distinctive because it includes analyses and perspectives from *practitioners and family migrants* themselves, both directly and indirectly. Directly, because some of the authors can build on their relevant work experience in international or non-governmental organisations (Intzipeoglou & Nefeli Skotori, this volume) or have gone through the process themselves (Corradi & Desmet, this volume). These perspectives are also included indirectly, because various contributions are based on empirical research including interviews and/or ethnographic work with experts (Arapiles & Mekonnen, this volume), practitioners and migrants (Debruyne, this volume; Orsini & Merla, this volume; Belloni & Verschraegen, this volume). This bottom-up perspective enables the authors to unveil contradictions and messy realities on the ground. For instance, on the one hand, family reunification applications are often filtered by governmental actors aiming to protect the Western value of gender equality – thus excluding couple configurations that would endanger that value. On the other hand, the implementation of regulations often reproduces inequality and dependency in itself, at times leading to violence within couples (Orsini & Merla, this volume).

This book analyses family reunification in the European Union. This geographic focus reflects a common regulatory framework adopted at the EU level and through the jurisprudence of the Court of Justice of the European Union (CJEU) and the ECtHR. These rules substantially shape how different European countries implement family reunification in practice, in spite of some variance. While being firmly rooted in Europe, authors throughout the book argue for the importance of considering family reunification through a transnational lens. Case law studies reveal how courts and administrations in Europe are confronted with a diversity of family relationships established abroad (Bruijnen, this volume; Den Haese & Verhellen, this volume). The studies focusing on the experience of families (Christ & Etzold, this volume), social workers (Debruyne, this volume) and the material aspect of the administrative demarches in place (Belloni & Verschraegen, this volume) highlight that, by its very nature, family reunification spans borders and cannot be properly accounted for without considering realities beyond Europe.

5. A guided tour of the chapters

Setting the scene

The contributions in this book study family reunification from the perspective of various disciplines. Yet, each field has its own vocabulary and approach, and it is not always straightforward to engage with fields one is less familiar with. To enhance future dialogue and collaboration, the book therefore kicks off with three chapters that explain key concepts and sketch the contours of their domain. These chapters, each (co-)written by an editor of this volume, offer a beginner's introduction to three main fields that intersect in family reunification policies and realities: migration law, private international law and social sciences.

In the first chapter, *Desmet* provides an overview of the fragmented legal frameworks governing family reunification in Europe. At the level of the European

Union, the two main legal instruments – the Citizens Directive (on reunification with Union citizens who made use of their freedom of movement) and the Family Reunification Directive (on reunification with third-country nationals) – are supplemented with specific rules for particular categories. The chapter also briefly discusses relevant norms adopted by the United Nations and the Council of Europe.

In the second chapter, *Den Haese and Verhellen* link family reunification procedures to the field of private international law. Private international law rules determine whether a family relationship established in State A has legal consequences in State B. The authors provide an overview of the multitude of rules and case law on the cross-border recognition of documents concerning migrants' personal status (e.g. name, age, marriage, filiation), which is a prerequisite for family reunification.

In the third chapter, *Belloni and Cleton* provide a genealogy of the study of family reunification in the social sciences. They guide the reader among the most important theoretical debates that have inspired scholars' understanding of the way family reunification is categorised, managed and experienced by different configurations of social actors, such as migrants, citizens, social workers, NGOs, street-level bureaucrats and policy makers.

Unveiling inequalities

Part II of the book delves deeper into how inequalities are shaped and produced by family reunification regulations. *Groenendijk* first looks back, giving a historical overview of the development of family reunification rules. Analysing the current fragmentation of family reunification policies, as well as available empirical evidence on their effects on (in)equality, he also looks forward and suggests that various features of family reunification rules seem to violate the fundamental legal principles of equality and non-discrimination.

Whereas Groenendijk adopts a doctrinal legal perspective, *de Hart* arrives at a similar conclusion through a socio-legal analysis of the racialised, gendered and colonial roots and consequences of family migration policies. She calls upon legal scholars to take up this intersectional perspective on family reunification and to think through its legal consequences, as she starts to do.

Adopting a metalegal perspective, *Olivero* concludes that the diverging rules on family reunification for different categories of children cannot be justified from an ethical point of view and lead to an ethically unjustified treatment of some categories of refugee children. Children accompanied by non-biological parents are paying the highest price.

The following parts of the book further analyse three main sources of inequalities created and reproduced in family reunification regimes. They relate to accessing family reunification rights, proving one's personal status and family ties, and implementing laws and policies in practice.

Accessing family reunification

Both legal and sociological analyses demonstrate that accessing family reunification rights has become increasingly difficult. This is even the case for the more privileged category of EU citizens who made use of their free movement rights and therefore benefit from more lenient family reunification rules. In her chapter, *Kroeze* analyses the conditions that EU citizens and their family members must fulfil to maintain such family reunification rights upon return of the EU citizen to their home state and compares these with the requirements that an EU citizen must fulfil to complete an expulsion order. As these conditions are developed through subsequent and often complex cases of the CJEU, knowing the circumstances under which family reunification rights are maintained becomes a complicated and continuously evolving enterprise.

Štýbnarová untangles another legal knot in the rules on family reunification with EU citizens, relating to the so-called relationship triangle: can a third-country national qualify for a derived residence right as a durable partner of an EU citizen if they are formally married to another person? Based on an analysis of the relevant case law of the ECtHR and the CJEU and a review of cases in the UK and Czechia, she argues for a substance-oriented (focusing on the length of cohabitation and the intention to live together) rather than a formal (the impediment of ongoing marriage) approach.

Other categories of migrants, such as applicants for international protection, do not have family reunification rights. Yet the Dublin III Regulation contains a 'humanitarian clause', giving states the discretionary competence to reunify families based on cultural and humanitarian considerations. *Intzipeoglou and Nefeli Skotori* show how states apply this clause very reluctantly, and they relate this to the upholding of occidental cultural values on family and familial dependency.

Finally, *Della Puppa* provides a sociological and historical analysis of family reunification policies in Italy, showing how the Italian legal framework functions as a 'double device'. It demarcates which family members are included in the concept of family, on the one hand, and how the migrant family should contribute to the economy of the country of destination on the other. Della Puppa shows how expectations for family reunification and economic contributions differ for male and female migrants. While being accompanied by one's family is positively seen as a sign of integration for male migrants, the figure of the lone migrant is ideal for female migrants mostly employed in the care sector.

The first two contributions in this section emphasise the key relevance of case law to grasp the actually applicable rules on family reunification. Compounded by the already fragmented and complex nature of the legislation itself, the consequence of this is that legal knowledge, 'legal literacy' and/or adequate socio-legal support become important – and often necessary yet lacking – resources to actually access and enjoy family reunification rights. The latter two chapters reveal the cultural and ideological notions shaping family reunification laws and policies. In light of this complexity, the image of a labyrinth well describes the experience of families and practitioners who need to find their way through the myriad of regulations and practices on family reunification, as well as the experience of scholars trying to make sense of this phenomenon.

Proving family ties

Proving family ties has become an increasingly significant obstacle in family reunification procedures. This evidence obstacle may be a practical or administrative one, but it may also be due to the unfamiliarity with certain family ties established in a country outside the European Union.

Arapiles and Mekonnen examine the practical challenges Eritrean refugees face in their pursuit of family reunification, due to the absence of a well-functioning documentation system in Eritrea. They argue that the right to family reunification becomes unattainable for many Eritrean refugees, unless 'other' evidentiary standards are considered to establish the existence of a family relationship, when documentary evidence is lacking.

Belloni and Verschraegen also draw on empirical research with Eritrean and Somali refugee families living between Belgium, Italy and Ethiopia to argue that the family reunification process cannot be understood unless the capability of both migrants and their state of origin to produce documentary evidence of identity are taken into account. Refugees and their family members are confronted with 'the requirement to perform administrative citizenship' and are often trapped in administrative limbo.

Next to these administrative challenges, another private international law issue that may arise in a family reunification context concerns the confrontation with 'unknown' or 'foreign' legal institutes or concepts. In this regard, *Bruijnen* compares the legal frameworks on child and polygamous marriages in Belgian private international law and in the Family Reunification Directive, discussing the role of public policy in relation to the best interests of the child.

Even if evidence of a family relationship established abroad is presented, there is no guarantee that authorities in EU Member States will 'believe' that there is such a family tie. The fight against marriages of convenience, for instance, is high on the political agenda. *Ancite-Jepifánova* compares the interpretation of the concept of marriages of convenience at the EU level and in the UK. She argues that British marriage control practices target a much broader group of couples than those whose circumstances fit the definition of a marriage of convenience under the Citizens Directive and concludes that such measures may lead to the disruption of families of EU citizens in the UK, a situation she expects to further deteriorate after Brexit.

Navigating regimes

The last section of our volume provides diverse accounts of families' experiences of waiting for, being rejected, and succeeding with their reunification application. Drawing on sociological concepts, legal and social work debates, the authors illustrate how families 'navigate' legal and policy requirements surrounding family reunification. We refer here to the concept of social navigation as elaborated by Vigh: 'Due to the intersection of the multiple factors constituting it, our social environment is always emergent and unfolding, in consequence requiring of the agent the capacity to "adapt" and "read" "capricious environments"' (Vigh, 2009, p. 425). Navigation thus designates the capacity of people to interpret and react to shifting and unpredictable circumstances – in our case, the shifting legal requirements, the geo-political scenarios across which migration takes place as well as the changing family configurations across time.

Focusing on the case of Syrian and Eritrean refugees in Germany, *Christ and Etzold* illustrate how family life continues and stretches across borders in spite of long-term separation. Using a transnational lens, the authors identify three different types of refugee family configurations and analyse how these families respond to increasingly strict policy requirements.

Debruyne investigates the experiences of social workers as they try to make sense of the multi-layered regulations deriving from the interaction of the different levels of governance that regulate family reunification in Belgium. He uses the concept of 'welfare bricolage' to describe the complexity of provisions in which practitioners' and migrants' strategies are embedded.

Corradi and Desmet take a self-ethnographic approach to explore how a sudden change of policy in Belgium affected the possibility of one of the authors to be joined by her mother. While narrating the intimate history of the family trying to survive the legal regime, their essay explores both the unequal consequences of diverging national and EU norms and the feelings of injustice experienced by this separated family.

Orsini and Merla's contribution illustrates what can happen after families manage to reunite in Europe within securitised migration governance systems. Building on their research in the Belgian context, the authors systematically show how family reunification rules produce dependency within couples and may lead to domestic violence.

Throughout the section, the authors strike a balance between accounting for people's resourcefulness in dealing with increasingly strict requirements and recognising the limited possibilities they have to cope with shifting ground, represented by legal frameworks as well as biographical circumstances.

6. Concluding reflections

Overall, this volume shows, in different ways, that family reunification laws and policies often have undesirable and sometimes disastrous consequences, not only for families, who are kept separated for years, but also when they are finally reunited in circumstances that increase intra-family power imbalances. These are amplified by the fact that the residence right of family members remains 'dependent' during the first years on complying with the conditions for family reunification, which adds to the increased precarity of migration statuses (Ellermann, 2020; de Hart et al., 2022; Orsini & Merla, this volume). Whether the chapters draw on a doctrinal, human rights, socio-legal or ethical perspective, whether they use technical legal analyses or empirical methods, they all point to various kinds of inequalities created by the current family reunification regime in Europe, some of them enshrined in the law, some resulting from implementation. The family reunification regime consists of almost countless subregimes, special rules, exceptions and interpretations. Those seeking to navigate it end up struggling with enormous piles of paperwork and red tape, formal requirements that impede the actual enjoyment of their rights. Various features of the family reunification regime are thus not in line with the objectives of EU law on this topic, namely, to promote family reunification and recognise family relationships. More fundamentally, they seem to be at odds with basic principles of ethics, equality and human rights, as well as with legal principles of transparency and certainty. The human cost is enormous, as highlighted by civil society and actors working in the field (UNICEF et al., 2017; ECRE, 2023; IRC, 2023). These legal, socio-economic, gender and racial inequalities call for more research engagement.

Therefore, we suggest that future research on family reunification requires a threefold strategy, which we started to explore in this book. Rephrasing the famous statements by Marcus on multi-sited ethnography (1995), we propose a research agenda consisting of studies *following the laws*, *following the documents* and *following the people*. This suggestion builds on different bodies of knowledge rooted in legal sociology, legal anthropology, history of law and social studies, as well as various theoretical approaches, such as critical theory (e.g., Thornhill, 2004), the genealogical approach to law (e.g., Baxter, 1996; Leonard, 1990) and actor-network theory (e.g., Callon, 1999). Drawing on these theoretical traditions, this threefold strategy aims to orient future avenues for researchers investigating family reunification from multiple disciplinary backgrounds.

First, to account for the complexity of family reunification today, scholars need to consider the historical and societal development of laws as well as the interaction of different bodies of laws across and within countries ('follow the law' strategy). This means tracking how multiple layers of governance and laws (international, national, regional, local) influence families, through an intersectional approach (de Hart, this volume). Second, by 'following the documents', researchers of family migration can illuminate the non-human agency of bureaucratic and technological processes of administration and identification that crucially shape the possibilities of travelling, proving family ties and enjoying the right to respect for family life. With documents, we refer not only to paperwork and paper trails (Horton & Heyman, 2020) that accompany migrants' experience, but also to forms of digital and biomedical *evidence* (Heinemann et al., 2016) that are increasingly used in family reunification procedures. Finally, it is vital to go beyond the formal words of laws and documents in order to make sense of people's lived experiences and the administrative hurdles in their trajectories between places and institutional frameworks. By 'following the people' across time and space, scholars can discover new incoherences and inconsistencies in the labyrinth, seek to illuminate their complex structural and personal origins and possibly identify practices that are in line with the spirit of EU laws on family reunification. Future studies may combine two or three of these lines of investigation to explore interactions between legal environments, material practices and experiences of actors.

When following the laws, the documents and/or the people, this book shows the importance of combining migration law, private international law and social scientific analyses. Only a real 'joining of forces' between legal and social sciences and between doctrinal and empirical research can illuminate the subtle but persistent ways in which inequalities are reproduced for some specific social groups. Moving towards a truly interdisciplinary and comprehensive understanding of family reunification also implies the inclusion of fields of law (e.g. family law, social law) and social science perspectives (e.g. geography, psychology) that are less prevalent in this volume.

We should like to end this book with a few glimmers of hope. They come from the resilience of the persons who (have to) embark on these family reunification trajectories, their ability to 'do family' across and despite borders and their strength to persevere, even if it is because they are left with no other choice. These rays of hope also come from the social workers, lawyers and other professionals trying to help migrants and their families to navigate this multi-layered regime. Finally, they come from some – from a human rights perspective – 'hopeful' interpretations in judgements of national and European courts. Although they are only small drops in an ocean of increasingly restrictive policies, they could be a firm encouragement for further research. We thus hope that this book will be a companion for more critical research on family reunification, to reveal the stratified consequences of the many rules governing the everyday life of separated families.

References

Adamson, F. B., Triadafilopoulos, T., & Zolberg, A. R. (2011). The limits of the liberal state: Migration, identity and belonging in Europe. *Journal of Ethnic and Migration Studies, 37*(6), 843–859. https://doi.org/10.1080/1369183X.2011.576188

Ahlén, A. (2024). The effects of admission policies on rates of family migration in European states, 2008–2019. *Nordic Journal of Migration Research,* 14(3): 2, pp. 1–23. https://doi.org/10.33134/njmr.707

Amelina, A., & Horvath, K. (2020). Regimes of intersection: Facing the manifold interplays of discourses, institutions, and inequalities in the regulation of migration. *Migration Letters, 17*(4), 487–497. https://doi.org/10.59670/ml.v17i4.710

Baxter, H. (1996). Bringing Foucault into law and law into Foucault. *Stanford Law Review, 48*(2), 449–479. https://doi.org/10.2307/1229368

Berneri, C. (2017). *Family Reunification in the EU: The Movement and Residence Rights of Third Country National Family Members of EU Citizens.* Bloomsbury Publishing.

Bonjour, S., & de Hart, B. (2013). A proper wife, a proper marriage: Constructions of "us" and "them" in Dutch family migration policy. *European Journal of Women's Studies, 20*(1), 61–76. https://doi.org/10.1177/1350506812456455

Bonjour, S., & Duyvendak, J. W. (2020). The "Migrant with Poor Prospects": Racialized Intersections of Class and Culture in Dutch Civic Integration Debates. In M. Bulmer & J. Solomos (Eds.), *Migration and Race in Europe* (pp. 104–122). Routledge. https://doi.org/10.1080/01419870.2017.1339897

Buonfino, A. (2004). Between unity and plurality: The politicization and securitization of the discourse of immigration in Europe. *New Political Science, 26*(1), 23–49. https://doi.org/10.1080/0739314042000185111

Burgess, J. P., & Gutwirth, S. (Eds.). (2011). *A Threat Against Europe? Security, Migration and Integration.* VUB Press.

Callon, M. (1999). Actor-network theory – the market test. *The Sociological Review, 47* (Suppl 1), 181–195. https://doi.org/10.1111/j.1467-954X.1999.tb03488.x

Crenshaw, K. (1989). Demarginalizing the Intersection of race and sex: A black feminist critique of antidiscrimination doctrine, feminist theory and antiracist politics. *University of Chicago Legal Forum, 1989*(1), 139–167.

de Hart, B., van Rossum, W., & Sportel, I. (2013). Law in the everyday lives of transnational families: An introduction. *Oñati Socio-Legal Series, 3*(6), 991–1003.

de Hart, B., Verweij, E., & Arbaoui, Y. (2022). *Heb geduld. De betekenis van het afhankelijk verblijfsrecht in het dagelijks leven van huwelijksmigranten en hun partners.* https://acmrl.org/wp-content/uploads/2022/12/Rapport-afhankelijk-verblijfsrecht-def-5-12-2022-1.pdf

Dembour, M.-B. (2015). *When Humans Become Migrants: A Study of the European Court of Human Rights with an Inter-American Counterpoint.* Oxford University Press.

Den Haese, S. (2023). *Crossing Borders: Proving Your Personal Status Interactions Between Private International Law and Human Rights Law*. Eleven/Boom Juridisch.
Den Heijer, M. (2018). Visas and non-discrimination. *European Journal of Migration and Law*, *20*, 470–489. https://doi.org/10.1163/15718166-12340039
Ellermann, A. (2020). Discrimination in migration and citizenship. *Journal of Ethnic and Migration Studies*, *46*(12), 2463–2479. https://doi.org/10.1080/1369183X.2018.1561053
European Council on Refugees and Exiles (ECRE). (2023). *Not there yet: Family reunification for beneficiaries of international protection*. ECRE. https://ecre.org/wp-content/uploads/2023/02/AIDA-Family-Reunification-February-2023.pdf
Farcy, J. (2020). Equality in immigration law: An impossible quest? *Human Rights Law Review*, *20*(4), 725–744. https://doi.org/10.1093/hrlr/ngaa037
Friedery, R., Manca, L., & Roßkopf, R. (Eds.). (2018). *Family Reunification: International, European and National Perspectives*. Berliner Wissenschats-Verlag.
Geoffrion, K., & Cretton, V. (2021). Bureaucratic routes to migration: Migrants' lived experience of paperwork, clerks and other immigration intermediaries. *Anthropologica*, *63*(1), 1–28. https://doi.org/10.18357/anthropologica6312021184
Güdük, A., & Desmet, E. (2022). Legal consciousness and migration: Towards a research agenda. *International Journal of Law in Context*, *18*(2), 213–228. https://doi.org/10.1017/S1744552322000118
Heinemann, T., Helén, I., Lemke, T., Naue, U., & Weiss, M. G. (Eds.). (2015). *Suspect Families: DNA Analysis, Family Reunification and Immigration Policies*. Routledge.
Horton, S. B., & Heyman, J. (Eds.). (2020). *Paper Trails: Migrants, Documents, and Legal Insecurity*. Duke University Press.
Huysmans, J., & Squire, V. (2009). *Migration and Security: Handbook of Security Studies*. Routledge.
International Red Cross (IRC). (2023). *Upholding the right to family reunification for beneficiaries of international protection in Europe*. https://redcross.eu/positions-publications/upholding-the-right-to-family-reunification-for-beneficiaries-of-international-protection-in-europe
Jaskulowski, K. (2019). The securitisation of migration: Its limits and consequences. *International Political Science Review*, *40*(5), 710–720. https://doi.org/10.1177/0192512118799755
Jubany, O. (2017). *Screening Asylum in a Culture of Disbelief. Truths, Denials and Skeptical Borders*. Palgrave Macmillan.
Karyotis, G. (2007). European migration policy in the aftermath of September 11: The security – migration nexus. *Innovation: The European Journal of Social Science Research*, *20*(1), 1–17. https://doi.org/10.1080/13511610701197783
Klaassen, M. A. K. (2015). *The right to family unification: Between migration control and human rights* [Doctoral thesis, Leiden University]. Leiden University Repository. https://hdl.handle.net/1887/36049
Kofman, E. (2002). Contemporary European migrations, civic stratification and citizenship. *Political Geography*, *21*(8), 1035–1054.
Kroeze, H. (2021). *For whom I love I want to be known: The scope of EU citizens' family reunification rights: Addressing legal fragmentation in the European Union's multi-layered legal order* [Doctoral thesis, Ghent University].
Lawrance, B. N., & Stevens, J. (2017). *Citizenship in Question: Evidentiary Birth Right and Statelessness*. Duke University Press.
Leonard, J. D. (1990). Foucault: Genealogy, law, praxis. *Legal Studies Forum*, *14*(1), 3–26.
Marcus, G. E. (1995). Ethnography in/of the world system: The emergence of multi-sited ethnography. *Annual Review of Anthropology*, *24*(1), 95–117. https://doi.org/10.1146/annurev.an.24.100195.000523

Morris, L. (2003). Managing contradiction: Civic stratification and migrants' rights. *International Migration Review*, *37*(1), 74–100. https://doi.org/10.1111/j.1747-7379.2003.tb00130.x

Paterson, I., & Karyotis, G. (2022). "We are, by nature, a tolerant people": Securitisation and counter-securitisation in UK migration politics. *International Relations*, *36*(1), 104–126. https://doi.org/10.1177/0047117820967049

Saroléa, S., & Merla, L. (2021). Migrantes et sédentaires: Des familles ontologiquement différentes? In L. Merla, S. Saroléa, & B. Schoumaker (Eds.), *Composer avec les normes. Trajectoires de vie et agentivité de migrants face au cadre légal* (pp. 259–291). Academia L'Harmattan.

Seron, C., & Munger, F. (1996). Law and inequality: Race, gender. . . and, of course, class. *Annual Review of Sociology*, *22*(1), 187–212. https://doi.org/10.1146/annurev.soc.22.1.187

Spijkerboer, T. (2018). The global mobility infrastructure: Reconceptualising the externalisation of migration control. *European Journal of Migration and Law*, *20*(4), 452–469. https://doi.org/10.1163/15718166-12340038

Strik, T., de Hart, B., & Nissen, E. (2013). *Family Reunification: A Barrier or Facilitator of Integration? A Comparative Study*. European Commission.

Szreter, S., & Breckenridge, K. (2012). *Registration and Recognition: Documenting the Person in World History*. Oxford University Press. https://doi.org/10.5871/bacad/9780197265314.001.0001

Thorleifsson, C. (2017). Disposable strangers: Far-right securitisation of forced migration in Hungary. *Social Anthropology*, *25*(3), 318–334. https://doi.org/10.1111/1469-8676.12420

Thornhill, C. (2004). Critical theory and legal theory – a genealogical study. *King's Law Journal*, *15*(1), 23–43. https://doi.org/10.1080/09615768.2004.11423641

Tiilikainen, M., Hiitola, J., Ismail, A. A., & Palander, J. (Eds.). (2023). *Forced Migration and Separated Families: Everyday Insecurities and Transnational Strategies*. Springer International Publishing.

UNICEF, UNHCR, & IRC. (2017). *The way forward to strengthened policies and practices for unaccompanied and separated children in Europe*. https://data2.unhcr.org/en/documents/download/58434

Vandenbroucke, M. (2020). Legal-discursive constructions of genuine cross-border love in Belgian marriage fraud investigations. *Critical Discourse Studies*, *17*(2), 175–192. https://doi.org/10.1080/17405904.2020.1715233

Vigh, H. (2009). Motion squared: A second look at the concept of social navigation. *Anthropological Theory*, *9*(4), 419–438. https://doi.org/10.1177/1463499609356044

Wray, H. (2023). *Article 8 ECHR, Family Reunification and the UK's Supreme Court: Family Matters?* Bloomsbury Publishing.

Part I

Setting the scene

2 A right to family reunification in Europe

A guide to the labyrinth

Ellen Desmet

1. Introduction

This chapter offers a bird's-eye view to the current rules on family reunification at the European level.[1] The 'right to family reunification' can be understood as the right to entry and residence of a foreigner based on family ties with another person who has residence in the host state, the so-called sponsor. There is no single instrument regulating family reunification at the European or international level; rules are spread out over different legal instruments. Moreover, these rules (may) differ depending on, among others, the nationality, age, type of residence right, legal status, educational background and professional position of the sponsor, as well as the nationality, age and relationship of the family member.

In light of this complexity, this chapter aims to serve as an introductory guide to this legal labyrinth, by focusing on key legal provisions and landmark cases. Such a guide may be particularly useful for researchers, policy makers and practitioners who engage with family reunification from a perspective other than a strictly legal one. The chapter adopts a 'classical' legal-doctrinal approach. It focuses on the regulatory and judicial framework within migration law and human rights law that is relevant for family reunification. For a broader understanding, it is to be read in conjunction with the introductions to private international law (Den Haese & Verhellen, this volume) and social science perspectives on family reunification (Belloni & Cleton, this volume). Furthermore, this contribution aims to paint the overall picture in which the other chapters, which delve into the specificities of a particular regime or challenge, can be located. Overall, the chapter illustrates the excessively fragmented nature of family reunification rules, which leads to legal uncertainty as well as differential, and arguably discriminatory, treatment (see further Groenendijk, this volume; de Hart, this volume).

Often, chapters relating to fundamental aspects of life, such as family life, start with discussing the general human rights framework before turning to more specific provisions in, for instance, EU law. Looking at the current state of human rights law in relation to family reunification, it makes more sense to do otherwise. The human

1 For a historical overview, see Groenendijk (this volume).

DOI: 10.4324/9781003503217-3

right to respect for family life has only in limited circumstances been interpreted as implying a right to family reunification. When working in or researching family reunification, the provisions of EU law are therefore generally more relevant as the starting point, because various EU law instruments do provide a subjective right to family reunification – meaning that state authorities are obliged to grant family reunification when all the conditions are fulfilled.

As such, EU law provides a right to family reunification with EU citizens who have made use of their freedom of movement (3.1.1) and, in specific circumstances, also with 'static' EU citizens (3.1.2). The EU Family Reunification Directive contains the general framework for family reunification with third-country nationals residing in a Member State, including more lenient provisions for refugees (3.2.1). More favourable rules also exist for family reunification with certain economic migrants (3.2.2), as well as with economically active Turkish citizens in particular (3.2.3). The section on EU law closes with discussing the rules on family reunification with beneficiaries of temporary protection (those fleeing the war in Ukraine) (3.2.4) and the possibilities provided under the Dublin III Regulation to reunify families during the asylum procedure (3.2.5). This is followed by a succinct discussion of the current relevance of international and Council of Europe human rights law (4) and migration and refugee law (5), before drawing some conclusions (6). The next section (2) first introduces some key terminology and gives an overview of the various aspects that together constitute the legal regime on family reunification.

2. Disentangling rules on family reunification

When studying rules on family reunification, various issues must be distinguished: the definition of the sponsor and family members, the requirements for family reunification, the procedures thereto and the type of residence right acquired.

First, how are the sponsor and family members defined? The term *sponsor* (or 'reference person') refers to the person who is a national of or has a residence right in the host country, and who 'opens' the right to family reunification. The *family member* then aims to accompany or join[2] the sponsor in the host country. Importantly, in the legal field of family reunification, family is not defined uniformly; not everyone has the same family. Who is considered a family member varies with the applicable family reunification regime. Broader and narrower definitions apply, encompassing or excluding certain ascendents, extra-marital partners or blood relatives. Sometimes, a distinction is made between family reunification in the literal sense of the word (where the family relationship existed before the sponsor's entry in the host state) and family formation (where the family relationship arose after the sponsor's entry, such as in marriage migration). Unless indicated otherwise, the term 'family reunification' in this chapter encompasses both situations.

2 'Accompanying' indicates that the family member travels together with the sponsor; 'joining' refers to situations where the family member moves at a later moment.

Second, the *requirements* to be fulfilled to enjoy family reunification are diverse. These conditions may relate to the sponsor (e.g., socio-economic conditions, waiting period), the family member (e.g., not being a danger to health or public order, integration requirements) and the relationship between both (e.g., living together). The challenges related to proving one's identity and family ties that typically fall under the rules of family law and private international law are discussed in other contributions (Den Haese & Verhellen, this volume; Arapiles & Mekonnen, this volume; Belloni & Verschraegen, this volume).

Third, which *procedures* need to be followed? These procedures may again vary, depending, for instance, on the nationality of the family member (e.g., EU citizen or not) and on whether the application is submitted abroad or in the host country.

Fourth, which type of *residence right* follows from the granting of family reunification? The family member will first receive a temporary residence right, which may be terminated if the conditions for family reunification are not complied with anymore. Such a 'dependent residence right' may turn out to be problematic, for instance, in cases of domestic violence (de Hart et al., 2022; Orsini & Merla, this volume). A related question thus concerns the situations in which a residence right based on family reunification may be withdrawn or ended (e.g., because of fraud, not fulfilling the conditions anymore).

Due to the restrictions in terms of length, this chapter focuses on the definition of sponsors, the definition of family members, and the substantive requirements they must fulfil.

3. European Union law

The importance of family life is recognised by the Charter of Fundamental Rights of the European Union (Charter). The Charter applies to all actions by institutions of the European Union and by the Member States when implementing Union Law.[3] The Charter guarantees the right to respect for private and family life[4] and provides that the child's best interests must be a primary consideration in all actions relating to children[5] – thus also in family reunification cases (Klaassen & Rodrigues, 2017). Moreover, children have the right to maintain on a regular basis a personal relationship and direct contact with both parents, unless that is contrary to their interests.[6] The Charter does not explicitly mention a right to family reunification for migrants.

Nevertheless, the strongest provisions at the supranational level guaranteeing a right to family reunification are found in other provisions of substantive EU law: EU treaties, regulations and directives. These provisions are interpreted, in a legally binding way, by the Court of Justice of the European Union (CJEU). The Court's case law has led to nuances and specifications, as well as to the identification of additional situations in which family members hold a right to family

3 Article 51(1) Charter.
4 Article 7 Charter.
5 Article 24(2) Charter.
6 Article 24(3) Charter.

reunification, especially regarding reunification with EU citizens. This growing body of case law further complexifies the already fragmented legal landscape on family reunification and may make it difficult for people to know whether or not they are entitled to family reunification under EU law (for general overviews, see Berneri, 2017; Kroeze, 2021).

To identify the applicable family reunification regime at the level of EU law, a phased approach is required. The first relevant element concerns the nationality of the sponsor, as different regimes exist for family reunification with EU citizens and assimilated nationalities (3.1) and with third-country nationals (3.2). Pursuant to Article 20 TFEU, 'every person holding the nationality of a Member State shall be a citizen of the Union'. Following the creation of the European Economic Area (EEA), nationals of Iceland, Liechtenstein and Norway have been fully assimilated to EU citizens, following the same residence rules. Based on a 1999 treaty, Swiss nationals are also treated the same as EU citizens in terms of the free movement of persons. Consequently, in this chapter, the term 'EU citizens' should be understood as 'EU citizens, other EEA nationals and Swiss nationals'.

3.1 Family reunification with EU citizens

When the sponsor holds the nationality of an EU Member State or an assimilated country, the next question determining the applicable family reunification regime is whether the sponsor has made use of their right of free movement and residence within the European Union. EU citizens who have made use of their free movement rights are called 'mobile' EU citizens; they fall within the scope of EU law. By contrast, 'static' EU citizens fall – in principle – exclusively under national law. Nevertheless, in certain situations, the CJEU has nuanced this strict division between mobile and static EU citizens and has applied EU law to the latter as well.

3.1.1 Family reunification with mobile EU citizens

Definition of the sponsor – According to Article 21 TFEU, EU citizens 'shall have the right to move and reside freely within the territory of the Member States', subject to the conditions laid down in the Treaties and in implementing legislation. The most important implementing instrument is the Citizens Directive (2004/38/EC) – which should not be interpreted restrictively.[7] Article 7(1) of this Directive provides that EU citizens have a right of residence for more than three months in another Member State if they (i) are workers or self-employed in the host Member State (extended by the CJEU to jobseekers)[8]; or (ii) have sufficient resources for

7 CJEU, 25 July 2008, C-127/08, *Metock*, ECLI:EU:C:2008:449. For guidance of the Commission on the Directive's transposition and application, see European Commission, Communication from the Commission to the European Parliament and the Council on guidance for better transposition and application of Directive 2004/38/EC on the right of citizens of the Union and their family members to move and reside freely within the territory of the Member States, 2 July 2009, COM(2009) 313 final.

8 CJEU, 26 February 1991, C-292/89, *Anthonissen*, ECLI:EU:C:1991:80.

themselves and their family members not to become a burden on the social assistance system of the host Member State, as well as a sickness insurance; or (iii) are students with a sickness insurance; or (iv) are family members accompanying or joining an EU citizen who falls under one of the three previous categories. Article 7(2) of the Directive extends this residence right of more than three months to family members who are not nationals of a Member State, if they accompany or join an EU citizen who satisfies the conditions of one of the first three categories. In other words, both family members who themselves have the nationality of an EU Member State (e.g., a French partner)[9] and family members who are third-country nationals (e.g., a Brazilian partner),[10] have a right to family reunification with a mobile EU citizen (e.g., a Portuguese engineer working in Germany). Pursuant to CJEU case law, EU citizens who reside in their home Member State, but who provide services in other Member States (Article 56 TFEU), also fall under the scope of EU law and are entitled to the accompanying family reunification rights.[11]

Definition of family members – The following 'core' family members are entitled to family reunification with workers, self-employed persons, jobseekers and holders of sufficient resources: (i) the spouse – which includes same-sex marriages contracted in other EU Member States[12]; (ii) the partner with a registered partnership; (iii) children who are under the age of 21 or dependent, and those of the spouse or partner; and (iv) dependent parents, and those of the spouse or partner.[13] Students, on the other hand, only have the right to be joined by their spouse, registered partner and dependent children (and thus not by their dependent parents).[14] In case the mobile EU citizen is a minor, they are entitled to be accompanied by the parent who is their carer.[15] The Citizens Directive recognises the relevance of 'other' family members, by providing that Member States 'shall' facilitate the entry and residence of (i) any other family members who are dependents or members of the household of the EU citizen, or where serious health grounds require the personal care of the family member by the EU citizen; and (ii) the partner with whom the EU citizen has a durable relationship, duly attested.[16]

Substantive requirements – The 'core' family members identified earlier are entitled to accompany or join the mobile EU citizen without any additional substantive requirements. These lenient provisions can be explained by the fact that the European Union wants to stimulate its citizens to make use of their free movement rights. EU citizens will be more inclined to move to another EU country if

9 Article 7(1)(d) Citizens Directive.

10 Article 7(2) Citizens Directive.

11 CJEU, 11 July 2002, C-60/00, *Carpenter*, ECLI:EU:C:2002:434.

12 CJEU, 5 June 2018, C-673/16, *Coman*, ECLI:EU:C:2018:385. See Den Haese and Verhellen (this volume).

13 Article 2(2) Citizens Directive.

14 Article 7(4) Citizens Directive. The Member States must facilitate the family reunification of the students' dependent parents and those of their spouse/partner (Article 3(2) Citizens Directive).

15 CJEU, 19 October 2004, C-200/02, *Zhu and Chen*, ECLI:EU:C:2004:639.

16 Article 3(2) Citizens Directive. See CJEU, 5 September 2012, C-83/11, *Rahman and Others*, ECLI:EU:C:2012:519.

they can easily be accompanied or joined by their family members. The freedom of movement and residence of EU citizens and their family members may only be restricted on grounds of public policy, public security or public health.[17]

What happens, though, if the Portuguese engineer working in Germany moves back to Portugal, on the one hand, or acquires the German nationality on the other? Do they then continue to benefit from the beneficial provisions of EU law, or do they fall exclusively under the family reunification rules of the national Portuguese or German legislation? The CJEU has held that the residence right acquired by family members (e.g., the French or the Brazilian partner) under EU law, continues to exist, both when the sponsor returns to the home state[18] and when they become a national of the host state.[19] The CJEU has thus extended the application of EU law from *cross-border* situations to certain *post-cross-border* situations (return to the home state and acquiring the nationality of the host state) (Kroeze, 2021).

3.1.2 Family reunification with static EU citizens

Because static EU citizens have not made use of their right of free movement and residence, they – in principle – do not fall within the scope of EU law: their family reunification rights are determined by national legislation. The resulting legal landscape in Europe is one of fragmentation: some countries have extended the more beneficial rules applicable to mobile EU citizens to their static nationals; other countries maintain minor or major differences between mobile and static EU citizens regarding family reunification, which may amount to a so-called reverse discrimination (Guild, 2019; Groenendijk, this volume; Corradi & Desmet, this volume).

In certain cases concerning static EU citizens, the CJEU has derived a residence right for a family member directly from Article 20 TFEU, the provision that establishes Union citizenship (rather than Article 21 TFEU on free movement rights). There are thus also *non-cross-border* situations in which EU family reunification rights apply (Kroeze, 2021). In the landmark case of *Ruiz Zambrano*, the Court held that the Colombian (third-country national) parents of a Belgian static child should have a right of residence in Belgium, because deciding otherwise would 'deprive those children of the genuine enjoyment of the substance of rights attaching to the status of European Union citizen'.[20] In *Dereci*, the Court clarified that this criterion refers to situations in which the EU citizen has to 'leave not only the territory of the Member State of which he is a national but also the territory of the Union as a whole'.[21] This line of reasoning has been further developed and nuanced in numerous cases, in which the dependency of the static EU citizen on the third-country

17 Article 27 Citizens Directive.

18 CJEU, 7 July 1992, C-370/90, *Surinder Singh,* ECLI:EU:C:1992:296; CJEU, 12 March 2014, C-456/12, *O. & B.*, ECLI:EU:C:2014:135. See Guild (2019).

19 CJEU, 14 November 2017, C-165/16, *Lounes*, ECLI:EU:C:2017:862.

20 CJEU, 8 March 2011, C-34/09, *Ruiz Zambrano*, ECLI:EU:C:2011:124, § 45.

21 CJEU, 15 November 2011, C-256/11, *Dereci*, ECLI:EU:C:2011:734, § 66.

national family member appears as a crucial element to be granted a residence right derived from Article 20 TFEU. The CJEU readily accepts the existence of a relationship of dependency when it concerns minor EU citizens, but does so only in very exceptional circumstances for adults.[22] In 2023, the CJEU extended this line of case law to establish a derived right of residence for a third-country national parent of a minor EU citizen who has never resided in the territory of the European Union, but will reside with their parent in the Member State of their nationality.[23]

3.2 *Family reunification with third-country nationals*

3.2.1 The Family Reunification Directive: general provisions and family reunification with refugees

The 2003 Family Reunification Directive (2003/86/EC) is the general instrument regulating family reunification with third-country nationals in the EU and has been characterised as a 'surprising anchor in a sensitive field' (Groenendijk & Strik, 2022). It is applicable in 25 Member States only, with Denmark and Ireland having opted out. The directive provides minimum standards that always apply (in the form of 'shall' clauses), while leaving quite some room for discretion to the Member States (in the form of 'may' clauses) to demarcate the actual boundaries of family reunification rights. The CJEU has consistently emphasised that it is the objective of the Family Reunification Directive to *promote* family reunification, and that the directive aims to provide protection to third-country nationals, in particular minors.[24] In a 2014 Communication, the European Commission provided guidance to the Member States on how to apply the directive.[25]

Definition of the sponsor – To qualify as a sponsor, the third-country national must have a residence permit of one year or more and have reasonable prospects of obtaining a permanent residence right.[26] The Family Reunification Directive

22 See, among others, CJEU, 6 December 2012, C-356/11 and C-357/11, *O., S. and L*, EU:C:2012:776; CJEU, 10 May 2017, C-133/15, *Chavez-Vilchez*, ECLI:EU:C:2017:354; CJEU, 8 May 2018, C-82/16, *K.A. and Others*, ECLI:EU:C:2018:308.

23 CJEU 22 June 2023, C-459/20, *X.*, ECLI:EU:C:2023:499.

24 See, e.g., CJEU, 4 March 2010, C-578/08, *Chakroun*, ECLI:EU:C:2010:117, § 43; CJEU, 6 December 2012, C-356/11 and C-357/11, *O., S. and L*, EU:C:2012:776, § 69; CJEU, 13 March 2019, C-635/17, *E.*, EU:C:2019:192, § 45. See also Article 5(5) Family Reunification Directive (obliging Member States to have due regard to the best interests of the child when examining an application).

25 European Commission, Communication from the Commission to the European Parliament and the Council on guidance for application of Directive 2003/86/EC on the right to family reunification, 3 April 2014, COM(2014) 210 final. Both the European Commission and the European Migration Network (2017) have issued summary reports on the implementation of the directive across Member States. See European Commission, Report from the Commission to the European Parliament and the Council on the Application of Directive 2003/86/EC on the right to family reunification, 8 October 2008, COM(2008) 610 final; European Commission, Report from the Commission to the European Parliament and the Council on the Implementation of Directive 2003/86/EC on the right to family reunification, 29 March 2019, COM(2019) 162 final.

26 Article 3(1) Family Reunification Directive.

enshrines specific, more favourable provisions for family reunification with recognised refugees – given that they cannot enjoy their family life in their country of origin (see generally ECRE, 2023a; Nicholson, 2018, 2021). Excluded, however, from the application of the Directive are applicants for refugee status, applicants for and beneficiaries of temporary protection, as well as applicants for and beneficiaries of 'a subsidiary form of protection in accordance with international obligations, national legislation or the practice of the Member States'.[27] Even though this provision does not refer to the EU subsidiary protection status (as this was only introduced a year later, in 2004), the CJEU has held that the Family Reunification Directive does not apply to persons with a EU subsidiary protection status.[28] This does not prevent Member States from adopting more favourable provisions in their national legislation and, for instance, extend family reunification rights to beneficiaries of subsidiary protection.[29] The latter has been recommended as a good practice (Council of Europe Commissioner of Human Rights, 2017).

Definition of family members – The family members of a third-country national are defined more narrowly than those of a mobile EU citizen (see Section 3.1.1). Only the spouse and the unmarried dependent minor children of the sponsor or spouse over which the latter have custody, 'shall' be entitled to family reunification.[30] The CJEU has specified that the minority of a child applying for family reunification must be determined in relation to *the date of submission* of the application for family reunification, and not the date of *decision* on the application.[31] Otherwise, the applicant would be dependent on the working speed of the national immigration authorities, which would not be in line with the right to respect for family life and the best interests of the child (Articles 7 and 24(2) of the Charter) and the overall objective of the directive to promote family reunification.[32] On top, Member States 'may' extend family reunification rights with third-country nationals to dependent parents, adult unmarried children who are dependent because of their state of health, unmarried registered or unregistered partners and the same two categories of their children (minor children and dependent adult unmarried children).[33]

The *family members of refugees* who 'shall' (spouse and minor unmarried children) and 'may' be entitled to family reunification are the same as those in the

27 Article 3(2) Family Reunification Directive. Family members of EU citizens are also excluded since they fall under the Citizens Directive. Article 3(3) Family Reunification Directive.

28 CJEU, 7 November 2018, C-380/17, *K., B.*, ECLI:EU:C:2018:877, §§ 26–33. For a critical reflection, see Groenendijk and Strik (2022, pp. 311–312).

29 Article 3(5) Family Reunification Directive.

30 Article 4(1) Family Reunification Directive.

31 CJEU, 16 July 2020, C-133/19, C-136/19 and C-137/19, *B.M.M. and others*, ECLI:EU:C:2020:577, § 47.

32 Moreover, an appeal against a negative decision on the family reunification application of a minor child cannot be declared inadmissible on the single ground that the child has turned 18 during the court proceedings. CJEU, 16 July 2020, C-133/19, C-136/19 and C-137/19, *B.M.M. and others*, ECLI:EU:C:2020:577, § 58.

33 Article 4(2)–(3) Family Reunification Directive.

general provisions.[34] Also here, the CJEU held that the minority of a child applying for family reunification with a refugee sponsor must be established in relation to the *date of submission* of the application for international protection of the parent, on the condition that the family reunification application was submitted within a reasonable period of, in principle, three months after the parent was recognised as a refugee.[35] In addition, Member States 'may' authorise family reunification of other family members if they are dependent on the refugee.[36]

When the refugee sponsor is an *unaccompanied minor*, their parents 'shall' be entitled to family reunification, whereas – in case no parents can be traced – their legal guardian or any other family member 'may' be authorised to family reunification.[37] No mention is made of siblings. In 2018, the CJEU held in *A. and S.* that a person who was a minor at the time of submission of the application for international protection, but turns 18 during the asylum procedure and is then granted refugee status, must be considered an unaccompanied minor in the context of the Family Reunification Directive – and is thus entitled to be reunified with their parents,[38] if the latter submit their application within a reasonable period of, in principle, three months.[39] Chronologically, this was the first case in which the Court pronounced on the qualification as a minor in the context of family reunification proceedings.[40] These judgements have increased the protection of minors, young adults and their families in the context of family reunification, in line with the overall purpose of the Family Reunification Directive and children's rights.

Substantive requirements – In general, Member States 'may' (and in practice mostly do) require that the family member, when submitting the application, provides evidence that the sponsor has (i) decent accommodation, (ii) sickness insurance covering the sponsor and their family members and (iii) 'stable and regular' resources which are 'sufficient' to maintain the sponsor and their family members without recourse to the social assistance system of the host state.[41] In the 2010 landmark case of *Chakroun*, the CJEU held that the possibility for states to impose an income requirement must be interpreted strictly, 'since authorization of family reunification is the general rule'.[42] Moreover, the margin for manoeuvre left to Member States may not lead to an undermining of 'the objective of the Directive, which is to promote family reunification, and the effectiveness thereof'.[43] Conse-

34 Article 10(1) Family Reunification Directive.
35 CJEU, 1 August 2022, C-279/20, *XC*, ECLI:EU:C:2022:618, § 54.
36 Article 10(2) Family Reunification Directive.
37 Article 10(3) Family Reunification Directive.
38 CJEU, 12 April 2018, C-550/16, *A. and S.*, ECLI:EU:C:2018:248, § 64.
39 Ibid., § 61.
40 Followed by the cases of *B.M.M.* and *XC* mentioned earlier. See CJEU, 1 August 2022, C-273/20 and C-355/20, *SW and Others*, ECLI:EU:C:2022:617, which elaborates on the requirement of a 'real family relationship' in the case of family reunification of a parent with an unaccompanied minor with refugee status.
41 Article 7(1) Family Reunification Directive.
42 CJEU, 4 March 2010, C-578/08, *Chakroun*, ECLI:EU:C:2010:117, § 43.
43 Ibid.

quently, in order to determine whether resources are 'sufficient', Member States may indicate a certain sum as a reference amount, but they may not automatically reject all applications below this threshold.[44] Member States are thus obliged to carry out an individualised assessment *in concreto* of the resources requirement in each case.[45] To assess whether the resources of the sponsor are 'stable and regular', the CJEU has allowed Member States to make a prospective assessment of the likelihood that the sponsor will retain the necessary resources in the year following the date of submission of the application, based on the pattern of the sponsor's income in the six months preceding the submission.[46]

Moreover, Member States may impose a waiting period, requiring sponsors to have stayed lawfully on their territory for a certain period (not exceeding two years), before their family members may join them.[47] Finally, Member States may also require the family members to comply with certain integration measures,[48] if these measures aim at facilitating the family members' integration, and thus not at 'filtering' persons who will be able to exercise their right to family reunification.[49]

When it concerns family reunification of the spouse and/or children *with a refugee*, the substantive requirements are more lenient. First, Member States 'shall' not require that the refugee sponsor complies with the aforementioned socio-economic requirements (accommodation, sickness insurance, resources). However, they 'may' require the sponsor to fulfil these requirements if the family reunification application is not submitted within three months after the granting of refugee status.[50] This period of three months is the minimum standard, and there may be circumstances which render a late submission objectively excusable.[51] Yet, even longer time periods often turn out to be too short for refugee sponsors to trace their family members, gather all the necessary paperwork and obtain an appointment for the family members with the consulate or embassy (Debruyne, this volume; Christ & Etzold, this volume). It has therefore been recommended to '[a]bolish short time limits for family reunification applications, unless they are adapted to permit a first provisional application to be made by the refugee him- or herself in the country of asylum, allowing documentation and details to be submitted later' (Council of Europe Commissioner of Human Rights, 2017, p. 9). In addition, no waiting

44 Ibid., § 48.

45 In line with the individual proportionality test enshrined in Article 17 of the Family Reunification Directive.

46 CJEU, 21 April 2016, C-558/14, *Khachab*, ECLI:EU:C:2016:285, § 48.

47 Article 8 Family Reunification Directive.

48 Article 7(2) Family Reunification Directive.

49 CJEU, 9 July 2015, C-153/14, *K. and A.*, ECLI:EU:C:2015:453, § 57.

50 Another exception (yet less relevant in practice) to this exemption from socio-economic requirements is the situation where family reunification is possible in a third country with which the sponsor and/or family member has special links. Article 12(1) Family Reunification Directive.

51 CJEU, 7 November 2018, C-380/17, *K., B.*, ECLI:EU:C:2018:877.

period can be imposed on the refugee sponsor,[52] and integration requirements may only be applied once the family members have been granted family reunification.[53]

3.2.2 Family reunification with EU Blue Card holders, intra-corporate transferees and researchers

Three EU directives on economic migration of third-country nationals include more favourable provisions on family reunification, compared to the general framework laid out in the Family Reunification Directive. These directives apply in all EU Member States, except Denmark and Ireland. They relate to particular situations of labour migration.

The EU Blue Card Directive aims to attract and retain highly qualified workers from third countries. The original directive from 2009[54] was replaced by a revised EU Blue Card Directive in 2021[55] that has become effective as from 19 November 2023, the deadline for Member States to transpose the new directive.[56] The Intra-Corporate Transferees (ICT) Directive of 2014 defines an 'intra-corporate transfer' as a temporary secondment of more than 90 days of a third-country national (manager, specialist or trainee employee) who, at the time of application, resides outside the territory of the EU Member States (e.g., an Indian national residing in India), from an undertaking established outside the territory of a Member State (e.g., mother firm in India), and to which the third-country national is bound by a work contract prior to and during the transfer, to an entity belonging to the undertaking or to the same group of undertakings which is established in that Member State (e.g., entity of the same firm in Italy). Where applicable, the mobility between host entities established in one or several second Member States (e.g., other entities in France and Croatia) is also covered.[57] The Students and Researchers Directive of 2016 aims to promote the Union as 'an attractive location for research and innovation' and 'a world centre of excellence for studies and training'.[58] The more

52 Article 12(2) Family Reunification Directive.

53 Article 7(2) Family Reunification Directive.

54 Council Directive 2009/50/EC of 25 May 2009 on the conditions of entry and residence of third-country nationals for the purposes of highly qualified employment (hereinafter: EU Blue Card Directive 2009).

55 Directive (EU) 2021/1883 of the European Parliament and of the Council of 20 October 2021 on the conditions of entry and residence of third-country nationals for the purpose of highly qualified employment, and repealing Council Directive 2009/50/EC (hereinafter: EU Blue Card Directive 2021).

56 Article 30 EU Blue Card Directive 2021.

57 Article 3(b) Directive 2014/66/EU of the European Parliament and of the Council of 15 May 2014 on the conditions of entry and residence of third-country nationals in the framework of an intra-corporate transfer (hereinafter: ICT Directive).

58 Recitals 8 and 14 of the preamble, Directive (EU) 2016/801 of the European Parliament and of the Council of 11 May 2016 on the conditions of entry and residence of third-country nationals for the purposes of research, studies, training, voluntary service, pupil exchange schemes or educational projects and au pairing (recast) (hereinafter: Students and Researchers Directive).

favourable rules on family reunification only apply to researchers, and thus not to other categories under the scope of the directive (students, school pupils, trainees, volunteers, au pairs).[59]

Within the focus of this chapter, the more favourable provisions for family reunification with EU Blue Card holders, intra-corporate transferees and researchers relating to the eligibility of the sponsor and integration requirements for family members will be looked at.[60]

Definition of the sponsor – By way of derogation from the Family Reunification Directive, the sponsor under these three directives is not required to have reasonable prospects of obtaining the right of permanent residence, nor can a minimum period of residence (waiting period) be imposed. This allows family members of these economic migrants to directly accompany them.[61] The 2021 EU Blue Card Directive adds that family reunification with an EU Blue Card holder cannot be made dependent on holding a residence permit for a validity of one year or more.[62]

Substantive requirements – Moreover, Member States can only apply integration measures upon family members *after* they have been granted family reunification.[63]

3.2.3 Family reunification with economically active Turkish citizens

The legal position of Turkish citizens in the EU is covered not only by immigration legislation but also by the EU-Turkey Association Agreement (Ankara Agreement) of 1963 and has therefore been characterised as 'particularly complex' (Peers, 2016). The Ankara Agreement aimed to progressively realise free movement of workers, services and establishment between the EU and Turkey.[64] The Agreement itself does not include rights regarding family reunification. However, a 1970 Additional Protocol to the Agreement includes a standstill provision, according to which the parties cannot introduce any new restrictions on the freedom of establishment and the freedom to provide services.[65] Whereas this provision applies to *self-employed* persons, a similar standstill clause was adopted regarding conditions for access to employment for Turkish *workers* and their family members in 1980.[66]

59 Article 26 Students and Researchers Directive.

60 Other more lenient provisions relate to the processing times of the family reunification application, intra-EU mobility, the validity of the residence permit, access to the labour market, and the possibility for the family member to obtain an autonomous residence permit.

61 Article 15(2) EU Blue Card Directive 2009; Article 17(2) EU Blue Card Directive 2021; Article 19(2) ICT Directive; Article 26(2) Students and Researchers Directive.

62 Article 17(2) EU Blue Card Directive 2021.

63 Article 15(3) EU Blue Card Directive 2009; Article 17(3) EU Blue Card Directive 2021; Article 19(3) ICT Directive; Article 26(3) Students and Researchers Directive.

64 Agreement establishing an Association between the European Economic Community and Turkey, signed in Ankara on 12 September 1963, entry into force on 1 December 1964, OJ L 217, 29 December 1964.

65 Article 41(1) Additional Protocol, signed on 23 November 1970, entry into force on 1 January 1973, OJ L 293, 29 December 1972.

66 Article 13 Decision 1/80 of the Association Council of 19 December 1980 on the Development of the Association.

Consequently, the EU and its Member States cannot introduce new limitations on access to these free movement rights of Turkish citizens.

The CJEU has 'stirred the water' (Adamo, 2016) around the conditions for family reunification for Turkish nationals, leading to a 'transformation' (Peers, 2014) of these rules. In the *Dogan* case, the Court extended its case law on the standstill provision from self-employed persons to *spouses* of such persons.[67] According to the Court, where national legislation made family reunification 'difficult or impossible', the decision of a Turkish national to establish himself as a self-employed person could be 'negatively affected', given that he would 'find himself obliged to choose between his activity in the Member State concerned and his family life in Turkey'.[68] A restriction can only be justified by an overriding reason in the public interest. Moreover, the restriction must be suitable to achieve the legitimate objective pursued and proportional.[69] In 2016, the Court extended this reasoning to the standstill clause of workers as well as to *other family members*, when assessing an integration requirement in Danish law for Turkish children.[70] As a consequence, conditions on family reunification cannot be made stricter with respect to sponsors that fall under the scope of the Ankara Agreement (i.e., economically active citizens): such stricter limitations in national legislation have been invalidated by the CJEU. Peers (2015) discusses more in detail how the two bodies of law (the Family Reunification Directive, on the one hand, and the Ankara agreement and subsequent instruments, on the other) interact in relation to the definition of the sponsor, the definition of family members, substantive requirements and the status of family members.

3.2.4 Family reunification with beneficiaries of temporary protection

Temporary protection is an exceptional procedure to provide immediate and temporary protection to displaced persons from non-EU countries who are unable to return to their country of origin, in the event of an (imminent) mass influx.[71] On 4 March 2022, the Council of the EU activated the Temporary Protection Directive (2001/55/EC) for the first time, namely for persons displaced from Ukraine as a result of the Russian military invasion.[72] All EU Member States are bound by the temporary protection regime, except for Denmark.

67 CJEU, 10 July 2014, C-138/13, *Dogan*, ECLI:EU:C:2014:2066.

68 Ibid., § 35.

69 Ibid., § 37. See also CJEU, 7 November 2013, C-225/12, *Demir*, ECLI:EU:C:2013:725.

70 CJEU, 12 April 2016, C-561/14, *Genc*, ECLI:EU:C:2016:247.

71 Article 2(a) Temporary Protection Directive.

72 Council of the European Union, Council Implementing Decision (EU) 2022/382 establishing the existence of a mass influx of displaced persons from Ukraine within the meaning of Article 5 of Directive 2001/55/EC, and having the effect of introducing temporary protection, 4 March 2022 (hereinafter: Council Implementing Decision). See also European Commission, Communication from the Commission on Operational guidelines for the implementation of Council implementing Decision 2022/382 establishing the existence of a mass influx of displaced persons from Ukraine within the meaning of Article 5 of Directive 2001/55/EC, and having the effect of introducing temporary protection, 21 March 2022, 2002/C 126 I/01.

Definition of the sponsor – Temporary protection applies to Ukrainian nationals residing in Ukraine before 24 February 2022, stateless persons and third-country nationals who benefited from international or equivalent national protection in Ukraine before that same date, and family members of these categories of persons.[73] Temporary protection or adequate national protection should also apply to stateless persons and third-country nationals who had a permanent residence permit in Ukraine before 24 February 2022 and are unable to return in safe and durable conditions to their country or region of origin.[74] Family members of the latter category are not covered, though. The rules on family reunification are therefore particularly relevant for these family members (see generally Milios, 2023).

Definition of family members – The temporary protection regime considers as family members: (i) the spouse or the unmarried partner in a stable relationship,[75] (ii) the minor unmarried children of the sponsor or their spouse, and (iii) other 'close relatives' – a term not further defined[76] – who lived together as part of the family unit and were wholly or mainly dependent on the person enjoying temporary protection.[77] A transversal requirement is that the family already existed in Ukraine before 24 February 2022 – thus excluding family formation. Compared to the family of refugees under the obligatory provisions of the Family Reunification Directive, the family of beneficiaries of temporary protection is thus defined somewhat broader, with the inclusion of unmarried partners and dependent close relatives.

Substantive requirements – There are no substantive requirements for family reunification with beneficiaries of temporary protection.

3.2.5 The possibility of reunifying families under the Dublin III Regulation

The Dublin III Regulation (No. 604/2013) provides rules to determine which EU Member State is responsible for assessing an application for international protection. Although the Dublin system does not include an explicit *right* to family reunification, various provisions may lead to the reunification of family members during the asylum procedure. This is particularly relevant because persons seeking international protection are excluded as sponsors in the Family Reunification Directive until they have been recognized as a refugee (see Section 3.2.1).

The Dublin III Regulation makes a distinction between 'family members' and 'relatives'. 'Family members' include the spouse and unmarried partner in a

73 Article 2(1) Council Implementing Decision.

74 Article 2(2) Council Implementing Decision.

75 On the condition that national legislation or practice treats unmarried couples in a way comparable to married couples. This may lead to divergent approaches as well as additional obstacles in certain Member States for same-sex couples (Milios 2023, p. 228).

76 Milios (2023) pleads for a broad interpretation of the term 'close relatives', going beyond the relationships covered by the term 'relatives' in Article 2(h) of the Dublin III Regulation (aunts, uncles and grandparents) (see Section 3.2.5). The question thus arises what weight is to be attached to the additional adjective 'close' in the Temporary Protection Directive.

77 Article 15 Temporary Protection Directive; Article 2(4) Council Implementing Decision.

stable relationship,[78] as well as the minor unmarried children, insofar as the family already existed in the country of origin, and these family members are present on the territory of an EU Member State.[79] For unmarried minors, 'family members' are defined as the father, mother or another legally responsible adult.[80] The Commission proposal for a Regulation on Asylum and Migration Management (RAMM) in the EU Pact on Migration and Asylum positively extended the definition of 'family members' by including siblings of the applicant, as well as family relations formed in transit zones.[81] When establishing its negotiating position for the trilogues, the Council removed the inclusion of siblings as family members (ECRE, 2023b), and this was maintained in the final text.[82] The term 'relatives' in the Dublin III Regulation refers to aunts, uncles or grandparents of the applicant for international protection who are present on the territory of a Member State.[83]

The Dublin rules can lead to family reunification following the hierarchical criteria, on the one hand, and by using the discretionary clauses, on the other. The Dublin III Regulation provides a set of criteria that must be checked one by one in the sequence established by the regulation; the first criterion that is fulfilled designates the responsible Member State.[84] These hierarchical criteria try to take the reality of families dispersed across the EU into account. First, when an applicant for international protection is an unaccompanied minor, the Member State responsible shall be that where a family member or sibling is legally present.[85] In subsidiary order, the Member State responsible is that where a relative of the minor is legally present, if it is established that the relative can take care of the minor.[86] Both provisions explicitly require the reunification to be in the best interests of the child. In the absence of a family member, sibling or relative, the Member State responsible under the RAMM Regulation is the one where the unaccompanied minor's application for international protection was *first registered*, instead of previously that where the minor *has lodged* their application.[87] Second, the state responsible is the one where a family member resides who is a beneficiary of international protection or, as the new RAMM Regulation adds, who resides there on the basis of a long-term residence permit.[88] Third, the state responsible is the one where a family member resides whose application for international protection has

78 When the latter are treated comparably to married couples in the law or practice of the Member State concerned.

79 Article 2(g) Dublin III Regulation.

80 Ibid.

81 Article 2(g) Proposal for a Regulation of the European Parliament and of the Council on asylum and migration management and amending Council Directive (EC) 2003/109 and the proposed Regulation (EU) XXX/XXX [Asylum and Migration Fund], COM/2020/610 final.

82 Article 2(8) Regulation (EU) 2024/1351 of the European Parliament and of the Council of 14 May 2024 on asylum and migration management, amending Regulations (EU) 2021/1147 and (EU) 2021/1060 and repealing Regulation (EU) No 604/2013.

83 Article 2(h) Dublin III Regulation; Article 2(9) RAMM Regulation.

84 Article 7 Dublin III Regulation; Article 24 RAMM Regulation.

85 Article 8(1) Dublin III Regulation; Article 25(2) RAMM Regulation.

86 Article 8(2) Dublin III Regulation; Article 25(3) RAMM Regulation.

87 Article 8(4) Dublin III Regulation; Article 25(5) RAMM Regulation.

88 Article 9 Dublin III Regulation; Article 26 RAMM Regulation.

not yet been decided upon in first instance.[89] In both cases, the persons concerned must express their desire in writing to join the family member in the other state. Only after these rules have been applied can the other criteria (issue of residence documents or visas, entry and/or stay, etc.) be considered.

Moreover, according to the 'discretionary clause' of Article 17(2) of the Dublin III Regulation, a Member State may be requested to take charge of the applicant 'in order to bring together any family relations, on humanitarian grounds based in particular on family or cultural considerations'.[90] This provision is only to a limited extent applied on the ground, however (Intzipeoglou & Nefeli Skotori, this volume).

4. International and Council of Europe human rights law

4.1 Explicit references to family reunification

In its current state, human rights law does not include a subjective right to family reunification. The Convention on the Rights of the Child (CRC) does establish a procedural obligation to examine family reunification applications of children or their parents 'in a positive, humane and expeditious manner'.[91] This is today 'the strongest explicit commitment to family reunification in international law' (Palander et al., 2023, p. 17). Moreover, states must ensure that a family reunification application does not entail adverse consequences for the applicants and their family members.[92] With respect to refugee and asylum-seeking children in particular, states are required to assist in family tracing and family reunification.[93] According to the UN Committee on the Rights of the Child, the term 'family' must be interpreted broadly, including biological, adoptive or foster parents or, where applicable, members of the extended family or community.[94]

Moreover, states are obliged to facilitate family reunification with foreign workers, if they are a party to the Migrant Workers' Convention (which no EU Member State is, though) and/or the Revised European Social Charter.[95] The

89 Article 10 Dublin III Regulation; Article 27 RAMM Regulation. Article 11 Dublin III Regulation, establishes a 'family procedure' for cases in which 'several family members and/or minor unmarried siblings submit applications for international protection in the same Member State simultaneously, or on dates close enough for the procedures for determining the Member State responsible to be conducted together, and where the application of the criteria set out in this Regulation would lead to their being separated'. See also Article 28 RAMM Regulation.

90 Compare Article 35 RAMM Regulation: 'on humanitarian grounds based in particular on meaningful links regarding family, social or cultural considerations'.

91 Article 10(1) CRC. Moreover, states must ensure that such an application does not entail adverse consequences for the applicants and their family members.

92 Ibid.

93 Article 22(2) CRC.

94 CRC Committee, General Comment No. 14 on the right of the child to have his or her best interests taken as a primary consideration (art. 3, para. 1), 29 May 2013, UN Doc. CRC/C/GC/14, § 59. See also Article 5 CRC.

95 Article 44(2)–(3) International Convention on the Protection of the Rights of All Migrant Workers and Members of their Families (ICPMW); Article 19(6) Revised European Social Charter.

provisions on family reunification in the Migrant Workers' Convention relate to spouses or couples with a relationship equivalent to marriage, as well as their dependent unmarried children.[96] The Revised European Social Charter does not define 'family'.

4.2 The right to respect for family life and the prohibition of discrimination

The provisions enshrining human rights differ from the rules providing a right to family reunification that have been explained before. These human rights provisions may lead to obligations in relation to family reunification, yet this is currently far from always the case (see generally Klaassen, 2015).

The right to respect for family life is guaranteed by multiple international and European human rights treaties, such as Article 17 of the International Covenant on Civil and Political Rights (ICCPR) and Article 8 of the European Convention on Human Rights (ECHR).[97] According to the European Court of Human Rights (ECtHR), the existence of 'family life' within the meaning of Article 8 ECHR 'is essentially a question of fact depending upon the real existence in practice of close personal ties' (on 'doing family', see Belloni & Cleton, this volume).[98] Generally, the Court considers as family life the relationships between spouses and unmarried partners (with no discrimination allowed based on sexual orientation)[99] as well as between parents and children. Beyond the nuclear family, the Court requires additional elements of dependency, consisting of 'more than the normal emotional ties'.[100] In their contribution to this volume, Den Haese and Verhellen explain how the case law of the ECtHR interacts with rules of private international law on the recognition of a (change in) personal status obtained abroad.

Both the UN Human Rights Committee[101] and the ECtHR[102] have only in limited circumstances identified a positive obligation for states to allow family reunification. The cautious jurisprudence of the ECtHR took off with the landmark case of *Abdulaziz, Cabales and Balkandali*, in which the Court held that the obligations imposed under Article 8 ECHR do not include a right of married couples to choose their country of residence (see also de Hart, this volume).[103] The Court applies the so-called elsewhere approach, in which applicants are required to show that there are obstacles to establishing family life in their home countries or that there

96 Article 44(2) ICPMW.

97 See also Article 23 ICCPR, recognizing family as 'the natural and fundamental group unit of society', requiring its protection.

98 ECtHR, 12 July 2001, *K and T. v. Finland*, No. 25702/94, § 150.

99 ECtHR, 23 February 2016, *Pajić v. Croatia*, No. 68453/13.

100 See, e.g., ECtHR, 30 June 2015, *A.S. v. Switzerland*, No. 39350/13.

101 See, e.g., Human Rights Committee, 20 August 2010, *El-Hichou v. Denmark*, Comm. No. 1554/2007, UN Doc. CCPR/C/99/D/1554/2007.

102 See, e.g., ECtHR, 21 December 2001, *Şen v. the Netherlands*, No. 31465/96; ECtHR, 1 December 2005, *Tuquabo-Tekle and Others v. the Netherlands*, No. 60665/00.

103 ECtHR, 24 April 1985, *Abdulaziz, Cabales and Balkandali v. The United Kingdom*, Nos 9214/80, 9473/81, 9474/81, § 68.

are 'special reasons' why this cannot be expected from them.[104] For the ECtHR, identifying state obligations in the context of family reunification implies that a 'fair balance . . . has to be struck between the competing interests of the individual and of the community as a whole', in which the State enjoys 'a certain margin of appreciation'.[105] In this balancing exercise, various factors are to be taken into account, including the extent to which family life is effectively ruptured, the extent of the ties in the host state, the existence of insurmountable obstacles to one or more family members living in the country of origin, factors of immigration control and of public order and whether family life was created at a moment that the persons involved were aware of the precarious immigration status.[106] When children are involved, additional relevant factors include the age of the children, their situation in the country of origin and their degree of dependence on their parents.[107]

In relation to refugees, the ECtHR accepts that there are unsurmountable obstacles to establishing family life in their home country, given their well-founded fear of persecution upon return. This, in principle, implies a positive obligation for the host state to admit refugees' family members.[108] Regarding family reunification with persons enjoying subsidiary or temporary protection, the ECtHR decided in 2021 in *M.A. v. Denmark* that a three-year waiting period for applying for family reunification, without an individualized assessment, constituted a violation of Article 8 ECHR – even though the Court also emphasized the wide margin of appreciation of States in this area.[109] In *M.T. and Others v. Sweden* of 2022, the ECtHR then held that the suspension of family reunification in Sweden between 2016 and 2019 for subsidiary protection holders did *not* violate Article 8 ECHR, among others because an individualized assessment was (arguably) provided and the suspension had been of a temporary nature.[110] Moreover, in the view of the Court, the differential treatment of subsidiary protection holders and recognized refugees did not entail a violation of the prohibition of discrimination (Article 14 ECHR, alone or in conjunction with Article 8).[111] Also more generally, the ECtHR has been criticised for its restrictive approach and its inconsistent case law on Article 8 ECHR in (family) migration cases (Dembour, 2015; Klaassen, 2019; Milios, 2018).[112] By

104 Ibid.

105 ECtHR, 19 February 1996, *Gül v. Switzerland*, No. 23218/94, § 38.

106 ECtHR, 31 January 2006, *Rodrigues da Silva and Hoogkamer v. the Netherlands*, No. 50435/99, § 39.

107 ECtHR, 21 December 2001, *Şen v. the Netherlands*, No. 31465/96, § 37.

108 ECtHR, 12 October 2006, *Mubilanzila Mayeka and Kaniki Mitunga v. Belgium*, No. 13178/03, § 75; ECtHR, 10 July 2014, *Tanda-Muzinga v. France*, No. 2260/10, § 73. See also Groenendijk and Strik (2022, p. 322). See also ECtHR, 4 July 2023, *B.F. v. Switzerland*, Nos. 13258/18, 15500/18, 57303/18 and 9078/20, on the additional requirement of non-reliance on social assistance imposed by Switzerland on refugees '*sur place*', i.e., refugees where the grounds for refugee status arose *after* the departure from their countries of origin.

109 ECtHR, 9 July 2021, *M.A. v. Denmark* [GC], No. 6697/18.

110 ECtHR, 20 October 2022, *M.T. and Others v. Sweden*, No. 22105/18.

111 Ibid. For a critique, see Cowan (2022).

112 The 'rights holders' in these cases before the ECtHR are the sponsors, present in a Council of Europe country. Palander (2023) suggests that also the rights of family members abroad could

contrast, in *Biao v. Denmark*, the ECtHR did find a violation of the prohibition of discrimination, laid down in Article 14 ECHR, in conjunction with the enjoyment of the right to respect for family life of Article 8 ECHR, because of the difference in treatment in the family reunification rules between persons born with the Danish nationality and those who acquired it later in life (and were thus migrants).[113]

4.3 Children's rights law

Transversally, the rights of the child, as primarily enshrined in the Convention on the Rights of the Child, should be applied in all family reunification cases. Particularly relevant are the requirement that the best interests of the child are a 'primary consideration' in all actions concerning children[114] and the prohibition of family separation (see more elaborately Boreil et al., 2020).[115]

5. International migration and refugee law

Neither the 1951 Refugee Convention nor its 1967 Protocol mention family reunification. Nonetheless, in its Final Act, the Conference drafting the convention recommended governments to take the necessary measures to protect the refugee's family, given that the 'unity of the family . . . is an essential right of the refugee'.[116] In addition, various soft law instruments on migration include a political commitment to facilitate family reunification. Pursuant to the New York Declaration for Refugees and Migrants, adopted in 2016 by the UN General Assembly, states 'will consider facilitating opportunities for safe, orderly and regular migration, including, as appropriate. . . family reunification'.[117] This Declaration has been further developed in the Global Compact for Safe, Orderly and Regular Migration (GCM), on the one hand, and the Global Compact for Refugees (GCR), on the other. One of the actions in the GCM to expand pathways for regular migration (Objective 5) reads, 'Facilitate access to procedures for family reunification for migrants at all skills levels through appropriate measures that promote the realisation of the right of family life and the best interests of the child'.[118] Even though the action positively refers to migrants 'at all skills levels', its overall formulation has been considerably weakened during the drafting process – indicating its politically sensitive nature (Groenendijk, 2018; Desmet, 2020). The GCR promotes family reunification

fall within the jurisdiction of the ECHR contracting partners, based on a functional criterion of extraterritorial jurisdiction.

113 ECtHR, 24 May 2016, *Biao v. Denmark* [GC], No. 38590/10.

114 Article 3(1) CRC.

115 Article 9(1) CRC.

116 Final Act of the United Nations Conference of Plenipotentiaries on the Status of Refugees and Stateless Persons, 25 July 1951, UN Doc. A/CONF.2/108/Rev.1, IV, B.

117 UN General Assembly, New York Declaration for Refugees and Migrants, 3 October 2016, UN Doc. A/RES/71/1, § 79 (hereinafter: New York Declaration).

118 UN General Assembly, Global Compact for Safe, Orderly and Regular Migration, Objective 5: Enhance availability and flexibility of pathways for regular migration, paragraph 21, i)., Resolution 73/195, 11 January 2019, UN Doc. A/RES73/195.

as a complementary pathway for admission,[119] following states' commitment in the New York Declaration to consider 'flexible arrangements to assist family reunification' with refugees.[120]

6. Concluding reflections

To know whether you have a right to family reunification in Europe is far from evident, given the complexity and fragmentation of the relevant rules. Legal instruments define the sponsors and family members eligible for family reunification differently. They are mostly limited to a variation of the Western nuclear family. Such an approach neither reflects sociological changes in family models nor does it take the realities of extended families into account (Saroléa & Merla, 2021; Christ & Etzold, this volume; Intzipeoglou & Skotori, this volume). The importance of extended families is often associated with 'non-Western' countries. In this sense, it is remarkable that the Citizens Directive does recognise the relevance of 'other' family members of mobile EU citizens, whose family reunification is to be 'facilitated'.[121] Moreover, substantive (and procedural) requirements may hinder persons in enjoying their family reunification rights. These diversified rules lead to pressing questions from an equality and non-discrimination perspective, which are further addressed in this volume from both a legal (Groenendijk) and socio-legal (de Hart) perspective.

References

Adamo, S. (2016). Keeping up with the (Turkish) family: Integration requirements for family reunification in Genc. *EU Law Analysis*. http://eulawanalysis.blogspot.be/2016/04/keeping-up-with-turkish-family

Berneri, C. (2017). *Family Reunification in the EU: The Movement and Residence Rights of Third Country National Family Members of EU Citizens*. Bloomsbury Publishing.

Boreil, F., Desmet, E., Dimitropoulou, G., & Klaassen, M. (2020). *Family Reunification for Refugee and Migrant Children: Standards and Promising Practices*. Council of Europe.

Council of Europe Commissioner for Human Rights. (2017). *Realising the right to family reunification of refugees in Europe*. Council of Europe. www.refworld.org/docid/5a0d5eae4.html

Cowan, C. (2022). *M.T. and Others vs. Sweden*: The right to family reunification – does subsidiary protection lead to a subsidiary right to family life? *Strasbourg Observers*. https://strasbourgobservers.com/2022/11/29/m-t-and-others-vs-sweden-the-right-to-family-reunification-does-subsidiary-protection-status-lead-to-a-subsidiary-right-to-family-life/

de Hart, B., Verweij, E., & Arbaoui, Y. (2022). *Heb geduld. De betekenis van het afhankelijk verblijfsrecht in het dagelijks leven van huwelijksmigranten en hun partners*. https://acmrl.org/wp-content/uploads/2022/12/Rapport-afhankelijk-verblijfsrecht-def-5-12-2022-1.pdf

119 UN General Assembly, Report of the United Nations High Commissioner. Part II. Global compact on refugees. UN Doc. A/73/12 (Part II) (2018), § 95.

120 New York Declaration, § 79.

121 The Belgian legislator has granted these 'other' family members of EU citizens a *right* to family reunification. Articles 47/1–47/4 Aliens Act.

Dembour, M.-B. (2015). *When Humans Become Migrants: A Study of the European Court of Human Rights with an Inter-American Counterpoint*. Oxford University Press.
Desmet, E. (2020). Het migratiepact: Aanleidingen voor de crisis en beleidsuitdagingen voor België. In T. Moonen, E. Desmet, & T. Ruys (Eds.), *Het migratiepact: Kroniek van een crisis* (pp. 7–36). Die Keure.
European Council on Refugees and Exiles (ECRE). (2023a). *Not there yet: Family reunification for beneficiaries of international protection*. ECRE. https://ecre.org/wp-content/uploads/2023/02/AIDA-Family-Reunification-February-2023.pdf
European Council on Refugees and Exiles (ECRE). (2023b). *Reforming EU asylum law: The final stage. ECRE's analysis of the most important unresolved issues in the legislative reform of the common European asylum system (CEAS) and recommendations to the co-legislators*. ECRE. Policy-Parper-Reforming-EU-Asylum-Law-the-Final-Stage-August-2023.pdf (ecre.org)
European Migration Network (EMN). (2017). *EMN synthesis report for the EMN focussed study 2016. Family reunification of third-country nationals in the EU plus Norway: National practices*. https://emnbelgium.be/sites/default/files/publications/FINAL_00_family_reunification_synthesis_report_final_en_print_ready.pdf
Groenendijk, K. (2018). GCM Commentary: Objective 5: Enhance Availability and Flexibility of Pathways for Regular Migration. In E. Guild & T. Basaran (Eds.), *The UN's Global Compact for Safe, Orderly and Regular Migration: Analysis of the Final Draft, Objective by Objective* (pp. 19–20). University of London.
Groenendijk, K., & Strik, T. (2022). Directive 2003/86 on the Right to Family Reunification: A Surprising Anchor in a Sensitive Field. In E. Tsourdi & P. De Bruycker (Eds.), *Research Handbook on EU Migration and Asylum Law* (pp. 306–326). Edward Elgar. https://doi.org/10.4337/9781786439635.00023
Guild, E. (2019). EU citizens, foreign family members and European Union law. *European Journal of Migration and Law*, *21*(3), 358–373. https://doi.org/10.1163/15718166-12340055
Klaassen, M. A. K. (2015). *The right to family unification: Between migration control and human rights* [Doctoral thesis, Leiden University]. Leiden University Repository. https://hdl.handle.net/1887/36049
Klaassen, M. A. K. (2019). Between facts and norms: Testing compliance with Article 8 ECHR in immigration cases. *Netherlands Quarterly of Human Rights*, *37*(2), 157–177. https://doi.org/10.1177/0924051919844387
Klaassen, M. A. K., & Rodrigues, P. (2017). The best interests of the child in EU family reunification law: A plea for more guidance on the role of article 24(2) charter. *European Journal of Migration and Law*, *19*(2), 191–218. https://doi.org/10.1163/15718166-12340007
Kroeze, H. (2021). *For whom I love I want to be known: The scope of EU citizens' family reunification rights: Addressing legal fragmentation in the European Union's multi-layered legal order* [Doctoral thesis, Ghent University].
Milios, G. (2018). The immigrants and refugees' right to "family life": How relevant are the principles applied by the European Court of human rights? *International Journal of Minority and Group Rights*, *25*(3), 401–430. https://doi.org/10.1163/15718115-02503001
Milios, G. (2023). The Right to Family Reunification Under the Temporary Protection Directive and Council Decision 2022/382: Preserving Family Unity for the Beneficiaries of Temporary Protection. In S. Carrera & M. Ineli-Ciger (Eds.), *EU Responses to the Large-Scale Refugee Displacement from Ukraine: An Analysis on the Temporary Protection Directive and Its Implications for the Future EU Asylum Policy* (pp. 225–235). European University Institute.
Nicholson, F. (2018). *The "Essential Right" to Family Unity of Refugees and Others in Need of International Protection in the Context of Family Reunification*. UNHCR.
Nicholson, F. (2021). The Right to Family Reunification. In C. Costello, M. Foster, & J. McAdam (Eds.), *The Oxford Handbook of International Refugee Law* (pp. 988–1006). Oxford University Press.
Palander, J. (2023). Recognizing Insecurities of Family Members Abroad: Human Rights Balancing in European and Finnish Case Law. In M. Tiilikainen, J. Hiitola,

A. A. Ismail, & J. Palander (Eds.), *Forced Migration and Separated Families: Everyday Insecurities and Transnational Strategies* (pp. 43–61). Springer. https://doi.org/10.1007/978-3-031-24974-7_3

Palander, J., Baraka, U., Gustafsson, H., & Kvalvaag, A. M. (2023). International Human Rights Frameworks in Relation to National Family Reunification Policy and Administrative Practice. In M. Tiilikainen, J. Hiitola, A. A. Ismail, & J. Palander (Eds.), *Forced Migration and Separated Families: Everyday Insecurities and Transnational Strategies* (pp. 15–37). Springer. https://doi.org/10.1007/978-3-031-24974-7_2

Peers, S. (2014). The CJEU transforms family reunion for Turkish citizens. *EU Law Analysis*. http://eulawanalysis.blogspot.nl/2014/07/thecjeu-transforms-family-reunion-for.html

Peers, S. (2015). EU Migration Law and the EU/Turkey Association Agreement. In D. Thym & M. Zoeteweij-Turhan (Eds.), *Rights of Third-Country Nationals Under EU Association Agreements: Degrees of Free Movement and Citizenship* (pp. 202–222). Brill Nijhoff.

Peers, S. (2016). *EU Justice and Home Affairs Law: Volume I: EU Immigration and Asylum Law*. Oxford University Press.

Saroléa, S., & Merla, L. (2021). Migrantes et sédentaires: Des familles ontologiquement différentes? In L. Merla, S. Saroléa, & B. Schoumaker (Eds.), *Composer avec les normes. Trajectoires de vie et agentivité de migrants face au cadre légal* (pp. 259–291). Academia L'Harmattan.

3 Personal status across borders

Family reunification procedures meet private international law

Sarah Den Haese and Jinske Verhellen

1. Introduction

The terms and conditions to apply and qualify for family reunification in Europe can be found most importantly in the Family Reunification Directive (2003/86/EC), the Citizens Directive (2004/38/EC) and national legislation (Desmet, this volume). This legal framework on family reunification adopts a narrow understanding of the family: only the spouse, registered partner and the underage, unmarried biological or adopted children[1] are eligible for family reunification. These family ties have to be demonstrated by official documents like marriage certificates and birth certificates. Yet migrants regularly find themselves confronted with huge difficulties or even the impossibility of submitting a document to provide evidence of their personal or family status. Moreover, in some cases the foreign family relationship does not fit into the categories of the rules on family reunification. The Islamic institution of *kafala* – a child protection measure – is a well-known illustration of the latter (see later in this chapter).

In this chapter, the notion 'personal status' encompasses all the legal elements that identify a person as an individual and as a member of a family. This concept covers the elements of personal status in the strict sense (e.g., name, gender, age), but also family status (e.g., marriage, partnership, filiation and adoption) (Pfeiff, 2017, p. 35; de Groot, 2021).

The cross-border recognition of facts and documents concerning migrants' personal status is a prerequisite for family reunification. It brings family reunification procedures into the field of private international law. Private international law rules determine whether a family relationship established in State A has legal consequences in State B. What are the grounds to grant or refuse recognition in France, Italy or Spain of a marriage concluded in Somalia, Pakistan or Ivory Coast?

This chapter will first link family reunification procedures to the specific field of private international law (Section 2): what is private international law, and where can private international law rules be found? Subsequently, we will discuss the

1 When the sponsor is an EU citizen, the dependent direct relatives in the ascending line and those of his/her/their spouse or registered partner also qualify for family reunification. This is not the case for family reunification with a third-country national.

DOI: 10.4324/9781003503217-4

interactions between private international law and European human rights law (Section 3) as well as the interactions between private international law and EU law (Section 4). The aim of this chapter is to highlight the importance and potential of private international law in a migration context and to unravel its complexity for legal scholars, social scientists and actors in the field.

2. Recognition of personal status: a prerequisite for family reunification

2.1 Entering the field of private international law

Questions regarding the validity of a family relationship obtained abroad belong to the field of private international law. The fundamental objective of this field of law is to guarantee the continuity across borders of one's personal status and to avoid limping situations, in which the personal status is considered lawful and valid in one legal order, but not in another. An example of such a limping legal relationship is the existence of a child marriage concluded in Syria versus the non-recognition of this marriage in, e.g., Portugal. Hence, this couple is married in Syria but not in Portugal. In principle, cross-border mobility in general,[2] and migration in particular, should not lead to a loss of one's personal status. However, the current family reunification policies put considerable strain on this core mission of private international law because there is a persistent tension between successfully maintaining cross-border family life and upholding the interests of States in controlling migration (Verhellen, 2018).

Private international law rules determine under which formal and substantive conditions a foreign judgement (e.g., divorce decree or guardianship decision) or authentic document (e.g., birth or marriage certificate) can be recognised in another country. The most important formal requirement is the proof of authenticity of the foreign document. Depending on the country of origin, this includes the legalisation of the document or the attachment of an apostille seal (see later in this chapter).[3] In turn, public policy is an important substantive requirement on the basis of which fundamental values and norms can be protected. So, the question whether, and under which conditions, the aforementioned child marriage celebrated in Syria (or in a Turkish refugee camp) can be recognised in an EU country, is a question of private international law (Bruijnen, this volume). Its recognition is a precondition for family reunification.

2 Not every mobility across borders contains a migration element. The decision of two Italian nationals, living and working in Italy, to make use of a Russian surrogacy agency to become the parents of a child, has little to do with migration law.

3 Legalisation is often a long and costly process. To enhance the cross-border mobility of documents, the Hague Conference of Private International Law introduced a simplified form of legalisation in the 1961 Apostille Convention. Where legalisation requires a chain of signatures, the 1961 Apostille Convention allows a Contracting State to legalise a document with a single stamp or sticker, known as an 'apostille'.

Private international law rules provide for the criteria to grant or to refuse recognition of a personal status obtained abroad. Contrary to what one might expect in this cross-border context, each State has its own private international law rules in place. However, throughout the years, more and more countries have engaged in international co-operation in the field of private international law to enable the cross-border movement of persons and families. Next, we will give a brief overview of the existing international and European legal framework in this field. Both the Hague Conference of Private International Law[4] (HCCH) and the European Union have taken – and are currently still taking – steps to harmonise domestic private international law rules. Besides these specific private international law instruments, we will also refer to the Refugee Convention, which is the only other convention that encompasses a private international law provision on the personal status of refugees. At the UN level, the Global Compact for Migration[5] refers to the issue of personal status of migrants in general. In its Objective 4 (para. 20), the Compact commits 'to fulfil the right of all individuals to a legal identity by providing all . . . nationals with proof of nationality and relevant documentation, allowing national and local authorities to ascertain a migrant's legal identity' and 'to ensure . . . that migrants are issued adequate documentation and civil registry documents, such as birth, marriage and death certificates, at all stages of migration, as a means to empower migrants to effectively exercise their human rights'.

2.2 HCCH Conventions

The HCCH has drafted several instruments regarding the cross-border portability of personal statuses. In a family reunification context, especially the rules on the recognition in the country of destination of a family relationship established in the country of origin, are crucial.

To limit the administrative hurdles for people, the *1961 Apostille Convention* (currently 216 Contracting Parties – including all EU Member States[6]) abolished the traditional requirement of legalisation for documents circulating between Contracting States and replaced it by the apostille. By introducing the apostille certificate, people no longer need to collect legalisation in the form of a string of signatures and/or stamps, which is often a long and costly process.[7] Instead, a

4 The HCCH is composed of 91 members: 90 States and the European Union (situation on 6 January 2023). See www.hcch.net/en/about.

5 UN General Assembly, Global Compact for Safe, Orderly and Regular Migration, 11 January 2019, UN Doc. A/RES73/195.

6 For the latest status table on the number of Contracting Parties to these conventions, see hcch.net.

7 Often, legalisation involves two steps. Step 1: one or more authorities in State A check that the document has been signed by the relevant official authority in State A. In Belgium, a document issued by the municipality (e.g., a marriage or birth certificate) must first be signed by the major, alderman or delegated official of that municipality. Afterwards, the Federal Service of Public Affairs places a stamp or sticker on the document. This shows State B that the document has been issued by

certificate issued by a Competent Authority[8] in the country where the document was drafted suffices to certify the document's authenticity. For instance, when submitting a Moroccan marriage certificate in Belgium, an apostille suffices to prove its formal authenticity. For a document from Somalia, however, legalisation will still be needed, as Somalia has not ratified the Apostille Convention.

Throughout the years, the HCCH also developed matter-specific instruments. On 1 May 1991, the *1978 Marriage Convention* entered into force. This Convention, encompassing rules on the celebration and recognition of marriages, never fulfilled its full potential, as it was only ratified by Australia, Luxembourg and the Netherlands. More successful are the *1993 Hague Adoption Convention* (currently 106 Contracting Parties) and the *1996 Hague Child Protection Convention* (currently 54 Contracting Parties).[9] All three conventions – as all other conventions of the HCCH – aim at unifying the domestic private international law rules.[10]

The 1993 Adoption Convention, however, also deals with the migratory status of the child in the country of the prospective adoptive parents. Cooperation between the Central Authorities of the State of origin of the child and the State of residence of the adoptive parents ensures that the adoption can only take place once it has been determined that the child is authorised to enter and reside permanently in the receiving State.[11] By contrast, the 1996 Child Protection Convention does not deal with this 'family reunification aspect' and stipulates that 'it does not apply to decisions on the right of asylum and on immigration'.[12] However, this does not mean that issues of parental responsibility or measures for the protection of children (such as *kafala* or guardianship decisions) are excluded from its scope of application for the mere fact that they arise in a context of asylum or immigration (Lagarde, 1996, § 36). So, the question whether a Moroccan *kafala* decision on the basis of which a Moroccan couple living in Spain accepts the responsibility to take care of a Moroccan orphan, can be recognised in Spain has to be assessed under the criteria of the 1996 Convention. The question whether and under which conditions that child can live in Spain must be assessed under the applicable migration law rules (see Section 4.3).

Currently, the HCCH is working on a general private international law instrument on legal parentage, including international surrogacy.[13]

---

a Competent Authority in State A. Step 2: State B checks the formal validity of the document and legalises the document with a stamp or sticker. Usually, this is done by an embassy, consulate-general or honorary consul of State B in State A.

8 A list of Competent Authorities can be found on the website of the HCCH. Retrieved 14 July 2023, from www.hcch.net/en/instruments/conventions/authorities1/?cid=41.

9 For the latest status table on the number of Contracting Parties to these conventions, see hcch.net.

10 Article 1 Statute of the Hague Conference on Private International Law.

11 Articles 17(d) and 18 1993 Hague Convention.

12 Article 4(j) 1996 Hague Convention.

13 For more information. Retrieved 10 January 2023, from www.hcch.net/en/projects/legislative-projects/parentage-surrogacy.

2.3 European Regulations

At the level of the European Union, the *Regulation on Public Documents*[14] further reduces the administrative hurdles related to legalisation and translation of documents. This Regulation provides a simplified circulation system for public documents issued by the authorities of a Member State that have to be presented to the authorities of another Member State. It builds on the principle of mutual trust and the assumption that equivalent legal guarantees exist in all EU Member States.

The scope of the Regulation comprises documents concerning birth, a person being alive, death, name, marriage, divorce, registered partnership, parenthood, adoption, domicile and/or residence, and nationality (Article 2). For such public documents, the formalities required for their cross-border circulation are simplified: no legalisation or similar formality (such as an apostille) is necessary (Article 4). Moreover, public documents issued in one Member State are exempted from a sworn translation for usage in another Member State when the document is accompanied by a multilingual standard form included in the Regulation (Article 6).

The Regulation's scope of application is, however, narrow. First, it only governs the circulation of such public documents within the European Union and only applies to public documents issued by the authorities of a Member State. Consequently, it primarily simplifies the family reunification procedure of EU citizens. However, the Regulation could also impact the family reunification of third-country nationals if they have family ties that are created in an EU State of transit. For instance, children born in a refugee camp in Greece, who have their birth registered there, benefit from the Regulation when presenting their Greek birth certificate in Germany, France or the Netherlands (Corneloup & Verhellen, 2021, p. 521; Ho-Dac et al., 2023). The nationality of the person is irrelevant. Decisive is the issuing authority. The birth of a non-EU national falls within the scope of the Regulation if the issuing authority is the authority of a Member State. Second, it is not a Regulation on the recognition of personal status itself (the content, known as *negotium*), but on the recognition of the public document attesting these personal or family status events (the *instrumentum* delivered by a public authority). As such, the Regulation only deals with the authenticity of foreign documents and not with the validity of their content. Article 2.4 clearly states that '[t]his Regulation does not apply to the recognition in a Member State of legal effects relating to the content of public documents issued by the authorities of another Member State'. Rules regarding the recognition of the legal personal status itself, obtained in another EU Member State, must therefore be sought elsewhere: either in other EU law or in national law.

Several EU Regulations deal with this intra-EU recognition of judicial decisions and certain public documents. Within the context of this chapter, the *Brussels IIter*

14 Regulation (EU) 2016/1191 of the European Parliament and of the Council of 6 July 2016 on promoting the free movement of citizens by simplifying the requirements for presenting certain public documents in the European Union and amending Regulation (EU) No 1024/2012, *OJ L* 200, 26 July 2016, pp. 1–136.

Regulation should be mentioned.[15] The recognition in an EU Member State of a divorce, guardianship or foster care arrangement pronounced in another Member State falls within the scope of this Regulation. For instance, Belgian authorities have to assess an Italian judgement assigning a guardian to an unaccompanied minor in the light of this Regulation. A new guardianship/custody decision cannot be taken without considering the Italian judgement. The content and effects of the Italian decision must be recognised without any special procedure in Belgium, and the grounds for refusing recognition are limited and enlisted in Article 39 Brussels IIter Regulation. For instance, recognition shall be refused 'if such recognition is manifestly contrary to the public policy of the Member State in which recognition is invoked, taking into account the best interests of the child' or if the guardianship decision was given 'without the child who is capable of forming his or her own views having been given an opportunity to express his or her views', either directly, or through a representative or an appropriate body (Article 21 Brussels IIter).

The European Union is currently working on a Regulation aimed at harmonising the rules of private international law relating to parenthood in order to strengthen the protection of the fundamental rights of children in cross-border situations, including their right to an identity and to a private and family life.[16] The explanatory memorandum refers to the issue of limping situations: 'an estimated 2 million children may currently face a situation in which the recognition of their parenthood as established in one Member State is not recognised for all purposes in another Member State. . . . This non-recognition can have significant adverse consequences for children. It hinders their fundamental rights in cross-border situations and may result in the denial of the rights that they derive from parenthood under national law'. As the recognition of the legal parent–child relationship is a prerequisite for family reunification, the non-recognition can prevent the family from moving within the EU as family reunification may be refused. If a woman wants to move from the Netherlands to Lithuania with her family because of work, she will have to overcome different hurdles depending on her sexual orientation. If she is married to a woman, the *Coman* case (see Section 4.2) will make it possible for her wife to obtain a right of residence in Lithuania. If they have a child, the principles laid out in the *V.M.A.* case (see Section 4.2) must be applied pending the entry into force of a regulation on parenthood.

2.4 Refugee Convention

The Refugee Convention does not contain a specific reference to family reunification for refugees (Darling, 2019, p. 255). However, there is an important provision in this convention with regard to refugees' personal status.

15 Council Regulation (EU) 2019/1111 of 25 June 2019 on jurisdiction, the recognition and enforcement of decisions in matrimonial matters and the matters of parental responsibility, and on international child abduction (recast), *OJ L* 178, 2 July 2019, pp. 1–115.

16 Proposal for a Council Regulation on jurisdiction, applicable law, recognition of decisions and acceptance of authentic instruments in matters of parenthood and on the creation of a European Certificate of Parenthood, 7 December 2022, COM(2022) 695 final.

Article 12(1) of the Refugee Convention stipulates that 'the personal status of a refugee shall be governed by the law of the country of his domicile or, if he has no domicile, by the law of the country of his residence'. This provision is a private international law rule, or conflict rule. It determines directly the applicable law for the personal status of refugees and uses the domicile and, subsidiarily, the residence of the refugee as connecting factor. In areas where domestic (or European or international) private international law rules use 'nationality' as the connecting factor, the Refugee Convention obliges national authorities to apply the law of the country where the refugee is domiciled or has his/her/their habitual residence. Deciding otherwise disregards the need for protection against the government of the country one had to flee. For instance, the question whether the name of an Iraqi refugee changes after her marriage in Belgium to a Belgian citizen, will be determined by the law of the country where the Iraqi woman resides (not by her national Iraqi law[17]). Or, when a Syrian refugee marries another Syrian refugee in Belgium, Belgian marriage law will govern the marriage conditions (and not Syrian law, the law of their nationality[18]).

However, Article 12(1) should not result in forcing refugees to give up their status-based acquired rights (Hathaway, 2021, p. 249). The second paragraph of Article 12 provides for the protection of 'rights previously acquired by a refugee and dependent on personal status, more particularly rights attaching to marriage'. This provision expresses the principle of 'acquired or vested rights'. The respect for previously acquired rights, however, is not absolute. Article 12(2) provides for a public policy limitation: the right in question must be 'one which would have been recognized by the law of that State had he not become a refugee'. States should not be required to respect rights previously acquired by a refugee when these rights are contrary to their own law (Chetail, 2014, pp. 471–472).

3. Interactions between private international law and human rights law

3.1 Introduction

Private international law rules do not operate in a vacuum. The result after application of these rules must respect the rights and guarantees enshrined in the European Convention on Human Rights (ECHR). In her PhD research, Den Haese (2023) examined whether and to what extent human rights law can be invoked to obtain or prevent the recognition of a (change in) personal status obtained abroad. By thoroughly collecting (Den Haese, 2023, pp. 57–58) and examining case law of the ECtHR, she was able to distil some general principles. Next, we briefly discuss these principles, by focusing on 10 judgements of the European Court of Human Rights (ECtHR).

17 Which would normally be applicable in accordance with Article 38 Belgian Code of PIL.

18 Which would normally be applicable in accordance with Article 46 Belgian Code of PIL.

3.2 The right to receive a decision on family ties within a reasonable time

The cases of *Hussin v. Belgium*,[19] *Sylvester v. Austria (No. 2)*[20] and *Dadouch v. Malta*[21] illustrate that the right to have your case dealt with within a reasonable time[22] does not only apply to proceedings on the merits of the case but also to proceedings needed in order to get a foreign document recognised and/or enforced in another State. In *Hussin v. Belgium*, the Belgian courts needed 5,5 years to refuse the recognition of a German judgement establishing paternity. In *Sylvester v. Austria (No. 2)*, a little over 5 years passed until it was finally decided that the divorce decree pronounced in the USA could not be recognised in Austria. In *Dadouch v. Malta*, the applicant waited 2,5 years to get the news that his marriage celebrated in Russia could not be recognised in Malta.

The (non-)recognition of a family tie established abroad within a reasonable time can have far-reaching consequences (Baldassar, 2007; Belloni, 2020; Beloni & Verschraegen, this volume; Belloni & Cleton, this volume). The non-recognition of filiation can prevent parents from reuniting with their children. Consequently, parents can involuntarily be forced to watch their children grow up from a distance. The decision to refuse the validity of a divorce obtained abroad can make it impossible for the person(s) concerned to remarry and continue his/her/their life. The non-recognition of a marriage celebrated abroad can lead to the situation where spouses cannot live in the same country, and this for many years.

According to the ECtHR,

> the reasonableness of the length of the proceedings must be assessed in the light of the circumstances and with reference to the following criteria: the complexity of the case, the conduct of the applicant and the relevant authorities and what was at stake for the applicant in the dispute.[23]

Consequently, the seized State has the right to verify the authenticity and validity of a foreign document but must do so without any unnecessary delays. In the words of the ECtHR: 'In cases relating to civil status special diligence is required in view of the possible consequences which the excessive length of proceedings may have, notably on the enjoyment of the right to respect for family life'.[24] The fact that the (un)necessary delays have far-reaching consequences on people's family life must be taken into account by the authorities ruling on the validity of family ties established abroad, for instance, in the context of family reunification procedures.

19 ECtHR, 6 May 2004, *Hussin v. Belgium*, No. 70807/01 (inadmissible).
20 ECtHR, 3 February 2005, *Sylvester v. Austria (no. 2)*, No. 54640/00.
21 ECtHR, 20 July 2010, *Dadouch v. Malta*, No. 38816/07.
22 Enshrined in Articles 6 and 8 ECHR.
23 ECtHR, 6 May 2004, *Hussin v. Belgium*, No. 70807/01 (admissibility decision), § 14 and ECtHR, 3 February 2005, *Sylvester v. Austria (No. 2)*, No. 54640/00, § 28.
24 ECtHR, 3 February 2005, *Sylvester v. Austria (No. 2)*, No. 54640/00, § 32.

3.3 The right to recognition of an adoption obtained in good faith and serving the best interests of the child

In *Wagner and J.M.W.L. v. Luxembourg*,[25] the ECtHR looked into the decision of the Luxembourg authorities to refuse the recognition of an adoption order pronounced in Peru in accordance with Peruvian law. The case illustrates that the ECtHR does not oblige the Member States of the Council of Europe to recognise all adoptions obtained abroad without any form of control (Kinsch, 2010, p. 275). On the contrary, the ECtHR made it very clear that every (international) adoption should serve the best interests of the child concerned and that a non-recognition could be justified. However, in this case, the ECtHR stressed the fact that Ms. Wagner had acted in good faith and that she could legitimately expect that Luxembourg would recognise the adoption pronounced in Peru given that the adoption complied with all the rules and requirements laid down by Peruvian law and the attitude of the Luxembourg authorities for many years.[26] In addition, the ECtHR emphasised the social reality of the situation. The obstacles encountered in their daily life and the lack of legal protection of their relationship made it not possible for the child to fully integrate into the adoptive family.[27]

Wagner and J.M.W.L. v. Luxembourg illustrates the positive obligations arising under Article 8 ECHR. Article 8 ECHR does not only protect people against arbitrary interference with their private and/or family life (negative obligation) but also compels Contracting States to take appropriate steps to ensure the right to respect for private and family life (positive obligation). In the words of the ECtHR:

> where the existence of a family tie with the child has been established, the State must act in a manner calculated to enable that tie to be developed and establish legal safeguards that render possible the child's integration in his family.[28]

Even though Article 8 ECHR cannot be interpreted as entailing a general obligation for a State to authorise family reunion on its territory (see also Desmet, this volume),[29] the social reality of the situation can oblige Contracting States to recognise the personal status created abroad and grant a right of residence.

3.4 No obligation to recognise a polygamous marriage

Polygamy does not only occur in countries allowing people to have more than one spouse. In practice, polygamy is often the result of the non-recognition of the

25 ECtHR, 28 June 2007, *Wagner and J.M.W.L. v. Luxembourg*, No. 76240/01.

26 Ibid., § 130.

27 Ibid., §§ 132–133.

28 Ibid., § 119. See also ECtHR, 4 October 2012, *Harroudj v. France*, No. 43631/09, § 41 and ECtHR, 16 December 2014, *Chbihi Loudoudi and Others v. Belgium*, No. 52265/10, § 89.

29 See, for example, ECtHR, 24 May 2016, *Biao v. Denmark*, No. 38590/10, § 117.

dissolution of the previous marriage or the fact that one of the spouses remarried before his/her/their previous marriage was lawfully dissolved. In *Green and Farhat v. Malta*,[30] the ECtHR scrutinised the decision of the Maltese authorities to refuse the recognition of a polygamous marriage celebrated in Libya. The female applicant in this case, Ms. Green, a Maltase national, married another Maltese national in 1978. In 1980, the applicant moved to Libya and converted to Islam. In accordance with Libyan law, her first marriage was declared null and void and she was given the permission by a Libyan court to (re)marry in Libya. In August 1980, Ms. Green married her second husband in accordance to the rites of Islam and in conformity with Libyan law. For more than 20 years, the applicants lived as a lawfully married couple in Libya. After her father became ill, Ms. Green and her second husband wanted to move to Malta. The Maltese authorities, however, refused to recognise their marriage. According to the Maltese courts, Ms. Green was still married to her first husband, as the Libyan decision, which declared her first marriage null and void, could not be recognised in Malta. In its inadmissibility decision, the ECtHR came to the conclusion that Malta had struck a fair balance between the competing interests at stake. The ECtHR accepted that Malta deemed it necessary not to recognise the marriage concluded in Libya in order to prevent disorder and protect the rights of others.[31]

3.5 No obligation to recognise child marriages

In 2015, a (religiously) married couple initiated proceedings against Switzerland and claimed that the Swiss authorities had violated their right to respect for family life by expelling the husband to Italy. At the time of the marriage, the wife was 14 years old and the husband 18 years old. The ECtHR ultimately decided that Switzerland had not violated Article 8 because the marriage was invalid under Afghan law (national law of both spouses) and was incompatible with Swiss *ordre public*:

> Article 8 of the Convention cannot be interpreted as imposing on any State party to the Convention an obligation to recognise a marriage, religious or otherwise, contracted by a 14-year-old child. Nor can such obligation be derived from Article 12 of the Convention.[32]

3.6 No obligation to recognise same-sex marriages, but obligation to protect same-sex unions

As there is currently no consensus within the Council of Europe regarding the validity of same-sex marriages, the question arises whether a same-sex marriage

30 ECtHR, 6 July 2010, *Green and Farhat v. Malta*, No. 38797/07 (admissibility decision).
31 Ibid., p. 11.
32 ECtHR, 8 December 2015, *Z.H. and R.H. v. Switzerland*, No. 60119/12, § 44.

lawfully contracted in one Member State must be recognised in all other Member States. In *Orlandi and Others v. Italy*,[33] the ECtHR answered this question: Member States are under no obligation to recognise a same-sex marriage contracted abroad as a marriage if same-sex marriage is not provided for in domestic law. Moreover, the ECtHR explicitly accepted that States have a legitimate interest in avoiding domestic restrictions on same-sex marriage to be circumvented.[34] However, Member States must have a legal framework in place providing for the recognition and protection of same-sex unions. Consequently, same-sex couples lawfully married abroad have the right to have their marriage converted into a registered partnership or civil union with the aim of having their relationship legally protected.

3.7 No obligation to convert kafala into adoption

As mentioned earlier, 'other' family relations can be at stake in family reunification procedures, such as the *kafala*, which is an Islamic legal institution with the aim of protecting children (temporarily) deprived of a family environment. In the case of *kafala*, the care of a child (*makful*) is transferred from the biological parents to another person or other persons (*kafil*), as long as they are Muslims. The *kafil* can be a family member of the child (intrafamily *kafala*). *Kafala* can also be extra-family if the *kafil* is a third person who is not a relative of the *makful*. *Kafala* is a commitment to take responsibility for the protection, education and maintenance of an abandoned child as a father would for his own child. *Kafala* does not entail a filiation bond or inheritance rights. *Kafala* ends when the child reaches the age of majority (or until marriage in the case of girls) or when a judge terminates it (ISS, 2020; Yassari, 2015).

In *Harroudj v. France* and *Loudoudi v. Belgium*,[35] the ECtHR made it clear that although the relationship between a child placed in *kafala* care and the *kafil(s)* falls under the notion 'family life', Member States are under no obligation to convert *kafala* into an adoption. In both cases, the applicants requested the full adoption of the child placed in *kafala* care to obtain stronger legal effects than the more limited ones attached to *kafala*. Both France and Belgium refused to grant an adoption. Unlike in *Wagner and J.M.W.L. v. Luxembourg* (see Section 3.2), the ECtHR was not faced with the non-recognition of a change in personal status validly obtained abroad but with the decision not to establish a new legal status in order to avoid the creation of a limping legal relationship. Due to the fact that adoption is prohibited in the country of origin (Algeria in *Harroudj* and Morocco in *Loudoudi*), that country would not award any consequences to the adoption pronounced in Europe. In both cases, the ECtHR came to the conclusion that there was no violation of Article 8 ECHR.

33 ECtHR, 14 December 2017, *Orlandi and Others v. Italy*, Nos. 26431/12, 26742/12, 44057/12 and 60088/12.

34 Ibid., § 207.

35 ECtHR, 4 October 2012, *Harroudj v. France*, No. 43631/09 and ECtHR, 16 December 2014, *Chbihi Loudoudi and Others v. Belgium*, No. 52265/10.

In this context, it should be emphasised that the aforementioned 1996 Child Protection Convention also encompasses rules regarding the recognition of decisions on the provision of care by *kafala* as a measure related to the protection of children (Article 3, e). This inclusion of *kafala* led to Morocco being the first signatory State. Under the 1996 Convention, States may recognise the *kafala* obtained abroad, but the Convention does not entail an obligation on States to provide a right of residence for children under *kafala* (see Section 2.2 for the difference with adoption). The recognition of the *kafala*, which is not accompanied by the granting of a residence right, is a well-known illustration of insufficient coordination between migration law and private international law (Corneloup et al., 2017, p. 24).

3.8 Unaccompanied minors and the principle of presumption of minority

In order to benefit from the additional guarantees offered to unaccompanied minors or to qualify for family reunification, States request proof of minority. Individuals seeking international protection and claiming to be a minor are often forced to undergo a radiological age assessment test. The use of X-rays to determine age is a controversial topic (e.g., Hjern et al., 2012; Mateja et al., 2018; Aarseth et al., 2022).

In *Darboe and Camara v. Italy*,[36] the ECtHR ruled for the first time on the impact of medical age assessment tests on the fundamental rights of young refugees and migrants.[37] The applicant in this case, Darboe, had undergone an X-ray examination of his left wrist and hand in Italy. He claimed to be 17 years old. The medical report stated that he was 18 years old. Darboe stated that his consent to undergo this examination had not been acquired, that he had not been provided with a copy of the medical report, that no margin of error was indicated in the report and that no administrative or judicial decision regarding his age assessment had been communicated to him, making it impossible to lodge an appeal. In addition, no legal guardian had been appointed to assist him and safeguard his rights.[38]

The ECtHR took a procedural approach (Simon & Klaassen, 2022): qualifying the presumption of minority as an inherent element of the protection of the right to respect for private life,[39] the Court examined whether this presumption of minority and the corresponding procedural safeguards were respected. The ECtHR identified two procedural safeguards: 1) the appointment of a legal guardian or representative and 2) the right to information. Taking into account that Italy had failed to promptly appoint a legal guardian, that Darboe was placed in a reception centre for adults, that his medical report was not served on him and that it was not possible for him to lodge an appeal against the outcome of the age assessment test, the ECtHR concluded that Article 8 ECHR had been violated.[40]

36 ECtHR, 21 July 2022, *Darboe and Camara v. Italy*, No. 5797/17.
37 Followed by ECtHR, 14 September 2023, *Diakitè v. Italy*, No. 44646/17.
38 ECtHR, 21 July 2022, *Darboe and Camara v. Italy*, No. 5797/17, §§ 8–13, §§ 15–21 and §§ 143–144.
39 Ibid., § 153.
40 Ibid., §§ 143–150 and § 157.

In this case, the ECtHR unfortunately stated that 'its task [is] not to speculate on whether or not the applicant was a minor at the time of his arrival in Italy, or whether he submitted any documents to prove his age'.[41] Indeed, the presumption of minority should be the starting point, but if migrants effectively have documents to prove their minority, these should be taken into account. Having a date of birth that is the same in the country of birth and the country of destination serves the interests of cross-border continuity and avoids legal limbo.

4. Interactions between private international law and EU law

4.1 Introduction

Where the Council of Europe has neither the aspiration nor the capacity to harmonise (domestic) private international law rules, this is not the case for the European Union. The instruments discussed earlier illustrate this (see Section 2.3). In addition, general EU principles, like EU citizenship (Article 20 TFEU), the principle of non-discrimination (Article 18 TFEU) and the right to move freely within the territory of the Member States (Article 21 TFEU) can impose the obligation on Member States to recognise a (change in) family ties validly established abroad. Next we will discuss five rulings of the Court of Justice of the European Union (CJEU), dealing with the recognition of family ties in family reunification proceedings and the absence of documentary evidence to prove family ties.

4.2 Recognition of same-sex marriage for the purpose of family reunification

In *Coman and Others*,[42] the CJEU had to rule on the cross-border portability of a same-sex marriage validly contracted in Belgium. At the time of the marriage, Mr. Coman – a Romanian and American national – had his habitual residence in Brussels (Belgium). As same-sex marriage is not possible in Romania,[43] the question arose whether the Romanian authorities were under the obligation to recognise the marriage celebrated in Belgium and grant the husband of Mr. Coman the right to reside in Romania for more than three months as the couple wished to move to Romania.[44]

Although the recognition of a marriage validly contracted in another EU Member State is governed by domestic private international law rules, the decision not to recognise a foreign marriage falls within the scope of EU law because it can prevent an EU national from exercising their right of free movement. The CJEU first determined that even though the request for family reunification in an EU Member

41 Ibid., § 131.

42 CJEU, 5 June 2018, C-673/16, *Relu Adrian Coman and Others*, ECLI:EU:C:2018:385.

43 Article 259(1) Romanian Civil Code states: 'Marriage is the union freely consented to a man and a woman'. Article 227(2) clarifies that 'marriages between persons of the same sex entered into or contracted abroad by Romanian citizens or by foreigners shall not be recognised in Romania'. See CJEU, 5 June 2018, *Coman and Others*, ECLI:EU:C:2018:385, §§ 7–8.

44 Article 7(1)(d) juncto Article 2(2)(a) Citizens Directive.

State of which one of the spouses is a national does not fall within the scope of the Citizens Directive, the Directive must be applied by analogy.[45] The CJEU subsequently came to the conclusion that a same-sex spouse falls within the notion of 'spouse' in Article 2(2)(a) of the Citizens Directive. The CJEU invoked two reasons to justify its decision. First, the term 'spouse', within the meaning of the Citizens Directive, is gender-neutral and may therefore cover the same-sex spouse of an EU citizen.[46] Second, when comparing Article 2(2)(a) and Article 2(2)(b) of the Citizens Directive, it is clear that a Member State cannot rely on its national law as justification for refusing to recognise in its territory a marriage concluded by a third-country national with an EU citizen of the same sex in another Member State in accordance with the law of that State.[47] The freedom of movement of EU citizens cannot vary from one Member State to another depending on whether or not national law allows marriage by persons of the same sex (Kochenov & Belavusau, 2019; Kroeze & Safradin, 2019).[48]

More recently, in *V.M.A.*,[49] the CJEU was confronted with the issue of same-sex parenthood: V.M.A., a Bulgarian woman, and K.D.K., a British woman, married in Spain. Their daughter was born in Spain; the Spanish birth certificate mentioned both women as mother of the child. V.M.A. applied to the Sofia municipality in Bulgaria for a birth certificate for the child. The municipality refused to issue a birth certificate because it had no information concerning the identity of the child's biological mother and a reference to two female parents on a birth certificate was contrary to the public policy of Bulgaria, which does not permit marriage between two persons of the same sex. The CJEU ruled that any Member State has to recognise the parent–child relationship between a child and the two persons of the same sex designated as parents in a birth certificate issued by another Member State in the context of free movement – even if this Member State does not know the concept of parenthood of persons of the same sex in its own law. Moreover, it has to issue an identity document, such as a passport, to the child if they are a national of the host State.

Although the facts in this case do not have immediate links with family reunification or other residence procedures, the CJEU examines – in the final paragraphs of its judgement[50] – the hypothesis that the child is not of Bulgarian nationality. According to the Court, both the child and the spouse of V.M.A. must, irrespective of their nationality and whether or not they themselves are EU citizens, 'be regarded by all Member States as being, respectively, the spouse and the direct descendant within the meaning of Article 2(2)(a) and (c) of Directive 2004/38, and,

45 CJEU, 5 June 2018, *Coman and Others*, ECLI:EU:C:2018:385, §§ 20 and 25.
46 Ibid., § 35.
47 Ibid., § 36.
48 Ibid., § 39.
49 CJEU, 14 December 2021, C-490/20, *V.M.A.*, ECLI:EU:C:2021:1008. Followed by CJEU 24 June 2022, C-2/21, *Rzecznik Praw Obywatelskich*, ECLI:EU:C:2022:502, on a dispute between the Polish national ombudsman and the civil Kraków registry over the refusal to register a Spanish birth certificate in the Polish registers.
50 CJEU, 14 December 2021, C-490/20, *V.M.A.*, ECLI:EU:C:2021:1008, §§ 67–68.

therefore, as being V.M.A.'s family members'. In this respect, the Court follows the line taken in Coman, giving a specific Union law interpretation to the concepts of 'spouse' and 'direct descendant' used in the Citizens Directive.

4.3 Recognition of kafala for the purpose of family reunification

After having provided clarification on the notion 'spouse' (see Section 4.2), the CJEU was seized to take a stand on the notion 'direct descendent'. In *SM*,[51] the question arose whether a child placed under *kafala* care falls under the notion 'direct descendant'[52] or must be considered an 'other family member'[53] within the Citizens Directive. The qualification as a 'direct descendent' is not without importance. A 'direct descendent' enjoys a quasi-automatic right to enter and reside within the EU.[54] Other family members can only rely upon the obligation of Member States to facilitate the entry and residence on their territory. The host Member State shall undertake an extensive examination of the personal circumstances and shall justify any denial of entry or residence.[55]

The CJEU ultimately held that children placed under *kafala* care must be regarded as other family members within the Citizens Directive. If it is established that the *kafil* and *makfoul* live a genuine family life and relocation of the child serves the best interests of that child, the child will – in principle[56] – be granted a right of entry and residence in order to enable it to live with its guardian in his/her/their host Member State.[57]

4.4 Unmarried status of a child refugee: not a condition for family reunification

The CJEU ruled on whether a refugee child must be 'unmarried' in order to exercise the right to family reunification with his/her/their parents as an 'unaccompanied minor' pursuant to Article 10(3)(a) of the Family Reunification Directive.[58]

The daughter of X, a Palestinian woman, married at the age of 15 in Lebanon with Y.B., who has a valid residence permit in Belgium. The Belgian migration authorities did not recognise the marriage, as the child marriage was considered to be incompatible with public policy. The Belgian Guardianship Service deemed X's daughter to be an unaccompanied foreign minor and assigned her a guardian.

51 CJEU, 26 March 2019, C-129/18, *SM*, ECLI:EU:C:2019:248.
52 Article 2(2)(c) Citizens Directive.
53 Article 3(2)(a) Citizens Directive.
54 Opinion of Advocate General Campos Sánchez-Boordona in CJEU, 26 February 2019, C-129/18, *SM*, ECLI:EU:C:2019:140, §§ 67 and 91.
55 Article 3(2) Family Reunification Directive and opinion of Advocate General Campos Sánchez-Boordona in CJEU, 26 February 2019, C-129/18, *SM*, ECLI:EU:C:2019:140, § 91.
56 If the receiving Member State suspects child trafficking, (sexual) exploitation or abuse, forced labour, . . . the Member State can restrict the right of entry and residence. See CJEU, 26 March 2019, C-129/18, *SM*, ECLI:EU:C:2019:248, § 70.
57 CJEU, 26 March 2019, C-129/18, *SM*, ECLI:EU:C:2019:248, § 71.
58 CJEU, 17 November 2022, C-230/21, *X*, ECLI:EU:C:2022:887.

X's daughter lodged an application for international protection with the Belgian authorities and was recognised as a refugee. X, as the mother of the minor refugee recognised in Belgium, then applied for a family reunification visa at the Belgian embassy in Lebanon. The Belgian migration authorities rejected the visa application because the daughter was married and she was no longer a member of her parents' nuclear family. For the Belgian authorities, the daughter was unmarried for the purposes of her personal status, but married for the purposes of family reunification (Frasca & Carlier, 2023, p. 374). This paradox as a result of applying different legal frameworks (private international law and migration law), was highlighted by Advocate General Szpunar:

> A Member State's refusal to recognise a marriage involving a minor for public policy reasons whilst accepting that that marriage is effective as regards the right to family reunification would, in my view, be contrary both to the objective of family reunification and that of the prevention of forced marriages.
>
> Such a solution would mean that the State could deny that minor the right to family reunification with his or her ascendant relatives and refrain from protecting that minor from a marriage which that Member State itself accepts as being contrary to public policy.
>
> The minor would then be in a paradoxical situation in which his or her marriage could not have any legal effect in the territory of the Member State, whilst increasing his or her dependence on the unrecognised spouse, since the minor would be unable to enjoy the right to family reunification with his or her ascendant relatives.[59]

The CJEU ruled that migration authorities cannot add marital status to the definition of unaccompanied refugee minor in Article 10(3)(a) in conjunction with Article 2(f) of the Family Reunification Directive. An unaccompanied refugee minor residing in a Member State does not have to be unmarried in order to acquire the status of sponsor for the purposes of family reunification with his/her/their first-degree relatives in the direct ascending line.

4.5 Absence of documentary evidence

People applying for family reunification are expected to submit documentary evidence.[60] By providing documents, they can prove their age, marital status, filiation, etc. For people who obtained refugee or subsidiary protection status, it is often impossible (or at least very difficult) to submit (authentic) documents.

In the aforementioned case on the unmarried status of refugee children,[61] the CJEU also emphasises that the marital status of an unaccompanied refugee child may often be difficult to establish, 'particularly in the case of refugees from

59 Ibid., §§ 58–60.

60 See, e.g., Article 5(2) Family Reunification Directive.

61 CJEU, 17 November 2022, C-230/21, *X*, ECLI:EU:C:2022:887.

countries which are unable to issue reliable official documents'. Therefore, not restricting the benefit of family reunification only to unmarried unaccompanied refugee children is, according to the Court, 'also consistent with the principles of equal treatment and legal certainty, since it ensures that the right to family reunification does not depend on the administrative capabilities of the country of origin of the person concerned'.[62]

In 2019,[63] the CJEU was seized by a District Court in the Netherlands with the question whether an application for family reunification can be rejected solely on the ground that the sponsor has not provided official documentary evidence of the death of the minor's biological parents (see Arapiles & Mekonnen, this volume).[64] An Eritrean woman had submitted a statement from the Eritrean Liberation Front stating that she is the aunt and guardian of the child since the death of his biological parents. After having established that the CJEU had jurisdiction to issue a preliminary ruling,[65] the CJEU stressed the objective pursued by the Family Reunification Directive, namely, the promotion of family reunification.[66] National practices undermining this objective are prohibited. However, both the sponsor and the members of the family concerned by the application for family reunification are obliged to cooperate with the competent national authorities.[67] When official documentary evidence of the family relationship cannot be provided, the persons concerned must provide a reasonable explanation.[68] The fact that documentary evidence is lacking cannot be the sole reason for rejecting an application for family reunification.[69] The national authorities must take into consideration the specific circumstances of the sponsor and the minor and the particular difficulties they have encountered, according to their testimony, before and after fleeing their country of origin.[70] The Family Reunification Directive requires applications for family reunification to be examined on a case-by-case analysis and obliges Member States to take into account other evidence of the existence of a family relationship.[71] The national authorities are only entitled to reject the application if the sponsor flagrantly fails to fulfil their obligation to cooperate or it is clearly apparent that the application for family reunification is fraudulent.[72]

62 Ibid., § 46.
63 CJEU, 13 March 2019, C-635/17, *E.*, ECLI:EU:C:2019:192.
64 Ibid., § 44.
65 Although the Family Reunification Directive is not applicable to third-country family members of a beneficiary of subsidiary protection, the CJEU decided that it had jurisdiction to give a preliminary ruling since the Dutch legislature had chosen to apply the rules applicable to refugees under the Family Reunification Directive to beneficiaries of subsidiary protection. See CJEU 13 March 2019, C-635/17, ECLI:EU:C:2019:192, *E.*, §§ 34, 35 and 38.
66 Ibid., § 45.
67 Ibid., § 61.
68 Ibid., § 62.
69 Ibid., § 69.
70 Ibid., § 81.
71 Ibid., § 68.
72 Ibid., § 67.

5. Conclusion

This chapter discussed how personal status in a cross-border context brings a private law dimension to the family reunification procedures. The recognition in country A of the validity of a personal status established in country B is a private international law issue in a migration context. The application of the rules on family reunification implies knowledge of the private international law rules which are spread across different legal instruments.

Without always explicitly identifying it as private international law, a growing awareness of personal status issues in a cross-border context can be observed, both in legal and social scholarship and case law. Regarding the latter, we highlighted a few landmark decisions of the ECtHR and the CJEU that, for the moment, approach this private international law issue from different legal angles: the fundamental rights perspective (ECtHR) and free movement perspective (CJEU). According to us, these two approaches will, in time, converge in the human rights commitment of guaranteeing cross-border continuity of migrants' personal status.

Private international law and migration law interact, albeit based on different normative objectives: private international law aims at as much continuity of personal status across borders, whereas family reunification procedures are embedded in strict migration policies that often lead to discontinuity of personal status. Private international law and migration law scholars are increasingly aware of these interactions and these tensions. We encourage legal scholars and scholars in social sciences to join forces to think and go beyond these opposing normative choices.

References

Aarseth, S., Sund, T., Ording Müller, L., & Bring, J. (2022). Erroneous age assessment of young asylum seekers. *Tidsskriftet Den Norske Legeforening*. https://tidsskriftet.no/en/2022/08/opinions/erroneous-age-assessment-young-asylum-seekers

Baldassar, L. (2007). Transnational families and the provision of moral and emotional support: The relationship between truth and distance. *Identities: Global Studies in Culture and Power, 14*(4), 385–409. https://doi.org/10.1080/10702890701578423

Belloni, M. (2020). When the phone stops ringing: On the meanings and causes of disruptions in communication between Eritrean refugees and their families back home. *Global Networks, 20*(2), 256–273. https://doi.org/10.1111/glob.12230

Chetail, V. (2014). Les relations entre droit international privé et droit international des réfugiés: Histoire d'une brève rencontre. *Journal de Droit International, 141*, 447–475.

Corneloup, S., Heiderhoff, B., Honorati, C., Jault-Seseke, F., Kruger, T., Rupp, C., van Loon, H., & Verhellen, J. (2017). *Private international law in a context of increasing international mobility: Challenges and potential* (pp. 1–47). Study for the European Parliament. www.europarl.europa.eu/RegData/etudes/STUD/2017/583157/IPOL_STU(2017)583157_EN.pdf

Corneloup, S., & Verhellen, J. (2021). SDG 16: Peace, Justice and Strong Institutions. In R. Michaels, V. Ruiz Abou-Nigm, & H. van Loon (Eds.), *The Private Side of Transforming the World: UN Sustainable Development Goals 2030 and the Role of Private International Law* (pp. 505–540). Intersentia.

Darling, E. (2019). The Rights to Refugee Family Reunion. In S. Singh Juss (Ed.), *Research Handbook on International Refugee Law* (pp. 253–267). Edward Elgar Publishing. https://doi.org/10.4337/9780857932815.00025

de Groot, D. (2021). *The Many Faces of Civil Status Recognition: A Legal Analysis in the Light of EU Citizenship and the Case Law of the European Court of Justice and the European Court of Human Rights*. ProefschriftMaken.

Den Haese, S. (2023). *Crossing Borders: Proving Your Personal Status. Interactions Between Private International Law and Human Rights Law*. Eleven/Boom Juridisch.

Frasca, E., & Carlier, J.-Y. (2023). The best interests of the child in ECJ asylum and migration case law: Towards a safeguard principle for the genuine enjoyment of the substance of children's rights? *Common Market Law Review*, *60*, 345–389.

Hathaway, J. C. (2021). *The Rights of Refugees Under International Law*. Cambridge University Press. https://doi.org/10.1017/9781108863537.004

Hjern, A., Brendler-Lindqvist, M., & Norredam, M. (2012). Age assessment of young asylum seekers. *Acta Paediatrica*, *101*, 4–7. https://doi.org/10.1111/j.1651-2227.2011.02476.x

Ho-Dac, M., Bernard, E., Gössl, S. L., Melcher, M., & Nord, N. (2023). Reassessing regulation (EU) 2016/1191 on public documents in the light of EU citizenship. *Papers di Diritto Europeo*, 111–143. https://www.papersdidirittoeuropeo.eu/wp-content/uploads/2023/02/Ho-Dac_Bernard-Goessl-Melcher-Nord_Papers-di-diritto-europeo-2023-numero-speciale-special-issue.pdf

International Social Service (ISS). (2020). *Kafalah: Preliminary analysis of national and cross-border practices*. www.iss-ssi.org/index.php/en/news1/456-kafalah-preliminary-analysis-on-national-and-cross-border-practices

Kinsch, P. (2010). Recognition in the Forum of a Status Acquired Abroad – Private International Law Rules and European Human Rights Law. In K. Boele-Woelki & K. Siehr (Eds.), *Convergence and Divergence in Private International Law, Liber Amicorum Kurt Siehr* (pp. 232–275). Eleven International Publishing. https://papers.ssrn.com/sol3/papers.cfm?abstract_id=1743681

Kochenov, D., & Belavusau, U. (2019). *Same-sex spouses in the EU after Coman: More free movement, but what about marriage?* (EUI Department of Law Research Paper No. 2019/03, University of Groningen Faculty of Law Research Paper No. 34/2019). http://dx.doi.org/10.2139/ssrn.3468257

Kroeze, H., & Safradin, B. (2019). Een overwinning voor vrij verkeersrechten van regenboogfamilies in Europa: Het langverwachte Coman-arrest. *Nederlands Tijdschrift voor Europees Recht*, 1–2, 51–59. https://doi.org/10.5553/NtER/138241202019025102008

Lagarde, P. (1996). Explanatory report on the 1996 Hague child protection convention. *Proceedings of the Eighteenth Session, II*. https://www.hcch.net/en/publications-and-studies/details4/?pid=2943

Mateja, S., Sauer, B., & Gornik, B. (2018). *Unaccompanied Children in European Migration and Asylum Practices: In Whose Best Interests?* Routledge.

Pfeiff, S. (2017). *La portabilité du statut personnel dans l'espace européen: De l'émergence d'un droit fondamental à l'élaboration d'une méthode européenne de la reconnaissance*. Bruylant.

Simon, D., & Klaassen, M. (2022). *Age Assessment and the Presumption of Minority as a Prerequisite for Effective Human Rights Protection of Asylum Seekers: A Discussion of Darboe and Camara v. Italy*. Strasbourg Observers.

Verhellen, J. (2018). Cross-border portability of refugees' personal status. *Journal of Refugee Studies*, *31*(4), 427–443. https://doi.org/10.1093/jrs/fex026

Yassari, N. (2015). Adding by choice: Adoption and functional equivalents in Islamic and Middle Eastern law. *The American Journal of Comparative Law*, *63*(4), 927–962. https://doi.org/10.5131/AJCL.2015.0028

4 Families, family norms and policies

Insights from the social sciences

Milena Belloni and Laura Cleton

0. Introduction

This chapter intends to guide non-social scientists across the most relevant theoretical discussions that have shaped the debate of family reunification in the field. Namely, we focus on three key contributions that social sciences have offered to the understanding of family reunification: the importance of recognising how legal frameworks of family reunification contain and shape specific gendered, racialised and classed conceptions of 'the nation'; the significance of investigating the agency of families, officials and practitioners to understand how laws are implemented and how individuals, families and groups respond to them; the relevance of studying family reunification across national borders. We aim to show that these three theoretical contributions are valuable not only for social scientific debates, but also for legal scholarship and policy. After providing a brief genealogy of the study of family reunification, we draw on a wide range of socio-legal (see Feenan, 2013 for a review) and social studies to elucidate the meaning of commonly used concepts, such as the culturalisation of migration law, agency and structure and transnationalism. This allows us to provide an overview of the most relevant academic and societal debates on the topic of migrant families and family reunification and to suggest some ways ahead.

1. Studying families in migration

While anthropology and sociology have always been concerned with ideas of family, family structure, norms and kinship (see, e.g., Fox, 1967; Parkin & Stone, 2004), migration studies have started to deal more systematically with family migration only in the 1980s. Until then, as Kofman (2004) explains, international migration was primarily analysed through an economic perspective – the dominant paradigm in migration studies at large until the late 1970s. In this paradigm, individuals constitute the unit of analysis, and families are merely an aggregate of individual behaviours. Early studies moreover tended to assume that men are 'primary migrants' who respond to opportunities by moving for work, while women are 'secondary migrants' who passively follow their male relatives (Morokvásic, 1984; Kofman et al., 2000). Empirically, this resulted in limited attention to the lived realities of migrant families and few critical assessments of the laws and policies

DOI: 10.4324/9781003503217-5

regulating their migration. Theoretically, it also meant that gender, family and sexuality were often ignored in discussions on the politics of belonging, nationhood and migration (Bonjour & Cleton, 2021). It was not before the 'New Economics of Labor Migration' paradigm emerged in the late 1980s (Stark & Bloom, 1985) that migration scholars started to focus more specifically on families as decision-making actors who balance risks and opportunities of migration. Internal power dynamics and negotiation processes within families became objects of study only later (i.e., Rodenburg, 1997; de Haas & Fokkema, 2010). With a few rare pioneers in the 1980s and 1990s (e.g., Bhabha & Shutter, 1994), the scholarship on family migration and family reunification in Europe kicked off in the 2000s. Inspired by the work of feminist scholars on colonial empire and the nation state (Yuval-Davis, 1997; Stoler, 2002), contemporary scholars drew attention to the intricate linkages between membership to nation states, belonging and the intimate life of families. They show that collective identities and boundaries – whether national, cultural or racial – are crucially shaped by value-ridden ideas surrounding gender, sexuality and reproduction. Indeed, the decision of what kind of family is allowed to enter the nation is closely related to concerns for the future of the national identity: families are seen as core to the survival and reproduction of the nation as a demographic body and as a cultural and racial entity (van Walsum, 2008; Myrdahl, 2010; Wray, 2011). This crucial interlinkage between families, family migration and the reproduction of the nation makes the regulation of family reunification – perhaps more so than other immigration and naturalisation policies – crucial sites of contestation and political struggle (Moret et al., 2019).

2. Constructing the nation through family reunification laws and policies

In the last three decades, social scientists and socio-legal scholars at large working on migration governance have unravelled the conventional assumption that law and its resulting policies are neutral and unbiased (see de Hart, this volume). For family reunification in particular, sociological and anthropological approaches to law have shown that legal provisions and resulting policies in the Global North convey predefined ideas of particular kinds of family that are more 'desirable' and thus eligible for admission in the nation (Mustasaari, 2015; Kraler & Bonizzoni, 2010; Horsti & Pellander, 2015; Strasser et al., 2009; see also de Hart, this volume). By critically interrogating perceptions of the 'genuineness' of relationships, as well as norms related to the 'dependency' between family members, these scholars have demonstrated how historically rooted societal values and political discourses shape the way policies are written and put in practice.

Until the 2000s, social scientists mostly accounted for changes in how migration laws were operated and implemented by policy makers in terms of a rational balancing of economic interests, electoral volatility, and juridical constraints (e.g., Cornelius et al., 2004). Such approaches paid less attention to the fact that states have historically always used immigration policies as a tool to foster specific ideas of national identity (i.e., Zolberg, 2006). In the 2000s, societal and policy debates within Western Europe on immigration in general and family migration in particular brought this relation between immigration and national identity, societal cohesion and diversity to the forefront of academic discussions. Kofman (2005) and Adamson and colleagues (2011) argue that these developments meant that immigration, both as a topic of societal debate and policy regulation, effectively 'culturalised': family reunification policies and debates de facto define group boundaries and group membership. Increasingly, politicians and citizens alike started to question whether family migrants could successfully integrate in Europe, and whether the gender and family norms of these 'foreign' families who sought to reunite were in line with alleged 'European' gender and family values. These discussions have been omnipresent in public debates in the last 20 years. Social scientists and socio-legal scholars together have convincingly shown that family migration policies are problematizing certain kinds of families as 'non-belonging' (Bonjour & Kraler, 2015): dominant gender norms, racial hierarchies and class differences shape the outcomes of debates on family migration policies and laws, and therefore affect family migrants' trajectories and opportunities (Bonjour & de Hart, 2013).

European governments impose restrictions on who can act as a sponsor for family reunification and in doing so introduce a hierarchy based on the sponsors' legal status. This 'stratification of family migration rights' (Kraler & Bonizzoni, 2010) closely reflects the degree to which sponsors are considered 'insiders' in the nation. This belonging and membership of sponsors is first and foremost assessed by formal citizenship and residency status. Unsurprisingly, family reunification rights are usually strongest for those who hold formal citizenship status, although important exceptions arise in various countries (see Corradi & Desmet, this volume, about family reunification rights in Belgium for static versus mobile EU citizens). Bonjour and Block (2016) highlight the importance of ethno-racial imaginations of these citizens for family reunification rights. They argue that, as more residents of immigrant background request reunification with their family members, policy makers in the EU started to question the legitimacy of their family projects. This, in turn, resulted in the restriction of family migration rights, in the form of additional requirements (see later in this chapter, also De Haas et al., 2018). In debates on family migration across Europe, authors argue that norms on gender, sexuality and ethnicity serve not only to keep 'outsiders' out, but also to turn 'insiders' – either citizens with a migrant background or native citizen women and men – into (partial) outsiders, without a legitimate claim to family life (Bonjour & de Hart, 2013; Myrdahl, 2010; Kofman et al., 2015). Authors, such as Bonjour and Block (2016), Wray (2011), and Myrdahl (2010) indeed point to the crucial importance of perceptions of belonging to the nation and argue that these are intricately connected to 'Western family norms' shaped by gender equality, freedom of choice and individual autonomy. As particular families of immigrant background – especially those with a Muslim background – are seen as deviating from these norms, they are constructed as not belonging in Europe (Grillo, 2008; Bonjour & de Hart, 2013). Such conceptualisations of family reunification and applicant families led to a series of restrictions to the right to family reunification, including tightened income, age and integration requirements (Wray, 2011; Carver, 2016).

Beyond imposing restrictions to sponsors, family migrants who are deemed to not belong to the nation are increasingly subject to strict integration requirements. In the Netherlands, the so-called champion of said requirements (De Haas et al., 2018), this takes the form of obligatory courses and/or tests that can happen pre- and post-departure, and deal with learning the national language and transmitting 'core values', institutions, and customs of the receiving society. While the proponents of these requirements argue that they solve particular 'problems' that arise when integrating (family) migrants (Strasser et al., 2009), research shows that their effects are more controversial. Goodman (2010), for example, argues that they often set exceptionally high barriers for obtaining legal status and are mobilised to prevent and limit migration, not to accelerate settlement and integration. Even more so, social scientists argue that these tests follow an implicit racial logic, as they target immigrants selectively based on an alleged lack of 'knowledge' and 'values' corresponding to those allegedly dominant in the Global North. For the Dutch integration tests in particular, Blankvoort and colleagues (2021) indeed show that civic integration programmes reproduce a colonial logic that constructs the Dutch nation state and its citizens as inherently modern and superior as opposed to the unmodern, threatening 'Other'.

Anthropologists, sociologists, political scientists as well as socio-legal scholars more widely have written at length about the rationales and implication of deciding on which family members are allowed to reunite with their sponsors (see Bonjour & Cleton, 2021 for an overview). A good share of these debates focuses on the reunification of partners across borders. These scholars show that, while several European countries allow for the reunification of non-marital partners, both homosexual and heterosexual, a monogamous, married, heterosexual couple is still the norm (Strasser et al., 2009). This means that couples who do not fit this definition and cannot live up to its normative ideals are subject to severe scrutiny by the state (D'Aoust, 2013; Wray, 2011; Chauvin et al., 2019). Such scrutiny often results in having to submit additional proofs of their relationship, by means of interviews in which they are assessed on knowledge about each other's lives and preferences (Challborn & Harder, 2019) and submitting proofs on intimacy (ibid.; see also Chauvin et al., 2019 for homosexual couples). Scholars explain such severe scrutiny by pointing to the normative expectations about marriage and intimacy at play while regulating movement across borders. Having started already within colonial times, racial hierarchies were secured by positioning Western, 'civilised' marriages and family forms as superior, as scholars like van Walsum (2008) and Stoler (2002) argue. Present-day, ethno-racial discourses on 'genuine marriages' resemble something similar, as they are measured against notions of what Giddens (1992) calls 'pure relationships'. These ideas of relationships, dominant in the Global North, are characterised by equality among partners, a fair power balance and autonomy. Family migrants, in turn, are assessed based on such norms, as it allegedly proves whether their relationship is 'genuine' or not. One way in which this materialises is the importance of a 'love marriage': a partnership that is chosen freely by two individuals, without interference of parents or other family members, and not based on material motives. Love therefore becomes the criterion for distinguishing 'genuine' from 'false' marriage migration claims, and a justification to impose restrictions on marriages that are understood as 'arranged', 'sham' or 'forced' (Wray, 2006, 2011; Eggebø, 2013; Bonjour & de Hart, 2013; D'Aoust, 2013; Andrikopoulos, 2021; Staver & Eggebø, 2023).

Finally, scholars have argued that ideas on 'dependency' within families permeate family reunification law and policies and warned against their adverse consequences. EU member states severely limit reunification of family members beyond the nuclear family, such as (grand)parents, siblings, adult children, aunts, uncles and cousins: they are only admitted in case of extreme financial or emotional dependency (Strasser et al., 2009). Horsti and Pellander (2015) argue that this is the case because adults – especially elderly immigrants – are seen as a possible financial burden to the welfare state and should therefore not be admitted to the nation. In the European Union (EU), such fears feed into a longer debate on the alleged dependency of migrant families on state welfare budgets, which played a significant role in migration policy making over the last decades (Kofman, 2018). While family migrants should thus not be dependent on the (welfare) state, family reunification laws at the same time exacerbate (financial) dependency within families. Kofman's (ibid.) review shows that family reunification is always accompanied by various requirements, such as the sponsor having sustainable income and housing. These requirements imply that the sponsor bears (financial) responsibility for their family members. This led Luibhéid (2008) to argue that the resulting financial dependency within families in fact reflects a broader 'neoliberal governmentality'. Building on Foucault's work, she argues that the responsibility for care and support is transferred from the welfare state to individual families, effectively disciplining them to fulfil their own needs and to avoid action on the part of the state. Social scientists have warned against such imposed dependency of family members (Eggebø, 2010; Pellander, 2015) and showed that it reproduces intra-familial inequalities and might exacerbate (gender-based) violence (Liversage, 2012). While the dependency between minor children and their parents is automatically assumed, reaching the age of majority is vice versa considered as an automatic transition to adulthood and hence independence (see also Gonzales, 2011). Yet, under certain circumstances, minor children are also excluded from reunification. Mustasaari (2015) argues that when they are married, they are seen as having started their own family and are therefore allegedly 'independent' from their parents. Mustasaari (ibid.) challenges this assumption and points out that minors who marry and have children, whether voluntarily or under constraints, may arguably be more dependent on their family's support than ever before.

3. Structure and agency in family reunification

Most of the sociological and anthropological debates starting from the time of Durkheim, Radcliffe-Brown, Weber, and Simmel can be connected to the ongoing tension between structure and agency. The interaction between collective and individual actions, social norms and personal values, political organisation and individual conduct are some of the topics traditionally analysed through the lens of structure and agency. Social scientific literature on family reunification can likewise be analysed through this tension. This is why it is important to briefly define these concepts and to show how they play out in recent studies on the topic.

Despite their centrality in these debates, definitions of agency and structure remain contested. In a simplistic way, we could say that agency is normally understood as the space of manoeuvre that is left to individuals to pursue their aspirations and objectives, while structure refers to social patterns – institutionalised across time – through which individuals, groups interact among themselves and with society at large. Importantly, most scholars agree that these social patterns cannot simply be reduced to the aggregation of individual conducts. Similarly in migration literature, the idea of structure is often used to describe all the legal, socio-economic, political conditions that constrain the actions of individuals and groups. However, as several authors have pointed out, the binary distinction of agency and structure is misleading. As Bakewell (2010, p. 1695) summarises, drawing from Sewell:

> First, there is a tendency to reification in which social structures – such as states or cultural norms – come to be seen as rigid and beyond the reach of human agency. . . . Second, the metaphor of structure usually carries with it connotations of stability. Structure describes patterns of human interaction but often has little to say about how those patterns change over time.

Giddens's (1984) structuration theory is the most well known in attempting to overcome this duality between structure and agency. Giddens highlights that structure not only shapes social practice but is in turn reproduced and transformed by this practice. Hence, social structures are seen not just as constraints on individual actors but also enabling their actions. In this view, laws and legal frameworks are seen as contexts for opening and closing spaces of negotiation for migrant families and other actors involved in family reunification.

In response to more structuralist approaches that were fashionable until the 1970s, migration studies have become increasingly careful in considering migrants' agency, their capabilities to enact tactics across pressing regulatory frameworks. This literature that we briefly discuss in section 3.1 below has produced a wide number of accounts that show how migrant families manage to do family at a distance and the creative ways in which migrant families and mixed couples are able to navigate regulations (Martinez, 2023; Bolzman, 2023; Cienfuegos-Illanes & Brandhorst, 2023). However, it is important to note that the relationship between agency and structure is also crucial to interpret the conduct of street-level bureaucrats, as we illustrate in section 3.2. Their role cannot be reduced to implementing top-down regulations, but their interpretation and enactment of the law is key to interpreting how family migration happens in practice.

While we believe that all accounts of human conduct require a balanced consideration of structure and agency, it is interesting to notice that more recently several scholars point to the dangers of overstating agency of migrants (Scheel, 2022) and their families in a deeply unequal context as the one of family reunification. For instance, Corradi and Desmet (this volume) suggest that 'navigation' (Vigh, 2009, in Corradi & Desmet, this volume) may not be the correct term to describe the agency of migrants with a precarious legal status. They argue:

> The term captures the violent conditions and rapidly changing legal environment that characterises the migration landscape, as well as migrants' capacities to act in this context. It is true that you are not a passive victim and that you analyse what seems most convenient, assessing possible costs and benefits. But . . . I did not feel that I was 'navigating' because to me this sounds as if you are, at least to a certain extent, in control. A more appropriate term would be 'avoid drowning', which captures the survival modus in which you actually find yourself.

Although much of the literature uses the word 'strategies' to refer to the practices put in place by migrants to circumvent or meet restrictive policies, we prefer the word *tactics*, drawing from the work of De Certeau (2005). While 'strategies' are those produced by those in power, the word 'tactics' refers to the actions of 'the weak' (see Scott, 1985) that emerge within the spaces opened by those in power.

3.1 Doing family in spite of the obstacles

While legal and geographic borders keep families apart, scholars have increasingly analysed how care, parenthood and intimate relationships are transnationally enacted among separated families through information and communication technologies (ICTs), mobile phones and social media (Cienfuegos-Illanes et al., 2023; Baldassar & Merla, 2014). These transitional relationships – the support they provide as well as the pressure they put on migrants – influence their daily lives, their feeling of belonging to the hosting country, as well as a conventional definition of the family (Grillo, 2008). Several scholars working on family reunification and separated families have inquired how families engage in different tactics to fulfil or circumvent requirements. Given the consistent financial resources and documentation needed for applying for family visas, migrants have to cooperate with each other to navigate complex administrative procedures. In this labyrinth of requirements, educational level, social status and gender may significantly affect the chances of presenting successful applications (Bonizzoni, 2015; Hiiltola, 2019). Intermediaries, such as migrant support organizations and informal middlemen, also play an important part in migrants' experience of family reunification (Kim, 2011; López, 2021; Odasso, 2021a). A prosperous formal and informal migration industry consisting of such intermediaries has emerged to provide official and fake documents, to guide sponsors and applicants across the many offices responsible for legalising, translating and stamping certificates.

However, the obstacles to family reunification do not end when families are finally reunited. Della Puppa (2018) for instance shows how during the economic crisis, Bangladeshi families in Italy resorted to local and international mobility to maintain the housing, occupational and economic standards needed for renewing the family residence. Moving to countries where migrants have stronger social ties often allows breadwinners to protect the legal stay of the family, at the expenses of family unity. While some may try to circumvent the rules, others try to protest them. Odasso (2021b), for instance, has explored how citizen partners in mixed families ally among themselves and with non-governmental organisations (NGOs) to challenge restrictive policy regimes. Through their public calls for justice, they perform a form of 'intimate citizenship': a political engagement on the basis of their personal and private life (Bonjour & de Hart, 2021).

Besides fulfilling, circumventing and dissenting with policy requirements, many migrants simply adapt. Some scholars, for instance, studied the importance of memory in long-term family separation. Rousseau and colleagues (2004), for instance, show how refugees cultivate personal, familial or collective history in spite of the painful memories, as this is an opportunity to recreate a partial sense of continuity in exile. Other researchers investigated how restrictive requirements may be actively embraced by some migrants to redefine kin obligations. Olwig (2022), for instance, explored how Somali migrants renegotiated their family responsibilities for supporting distant relatives within their communities based on the impossibility to overcome biometric definitions of family.

While most studies have focused on the agency of couples in the process of family reunification, recent studies have highlighted how children and youth experience family reunification not necessarily as passive actors (Anschutz & Mazzucato, 2022; Belloni, 2020a). In centring the agency and experiences of children on the move, these studies contest the policy definition of what counts as family worthy of reunification. While family reunification is assumed to be between parents and children, the biographic experience of separated children shows how reunification with their parents living in Europe entails a separation from significant caregivers in the country of origin – such as grandparents, uncles, cousins – who have played a key role in the development of the children. To be in touch with these loved ones, youth engage in recurrent visits, phone calls and other transnational family dynamics (Anschutz & Mazzucato, 2022).

3.2 *Translating law to practice: street-level bureaucracy*

Next to investigating the interplay of structure and agency through the lives and experiences of family migrants, social scientists and socio-legal scholars have investigated 'law in action' by centring the work of lawyers, judges and others who implement the law. Most studies build on Lipsky's (1980) concept of 'street-level bureaucracy' to investigate everyday bureaucratic practices of those working at the frontline of policy implementation, and how these impact the outcomes of procedures (i.e., Alpes & Spire, 2014; Eule et al., 2019; Infantino & Sredanovic, 2022). This includes a wide array of actors, such as policy officers, NGO workers and social workers, but also lawyers and judges (see, for the latter, Dallara & Lacchei, 2021; Mascia, 2021). Exploring their agency often focuses on investigating personal *discretion* that is used to realise or detriment migrant families' rights. Within an increasingly dominant culture of disbelief (Jubany, 2011), the space for manoeuvre of bureaucratic and administrative staff active in different visa-, welfare- and migration-related organisations may be used to exclude families, rather than ensuring their rights.

In line with the aforementioned work on street-level bureaucrats in wider immigration bureaucracies, Mascia (2021) highlights the importance of the administration and organisational culture in frontline decision-making. She shows that bureaucrats' work is crucially guided by their collective representation of case law on family reunification, which differed from the court rulings per se. Infantino (2014) uncovers how consular staff rely on various 'implementation tricks' to bypass the fundamental right to respect for family life, and instead use the visa application as a mechanism to 'filter out' immigrants who are perceived as unwanted (see also Alpes & Spire, 2014). Indeed, especially in the well-established work on 'problematic marriages' (Staver & Eggebø, 2023), scholars argue unequivocally that the regulation of marriage migration to the EU is less concerned with 'measuring the authenticity of the relationship' than with 'evaluating the desirability of the migrant partner' (Maskens, 2015, p. 55). Wray (2006) was among the first to centre the tacit, normative assumptions of street-level bureaucrats and called this process 'moral gatekeeping', which refers to the intersection of immigration regulations with bureaucrats' moral understandings of how people ought to live their family life. Ever since, a vast body of social scientific scholarship showed what moral gatekeeping looks like in practice, arguing that their normative assumptions about proper family life, family practices and gender relations play a crucial role not only in the admission of family members, but also in the overall production of collective, national identities (Wray, 2011; Bonjour & de Hart, 2013; Eggebø, 2013; Pellander, 2015).

4. Overcoming methodological nationalism: a transnational approach

Much of the literature on family reunification has focused on state legislations at the national level, for good reasons. Foreigners' access to the possibility to reunite with their family members has often been represented as a potential threat to the racial, cultural and religious assumed homogeneity of the native population (i.e., Grillo, 2008; Bonjour & de Hart, 2013). Regulations over family reunification have therefore aimed to control the boundaries of the nation and its stereotyped identity by producing a hierarchy of citizenship among citizens and migrants. As the first section of this chapter also reflects, most research is therefore focused on specific countries' attitudes, rules and practices towards migrants' family reunification.

However, as some of the chapters in this book also argue, family reunification does not take place within the nation. It is an eminently *transnational* phenomenon (Scheel & Gutekunst, 2019). Families, as well as their dossiers and the complex policies they must navigate cross, overflow and blur state borders (Mitchell & Coutin, 2019). Until the late 1990s, studies within the social sciences at large and migration studies in particular tended to suffer from what Wimmer and Glick-Schiller (2002) call 'methodological nationalism': treating the nation state as a 'natural' unit of analysis and a necessary representation of modern society. Nation states become all-encompassing containers of social and political life and phenomena that across borders become invisible or non-relevant. Against this bias, a new paradigm called 'transnationalism' developed in social sciences since the

1990s. Although transnationalism is not an exclusive characteristic of migrant populations, this concept has become dominant in migration studies and allowed researchers to question key assumptions in their field. This transnational lens has, for instance, revealed the limitations of widespread dichotomies, such as external versus internal, national versus international, sending versus receiving countries, *sojourner* versus *settler*, citizen versus non-citizen, and highlighted that these categories often overlap or are continuous in practice.

In one of the most famous formulations of this concept, Glick-Schiller and colleagues (1992, p. ix) write that transnationalism can be used

> to emphasize the emergence of a social process in which migrants establish social fields that cross geographic, cultural, and political borders. Immigrants are understood to be transmigrants[1] when they develop and maintain multiple relations – familial, economic, social, organizational, religious, and political – that span borders. We came to understand that the multiplicity of migrants' involvements in both the home and host societies is a central element of transnationalism. Transmigrants take actions, make decisions, and feel concerns within a field of social relations that links together their country of origin and their country or countries of settlement.

While the transnational approach has had a significant impact on all aspects of migration, the literature on family reunification remains partly blind to the social, political and legal work that crosses national boundaries. In particular, we see potential in expanding these reflections in three main ways.

First, different state regulations transnationally intersect among each other and with rules at the international level, and therefore produce organisational, political and legal configurations that should be studied in their own right (Scheel and Gutekunst, 2019). The resulting 'transnational regime' (Cvajner et al., 2018) cannot be reduced to the sum of individual state regulations. For instance, structural possibilities to family reunification for refugee families result from the intersection of international refugee laws, the actions of humanitarian agencies working in the field, destination countries' as well as transit and countries of origin regulations and bureaucratic practices concerning freedom of movement, specific implementation of the universal right to family life (and specific hierarchies of priorities) and the definition of families (see Arapiles & Mekonnen, this volume; Belloni & Verschraegen, this volume).

Second, individuals and families separated by borders often have to organise their lives transnationally. While prolonged periods of separation may lead to weaker emotional bonds and trigger phenomena of family disruptions, such as divorce, limited child–parent relations and limited connections with extended family (Belloni, 2020b), it is also important to acknowledge how families adapt to separation and put in place tactics of doing family at a distance. Some studies have investigated family

1 The use of the word 'transmigrant' by these authors differs from recent usage of the term in media outlets that specifically refer to migrants waiting in border zones such as Calais and Ventimiglia.

dynamics by focusing simultaneously on members residing in the country of origin and destination (Baldassar, 2007; Mazzucato, 2009). Less frequent are studies that systematically map and explore how family members located across multiple countries interact, support each other, influence each other's migration pathways and maintain various kinds of family life at a distance. Further developing this approach has crucial policy implications. Street-level bureaucrats often assume that dependency (counted in number of Western Union receipts), sharing information among couples (facts referring to work life and private life) and having intimate conversations (reified by exchanging pictures and love statements) represent the key ingredients of a maintained family bond at a distance (e.g., Coe, 2011; López, 2021). However, it is important to acknowledge there are diverse ways of doing family across borders which depend on cultural arrangements, family structures and social practices (Andrikopoulos & Duyvendak, 2020). For instance, economic support cannot simply be reduced to direct remittances. Emigrants may, for instance, build a house back home, support extended family or provide practical service to their partners, children and the extended family. Moreover, family migrants' sponsors in destination countries may not share information about their living circumstances to avoid worrying loved ones. In sum, conceptions of what kind of intimate conversation among partners is suitable vary greatly from community to community.

There is a third aspect that we believe would be worth further consideration. Beyond regulations, organisations and families, *administrative dossiers* are key units of analysis to understand how transnationalism plays out in family reunification dynamics. In a more recent development of social theory, social scientists have argued that not only people and organisations have agency but also the material world. All actors – both human and non-human – act in a network and influence each other's actions (Latour, 2000). This idea has been applied to migration studies as well, since '[this approach] draws attention to the relations between the different actors involved in networks of border control, such as databases, fingerprints, migrants' bodies, directives, policy documents, European and national bureaucracies, and so forth' (Dijstelbloem & Broeders, 2015, p. 27). Using an actor-network theory approach helps to clarify how administrative dossiers are constructed in a transnational field, how dossiers travel across borders, how they can be translated and how the materiality of the dossier influences policy makers', street-level bureaucrats' and migrants' conduct in family reunification. The focus on the agency of papers, documents, bureaucratic procedures and paperwork (Borrelli & Lindberg, 2019; Geoffrion & Cretton, 2021; De Hertog & Belloni, 2023) moreover allows us to grasp how structural violence is often enacted on migrants and how state control is exercised through outsourcing of services and administrative practices (Borelli et al., 2023).

5. Conclusion

This chapter identified three key conceptual contributions of the work conducted across anthropology, sociology, political science and socio-legal studies to the understanding of family reunification in Europe. These three key debates concern the neutrality of legal frameworks, the interplay between structure and agency and the role of transnational dynamics in family reunification. We showed how family reunification should be considered as a socio-legal process constituted by laws and practices embedded in specific conceptions of citizenship, belonging and nationhood. These conceptions are not neutral and objective. They are shaped by values and assumptions related to ethnicity, race, gender and class. We then illustrated the importance of considering the co-constructive character of agency and structure in analysing family reunification in practice. We focused on how laws and legal frameworks have the ability to open and close spaces for manoeuvre for both migrant families and street-level bureaucrats alike. Finally, we argued for the significance of adopting a transnational perspective in the study of family reunification. While not disregarding the regulatory power of state regulations, we maintain that a more transnational approach to the topic of family reunification would allow both social scientists and legal scholars to 1) unpack the complexities of transnational migration regimes that families navigate, 2) recognise that family life does not stop if people are separated by borders and 3) see the potential of studying administrative dossiers and files, in particular how they are constructed and understood across borders.

References

Adamson, F. B., Triadafilopoulos, T., & Zolberg, A. R. (2011). The limits of the liberal state: Migration, identity and belonging in Europe. *Journal of Ethnic and Migration Studies*, *37*(6), 843–859. https://doi.org/10.1080/1369183X.2011.576188

Alpes, M. J., & Spire, A. (2014). Dealing with law in migration control: The powers of street-level bureaucrats at French consulates. *Social & Legal Studies*, *23*(2), 261–274. https://doi.org/10.1177/0964663913510927

Andrikopoulos, A. (2021). Love, money and papers in the affective circuits of cross-border marriages: Beyond the "sham"/"genuine" dichotomy. *Journal of Ethnic and Migration Studies*, *47*(2), 343–360. https://doi.org/10.1080/1369183X.2019.1625129

Andrikopoulos, A., & Duyvendak, J. W. (2020). Migration, mobility and the dynamics of kinship: New barriers, new assemblages. *Ethnography*, *21*(3), 299–318. https://doi.org/10.1177/1466138120939584

Anschütz, S., & Mazzucato, V. (2022). Reconceptualizing family reunification from a youth mobilities perspective: Transnational youth between Ghana and Belgium. *Children's Geographies*, *20*(2), 160–173. https://doi.org/10.1080/14733285.2021.1919998

Bakewell, O. (2010). Some reflections on structure and agency in migration theory. *Journal of Ethnic and Migration Studies*, *36*(10), 1689–1708. https://doi.org/10.1080/1369183X.2010.489382

Baldassar, L. (2007). Transnational families and the provision of moral and emotional support: The relationship between truth and distance. *Identities: Global Studies in Culture and Power*, *14*(4), 385–409. https://doi.org/10.1080/10702890701578423

Baldassar, L., & Merla, L. (2014). *Transnational Families, Migration and the Circulation of Care Understanding Mobility and Absence in Family Life*. Routledge.

Bhabha, J., & Shutter, S. (1994). *Women's Movement: Women Under Immigration, Nationality and Refugee Law*. Trentham Books.

Blankvoort, N., van Hartingsveldt, M., Laliberte Rudman, D., & Krumeich, A. (2021). Decolonising civic integration: A critical analysis of texts used in Dutch civic integration programmes. *Journal of Ethnic and Migration Studies*, *47*(15), 3511–3530. https://doi.org/10.1080/1369183X.2021.1893668

Belloni, M. (2020a). Family project or individual choice? Exploring agency in young Eritreans' migration. *Journal of Ethnic and Migration Studies*, *46*(2), 336–353. https://doi.org/10.1080/1369183X.2019.1584698

Belloni, M. (2020b). When the phone stops ringing: On the meanings and causes of disruptions in communication between Eritrean refugees and their families back home. *Global Networks*, *20*(2), 256–273. https://doi.org/10.1111/glob.12230

Bolzman, C. (2023). The Elderly in Transnational Family Configurations: Migration, Inter-Generational Relations and Care Support in Switzerland. In J. Cienfuegos, R. Brandhorst, & D. Fahy Bryceson (Eds.), *Handbook of Transnational Families Around the World* (pp. 3–18). Springer. https://doi.org/10.1007/978-3-031-15278-8_11

Bonizzoni, P. (2015). Uneven paths: Latin American women facing Italian family reunification policies. *Journal of Ethnic and Migration Studies*, *41*(12), 2001–2020. https://doi.org/10.1080/1369183X.2015.1037257

Bonjour, S., & Block, L. (2016). Ethnicizing citizenship, questioning membership: Explaining the decreasing family migration rights of citizens in Europe. *Citizenship Studies*, *20*(6–7), 779–794. https://doi.org/10.1080/13621025.2016.1191429

Bonjour, S., & Cleton, L. (2021). Co-constructions of Family and Belonging in the Politics of Family Migration. In E. Carmel, K. Lenner, & R. Paul (Eds.), *Handbook on the Governance and Politics of Migration* (pp. 161–172). Edward Elgar Publishing. https://doi.org/10.4337/9781788117234.00020

Bonjour, S., & De Hart, B. (2013). A proper wife, a proper marriage: Constructions of "us" and "them" in Dutch family migration policy. *European Journal of Women's Studies*, *20*(1), 61–76. https://doi.org/10.1177/1350506812456459

Bonjour, S., & De Hart, B. (2021). Intimate citizenship: Introduction to the special issue on citizenship, membership and belonging in mixed-status families. *Identities*, *28*(1), 1–17. https://doi.org/10.1080/1070289X.2020.1737404

Bonjour, S., & Kraler, A. (2015). Introduction: Family migration as an integration issue? Policy perspectives and academic insights. *Journal of Family Issues*, *36*(11), 1407–1432.

Borelli, C., Poy, A., & Rué, A. (2023). Governing asylum without "being there": Ghost bureaucracy, outsourcing, and the unreachability of the state. *Social Sciences*, *12*(3), 169. https://doi.org/10.3390/socsci12030169

Borrelli, L. M., & Lindberg, A. (2019). Paperwork performances: Legitimating state violence in the Swedish deportation regime. *Journal of Legal Anthropology*, *3*(2), 50–69. https://doi.org/10.3167/jla.2019.030204

Carver, N. (2016). "For her protection and benefit": The regulation of marriage-related migration to the UK. *Ethnic and Racial Studies*, *39*(15), 2758–2776. https://doi.org/10.1080/01419870.2016.1171369

Challborn, M. R., & Harder, L. (2019). Sex and the genuine marriage: Consummation and conjugality in Canadian citizenship. *Citizenship Studies*, *23*(5), 407–423. https://doi.org/10.1080/13621025.2019.1620686

Chauvin, S., Salcedo Robledo, M., Koren, T., & Illidge, J. (2021). Class, mobility and inequality in the lives of same-sex couples with mixed legal statuses. *Journal of Ethnic and Migration Studies*, *47*(2), 430–446. https://doi.org/10.1080/1369183X.2019.1625137

Cienfuegos-Illanes, J., & Brandhorst, R. (2023). Transnational Families: Entangled Inequalities and Emerging Challenges on the Global Scale. In J. Cienfuegos, R. Brandhorst, & D. Fahy Bryceson (Eds.), *Handbook of Transnational Families Around the World* (pp. 3–18). Springer.

Coe, C. (2011). What is love? The materiality of care in Ghanaian transnational families. *International Migration*, *49*(6), 7–24. https://doi.org/10.1111/j.1468-2435.2011.00704.x

Cornelius, W. A., Tsuda, T., Martin, P. L., & Hollifield, J. F. (Eds.). (2004). *Controlling Immigration: A Global Perspective* (2nd ed.). Stanford University Press.

Cvajner, M., Echeverría, G., & Sciortino, G. (2018). What Do We Talk When We Talk About Migration Regimes? The Diverse Theoretical Roots of an Increasingly Popular Concept. In A. Pott, C. Rass, & F. Wolff (Eds.), *Was ist ein Migrationsregime? What is a Migration Regime?* (pp. 65–80). Springer. https://doi.org/10.1007/978-3-658-20532-4_3

Dallara, C., & Lacchei, A. (2021). Street-level bureaucrats and coping mechanisms: The unexpected role of Italian judges in Asylum policy implementation. *South European Society and Politics*, *26*(1), 83–108. https://doi.org/10.1080/13608746.2021.1956161
D'Aoust, A. M. (2013). In the name of love: Marriage migration, governmentality, and technologies of love. *International Political Sociology*, *7*(3), 258–274. https://doi.org/10.1111/ips.12022
De Certeau, M. (2005). "Making Do": Uses and Tactics. In G. Spiegel (Ed.), *Practicing History: New Directions in Historical Writing After the Linguistic Turn* (pp. 213–223). Routledge.
De Haas, H., & Fokkema, T. (2010). Intra-household conflicts in migration decision-making: Return and pendulum migration in Morocco. *Population and Development Review*, *36*(3), 541–561. https://doi.org/10.1111/j.1728-4457.2010.00345.x
De Haas, H., Natter, K., & Vezzoli, S. (2018). Growing restrictiveness or changing selection? The nature and evolution of migration policies. *International Migration Review*, *52*(2), 324–367. https://doi.org/10.1111/imre.12288
Della Puppa, F. (2018). Ambivalent mobilities and survival strategies of Moroccan and Bangladeshi families in Italy in times of crisis. *Sociology*, *52*(3), 464–479. https://doi.org/10.1177/0038038518764622
Dijstelbloem, H., & Broeders, D. (2015). Border surveillance, mobility management and the shaping of non-publics in Europe. *European Journal of Social Theory*, *18*(1), 21–38. https://doi.org/10.1177/1368431014534353
Eggebø, H. (2010). The problem of dependency: Immigration, gender, and the welfare state. *Social Politics*, *17*(3), 295–322. https://doi.org/10.1093/sp/jxq013
Eggebø, H. (2013). A real marriage? Applying for marriage migration to Norway. *Journal of Ethnic and Migration Studies*, *39*(5), 773–789. https://doi.org/10.1080/1369183X.2013.756678
Eule, T. G., Borrelli, L. M., Lindberg, A., & Wyss, A. (2019). *Migrants before the law: Contested migration control in Europe*. Routledge. https://doi.org/10.1007/978-3-319-98749-1
Feenan, D. (2013). Exploring the "Socio" of Socio-Legal Studies. In D. Feenan (Ed.), *Exploring the "Socio" of Socio-Legal Studies* (pp. 3–19). Palgrave Macmillan. https://doi.org/10.1007/978-1-137-31463-5_1
Fox, R. (1967). *Kinship and Marriage: An Anthropological Perspective*. Cambridge University Press.
Geoffrion, K., & Cretton, V. (2021). Bureaucratic routes to migration: Migrants' lived experience of paperwork, clerks and other immigration intermediaries. *Anthropologica*, *63*(1), 1–28. https://doi.org/10.18357/anthropologica6312021184
Giddens, A. (1984). *The Constitution of Society*. Polity Press.
Giddens, A. (1992). *The Transformation of Intimacy: Sexuality, Love and Eroticism in Modern Societies*. John Wiley & Sons.
Glick-Schiller, N., Basch, L., & Blanc-Szanton, C. (1992). Transnationalism: A new analytic framework for understanding migration. *Annals of the New York Academy of Sciences*, *645*(1), 1–24. https://doi.org/10.1111/j.1749-6632.1992.tb33484.x
Gonzales, R. G. (2011). Learning to be illegal: Undocumented youth and shifting legal contexts in the transition to adulthood. *American Sociological Review*, *76*(4), 602–619.
Goodman, S. W. (2010). Integration requirements for integration's sake? Identifying, categorising and comparing civic integration policies. *Journal of Ethnic and Migration Studies*, *36*(5), 753–772. https://doi.org/10.1080/13691831003764300
Grillo, R. (2008). *The Family in Question: Immigrant and Ethnic Minorities in Multicultural Europe*. Amsterdam University Press. https://doi.org/10.5117/9789053568699
Hiitola, J. (2019). Locating forced migrants' resources: Residency status and the process of family reunification in Finland. *Social Inclusion*, *7*(4), 190–191. https://doi.org/10.17645/si.v7i4.2327

Horsti, K., & Pellander, S. (2015). Conditions of cultural citizenship: Intersections of gender, race and age in public debates on family migration. *Citizenship Studies*, *19*(6–7), 751–767. https://doi.org/10.1080/13621025.2015.1008998

Infantino, F. (2014). Bordering "fake" marriages? The everyday practices of control at the consulates of Belgium, France and Italy in Casablanca. *Etnografia e Ricerca Qualitativa*, *7*(1), 27–48.

Infantino, F., & Sredanovic, D. (Eds.). (2022). *The Perspectives of Implementation in Migration Policies: An Introduction*. Éditions de l'Université de Bruxelles.

Jubany, O. (2011). Constructing truths in a culture of disbelief: Understanding asylum screening from within. *International Sociology*, *26*(1), 74–94. https://doi.org/10.1177/0268580910380978

Kim, J. (2011). Establishing identity: Documents, performance, and biometric information in immigration proceedings. *Law and Social Inquiry*, *36*(3), 760–786. https://doi.org/10.1111/j.1747-4469.2011.01249.x

Kofman, E. (2004). Family-related migration: A critical review of European studies. *Journal of Ethnic and Migration studies*, *30*(2), 243–262. https://doi.org/10.1080/1369183042000200687

Kofman, E. (2005). Citizenship, migration, and the reassertion of national identity. *Citizenship Studies*, *9*(5), 453–467. https://doi.org/10.1080/13621020500301221

Kofman, E. (2018). Family migration as a class matter. *International Migration*, *56*(4), 33–46. https://doi.org/10.1111/imig.12433

Kofman, E., Phizacklea, A., Raghuram, P., & Sales, R. (2000). *Gender and International Migration in Europe: Employment, Welfare and Politics*. Routledge.

Kofman, E., Saharso, S., & Vacchelli, E. (2015). Gendered perspectives on integration discourses and measures. *International Migration*, *53*(4), 77–89. https://doi.org/10.1111/imig.12102

Kraler, A., & Bonizzoni, P. (2010). Gender, civic stratification and the right to family life: Problematising immigrants' integration in the EU. *International Review of Sociology*, *20*(1), 181–187. https://doi.org/10.1080/03906700903525792

Latour, B. (2000). When things strike back: A possible contribution of "science studies" to the social sciences. *British Journal of Sociology*, *51*, 107–123. https://doi.org/10.1111/j.1468-4446.2000.00107.x

Lipsky, M. (1980). *Street-level bureaucracy: The Dilemmas of the Individual in Public Services*. Russell Sage Foundation. https://doi.org/10.1177/003232928001000113

Liversage, A. (2012). Gender, conflict and subordination within the household: Turkish migrant marriage and divorce in Denmark. *Journal of Ethnic and Migration Studies*, *38*(7), 1119–1136. https://doi.org/10.1080/1369183X.2012.681455

López, J. L. (2021). *Unauthorized Love: Mixed-Citizenship Couples Negotiating Intimacy, Immigration, and the State*. Stanford University Press. https://doi.org/10.1177/00943061231191421v

Luibhéid, E. (2008). Sexuality, migration, and the shifting line between legal and illegal status. *GLQ: A Journal of Lesbian and Gay Studies*, *14*(2–3), 289–315. https://doi.org/10.1215/10642684-2007-034

Martinez, A. Z. (2023). Preserving a Sense of Family: Parents' and Children's Ritualized Transnational Family Practices Amongst Colombian Migrants to Santiago, Chile. In *Handbook of Transnational Families Around the World* (pp. 71–82). Springer.

Mascia, C. (2021). How bureaucracies shape access to rights: The implementation of family reunification in Belgium. *Journal of Ethnic and Migration Studies*, *47*(9), 2127–2143. https://doi.org/10.1080/1369183X.2020.1726734

Maskens, M. (2015). Bordering intimacy: The fight against marriages of convenience in Brussels. *The Cambridge Journal of Anthropology*, *33*(2), 42–58. www.jstor.org/stable/26370575

Mazzucato, V. (2009). Bridging Boundaries with a Transnational Research Approach: A Simultaneous Matched Sample Methodology 1. In M. Falzon (Ed.), *Multi-sited Ethnography* (pp. 215–231). Routledge.

Mitchell, J., & Coutin, S. B. (2019). Living documents in transnational spaces of migration between El Salvador and the United States. *Law & Social Inquiry*, *44*(4), 865–892. https://doi.org/10.1017/lsi.2018.27

Moret, J., Andrikopoulos, A., & Dahinden, J. (2021). Contesting categories: Cross-border marriages from the perspectives of the state, spouses and researchers. *Journal of Ethnic and Migration Studies*, *47*(2), 325–342. https://doi.org/10.1080/1369183X.2019.1625124

Morokvaśic, M. (1984). Birds of passage are also women . . . *International Migration Review*, *18*(4), 886–907. https://doi.org/10.1177/019791838401800402

Mustasaari, S. (2015). The "nuclear family paradigm" as a marker of rights and belonging in transnational families. *Social Identities*, *21*(4), 359–372. https://doi.org/10.1080/13504630.2015.1071699

Myrdahl, E. M. (2010). Legislating love: Norwegian family reunification law as a racial project. *Social & Cultural Geography*, *11*(2), 103–116. https://doi.org/10.1080/14649360903514368

Odasso, L. (2021a). Negotiating legitimacy: Binational couples in the face of immigration bureaucracy in Belgium and Italy. *Anthropologica*, *63*(1), 1–30. https://doi.org/10.18357/anthropologica6312021273

Odasso, L. (2021b). Family rights-claiming as act of citizenship: An intersectional perspective on the performance of intimate citizenship. *Identities*, *28*(1), 74–92. https://doi.org/10.1080/1070289X.2020.1723309

Olwig, K. F. (2022). The right to a family life and the biometric "truth" of family reunification: Somali refugees in Denmark. *Ethnos*, *87*(2), 275–289. https://doi.org/10.1080/00141844.2019.1648533

Parkin, R., & Stone, L. (2004). *Kinship and Family: An Anthropological Reader*. Blackwell Pub.

Pellander, S. (2015). "An acceptable marriage:" Marriage migration and moral gatekeeping in Finland. *Journal of Family Issues*, *36*(11), 1472–1489.

Rodenburg, J. (1997). *In the Shadow of Migration: Rural Women and their Households in North Tapanuli, Indonesia*. KITLV Press.

Rousseau, C., Rufagari, M. C., Bagilishya, D., & Measham, T. (2004). Remaking family life: Strategies for re-establishing continuity among Congolese refugees during the family reunification process. *Social Science & Medicine*, *59*(5), 1095–1108. https://doi.org/10.1016/j.socscimed.2003.12.011

Scheel, S. (2022). Reconfiguring desecuritization: Contesting expert knowledge in the securitization of migration. *Geopolitics*, *27*(4), 1042–1068. https://doi.org/10.1080/14650045.2020.1774749

Scheel, S., & Gutekunst, M. (2019). Studying marriage migration to Europe from below: Informal practices of government, border struggles and multiple entanglements. *Gender, Place & Culture*, *26*(6), 847–867. https://doi.org/10.1080/0966369X.2018.1489375

Scott, J. C. (1985). *Weapons of the Weak: Everyday Forms of Peasant Resistance*. Yale University Press.

Stark, O., & Bloom, D. E. (1985). The new economics of labour migration. *American Economic Review*, 173–178.

Staver, A. B., & Eggebø, H. (2023). Everything but the marriage certificate: Unmarried partners in Norwegian immigration regulation. *Social Politics: International Studies in Gender, State & Society*, *30*(4), 1018–1039. https://doi.org/10.1093/sp/jxad005

Stoler, A. L. (2002). *Carnal Knowledge and Imperial Power: Race and the Intimate in Colonial Rule*. University of California Press.

Strasser, E., Kraler, A., Bonjour, S., & Bilger, V. (2009). Doing family: Responses to the constructions of "the migrant family" across Europe. *The History of the Family*, *14*(2), 165–176. https://doi.org/10.1016/j.hisfam.2009.02.005

Van Walsum, S. (2008). *The Family and the Nation: Dutch Family Migration Policies in the Context of Changing Family Norms*. Cambridge Scholars Publishing.

Vigh, H. (2009). Motion squared: A second look at the concept of social navigation. *Anthropological Theory*, *9*(4), 419–438.

Wimmer, A., & Glick-Schiller, N. (2002). Methodological nationalism and beyond: Nation – state building, migration and the social sciences. *Global Networks*, *2*(4), 301–334. https://doi.org/10.1111/1471-0374.00043
Wray, H. (2006). An ideal husband? Marriages of convenience, moral gatekeeping and immigration to the UK. *European Journal of Migration and Law*, *8*(3–4), 303–320. https://doi.org/10.1163/157181606778882582
Wray, H. (2011). *Regulating Marriage Migration into the UK: A Stranger in the Home*. Ashgate Publishing. https://doi.org/10.4324/9781315604510
Yuval-Davis, N. (2008). *Gender & Nation*. Sage. (Original work published 1997)
Zolberg, A. R. (2006). *A Nation by Design: Immigration Policy in the Fashioning of America*. Harvard University Press.

Part II

Unveiling inequalities

5 Developing a right to family reunification, immigrant integration and equality in Europe

Kees Groenendijk

1. Introduction

1.1 Two personal experiences

My first encounter with a migrant for family reunification was in the early 1970s. As a lawyer practising in Amsterdam I assisted a young Russian client who fell in love and married a Dutch businessman in Moscow. She somehow managed to get an exit visa from the USSR authorities after being expelled from her job and her university. In the Netherlands she discovered that her husband was living with another woman. He accommodated his spouse in a barn. Being the wife of a Dutchman according to the Dutch nationality law at that time, she could simply opt for Dutch nationality and stay in the Netherlands forever. She decided, however, not to use this right and to return to her widowed mother and an uncertain future in the Soviet Union. It was my first experience with the tension and contradictions between intimate family relations of individuals and government's migration policies, inherent in families across state borders.

My most frightening experience was in autumn 2015 when 4,000 refugees from Syria were temporarily accommodated in large tents two miles from the Nijmegen university campus. My wife and I invited four Syrian men for dinner. During the dinner one of them was constantly trying to make calls on his mobile telephone. He explained to us: 'My wife and our two young daughters are still in Raqqa. In our house there is no more electricity and my wife, as an unaccompanied woman, is unable to go to a telephone shop. A former colleague just phoned me that the Russians today bombed another quarter of the city.' I will never forget the fear in his eyes. It took six months before he received his refugee status and another six months before the family was actually reunited and could begin to focus on integration in the Netherlands. He was relatively lucky. Many Syrian refugees in the European Union (EU) were entitled to family reunification but had to deal with governments unwilling or unable to realize that right in practice. They had to wait several years before being reunited with their loved ones and make a real start with their integration in their new home country (Council of Europe Commissioner for Human Rights, 2017, pp. 33–46).

DOI: 10.4324/9781003503217-7

1.2 What do the numbers tell us?

Since the 1980s family reunification has become a major ground for admission of immigrants in Europe.[1] During the decade 2010–2019 the total number of first residence permits issued by the 27 EU Member States to nationals from non-EU countries for family reunification varied between 500,000 and 800,000 per year with a peak in 2019. Between 30 and 40% of all first residence permits issued to third-country nationals in the EU were issued for family reasons. The last year before the pandemic, Morocco, India, Ukraine and Brazil were the top four countries of origin of family members. A third of those admitted were children aged less than 15 (Eurostat, 2021). Despite all the restrictive national policy measures, a considerable number of non-EU family members is thus admitted in the EU each year. Moreover, these numbers do not represent the full picture of the size of family migration: family members of mobile EU nationals, family members receiving international protection status and irregular family members are not covered.

1.3 Three questions

Today most family migrants, except the irregular ones, have a legal right to family reunification on the basis of EU law. But the recognition and the actual realization of that right is the outcome of a long battle between actors at the national and the international level. There is constant tension between states and their wish to decide who to admit and to select new immigrants on their expected economic contribution or presumed ability to integrate in the society, on the one hand, and the human right of everyone to marry and live with the partner of their choice on the other hand.

The focus of this chapter is on three questions, an historical one, an empirical one and a normative one:

1 How did the right to family reunification develop, and which actors contributed to its recognition?
2 What does empirical research tell us about the effects of measures aimed at restricting family reunification?
3 Are the differences in treatment in the current EU rules on family reunification justified?

2. The gradual development of a right to family reunification

2.1 First steps in international agreements

In the first major international codifications on migration after the Second World War, the 1949 International Labour Organization (ILO) Convention no. 97 on

1 It is estimated that in the 1970s and 1980s family migration counted for half of the total immigration of non-citizens in Germany (Kommission Zuwanderung, 2001, p. 188).

migrant workers and the 1951 Refugee Convention, there is not a single word on family reunification. The ILO Convention only once mentions family members. According to its Article 8, the protection against expulsion of a migrant worker who becomes disabled five years after admission also covers 'the members of his family who have been authorised to accompany or join him'. In the Final Act adopting the Refugee Convention family reunification was only the subject of a recommendation.

When countries in Western Europe (Belgium, France, Germany and the Netherlands) started to recruit workers from Mediterranean countries in the 1950s they did not have rules on family reunification in their national immigration law, only rules in their nationality law allowing foreign women to acquire the nationality of their husband at or after the marriage. Due to the efforts of the countries of origin of the Mediterranean workers, clauses on family reunification were included in some bilateral recruitment agreements. In practice these rules produced little effect, either because the workers did not have the required accommodation for their families or because immigration authorities and national courts of the recruiting countries interpreted these clauses as being not legally binding (Henke, 1976, p. 103; Block, 2016, p. 73). The first national rules on family reunification in the recruiting countries since the mid-1960s were laid down in administrative circulars, often unpublished (GISTI, 1976; Weil, 1991, p. 98ff; Joppke, 2005, p. 108 for France; Henke, 1976, p. 103 for Germany). Their actual application depended largely on the discretion of local authorities. In the Netherlands those administrative instructions were adopted under pressure of employers' organisations and Christian-Democrat and conservative politicians, not from left parties. The wives of Spanish workers were admitted only if they had a job and no children (Bonjour, 2009, p. 78; Van Walsum, 2008, p. 120ff). In Germany employers also realised that direct recruitment of the spouses of their workers was relatively cheap and enhanced their chances to retain their trained male foreign workers (Block, 2016, p. 75).

2.2 European Economic Community (EEC) free movement rules on paper and in practice

In 1960 the European Commission noted the negative effect of the barriers to family reunification on the integration of especially Italian workers in the other Member States. The next year the Italian Commissioner of Social Affairs, Lionello Levi Sandri, managed to include the right to family reunification for workers of other EEC Member States for the first time in a binding legal international document, EEC Regulation no. 15 on the free movement of workers (Böhning, 1972, p. 10; Goedings, 2006). The Commission in its proposal for this first regulation and the two related directives observed that the Treaty provisions of free movement of workers do not mention their family members at all. Nevertheless, the right to family reunification was considered essential on three grounds: firstly, humanitarian reasons requiring maintenance of family unity; secondly, family unity strongly assists workers in remaining in their employment; and, thirdly, being unable to be accompanied by one's family would be a serious obstacle to free movement.[2] Family unity explicitly trumped demographic and housing problems.[3]

This right to family reunification was confirmed and extended in the following regulation of 1964 at the time when the peak of the labour migration from Italy to other Member States was over (Böhning, 1972, p. 53). In the 1968 regulation the requirement of 'normal housing' was de facto dropped after pressure from Italy against the opposition by Germany and the Netherlands. In practice, however, most Member States continued to apply their national rules on waiting periods or housing requirements and did not take the EEC rules on family reunification serious until the late 1970s.

2.3 Defining the family

Since 1961, the right to family reunification in the EU rules of free movement covered the spouse, children under the age of 21 years, older dependent children and the couple's dependent parents and grandparents, irrespective of their nationality.[4] This wide definition of the family still applies to mobile EU citizens today. In 2004 it was extended to cover registered partners as well.[5]

Cases testing the limits of the EEC right to family reunification started to arrive before the Court of Justice only in the 1980s. Four of the first five cases concerned the reunification rights of non-European family members of Union citizens: *Morson & Jhanjan*, the first family reunification case to be referred by a national judge to the Court in Luxembourg in 1982 concerned Surinamese parents of static Dutch nationals. The other cases concerned the Senegalese wife of a Frenchman living in Germany (*Diatta* in 1983), the Togolese widow of a Belgian national (*Dzodzi* in 1988) and the Indian wife of a UK national (*Surinder Singh* 1990). The fifth case on the equal treatment of unmarried partners was the only one concerning the family relationship between two white Europeans (*Reed* in 1985).[6] The other four cases

2 In the original French version: '[L]es considérations humaines visant le maintien de l'intégrité des familles, l'unité familiale contribue puissamment à stabiliser les travailleurs dans leur emploi' and 'l'impossibilité pour le travailleur migrant de se faire accompagner de sa famille constitue un obstacle sérieux à la libre circulation'. Commission of the European Communities, Proposition de règlement et de directives concernant la libre circulation des travailleurs dans la Communauté, 25 June 1960, COM(60) 85, Annex II, p. 4/5.

3 'Quels que soient les inconvénients de l' immigration familiale pouvant découler de certaines situations démographiques ou de logement, ils demeurent certainement inférieurs à ceux de la rupture du noyau familial', Commission of the European Communities, Proposition de règlement et de directives concernant la libre circulation des travailleurs dans la Communauté, 25 June 1960, COM(60) 85, Annex III, p. 6.

4 Explicitly for the first time in Article 17 of Regulation 38/64 adopted on 25 March 1964.

5 Article 2(2)(b) Citizens Directive.

6 CJEU, 27 October 1982, C-35 and C-36/82, *Morson & Jhanjan*, ECLI:EU:C:1982:368; CJEU, 13 February 1985, C-267/83, *Diatta*, ECLI:EU:C:1985:67; CJEU, 18 October 1990, C-297/88 and C-197/89, *Dzodzi*, ECLI:EU:C:1990:360; CJEU, 7 July 1992, C-370/90, *Surinder Singh*, ECLI:EU:C:1992:296 and CJEU, 17 April 1986, C-59/85, *Reed*, ECLI:EU:C:1986:157.

are an indication of the treatment of non-European family members during the first decades after 1968 in the Member States concerned. The role of race in family migration law is discussed extensively in the chapter by de Hart in this book.

2.4 The wider effect of the EEC rules on family reunification

These rules on the right to family reunification over the decades influenced the rights of several large groups outside the personal scope of the early EEC regulations. In the 1960s governments of third states, national politicians and ministries of social affairs used the EEC model to plead for granting this treatment also to other workers. Workers from Spain – not an EEC Member State until 1985 – should receive the same treatment as workers from Italy with regard to family reunification. In 1965 the former chairman of the French *Office National d'Immigration* observed that 'the prestige of the EEC's legislation' forced Member States' governments to liberalize their system towards workers from non-Member States, too (Böhning, 1972, p. 23).

The relatively liberal Belgian Aliens Act of 1980 provided that the rules of the 1968 EEC Regulation on Free Movement applied to the family reunification with static Belgian citizens as well.[7] Twenty years later at least nine other Member States[8] had adopted the same rules on the family reunification with their static nationals in their legislation or case law, thus avoiding the thorny discussion on reverse discrimination of their own citizens. In many countries national sponsors account for half or more of the applications for family reunification (Walter, 2008, p. 2; Groenendijk, 2014, p. 173).[9] Consequently, this extension of the EU rules to family reunification with static national sponsors has far-reaching effects. In Belgium the extension was limited in 2011 with the introduction of income and housing requirements with the explicit aim to restrict family reunification with Belgian nationals of immigrant origin. The Belgian Constitutional Court in a judgement of 26 September 2013 held the difference in treatment to be justified, on the ground that mobile and static EU citizens are different cases.[10]

The former right of male citizens to be reunited with their foreign spouses under nationality law was in several European countries substituted by a right of all citizens to live with their family members on the basis of an extended application of the EU free movement rules in their national immigration law. These national rules also applied to the reunification of foreign men with female citizen sponsors, marriages traditionally considered as suspect, based on the presumption of economic rather than romantic motives. The drive for equal treatment in favour of men trumped the fear for male immigration. Not all Member States agreed with this

7 Article 4 Belgian Aliens Act of 15 December 1980.

8 Bulgaria, Czech Republic, Greece, Hungary, Italy, Lithuania, Poland, Slovenia and Spain.

9 See also Commission of the European Communities, Proposal for a Council Directive on the right to family reunification, 1 December 1999, COM(1999) 638 final.

10 Belgian Constitutional Court, 26 September 2013, No. 123/2013.

extensive application of EU rules as is illustrated by the strong opposition of Germany and the Netherlands against the 1999 proposal of the European Commission to codify this extension to static EU nationals in the Family Reunification Directive (Walter, 2008, p. 41; Strik, 2011, p. 86). Germany was eager to retain the competence to regulate the family reunification of *Spät-Aussiedler* (ethnic Germans emigrating from Russia, Romania and Kazakhstan). The Netherlands opposed this proposal because it wanted to retain its freedom to restrict the family reunification of naturalized Turkish and Moroccan Dutch nationals and of Surinamese-Dutch nationals.

After 1990, the free movement rules from 1968 also influenced the family reunification rights of third-country national sponsors in the EU. The relevant provisions were used by the Court of Justice to interpret the rules on family member in the EEC-Turkey association law (Groenendijk, 2013, p. 415), and the European Commission used these rules as a model when drafting its proposals for the Family Reunification Directive.[11] Even after these proposals were watered down by Member States, the influence of the 1968 rules on new EU migration law is undeniable.

2.5 Gradual liberalization of reunification rules in the 1970s and 1980s

The prolonged residence of foreign workers, the 1973 recruitment ban, which closed the possibility to return and come back to Western Europe, and the repeated political discussions on reducing family benefits for children living in the countries of origin all increased the demand for family reunification. The increased value of the principle of equal treatment and the liberalization of family norms influenced the political responses when NGOs, such as GISTI in France and IAF in Germany,[12] and lawyers started to campaign for more liberal national rules on family reunification (Bonjour, 2009; Van Walsum, 2008).

We see two different patterns. The first one can be observed in countries like Germany and France where the highest courts used clauses on family life in the national constitution to annul administrative circulars unreasonably restricting family reunification: the French Conseil d'État in 1978 and the German Bundesverfassungsgericht in 1987.[13] The second pattern is noticeable in countries like Denmark, the Netherlands and the UK, where such constitutional right and constitutional review are absent. In the latter countries NGOs, lawyers and national courts were and are more inclined to look to the ECHR and the Court in Strasbourg to perform this role. In 1985 the ECtHR gave its first judgement on family reunification in *Abdulaziz*, ruling that the UK family reunification provisions in breach of Articles 8 and 14 ECHR discriminated between male and female citizens, not on

11 Commission of the European Communities, Proposal for a Council Directive on the right to family reunification, 1 December 1999, COM(1999) 638 final, § 7.2.

12 GISTI is the Group d'information et de soutien des immigrés and IAF is an association of binational families.

13 Conseil d'État, 8 December 1978, case GISTI, CFDT and CGT, ECLI:FR:CEASS:1978:10097.19781208 and Bundesverfassungsgericht, 12 May 1987, 2 BvR 1227/83, BVerfGE 76, 1.

the basis of race.[14] Before that judgement national courts in many European countries (Belgium, France, the Netherlands, Switzerland and the UK) ruled that Article 8 ECHR did not apply in immigration cases. Apparently, the national judges were reluctant to interfere and protected the national sovereignty.

The role of a human rights perspective in the debate on family reunification was stimulated by further judgements by the ECtHR in *Berrehab* (1988) and *Gül* (1995) illustrating that Article 8 ECHR, which guarantees the right to respect for family life (not a right to family reunification) could protect admitted family members against expulsion and obliges states to admit family members of non-nationals in need of protection in case reunification in another country was not possible.[15] All three Strasbourg cases originated in countries without a constitutional clause protecting family life and without a right to family reunification in their national legislation (the UK, the Netherlands and Switzerland).

2.6 Turn towards more restrictive rules in the 1990s and after 9/11

These liberal legal developments at the European level during the 1990s met with political pressure at the national level for more restrictive rules on family reunification (Block & Bonjour, 2013; Bech et al., 2017). This pressure was induced by the growing numbers of asylum seekers from outside Europe, who after admission would be entitled to family reunification, by the increasing number of children of settled immigrants asking for family reunification and by the realization that an increasing share of the sponsors for family reunification were citizens of immigrant origin (Bonjour, 2009, p. 211; Block, 2016). In the Netherlands, soon after the change of the century, half of the sponsors were Dutch citizens of immigrant origin (Groenendijk, 2014, p. 173).

At the same time Member States empowered the EU in the Treaty of Amsterdam of 1997 to make binding legal rules on the admission of third-country nationals, 'including those for the purpose of family reunification'. Two years later the European Commission published its first proposal for a Directive on the right to family reunification of third-country nationals. The proposal was modelled partly after the free movement rules and influenced by the then relatively liberal French rules. The negotiations in Brussels lasted four years (1999–2003). The opposition of some Member States against the liberal proposal was reinforced by the increasing anti-immigrant mood after the 9/11 attacks. The result was a compromise. For the first time the right to family reunification for non-EU sponsors with their spouse and minor children was codified in EU law, if the conditions regarding income, housing or integration were met. These conditions do not apply when the sponsors are refugees according to a chapter of the directive with more favourable rules for reunification with refugees.

14 ECtHR, 28 May 1985, *Abdulaziz, Cabales and Balkandali v. the United Kingdom*, nos. 9214/80; 9473/81, 9474/81.

15 ECtHR, 21 June 1988, *Berrehab v. the Netherlands*, No. 10730/84 and ECtHR, 19 February 1996, *Gül v. Swltzerland*, No. 23218/94.

Shortly after the adoption the European Parliament, which at that time had no legislative power but was only consulted by the Council, asked the Court of Justice to annul the directive for violation of the ECHR. The initiative for the Parliament's action was taken by lawyers from the same French NGO (GISTI) which in 1978 successfully obtained annulment of the circular on family reunification by the Conseil d'État. In this first case before the EU Court Germany argued that the directive did not really provide binding rules, repeating the minimalistic interpretation of earlier international norms on this topic in recruitment agreements and Council of Europe migration instruments. The Court dismissed the Parliament's action. But in its judgement the Court confirmed that the directive provided a subjective right to family reunification, leaving no discretion if the requirements were met, a right going far beyond the protection of family life guaranteed by Article 8 ECHR.[16]

2.7 Visible effects of the 2003 Directive on national immigration rules and practice

In most Member States the transposition of the directive resulted in more liberal rules on family reunification in national law. By contrast, some Member States used the transposition of the directive as an occasion to introduce new restrictions. In France the national rules were made less liberal on seven points but just above the minimum level required by the directive (Groenendijk et al., 2007; Pascouau & Labayle, 2011; EMN, 2017). The Netherlands used the transposition to introduce new restrictions. Several Member States decided to apply the rules of this directive also to the family reunification with their own (static) citizens, thus at a level considerably below that of mobile EU nationals on the basis of the free movement rules.

The Member States bound by the directive after 2003 lost the competence to make their national law more restrictive than the minimum level prescribed by the directive. Two examples clearly illustrate this effect. Shortly after the adoption of the directive, the Netherlands introduced an unusually high 120% of the minimum income requirement, high fees for residence permits and an integration test abroad for family members of nationals from certain (not all) third countries. On all three issues the new national rules had to be withdrawn or amended after the CJEU held the rules to be incompatible with the directive.[17] A well-published action by the Dutch government in 2011 to raise support among Member States to reduce the right to family reunification under the directive failed bitterly. The action triggered the Commission Green Paper on the issue.[18] The reactions to that paper demonstrated the lack of support for amending the directive (Groenendijk & Strik, 2022).

16 CJEU, 26 June 2006, C-540/03, *Parliament v. Council*, ECLI:EU:C:2006:429.

17 CJEU, 4 March 2010, C-578/08, *Chakroun*, ECLI:EU:C:2010:117; CJEU, 9 July 2015, C-153/14, *K & A*, ECLI:EU:C:2015:453 and CJEU, 26 April 2012, C-508/10, *Commission v. The Netherlands*, ECLI:EU:C:2012:243.

18 European Commission, Green paper on the right to family reunification of third-country nationals living in the European Union (Directive 2003/86/EC), 15 November 2011, COM(2011)735 final.

Most Member States, apparently, felt not unduly restricted by the directive in the application of their national policies or were more afraid of opening a Pandora's box triggering requests for more liberal rules from the European Parliament and civil society.

This effect of the Family Reunification Directive is also illustrated by the series of very restrictive income, age and integration requirements introduced over the last decade in the national rules in Denmark and the UK, two states not bound by the directive. Repeated proposals by politicians of anti-immigration or conservative parties in other Member States to introduce similar restrictions failed because they were clearly incompatible with the directive.

Initial opposition among national immigration authorities and courts to the application of the directive considerably postponed the effect of the directive in practice. After the 2010 *Chakroun* judgement of the Court of Justice,[19] the Netherlands reduced the income requirement from 120 to 100% of the minimum income level, but the Immigration Service continued its very strict application of this requirement ('One euro short and reunification will be refused'), disregarding the explicit instruction of the Court of Justice to apply the proportionality test in each individual case. National courts only started to take this instruction seriously after it was repeated in the *Khachab* judgement in 2016 in a case from Spain,[20] ten years after the first Luxembourg judgement and six years after the second (*Chakroun*).

2.8 Privileged rules for family reunification of highly qualified workers

As part of a policy to make the EU more attractive for highly qualified workers from outside the EU, privileged rules for family reunification with such workers were included in three EU directives. The Blue Card Directive adopted in 2008 provides for seven favourable derogations from the general rules of the Family Reunification Directive: among others no pre-entry integration test, no waiting period, faster decision making and immediate access to employment for the family members. Similar privileges were included in the 2014 ICT-directive and for researchers in the 2016 Students and Researchers Directive. In the 2021 revision of the Blue Card Directive those privileges are further expanded on two points.[21] Each time, economic reasons (human capital needs) clearly outweighed restrictive tendencies that prevailed in many Member States. In the 2022 proposal for a recast of the Long-Term Residents Directive for the first time similar, more favourable derogations from the Family Reunification Directive are proposed primarily with the aim to support the integration of the immigrants.[22]

19 CJEU, 4 March 2010, C-578/08, *Chakroun*, ECLI:EU:C:2010:117.

20 CJEU, 21 April 2016, C-558/14, *Khachab*, ECLI:EU:C:2016:285.

21 Article 17(6) and (10) EU Blue Card Directive.

22 See Article 15(2)–(5) of the proposal in European Commission, Proposal for a Directive of the European Parliament and of the Council concerning the status of third-country nationals who are long-term residents (recast), 27 April 2022, COM(2022) 650 final, pp. 14, 25.

From this short overview of the development of family reunification law in Europe it is clear that each time national courts at first cautiously shielded the national rules against influences from international and EU law.[23] This happened in the first decade after the adoption of the 1968 Regulation on free movement of workers, with regard to Article 8 ECHR in the decades before the 1985 *Abdulaziz* judgement and in the first decade after the adoption of the EU Family Reunification Directive. Only from 2013 onwards, ten years after the adoption of the directive, did national courts start to make references to the Court of Justice asking for interpretation of the directive. This tendency prevented or postponed the effect of the international and EU law in practice.

3. Two empirical questions

Today a patchwork of national and EU rules determines the chances of being admitted for family reunification. For several decades, the nationality of the sponsor determined the chances of their family members being admitted. In recent years, the education level of the sponsor or the family member has become more relevant. Having higher education considerably reduces the requirements and administrative hurdles. Only family members or sponsors without such education continue to be confronted with the full set of conditions and restrictions. The lower the education the harder it is to meet integration and income requirements for family reunification.

The political arguments for allowing more liberal reunification rules for certain categories, generally, relate to the expected economic advantage the migrant will bring or the supposed ability of the sponsor or his family members to integrate in the host society. Besides, exceptions are made for refugees who cannot reunite with their families elsewhere. Since the early 1990s the main arguments for the introduction of new restrictions are the reduction of the numbers of family migrants and the need to assist the integration of admitted family members, avoiding them becoming a burden on society. Economic and cultural or ethnic arguments are used to justify both liberal and restrictive measures.

The latter development raises two types of questions. Firstly, empirical questions about expected and unexpected effect of the restrictive measures (Section 3). In this respect, the two main questions are: first, did the new higher requirements introduced in many European countries after 2001 result in the desired reduction of the number of family migrants and, second, did these requirements assist the integration of admitted family members? The second type of question is of a normative (legal or political) nature: Is there sufficient justification for the resulting sharp differences in treatment with regard to family reunification? That question will be discussed in Section 4.

23 For a similar defensive reaction to Council of Europe agreements granting rights to non-citizen immigrants, see Swart (1980).

3.1 The numbers

Governments tend to point to statistical data indicating a sharp decline in the number of admitted family migrants after the introduction of higher age and income requirements or the pre-entry integration test in several countries. The reduction was real, although the statistical data often overestimate the effects of the policy measures; because immigration peaked just before the introduction, the immigration was postponed rather than waived or family members arrived via other channels, as student, worker, via the 'EU-route' as the spouse of a mobile Union citizen,[24] or as an irregular migrant (Leerkes & Kulu-Glasgow, 2011; Kolbaşi-Muyan, 2017, p. 301; Wray et al., 2021). Often, the reduction was partly due to other factors, such as economic trends, changing marriage patterns or other policy changes implemented at about the same time. Regardless, the Eurostat data mentioned in the beginning of this chapter indicate that family migration from outside the EU increased considerably after 2011.

3.2 Reactions of sponsors and their family members to the restrictive measures

How sponsors reacted to these restrictive measures has been studied in several European countries: in Germany (Aybek et al., 2015; Block, 2016, 2021a), in the Netherlands (Kulu-Glasgow & Leerkes, 2009, 2013; Leerkes & Kulu-Glasgow, 2011; Kolbaşi-Muyan, 2017, 2020; de Hart & Besselsen, 2021), in France (Fresnota-Flot, 2015) and in the UK (Grant et al., 2015; Wray et al., 2021). Strik et al. (2013) presented a comparative view.

From the results it appears that *higher age requirements* for spouses and partners in some cases lead to giving up the idea of marriage or to definite emigration of the sponsor in order to realize family unity elsewhere. More often they result in a waiting period (putting the reunification on hold until both spouses reach the required age), in temporary reunification in the country of origin or in temporary irregular residence of the migrant family member in the country of destination (Kulu-Glasgow & Leerkes, 2013; Kolbaşi-Muyan, 2017, 2020). All these effects result in prolonged focus of the sponsor on the country where the spouse/partner or other family members are living. None of the observed reactions are likely to contribute to integration of the sponsor and the migrating spouse or partner.

As regards *income requirements* above the general minimum wage level (120% in the Netherlands from 2004 to 2010 and 140% since 2012 in the UK), researchers observed the following reactions: sponsors interrupting or ending their studies in order to accept employment, thus sacrificing long-term gains through education; changing a promising but low-paid job for a better-paid job with fewer career

24 The 'EU-route' refers to the possibility for EU citizens, unable to reunite with TCN family members on the basis of the national rules, to migrate to another Member State and realize reunification there under the more liberal EU rules on free movement.

prospects; taking a second job or working more hours; reducing social participation; relying more often on family or community members to obtain cooperation of employers for a temporary extension; or increasing working hours, in reality or only on paper (Leerkes & Kulu-Glasgow, 2011; Kolbaşi-Muyan, 2017, 2020; Grant et al., 2015). In the latter case the sponsor often has to pay the employer the extra monthly income tax and social contributions due. In the Netherlands, both national authorities and certain sponsors transgressed the law; the state did so by raising the income requirement to a level which violated EU law, which triggered some sponsors and their employers to pretend that the illegal high level was met. As a result of the gendered pay gap, female sponsors experience more difficulties to meet the required income level. Again, none of these patterns of behaviour will enhance the integration of the sponsors or of their family members.

Currently, three EU Member States require spouses to pass a *pre-entry language or integration test*, the Netherlands since 2006, Germany since 2007 and Austria since 2011. Denmark and France enacted a similar requirement. In Denmark the relevant provision never entered into force because of the high costs and relative ineffectiveness of language acquisition abroad. France, after some years, cancelled its pre-entry test and focussed on in-country integration after admission (Groenendijk, 2011). Studies on the Dutch and German tests report high costs and long delays, especially for family members with lower education (Aybek et al., 2015). In 2017 and 2018 circa 15,000 spouses had to postpone reunification with their partners in Germany solely because they failed the language test.[25]

In her qualitative study of how Turkish-Dutch sponsors cope with the family reunification hurdles, Kolbaşi-Muyan (2017) observed the overall increased dependency of sponsoring spouses on their family and the wider Turkish community for additional jobs, extension of contracts, support in finding a job or housing in Belgium or Germany for the EU-route or for moral support against criticism of the family of the spouse waiting in Turkey. She also observed that the confrontation with the new hurdles for reunification made the sponsoring spouses experience a double devaluation of their Dutch nationality. Firstly, they discovered that their Dutch nationality does not assist them in realizing reunification, since in the Netherlands the rules of the Family Reunification Directive for third-country nationals are applied to static Dutch nationals as well. Secondly, these sponsors experienced that, as a consequence of the equal treatment and standstill clauses in the EU-Turkey association law, the higher age limit did not apply and their spouses were exempted from the Dutch pre-entry integration test (and from the integration exam after entry).[26] Consequently, they started to value their Turkish nationality more than their Dutch one (Kolbaşi-Muyan, 2017, p. 315; 2020, p. 169). The devaluation of the nationality of the country of immigration for the first-generation migrants or of the country of birth for the second generation also occurred among other

25 Deutscher Bundestag, 2019, Drucksache 19/9692, p. 4.

26 Both exemptions were withdrawn in 2022 on the grounds that the new Integration Act of 2021 was compatible with EEC-Turkey association law.

immigrant groups in the Netherlands (de Hart & Besselsen, 2021, p. 52). A similar devaluation of the citizenship of naturalized immigrants as a result of measures to restrict family reunification was observed in Germany (Block, 2021a, 2021b; Block & Bonjour, 2013) and in France (Bonjour & Block 2018).

On the basis of these studies the answer to the two empirical questions is as follows: yes, the numbers of admitted family members declined in the first years after the introduction of the restrictions. But all three measures (higher age, income and pre-entry integration conditions) resulted in increased reliance and dependence of the sponsor on family and community networks for jobs, money and moral support. Moreover, the additional hurdles negatively impacted on the integration of the sponsors in their country of residence of which they often are citizens since birth. Governments, generally, tend to disregard these unwelcome outcomes of the relevant research or to selectively quote from it in the political debate.

4. Are differences in treatment in the current rules on family reunification law justified?

EU rules on family reunification developed over 60 years since 1961. Currently these rules are laid down in 11 different EU instruments (ten directives and the Dublin III Regulation). One of these instruments, the Temporary Protection Directive adopted in 2001, was never applied in practice until the Russian invasion in Ukraine in 2022, mainly because of a lack of solidarity among Member States and because the level of rights attached to the status was considered too high. Many Member States, after all, were afraid for possible consequences of the right to family reunification provided for persons with the temporary protection in that directive.

The EU rules for different categories of sponsors vary considerably: different rules for EU citizens and non-EU citizens, for mobile and static EU citizens, for third-country sponsors with or without high qualifications and for refugees and those with other, subsidiary or temporary forms of protection. Moreover, the 2003 Family Reunification Directive leaves considerable freedom to Member States to make further variations for specific categories of sponsors in their national law.[27] This patchwork and most of the resulting differences are understandable and even inevitable considering the historic development, the legislative process of the EU and the considerable differences in national rules and traditions between Member States. Making one EU Immigration Code was politically impossible and will remain so for the time being. Nevertheless, the question arises whether this patchwork and the resulting differences in treatment are legally, morally and politically acceptable.

My plea is for a systematic and critical review of the differences in treatment of third-country sponsors with regard to family reunification in the national law

27 Article 3(5) Family Reunification Directive explicitly allows Members States to adopt or maintain more favourable national rules.

of Member States. Not a plea for revision of the EU legislation. Such revision in the current political situation most probably would result in a general reduction of the right to family reunification. Within each Member State, NGOs, lawyers, researchers, immigration authorities, judges and politicians should critically consider whether the current differences in treatment of sponsors are compatible with the prohibition of racial discrimination in Article 1 and Article 2 of the UN Convention against Racial Discrimination (CERD) and with the more general prohibition of discrimination in Article 14 ECHR and in Article 21 of the EU Charter.

Leaving aside the differences in the family reunification rights of Union citizens and immigrants from outside the EU[28] and the differences between static and mobile Union citizens, I will focus here on three differences in treatment between categories of non-EU sponsors only on the basis of their nationality, residence status or education. These differences have to be justified in the light of the EU and international human rights standards just mentioned.

1 Difference in treatment between highly qualified workers and other sponsors

We noticed that in three EU legal migration directives sponsors with higher educational qualifications are entitled to a clearly better right to migrate or be reunited with close family members, since they are exempted from several of the legal and administrative hurdles of the Family Reunification Directive. This raises questions as to the fairness of applying these conditions and barriers only to third-country nationals with less education. Article 8(2) ECHR allows for the interference with the right to family life, which is 'necessary in a democratic society in the interests . . . of the economic wellbeing of the country'. The Court in Strasbourg allows the states, generally, a large discretion on this point. But does the economic self-interest sufficiently justify that spouses of highly qualified Brazilian, Chinese or Indian citizens admitted for employment are exempted from the pre-entry language and integration test, while the spouses of third-country nationals who were born and lived their whole life in the Member State have to pass the test before entry? And how could the less favourable treatment of spouses of static sponsors with Dutch or German nationality be justified?

2 Difference in treatment between refugees and beneficiaries of other forms of protection

The Family Reunification Directive provides for a privileged treatment for refugees only and appears to allow Member States to apply less favourable rules for beneficiaries of subsidiary protection. Elsewhere in EU law the rights of these two categories are aligned. Most Member States decided to apply the same favourable rules to both categories (EMN, 2017, p. 29). The main reason why Germany and

28 For an explicit effort to justify these differences on the ground of non-comparability of the situations, see CJEU, 2 September 2021, C-930/19, *X.*, ECLI:EU:C:2021:657.

several Scandinavian countries decided to apply less favourable rules was to postpone family reunification of the large number of Syrian nationals fleeing from the civil war in their country in 2015. The main argument advanced by governments is that the protection needs of the other categories are only temporary. The argument proved to be more wishful thinking than realistic considering the continuing war in Syria. In a 2021 judgement on a complaint of a Syrian national granted temporary protection in Denmark, the Court in Strasbourg held the difference in treatment to be justified. In case of a massive influx of refugees, a state may temporarily give priority to protection over family reunification. But the Court set a limit: a waiting period may not last more than two years. By postponing consideration of these applications for three years Denmark violated Article 8 ECHR.[29] This judgement may well have consequences for other requirements for family reunification of beneficiaries of international protection which de facto postpone or block family reunification such as income, housing or integration requirements.

3 Difference in treatment in Dutch and German law exempting spouses of rich and Western countries from pre-entry language test only on basis of their nationality

The UN Committee monitoring CERD in its report on the Netherlands in 2010 recommended that the Netherlands 'review this legislation with a view to abolishing the discriminatory application of the civic integration examination abroad to "non-Western" state nationals'. It held this difference in treatment to be incompatible with the CERD Convention.[30] The Council of Europe's European Commission against Racism and Intolerance (ECRI) repeatedly recommended 'that the Dutch authorities review the Civic Integration Abroad Act from the point of view of its conformity with the prohibition of discrimination on grounds of nationality, notably as concerns the system of exemptions'.[31] Human Rights Watch came to the same conclusion.[32] There is no treaty basis for this difference in treatment.[33] The Dutch government disregarded all reports and recommendations. On the contrary, it twice raised the level of the test. A year later a Dutch court asked the Court in Luxembourg whether this difference in treatment is compatible with the Family Reunification Directive. The Dutch government avoided a possible unwelcome answer by immediately granting a visa for family reunification to the Afghan

29 ECtHR, 9 July 2021, *MA v. Denmark*, no. 6697/18, § 145; but partly otherwise ECtHR, 20 October 2022, *M.T. and others v Sweden*, No. 22105/18.

30 Committee on the Elimination of Racial Discrimination, Concluding observations: Netherlands, 25 March 2010, CERD//C/NLD/CO/17-18, § 5.

31 European Commission against Racism and Intolerance, Third Report on the Netherlands, 29 June 2007, CRI(2008)3, §§ 50–58 and European Commission against Racism and Intolerance, Fourth Report on the Netherlands, 20 June 2013, CRI(2013)39, §§ 190–197.

32 Human Rights Watch. (2018). *The Netherlands: Discrimination in the name of integration*. www.hrw.org/en/node/82373/section/1.

33 For a discussion of the justifications mentioned by the German Bundesverwaltungsgericht, 30 March 2010, 1 C 8.09, ECLI:DE: BVerwG:2010: 300310U1C8.09.0, § 67, see Groenendijk (2012, p. 136ff).

spouse concerned.[34] The EU Court of Justice has never dealt with the question whether the unfavourable treatment of 'non-Western' spouses is compatible with Article 21 EU Charter, which prohibits discrimination on the ground of race, ethnic origin or language.[35] In 2021, the Court of Justice held that Article 21 EU Charter, in so far as it prohibits any discrimination based on ethnic origin, does not preclude a language condition 'which is applicable to all third-country nationals without distinction and from which it is not apparent that it places persons of a particular ethnic origin at a disadvantage'.[36] In the Netherlands, however, nationals of certain third countries with mainly white populations are exempted from the test. The ECtHR has repeatedly held that differences in treatment on the basis of nationality can only be justified by 'very weighty reasons'.[37]

From the empirical data presented, it is clear that the selective effect of the test varies considerably depending on the nationality of the spouse. Less than half of the spouses from Iraq and Sri Lanka pass the test the first time, while the pass rates for spouses from Russia and Ukraine are near 100%. The overall pass rate declined each time the level was raised or the scope of the test was extended. In the first years after 2006, 90% of the participants passed the first time they took the test. The pass rate declined to 80% after the test's level was raised in 2011. After the additions to the test in 2015 the pass rate now varies between 60 and 70%, quite similar to the pass rate of the German language test abroad.[38] In recent years only 50% of the participants with basic education, as opposed to 85% of the candidates with higher education, passed the first time they took the Dutch test (Zwanepol et al., 2020). Apparently, the test discourages family members with lower education. Each year thousands of spouses have to take and pay for the test two, three or more times before they are admitted (Groenendijk & Strik, 2022).

Language tests have a long history as an instrument for excluding undesired immigrants, starting with the US Chinese Exclusion Act (1882–1952), a model followed in Canada, South Africa and the centre piece of the 'Keep Australia White' policy from 1901 till 1957 (Bast, 2011; Groenendijk, 2011, p. 4).

The cumulation of exemptions for spouses of highly qualified third-country nationals and those from certain rich third countries makes it all the more questionable whether the application of the pre-entry test to other spouses is compatible with the right to family life, Article 8 and Article 14 ECHR and the general non-discrimination clause in the Protocol No. 12 of the ECHR.

EU rules on family reunification explicitly privilege sponsors with higher education, among others, by exempting their spouses from the pre-entry language and integration test. The compatibility with international and EU standards of both this

34 CJEU, 10 June 2011, C-155/11PPU, *Imran*, ECLI:EU:C:2011:387.

35 In June 2025, questions on the compatibility of the Dutch pre-entry integration test with the Family Reunification Directive and Articles 7, 21 and 52 of the EU Charter were referred to the CJEU, see case C-394/25.

36 CJEU, 10 June 2021, C-94/20, *Land Oberösterreich*, ECLI:EU:C:2021:477, § 63.

37 ECtHR, 16 September 1996, *Gaygusuz v. Austria*, No. 17371/90, and later case law.

38 In 2019 the pass rate for the German test was 66%, Deutscher Bundestag Druckache 19/18193, p. 14.

explicit exemption on the basis of class and the explicit exemption on the basis of nationality in the three Member States operating those pre-entry tests is subject to serious doubt, considering the views of the international and EU monitoring bodies.

Most family reunification rules on paper are colour-blind, but their effects in real life are not. Immigrants from certain non-EU countries and Union citizens of immigrant origin experience the negative effects of these rules far more often than other 'native' white Union citizens.

References

Aybek, C. M., Stassburger, G., & Yüksel-Kaptanoglu, I. (2015). Marriage Migration from Turkey to Germany: Risks and Coping Strategies of Transnational Couples. In C. M. Aybek & R. Muttarak (Eds.), *Spatial Mobility, Migration and Living Arrangements* (pp. 23–42). Springer. https://doi.org/10.25336/csp29399

Bast, J. (2011). *Aufenthaltsrecht und Migrationssteuerung*. Mohr Siebeck.

Bech, E., Borevi, K., & Mouritsen, P. (2017). A "civic turn" in Scandinavian family migration policies? Comparing Denmark, Norway and Sweden. *Comparative Migration Studies*, *5*(7). https://doi.org/10.1186/s40878-016-0046-7

Block, L. (2016). *Policy Frames on Spousal Migration in Germany: Regulating Membership, Regulating the Family*. Springer. https://doi.org/10.1007/978-3-658-13296-5

Block, L. (2021a). "(Im-)proper" members with "(im-)proper" families? Framing spousal migration policies in Germany. *Journal of Ethnic and Migration Studies*, *47*, 379–396. https://doi.org/10.1080/1369183X.2019.1625132

Block, L. (2021b). "I'm not entitled to be married in Germany? Am I German or am I not?" Narratives and discursive strategies of citizen sponsors in the German spousal migration context. *Identities*, *28*, 56–73. https://doi.org/10.1080/1070289X.2020.1723327

Block, L., & Bonjour, S. (2013). Fortress Europe of Europe of rights? The Europeanisation of family migration policies in France, Germany and the Netherlands. *European Journal of Migration and Law*, *15*, 203–224. https://doi.org/10.1163/15718166-12342031

Böhning, W. R. (1972). *The Migration of Workers in the United Kingdom and the European Community*. Oxford University Press. https://doi.org/10.1007/BF02917943

Bonjour, S. (2009). *Grens en gezin, Beleidsvorming inzake gezinshereniging in Nederland, 1955–2005*. Aksant. https://doi.org/10.18352/bmgn-lchr.7267

Bonjour, S., & Block, L. (2018). Ethnicizing citizenship, questioning membership: Explaining the decreasing family migration rights of citizens in Europe. *Citizenship Studies*, *20*(6–7), 779–794. https://doi.org/10.1080/13621025.2016.1191429

Council of Europe Commissioner for Human Rights. (2017). *Realising the right to family reunification of refugees in Europe*. Council of Europe. www.refworld.org/docid/5a0d5eae4.html

De Hart, B., & Besselsen, E. (2021). "Everything went according to the rules": Female citizen sponsors' legal consciousness, intimate citizenship and family migration law. *Identities: Global Studies in Culture and Power*, *28*, 37–55. https://doi.org/10.1080/1070289X.2020.1723310

EMN (European Migration Network). (2017). *Family reunification of third-country nationals in the EU plus Norway: National practices*. https://ec.europa.eu/migrant-integration/library-document/family-reunification-third-country-nationals-eu_en.

Eurostat. (2021). *Residence permits – statistics on first permits issued during the year*. Retrieved July 7, 2022, from https://ec.europa.eu/eurostat/statistics-explained/index.php?title=Residence_permits_-_statistics_on_first_permits_issued_during_the_year&oldid=507019

Fresnota-Flot, A. (2015). The bumpy landscape of family reunification: Experiences of first and 1.5-generation Filipinos in France. *Journal of Ethnic and Migration Studies*, *41*, 1152–1171. https://doi.org/10.1080/1369183X.2014.956711

GISTI. (1976). L'immigration familiale. *Droit Social*, *5*, 101–109.

Goedings, S. A. W. (2006). *Labor Migration in an Integrating Europe: National Migration Policies and the Free Movement of Workers, 1950–1968*. SDU.

Grant, S., Kofman, E., Peel, C., & Wray, H. (2015). *Family Friendly? The Impact on Children of the Family Migration Rules: A Review of the Financial Requirements*. Children's Commissioner for England.

Groenendijk, K. (2011). Pre-departure integration strategies in the European Union: Integration or immigration policies? *European Journal of Migration and Law*, *13*, 1–30. https://doi.org/10.1163/157181611X558191

Groenendijk, K. (2012). Are Third-Country Nationals Protected by the Union Law Prohibition of Discrimination on Grounds of Nationality? In K. Barwig & R. Dobbelstein (Eds.), *Den Fremden akzeptieren, Festschrift für Gisbert Brinkmann* (Schriften zum Migrationsrecht no. 6, pp. 131–142). Nomos Verlag. https://hdl.handle.net/2066/106563

Groenendijk, K. (2013). The Court of Justice and the Development of EEC-Turkey Association Law. In G. Jochum, W. Fritzemeyer, & M. Kau (Eds.), *Grenzüberschreitendes Recht – Crossing Frontiers, Festschrift für Kay Hailbronner* (pp. 413–428). C.F. Müller.

Groenendijk, K. (2014). Reverse Discrimination, Family Reunification and Union Citizens of Immigrant Origin. In E. Guild, C. Gortázar Rotaeche, and D Kostakopoulou (Eds.), *The Reconceptualization of European Union Citizenship* (pp. 169–188). Martinus Nijhoff.

Groenendijk, K., et al. (2007). *The Family Reunification Directive in EU Member States. The First Year of Implementation*. Wolf Legal Publishers.

Groenendijk, K., & Strik, T. (2022). Directive 2003/86 on the Right to Family Reunification: A Surprising Anchor in a Sensitive Field. In E. Tsourdi & P. De Bruycker (Eds.), *Research Handbook on EU Migration and Asylum Law* (pp. 306–326). Edward Elgar. https://doi.org/10.4337/9781786439635.00023

Henke, H. (1976). Die aufenthaltsrechtliche Stellung der Familienangehörigen ausländischer Arbeitnehmer. In G. Albrecht (Ed.), *Das Düsseldorfer Reformprogramm zum Ausländerrecht* (pp. 99–110). Europa Union Verlag.

Joppke, C. (2005). *Selecting by Origin: Ethnic Migration in the Liberal State*. Harvard University Press.

Kolbaşi-Muyan, G. (2017). *Interactions between family reunification and integration: Marriages of second generation Turkish Dutch from Turkey* [Dissertation, Middle East Technical University]. http://etd.lib.metu.edu.tr/upload/12620896/index.pdf

Kolbaşi-Muyan, G. (2020). Alienation of "Second Generation Turkish Dutch" in the Name of "Integration": Family Reunification Policies in the Netherlands. In M. Jesse (Ed.), *European Societies, Migration and the Law: The "Others" Among "Us"* (pp. 152–172). Cambridge University Press. https://doi.org/10.1017/9781108767637.009

Kommission Zuwanderung. (2001). *Zuwanderung gestalten – Integration fördern*. Bericht der Unabhängige Kommission "Zuwanderung".

Kulu-Glasgow, I., & Leerkes, A. (2009). *Internationale gezinsvorming begrensd? Een evaluatie van de verhoging van de inkomenseis en leeftijdseis bij migratie van buitenlandse partners naar Nederland*. WODC.

Kulu-Glasgow, I., & Leerkes, A. (2013). Restricting Turkish marriage migration? National policy, couples coping strategies and international obligations. *Migration Letters*, *10*, 369–382. https://doi.org/10.33182/ml.v10i3.135.

Leerkes, A., & Kulu-Glasgow, I. (2011). Playing hard(er) to get: The state, international couples, and the income requirement. *European Journal of Migration and Law*, *13*(1), 95–121. https://doi.org/10.1163/157181611X554267.

Pascouau, Y., & Labayle, H. (2011). *Conditions for Family Reunification Under Strain*. European Policy Centre.

Strik, T. (2011). *Besluitvorming over asiel- en migratierichtlijnen. De wisselwerking tussen nationaal en Europees niveau*. Boom Juridische uitgevers.
Strik, T., De Hart, B., & Nissen, E. (2013). *Family Reunification: A Barrier or Facilitator of Integration? A Comparative Study*. Wolf Publishers.
Swart, A. H. J. (1980). The legal status of Aliens: Clauses in Council of Europe instruments relating to the rights of aliens. *Netherlands Yearbook of International Law, 11*, 3–64. https://bit.ly/3LKcMOQ
Van Walsum, S. (2008). *The Family and the Nation: Dutch Family Migration Policies in the Context of Changing Family Norms*. Cambridge Scholars.
Walter, A. (2008). *Reverse Discrimination and Family Reunification*. Wolf Legal Publishers.
Weil, P. (1991). *La France et ses Ëtrangers. L'aventure d'une politique de l'immigration 1938–1991*. Calmann-Lévy.
Wray, H., Kofman, E., & Simic, A. (2021). Subversive citizens: Using EU free movement law to bypass the UK's rules on marriage migration. *Journal of Ethnic and Migration Studies, 47*, 447–463. https://doi.org/10.1080/1369183X.2019.1625140
Zwanepol, M., Onstenk, A., & Tazelaar, P. (2020). *Monitor basisexamen inburgering buitenland 2019*. Significant Public. https://open.overheid.nl/documenten/ronl-1cf6ba0c-674e-45ca-bd22-3a281bcd6749/pdf

6 How race and gender function in European family migration law

Betty de Hart

1. Introduction

In recent years, a growing literature has addressed the colonial and racialised roots of European migration law. This contribution builds on this literature and extends its analysis to European family migration law. It answers the question of how European family migration policy was informed by race as well as gender and continues to be a white male privilege. It does so in three steps. First, the literature on race and migration law has demonstrated how the concept of sovereignty, the states' formal rule-making authority to control migration, is a racial as well as a colonial concept. This contribution will demonstrate how it is also gendered. Second, it will discuss how the European Convention on Human Rights and the European Union migration law framework that have informed family migration, even if one would assume that both of these legal frameworks are gender and race neutral – and there is ample reason not to – have gendered and racialised effects. Third, although both of these legal frameworks rely on the sovereignty of states to control migration, Member States claim that their sovereignty is under attack and try to take back control; the way they do that is built on racialised and gendered notions of couples and families.

To explore the working of race and gender in family migration law, mixed-status couples are used as a lens through which to understand the world, its laws and regulations. They are an interesting object of study, especially for a legal scholar, because their 'mixedness' confuses and destabilises (legal) categories that have become fixed and essentialised in certain times and places; for example, European and native in the colonies, Union citizen and third-country national in the EU, citizen and non-citizen at the national level. Mixed-status couples or families unite these categories into one family; borders run through these families (Bonjour & de Hart, 2021). Hence, through the lens of mixed-status couples, it becomes clear how legal categories of Union citizens, third-country nationals and others are being produced and reproduced. It is not about who and what people are, but about how they are seen by lawmakers and socially constructed in law. Furthermore, mixed-status couples have always had an ambiguous and often problematic relationship with the law. On the one hand, mixed-status couples have been seen as key to sociocultural integration into society. Legally, this perception has been expressed into certain

DOI: 10.4324/9781003503217-8

legal privileges, e.g., privileged access to citizenship status for the foreign wives of male citizens. On the other hand, mixed-status couples have been seen as a threat to society and social cohesion and consequently met with the exclusionary side of the law. They were often seen as fraudulent, engaged in only to obtain the earlier mentioned legal privileges (de Hart, 2015). Several examples of this exclusionary side of law will be discussed in the last part of this contribution. These contradictory perceptions of mixed-status families have fundamentally informed the development of family migration law over time.

2. Challenging the colour-blindness of migration law

Traditionally, legal scholars are trained to see law in a specific way, still best exemplified by the image of Lady Justice, who is blind-folded. She does not see the person in front of her, who is before the law, does not see race, colour or gender. It is what law students are taught what law is. In the law curriculum at universities in many countries, race is hardly mentioned, except for the litany that every person is treated equally and that discrimination on grounds of race, gender or any other ground is prohibited (Fischer, 2022). This common ideal of what law should be, should not blind us for the role of law in constructing racialised and gendered identities. Migration law, that is designed to keep 'others' out and some in, is the perfect field to explore this role of law.

Critical race theory, developed in the US, has long argued that the notion of colour-blind law is problematic and makes it difficult to effectively address structural and institutional racism. It turns combatting racism into an individual responsibility, regulated by anti-discrimination law based on individual complaints (Delgado & Stefancic, 2017). Critical race theory understands race not as a biological category but as a social construction. Racialisation refers to the socio-historical process in which a certain group's social position is attributed to 'racial' characteristics at certain times and places. Thus, the concept of 'race' has no objective, inherent or fixed meaning and does not correspond to a biological or genetic reality. Rather, 'race' is a category invented by society and by social actors within society at certain times and places (Lopez, 1997).

More recently, migration law scholars in Europe have started to look critically at racialisation in migration law, inspired by Third World approaches to international law (Anghie, 2006) as well as postcolonial and decolonial approaches (Achiume, 2019; El-Enany, 2020; Spijkerboer, 2018; De Vries & Spijkerboer, 2021). However, family migration law has not received the attention it deserves. This is remarkable, as family migration remains one of the predominant forms of migration into the European Union and, more importantly, the concept of sovereignty in the European context was developed to a large extent in court decisions on family reunification.

Although there is certainly no shortage of critical legal analysis of family migration policies (e.g. Costello, 2016; Lambert, 2014; Groenendijk, 2006; Staver, 2013; Van Walsum, 2008; Wray, 2016), race as an analytical category is largely absent. However, already in 1994, Bhabha and Shutter (1994) critically analysed the racialised and gendered foundations of British immigration law, and others have demonstrated that immigration control continues to be infused with assumptions about race as well as gender (Van Walsum, 2008; Wray, 2016).

3. Sovereignty as a racial concept

In the past years, the concept of sovereignty in controlling migration has become increasingly challenged. Scholars such as Achiume (2019), Anghie (2006), Chetail (2014) and Dembour (2015) have questioned the claim that the right to control migration is based on international law and have explored its colonial and racialised roots. Chetail (2014) has argued that from the end of the nineteenth century until the mid-twentieth century immigration controls were primarily introduced for racial reasons. It is generally understood that the so-called sovereignty of states to control migration was first formulated in the American context, with the 1882 Chinese Exclusion Act and subsequent case law on this legislation. In discussing this Act ten years later, prominent European legal scholars of the *Institut de Droit International* confirmed the sovereign right of states to exclude undesirable aliens based on group characteristics: *une différence fondamentale de moeurs ou de civilations* (Rygiel, 2015). The exclusion of Chinese migrants on racial grounds was not limited to the US: the 1905 British Aliens Act, White Australian Policy 1905 and White Canada Policy 1923 were introduced for racial reasons (Calavita, 2000; Lee, 2010; Volpp, 2005), and in Europe, too, Chinese migrants met with extensive forms of exclusion. Modern forms of policing were developed to surveil Chinese migrants, including routine refusal of visas, obligatory registration with the immigration police, identity cards with photographs and fingerprinting. In the Netherlands, every year, from 1930 to 1942, the number of Chinese migrants in the country was counted (de Hart, 2019). This is why Zolberg (1997) wrote of a 'great wall against China' for this period.

These Chinese exclusion laws were not only based on racialization, but also on gender, sexuality and class, and fears of 'interracialised intimacies' (Haritaworn, 2007). Before the Second World War, Asian and Chinese men were seen as sexually aggressive and dangerous to white women, in the US as well as Europe (Lee, 2010). While in the US marriages between 'whites' and 'Chinese' were prohibited (Pascoe, 2009; Volpp, 2005), other countries used other forms of regulation to prevent mixture, such as the prosecution and incarceration of white women involved with Asian men (Backhouse, 1996; Ryan, 1999). In Europe state authorities warned against marriages between white women and Chinese men (Lorke, 2019; Stovall, 1998) and deported Chinese men as a preventive measure (Parker, 2016). Such race-based exclusionary policies remained in place for decades, in the Netherlands as late as the 1980s (de Hart, 2019).

4. Sovereignty as a colonial concept

Achiume's work (2019) especially has explored how sovereignty is a colonial concept. Colonialism allowed for the mass emigration to colonised states by white people, enhancing their economic opportunities. However, this freedom to travel to the colony was, for a long time at least, restricted to white males, as independent travel by women was highly scrutinised and controlled (Guy, 1991). As Stoler (2001) and McClintock (1995) have demonstrated, the colonial order was not merely a racial hierarchy, but also a gendered one.

Independence of the colonies led to the recategorisation of colonised citizens into noncitizens and occurred along both racialised and gendered lines. The Netherlands is a case in point. With the independence of Indonesia in 1949 and Suriname in 1975, special Acts on Citizenship transformed those who were considered 'native' or 'black' into Indonesian or Surinamese, and those considered white into Dutch citizens. The children of Dutch fathers and colonised women were granted Dutch citizenship; the children of Dutch mothers and colonised men became Indonesians or Surinamese (de Hart, 2015; Heijs, 1991; Jones, 2007).

The Dutch debate concerning decolonisation not only reflected anti-colonial sentiment, but also concerns over migration control. As long as Suriname remained part of the Kingdom of the Netherlands, the Dutch government could not exclude Surinamese inhabitants without discriminating between Dutch subjects. Once Suriname became independent in 1975, its inhabitants would be foreigners, and the Dutch government could legitimately refuse their admission. While before decolonisation, colonial citizens could move freely between the colony and the metropole, accompanied by their family members, this became much more difficult afterwards. This made family migration a difficult issue for former colonial citizens, including for those who remained Dutch citizens but whose family members became Surinamese. These changes affected the family lives of Dutch citizens of Surinamese descent in profound ways (Van Walsum, 2000).

In other words, decolonisation *created* the issue of family migration for those former colonial citizens. The case law of the two European courts: *Morson Jahjan* of the CJEU and *Abdulaziz* and *Jeunesse* of the ECtHR show the lasting effects of decolonisation for family reunification.[1] Although in *Jeunesse* the ECtHR took this colonial legacy into account, its positive decision was an exception to the rule that postcolonial citizens have no right to family reunification.[2]

5. Sovereignty as a gendered concept

States are assumed to have sovereignty not only in migration but also in nationality law. For women, their belonging to the nation was never stable or self-evident. Their exclusion was part and parcel of the construction of the nation-state (Cott, 1998; Yuval-Davis, 1997). Hence, sovereignty to control migration and nationality meant, for them, exclusion from the nation. Marriage to a foreign husband made women lose citizenship, turning them into foreign nationals, while foreign women who married a citizen husband automatically became citizens. The latter was not considered a right of migrant women but resulted from the right of citizen men to a home and a family. Only a few nations abolished gender discrimination in

1 CJEU, 27 October 1982, C-35/82 and C-36/82, *Morson Jhanjan*, ECLI:EU:C:1982:368; ECtHR, 3 October 2014, Grand Chamber, *Jeunesse v Netherlands*, No. 12738/10.

2 Ibid., *Jeunesse*, § 115.

nationality law before the Second World War: Russia in 1918, France in 1927 and the US in 1932. Most European countries were much later: the UK in 1948, Germany in 1953, the Netherlands in 1964, Greece in 1984 and Switzerland in 1992. States were often even later with granting citizen women equal rights in passing on their nationality to their children.

Karen Knop's work (2001) is foundational in understanding the reasons why this gender inequality in nationality law was important to states: they intended to preserve the unity of the family by having its members share the same, and only one, nationality, as dual nationality was considered an abnormality. Thus, a family could only have one nationality, that of the husband, who was the self-evident head of the family. Linked to the unity of nationality of the family was the *right to domicile*: family members could live together within the state of nationality (the right to enter) and could continue to do so (the right not to be expelled). When gender equality was introduced, this right to domicile was lost. A choice was made for *levelling down*: rather than granting foreign men the same rights to automatic nationality upon marriage as foreign women had had for decades, this easy access to nationality was taken away from foreign women. Consequently, formal gender equality was reached, but at a lower level. This choice was made because of continuing gender stereotypes: the idea that women should follow their husbands and not the other way around. Moreover, it was about racial stereotypes. Building on colonial discourses according to which racialised men preyed on and abused white women (McClintock, 1995; Stoler, 2002), states feared that foreign men would use marriages of convenience to gain access to citizenship, consequently endangering states' ability to control migration. Such foreign men were often seen as criminals and pimps and the citizen women involved as prostitutes (Bonjour & de Hart, 2013; de Hart, 2015).

The gender inequality in nationality law was challenged before the European Commission of Human Rights in the now largely forgotten case *Family K and W v. the Netherlands*, involving the family of a Dutch woman and British man from Hong Kong, very likely of Chinese descent. The complaint was dismissed because the Commission considered that the right to acquire a particular nationality was not covered by or sufficiently related to Article 8 of the European Convention on Human Rights (ECHR) or any other provision of that Convention.[3] Since then, the Court has changed its position and has ruled on discrimination in nationality law but not on gender discrimination.[4] In the landmark CJEU case *M.G. Tjebbes v. Minister v Buitenlandse Zaken*, the gendered background of loss of nationality by Dutch female emigrants abroad was ignored.[5]

3 ECtHR, 1 July 1985, *Family K. and W. v. the Netherlands*, No. 11278184.

4 Although in the case *Genovese v. Malta* the applicant claimed to be discriminated against on grounds of being born out of wedlock and gender of the parent, the Court based its decision of discrimination only on the first ground. ECtHR, 11 October 2011, *Genovese v. Malta*, No. 53124/09.

5 CJEU (Grand Chamber), 12 March 2019, C-221/17, *M.G. Tjebbes*, ECLI:EU:C:2019:189. See on this gender background: de Hart, B., & Mantu, S. (10 July 2017). Loss of Dutch nationality *ex lege*: EU law, gender and multiple nationality. *GlobalCit Blog*. https://globalcit.eu/loss-of-dutch-nationality-ex-lege-eu-law-gender-and-multiple-nationality/.

To sum up, the introduction of gender equality in nationality law resulted in the loss of the right to domicile. Together with the racial and colonial background of the concept of state sovereignty to control migration, it created the salient and sensitive issue of family migration, that may separate mixed-status families in ways that were not possible before. The next section explores how this affected the European Court of Human Rights (ECtHR) case law.

6. Family migration and the European Convention on Human Rights

After the Second World War, Article 8 ECHR, which protects the right to respect for family life, was adopted in reaction to the Nazi prohibitions of interracial marriages. The drafters of the Convention wanted to make sure that states would never interfere with the racial composition of families again: 'racial restrictions on the right to marriage made by totalitarian regimes should be absolutely prohibited' (Opsahl, 1973). Hence, the background of Article 8 ECHR was explicitly anti-racist. In the same period, UNESCO drafted a statement on race, also as an anti-racist response to the Nazi era of scientific racism. However, it did not mention colonialism or racial segregation policies of the US and South Africa (Brattain, 2007).[6] Hence, these anti-racist stances left ample room for states' concerns on the application of the ECHR in their colonial territories. Article 56, the so-called colonial clause, allowed states to not apply the ECHR to their colonies (Dembour, 2015; Demir-Gürsel, 2021).

At the same time, although Article 14 ECHR prohibited discrimination on the grounds of sex, among other grounds, gender equality was not high on the drafters' agenda. The early drafts of the Convention did not even contain a prohibition of gender discrimination (Duranti, 2016). On the contrary, Article 8's right to respect for family life was considered a right of male citizens only, as the drafting documents demonstrate:

> The father of a family cannot be an independent citizen, cannot feel free within his own country, if he is menaced in his own home and if every day, the State steals from his soul, or the conscience of his children.[7]

Against this background, it is not a coincidence that in the ECtHR's first major migration law decision, ruling that states had the sovereign right to control migration, the applicants were women. In this *Abdulaziz* case, three migrant women, citizens and permanent residents in the UK, claimed that the refusal to grant their husbands a residence permit by the UK government constituted race and gender discrimination (Article 14 ECHR). Race discrimination, as the admittance of the husbands was refused because the women and their parents were not born in the UK, a distinction that aimed to keep out former colonial subjects (Dummet &

6 UNESCO, Paris, July 1950, Statement on Race.

7 Report for Assembly Council of Europe, 1949.

Nicol, 1990). Gender discrimination because of the stricter immigration rules for male than for female spouses.[8] Men had to prove their marriage was not one of convenience and had to meet financial requirements that did not apply to female family migrants. This gender discrimination was based on the government's assumption that male migrants constituted a greater threat to the labour market than women, as men were expected to work and women to care.

Gender discrimination was thought unacceptable in the enforcement of a state's sovereign right to control migration, and the women won their case on these grounds. However, the ECtHR rejected the complaint based on race discrimination because it ruled that there were 'persuasive social reasons' for 'special treatment to those whose link with a country stems from birth within it'.[9]

It was in this case that the ECtHR confirmed the sovereign right of states to control migration with the famous phrase:

> As a matter of well-established international law and subject to its treaty obligations, a State has the right to control the entry of non-nationals into its territory.[10]

The Court also stated that:

> The duty imposed by Article 8 cannot be considered as extending to a general obligation on the part of a Contracting State to respect the choice by married couples of the country of their matrimonial residence and to accept the non-national spouses for settlement in that country.[11]

In other words: the right to domicile that, as discussed earlier, had been central in nationality law for so long, was not accepted in migration law even if the sponsor was a permanent resident or citizen. This is crucial to the further development of family migration law. And although the case was won on grounds of gender discrimination, this turned out to be a pyrrhic victory, as the response of the British government was to level down and to make it as difficult for men as for women to reunite with their spouses (Bhabha & Shutter, 1994).

Decades later, the justification of racial discrimination in migration law was questioned again, in *Biao v. Denmark*.[12] By then, family migration had become one of the most controversial topics on the European migration agenda, resulting in restrictive reforms of family migration policy in many Member States of the Council of Europe (Ruffer, 2011). These restrictive measures often targeted racialised

8 ECtHR, 28 May 1985, *Abdulaziz, Cabales and Balkandali v. The United Kingdom*, Nos. 9214/80; 9473/81; 9474/81.

9 Ibid., *Abdulaziz*, § 88. Proportionality refers to the need for states to strike a fair balance between the competing public and individual interests.

10 Ibid., *Abdulaziz*, § 67.

11 Ibid., § 68.

12 ECtHR, 24 May 2016, Grand Chamber, *Biao v. Denmark*, No. 38590/10.

others and must be understood against the background of the idea that the integration of migrants had failed and the anti-Muslim sentiments that emerged after the 9/11 terrorist attacks of 2001. The *Biao* case concerned the very strict Danish family reunification policy that required Danish sponsors to have been a Danish citizen for 28 years or more. It was widely criticised by international organisations such as the European Commission against Racism and Intolerance (ECRI) and the UN Committee on the Elimination of Racial Discrimination (CERD), cited by the Court.[13] The question before the ECtHR was whether this distinction between Danish Danes and naturalised Danes was justified.

Initially, the ECtHR rejected the complaint of racial discrimination. Referring to *Abdulaziz*, the Court considered the distinction not a racial one but one based on duration of nationality and that it was justified because it favoured persons who could be understood as having a closer link to Denmark.[14] The Grand Chamber, however, looking not only at the history and context of the policy but also its effects, ruled that the 28-years rule constituted indirect discrimination based on ethnicity and demanded 'very weighty reasons' to justify it. The Court distanced itself from *Abdulaziz*, considering: 'it is very difficult to reconcile the grant of special treatment with current international standards and developments'.[15] Hence, states have the sovereign right to control migration, but may not make explicit distinctions in the law based on racial or ethnic grounds between citizens. Nevertheless, this prohibition of racial discrimination has not played any significant role in addressing the racialised impact of international migration control (De Vries & Spijkerboer, 2021). Consequently, the *Biao* decision has not significantly changed Danish family migration policy: the Danish government's response was to reintroduce the so-called attachment criteria which also applied to Danish citizens, later replaced by a new 'integration requirement' with similar results (Gammeltoft-Hansen & Madsen, 2021); again, an example of levelling down.

Furthermore, although direct gender and racial discrimination in national migration laws of members of the Council of Europe is prohibited, the ECtHR's case law remains informed by gendered and racialised notions of family migration. Most of the ECtHR's case law deals with male foreign partners of women who are refused admittance or residence and, consequently, women who were expected to follow their partner to his country of origin (de Hart, 2009; Swart, 1990). The ECtHR thinks of nation-states as closed units to which migrants may be admitted as an exception to the rule and does not acknowledge that citizens develop family relations with migrants residing either within or outside the nation-state. As in *Abdulaziz*, the ECtHR's starting point remains that if family life was created at a time when the persons involved were aware that the immigration status of one of

13 ECRI, Fourth report on Denmark, 23 March 2012, CRI(2012)25; UN Committee on the Elimination of Racial Discrimination, Concluding observations: Denmark, 19 October 2006, UN Doc. CERD/C/DEN/CO/17.

14 ECtHR, 24 May 2016, Grand Chamber, *Biao v. Denmark*, No. 38590/10.

15 Ibid., *Biao*, § 131.

them was precarious, only in the most exceptional circumstances will removal of the family member constitute a violation of Article 8.[16] Consequently, the Court sees relationships of citizens with non-citizens as a potential threat to state sovereignty to control migration.

7. EU Family Reunification Directive

European Union law makes a distinction between Union citizens and their family reunification rights and so-called third-country nationals (TCNs), nationals from outside the EU, who have fewer rights to family reunification. Union citizens who have not used their right to free movement are referred to as 'static', and their family reunification rights remain outside of the scope of EU law, resulting in the fragmentation of family reunification rights (Staver, 2013). The initial aim of the Family Reunification Directive (2003/86/EC) was to treat TCNs equally to Union citizens as much as possible (Groenendijk, 2006). The original draft by the European Commission was relatively liberal; however, the 9/11 terrorist attacks had a profound impact on the final version. It is well documented that this resulted in Islamophobia throughout Europe, which highly affected the negotiation process (Hammarberg, 2011). The end result was a Directive that, many feared, was below the level of Article 8 ECHR (Groenendijk, 2006).

The Directive explicitly rejects gender and racial discrimination in recital n° 5 of the preamble. Nevertheless, the conditions of the Family Reunification Directive are not race and gender neutral in its effects. The integration requirement and the income requirement[17] are a case in point. Both provisions were introduced after lobby by the Dutch government that aimed to maintain room for its restrictive family migration policies to keep out mainly Turkish and Moroccan family migrants (Bonjour, 2014).

The integration requirement allows states to demand that family migrants learn the language before admission. The Dutch Integration Abroad Act, introduced in 2006, was the first, as well as the strictest, in requiring family migrants to successfully complete a computer exam at the embassy on Dutch language and knowledge of society. Austria, Germany, Denmark and France followed (Bonjour, 2014). Not all nationalities are obliged to integrate before admission. Germany and the Netherlands exempt certain 'western' nationalities: USA, Canada, Australia, Japan, New Zealand, South Korea and – for Germany – Israel. For this reason, the Dutch Integration Abroad exam met with criticism from legal scholars as well as human rights organisations (De Vries, 2012).[18] Alas, in the CJEU case *K and A* on the legitimacy of the Dutch Integration Abroad Act, the issue of discrimination was not addressed. The advocate-general (AG) merely stated that it was within the

16 See, e.g., ECtHR, 11 April 2006, *Useimov v. the Netherlands*, No. 61292/00; ECtHR, 31 July 2009, *Omoregie and Others v. Norway*, No. 265/07.

17 Article 7 Family Reunification Directive.

18 Human Rights Watch. (2008). *The Netherlands: Discrimination in the name of integration*. www.hrw.org/en/node/82373/section/1

discretion of Member States to treat certain nationals, such as from Canada and the United States of America, more favourably.[19] The AG did not take into account the political context in which the Integration Abroad Act was introduced, namely, that of increasing problematisation of the 'failed' integration of migrants of Muslim background and of family migration, nor its effects (Bonjour & Duyvendak, 2018).

Dutch data demonstrate that the Integration Abroad exam has clear selective effects. Education, age and nationality are determinants for the chances of successfully completing the exam. South Africans, Taiwanese, Ukrainians, Russians and Mexicans have the highest pass rate, while Iraqis, Nigerians, Afghans, Tunisians and Moroccans have the lowest pass rates (Zwanepol et al., 2021). The differences are significant: South Africans (who, due to the historical links between the Netherlands and South Africa, are mainly white) have a pass rate of 96% as compared to 54% for Iraqis (Zwanepol et al., 2021, p. 22). Data on the German Integration test show a similar pattern (Scholten et al., 2012).

The available data do not provide an adequate insight in the gendered effects of the Integration Abroad exams. The Dutch reports look at gender overall, demonstrating a female pass rate that is 6% higher than that of men (Zwanepol et al., 2021, p. 18). However, linking gender to nationality in an intersectional approach (Crenshaw, 1990), Afghan women should be compared to South African men. This would reveal that pass rates of females from certain nationality groups differ from that of men from other nationalities. In Afghanistan, less than 40% of women have completed secondary education; the available data do not reveal how that effects pass rates.[20]

The income requirement shows a similar pattern, both in terms of reasons for its introduction and its gendered and racialised effects. In 2004, the Netherlands government introduced a required income level of 120% of the minimum wage until, in 2010, after a CJEU decision, it was lowered to 100% of the minimum wage.[21] The Dutch income requirement was, just like the Integration Abroad Act, justified with reference to the lack of integration of Moroccan and Turkish youth (mainly Dutch citizens) 'still' marrying partners from the country of origin of their parents. These family migrants were considered 'migrants with poor prospects' (Kulu-Glasgow & Leerkes, 2011; Bonjour & Duyvendak, 2018). The UK Minimum Income Requirement (MIR) of 18.000 BP (121% of the British National Living Wage), introduced in 2012, was linked to the protection of national sovereignty and identity. It aimed at regulating family migration of 'deserving' and 'undeserving' social groups, built on both ethnic and class stereotypes, as well as reducing net migration (Sirriyeh, 2015).[22] The British Supreme Court acknowledges that

19 Opinion of Advocate General Kokott in CJEU, 19 March 2015, C-153/14, *K and A*, ECLI:EU:C:2019:192, § 38.

20 United Nations. (2022). *Progress on the sustainable development goals: The gender snapshot 2022* (p. 4). United Nations.

21 CJEU, 4 March 2010, C-578/08, *Chakroun*, ECLI:EU:C:2010:117.

22 The UK was at the time, even before Brexit, not bound to the Family Reunification Directive due to an opt-out.

income requirements for family migration have gendered and racialised effects. Although the Supreme Court held that the MIR did not violate Article 8 ECHR, it described it as a 'serious obstacle' to enjoying family life and a permanent impediment to many couples, affecting especially female sponsors and sponsors of certain ethnic groups.[23]

Studies on the income requirement in both countries confirm this. A study on the Dutch 2004 income requirement demonstrated its gendered effects: applications for family reunification dropped 37% overall; applications of male sponsors dropped 32%, those of female sponsors 48%. The group affected the most were Dutch female sponsors of Turkish background, who demonstrated a 57% drop in applications, compared to 22% for Dutch white males (WODC/INDIAC, 2009). A study of the British MIR demonstrated that the families impacted most constituted a young, well-educated group whose earnings were nonetheless relatively low, often because of childcare responsibilities and thus mainly affecting women (Grant et al., 2015).[24] Hence, it is inevitable that female sponsors have more difficulty than men to reunite with their family members, as the gender pay gap of 13% across the EU remains significant.[25] What these figures, because of a lack of intersectional data, do not reveal, is that female migrant sponsors, as migrants and as women, are the ones most affected by restrictive family migration policies, be it integration or income requirements (see also Staver, 2015; Pellander, 2021).

8. EU Member States taking back control of migration

In spite of the restrictive tendencies discussed so far, Member States increasingly complain that they have lost control in family migration, blaming either the CJEU, the ECtHR, or both (Farahat, 2022; Farahat & Leijten, 2022; Gammeltoft-Hansen & Madsen, 2021). States reclaim their sovereignty to control migration and take back control in ways that are again highly racialised and gendered. Mixed-status families composed of Union citizens and TCNs are constructed as 'monstrous families' (Guild, 2016), as contamination of the pure. Such discourses draw back on colonial discourses that served to maintain the racial and gendered order (Stoler, 2001) and aim to keep racialised groups out of the privileged family migration rights of Union citizens. The discourse on 'monstrous families' can be found in various EU Member States. Overall, states claim, mostly without any empirical substantiation, that fraud and abuse of rights frequently occur. Member States question intentions and emotions of migrant and mixed-status families. They reclaim their sovereign right to control family migration in three specific ways.

First, the Europe route. Union citizens who remain in their country of citizenship, so-called static citizens, are not covered by EU law, as they did not use their

23 Supreme Court, *MM (Lebanon) and others v. Secretary of State for the Home Department*, 22 February 2017. Hilary Term [2017] UKSC 10.

24 For Belgium, see Quené (2022).

25 Eurostat Equal Pay Fact Sheet 2022.

right to free movement. This means that a German woman in the Netherlands with a Moroccan partner is better off than a Dutch woman in the Netherlands with a Moroccan partner because the German woman profits from the more liberal family reunification rights of the Citizens Directive (Staver, 2013). For instance, no integration requirements apply for family members of Union citizens, and there is no strict income requirement as long as Union citizens have sufficient resources for themselves and their family members not to become a burden on the social assistance system of the host Member State (Article 7(1)(b) Citizens Directive). It is important to bring to mind that the European Commission in its first, 1999 proposal for the Family Reunification Directive had suggested to treat static citizens equally to Union citizens in terms of family reunification rights, in order to prevent 'reverse discrimination'. Some countries, such as Belgium, Austria and Spain, have treated static citizens and Union citizens equally for a considerable number of years, while Portugal still upholds this policy (Groenendijk, 2014). However, most Member States treat Union citizens more favourably than static citizens.

Consequently, some citizens and their TCN family members move to another EU country for some time in order to achieve that, after returning to the home state, the more liberal EU free movement rights still apply to them.[26] We should not exaggerate the extent to which this Europe route is being used: it is only those happy few with sufficient financial and social capital who can use it (Wray et al., 2021, see also Corradi & Desmet, this volume). Member States reproach the Europe route as 'abuse of rights', although the CJEU in *Metock* pointed out that it is perfectly legal.[27] Member States criticised this CJEU ruling, claiming that it undermined their right to control migration (Lansbergen, 2009).

Dutch authorities subjected couples that used the Europe route to intense scrutiny of their relationships and claimed, even if totally unfounded, that predominantly citizens of migration background made use of this route (Fernhout & Groenendijk, 2010). Prime Minister Cameron expressed the British concerns about EU citizens and their family reunion rights in a letter to the president of the EU Council in November 2015:

> We need to crack down on the abuse of free movement, an issue on which I have found wide support in my discussions with colleagues. This includes tougher and longer re-entry bans for fraudsters and people who collude in sham marriages. It means addressing the fact that it is easier for an EU citizen to bring a non-EU spouse to Britain than it is for a British citizen to do the same.
>
> (cited in Guild, 2016)

In response, the European Commission promised to restrict the family reunification rights of Union citizens with TCN family members. This only did not happen

26 CJEU, 7 July 1992, C-370/90, *Surinder Singh*, ECLI:EU:C:1992:296.

27 CJEU, 13 September 2008, C-127/08, *Metock*, ECLI:EU:C:2008:449.

because the UK left the EU (Guild, 2016). We may have been on the verge of another levelling down.

The second way to problematise family migration in gendered and racialised ways is through discourses on so-called anchor babies: the notion that TCN parents use children to claim residence rights (Bledsoe, 2004; Luibhéid, 2013). This discourse, too, goes back to colonial times when colonial authorities commonly assumed that racialised others instrumentalised children to obtain European white privileges (Stoler, 2002). It rests specifically on perceptions of migrant mothers using their sexuality to claim access to the nation and on heteronormativity about the right way to have children, namely, in marriage (Chock, 1996). The ECtHR uses the phrase 'trump card' to emphasise that the best interests of the child should not be regarded as generating a right of residence in all cases involving children.[28] A similar argument has been made in the context of the *Zambrano* or *Chavez-Vilchez* cases in which the CJEU acknowledged Union citizen children's right to reside in the territory of the Union with TCN parents, based on Article 20 TFEU.[29] Both Belgian and Dutch state authorities claimed that the number of false paternity claims had risen steeply after these CJEU decisions, again without any proof. Nevertheless, in 2018, the Belgian legislator introduced a new law to combat fraudulent paternity claims, while in the Netherlands, civil registrars started scrutinising paternity claims involving TCN parents.[30] In fact, statistics produced by the Dutch Immigration Service (IND) on the implementation of *Chavez-Vilchez* demonstrate that in 79% of the cases, the child lived with both parents.[31]

Third, marriages of convenience. The CJEU has indicated that the Citizens Directive did not prevent Member States from combating abuse of Community rights, including marriages of convenience. The Court did so in response to the Irish minister of justice's claim that the pressures of international migration necessitated a control of migration at the external EU borders.[32] Hence, controlling marriages of convenience was explicitly linked to the sovereignty to control migration (de Hart, 2017; Lansbergen, 2009). Marriages of convenience have been a long-term concern of Member States, and this concern was consequently translated into the Family Reunification Directive (Article 16) and the Citizens Directive (Article 35). The European Commission guidelines to the Citizens Directive discuss marriages of convenience extensively, supplemented by a *Handbook on Marriages of*

28 ECtHR, 8 February 2017, *El Ghatet v Switzerland*, No. 56971/10; see also ECtHR, 4 December 2012, *Butt v. Norway*, No. 47017/09, § 79; and the dissenting opinion to *Jeunesse*: 'There would also be a great risk that parents exploited the situation of their children in order to secure a residence permit for themselves' (§ 9 dissenting opinion).

29 CJEU, 8 March 2011, Case C-34/09, *Ruiz Zambrano* ECLI:EU:C:2011:124; CJEU, 10 May 2017, C 133-15, *Chavez-Vilchez*, ECLI:EU:C:2017:354.

30 NOS Nieuws, 31 August 2019, Ambtenaren gewaarschuwd op te letten voor schijnerkenning kinderen; Volkskrant, 31 August 2019, Ambtenaren speuren naar 'schijnouders' die baby's erkennen voor verblijfspapieren.

31 Period 10 May 2019–10 May 2020, Analyse *Chavez-Vilchez*, IND, October 2021, p. 32.

32 CJEU, 25 July 2008, C-127/08, *Metock*, ECLI:EU:C:2008:449.

Convenience.[33] Again, there was no empirical evidence that marriages of convenience were actually a substantial phenomenon, and Member States could not provide any statistics (EMN, 2012).[34]

There is by now a rich, mainly non-legal, literature that critically analyses the heteronormative family and gender norms used in surveilling marriages of convenience (e.g., Abrams, 2007; de Hart, 2017; Wray, 2015), although the role of race in this surveillance remains understudied (see, however, Lavanchy, 2014). However, it is largely, although not exclusively, interracialised mixed-status couples who are seen as 'unlikely' couples because of their racial, cultural and religious differences. Gender is relevant, too, as it is mainly the marriages involving white women with racialised others, rather than white men, that are considered fraudulent, often building on the gendered notion that she naively fell for it (de Hart, 2017). These discourses are more than just discourses; they have real-life, material effects for couples and families desiring to reunite: even if their applications are not rejected based on suspicions of the Europe route, anchor babies or marriage of convenience, they are confronted with increased scrutiny of their applications, resulting in longer procedures, court cases and separation of families, with prolonged uncertainty and higher emotional and financial costs as a result.

9. Concluding remarks

To sum up, race, colonialism and gender have been crucial to the concept of sovereignty and the development of family migration law. Race, decolonisation and gender worked together to create family migration as a policy issue and are at the heart of the rejection of the notion of the right to domicile in family migration law. While family migration law has become formally colour-blind and gender neutral, it also has become increasingly restrictive, not in spite of, but because it became colour-blind and gender neutral and its accompanying scaling-down effects. Race and gender continue to pop up everywhere: in the discourses on family migration policy and its effects and in the ways in which multi-level sovereignty games are being played within the EU. It moves around and is never not there; it is ingrained and institutionalised in the family migration system that we know today. Both in the effects of present-day family migration policy and the ways in which states try to take back control, white males are least affected. As in the past, white male privilege to choose a home and a family remains largely intact.

This is only part of the story, as this chapter has focussed on admittance of family members, the front door. However, more restrictive policies have also meant

33 Communication from the Commission to the European Parliament and the Council on guidance for better transposition and application of Directive 2004/38/EC on the right of citizens of the Union and their family members to move and reside freely within the territory of Member States, 2 July 2009, COM(2009) 313 final, § 4.2, pp. 15–17.

34 European Commission, Green paper on the right to family reunification of third-country nationals living in the European Union (Directive 2003/86/EC), 15 November 2011, COM(2011) 735 final, p. 7.

that increasingly, people are pushed out by the backdoor, through deportation policies (Griffiths, 2021) or are excluded from social welfare rights (De Jong & de Hart, 2021).

Legal scholars should address these issues more heads on. The reader may have noticed that this chapter heavily relied on other than legal disciplines, where issues of race and gender are more explicitly addressed. It is time that legal scholars and practising lawyers no longer beat around the bush but explicitly address gendered and racialised stereotypes underlying family migration law and its effects. To do so, we need an intersectional analysis linking race and gender as well as class. This requires not only legal analysis, but also adequate (quantitative) data to aid such an analysis. However, to a large extent, the material is already there, as the racialised and gendered notions can be found in official government publications, parliamentary debates as well as national and European case law.

If race, colonial legacies and gender are not explicitly addressed, legal scholars end up legitimising such discourses and their legal implications, even in their critical evaluations of family migration law. This is all the more urgent, as states' efforts to gain back control of migration demonstrate that established rights remain heavily contested and are never certain.

References

Abrams, K. (2007). Immigration law and the regulation of marriage. *Minnesota Law Review, 91*, 1625–1709.

Achiume, E. T. (2019). Migration as decolonization. *Stanford Law Review, 71*, 1509–1574.

Anghie, A. (2006). The evolution of international law: Colonial and postcolonial realities. *Third World Quarterly, 27*(5), 739–753.

Backhouse, C. (1996). The white women's labor laws: Anti-Chinese racism in early twentieth century Canada. *Law and History Review, 14*(2), 315–368. https://doi.org/10.2307/743786

Bhabha, J., & Shutter, S. (1994). *Women's Movement: Women Under Nationality, Immigration and Refugee Law*. Trentham Books.

Bledsoe, C. H. (2004). Reproduction at the margins: Migration and legitimacy in the New Europe. *Demographic Research, 3*, 87–116. https://doi.org/10.4054/DemRes.2004.S3.4

Bonjour, S. (2014). The transfer of pre-departure integration requirements for family migrants among member states of the European Union. *Comparative Migration Studies, 2*(2), 203–226. https://doi.org/10.5117/CMS2014.2.BONJ

Bonjour, S., & de Hart, B. (2013). A proper wife, a proper marriage: Constructions of "us" and "them" in Dutch family migration policy. *European Journal of Women's Studies, 20*(1), 61–76. https://doi.org/10.1177/1350506812456459

Bonjour, S., & de Hart, B. (2021). Intimate citizenship: Introduction to the special issue on citizenship, membership and belonging in mixed-status families. *Identities, 28*(1), 1–17. https://doi.org/10.1080/1070289X.2020.1737404

Bonjour, S., & Duyvendak, J. W. (2018). The "migrant with poor prospects": Racialized intersections of class and culture in Dutch civic integration debates. *Ethnic and Racial Studies, 41*(5), 882–900. https://doi.org/10.1080/01419870.2017.1339897

Brattain, M. (2007). Race, racism, and antiracism: UNESCO and the politics of presenting science to the postwar public. *American Historical Review, 112*(5), 1386–1413. https://doi.org/10.1086/ahr.112.5.1386

Calavita, K. (2000). The paradoxes of race, class, identity, and "passing": Enforcing the Chinese exclusion acts, 1882–1910. *Law & Social Inquiry, 25*(1), 1–40. https://doi.org/10.1111/j.1747-4469.2000.tb00149.x

Chetail, V. (2014). *International Migration Law*. Oxford University Press. https://doi.org/10.1093/law/9780199668267.001.0001

Chock, P. P. (1996). No new women. Gender, "alien" and "citizen" in the congressional debate on immigration. *PoLAR*, *19*(1), 1–9.

Costello, C. (2016). *The Human Rights of Migrants and Refugees in European Law*. Oxford University Press. https://doi.org/10.1093/acprof:oso/9780199644742.001.0001

Cott, N. F. (1998). Marriage and women's citizenship in the United States, 1830–1934. *The American Historical Review*, *103*(5), 1440–1474. https://doi.org/10.1086/ahr/103.5.1440

Crenshaw, K. W. (1990). A Black Feminist Critique of Anti-Discrimination Law and Politics. In D. Kairys (Ed.), *The Politics of Law: A Progressive Critique* (pp. 195–218). Pantheon.

de Hart, B. (2009). Love thy neighbour: Family reunification and the rights of insiders. *European Journal Migration and Law*, *11*(3), 248–249. https://doi.org/10.1163/138836409X12469435402774

de Hart, B. (2015). Regulating mixed marriages through acquisition and loss of citizenship. *The Annals of the American Academy of Political and Social Science*, *662*(1), 170–187. https://doi.org/10.1177/0002716215595390

de Hart, B. (2017). The Europeanization of love. The marriage of convenience in European migration law. *European Journal of Migration and Law*, *19*(3), 281–306.

de Hart, B. (2019). Regulating Dutch–Chinese marriages and relationships in the Netherlands (1920–1945). *The History of the Family*, *24*(3), 539–559. https://doi.org/10.1080/1081602X.2019.1633678

De Jong, J., & de Hart, B. (2021). Divided Families and Devalued Citizens: Money Matters in Mixed-Status Families in the Netherlands. In T. De Lange, W. Maas, & A. Schrauwen (Eds.), *Money Matters in Migration: Policy, Participation, and Citizenship* (pp. 297–316). Cambridge University Press. https://doi.org/10.1017/9781009042505.017

Delgado, R., & Stefancic, J. (2017). *Critical Race Theory: An Introduction*. New York University Press. https://doi.org/10.18574/nyu/9781479851393.001.0001

Dembour, M. (2015). *When Humans Become Migrants: Study of the European Court of Human Rights with an Inter-American Counterpoint*. Oxford University Press.

Demir-Gürsel, E. (2021). For the Sake of Unity: The Drafting History of the European Convention on Human Rights and Its Current Relevance. In H. Aust & E. Demir-Gürsel (Eds.), *The European Court of Human Rights*. Edward Elgar Publishing. https://doi.org/10.4337/9781839108341.00014.

De Vries, K. (2012). The Dutch Act on Integration Abroad: A Case of Racial or Ethnic Discrimination? In S. Morano-Foadi & M. Malena (Eds.), *Integration for Third-Country Nationals in the European Union* (pp. 324–345). Edward Elgar Publishing. https://doi.org/10.1163/15718166-12342110

De Vries, K., & Spijkerboer, T. (2021). Race and the regulation of international migration: The ongoing impact of colonialism in the case law of the European Court of Human Rights. *Netherlands Quarterly of Human Rights*, *39*(4), 291–307. https://doi.org/10.1177/09240519211053932

Dummett, A., & Nicol, A. G. (1990). *Subjects, Citizens, Aliens and Others: Nationality and Immigration Law*. Weidenfeld and Nicolson.

Duranti, M. (2016). *The Conservative Human Rights Revolution: European Identity, Transnational Politics, and the Origins of the European Convention*. Oxford University Press. https://doi.org/10.1093/acprof:oso/9780199811380.001.0001

El-Enany, N. (2020). *(B)ordering Britain: Law, Race and Empire*. Manchester University Press. https://doi.org/10.1093/ijrl/eeab022

European Migration Network. (2012). *Misuse of the Right to Family Reunification: Marriages of Convenience and False Declarations of Parenthood*. Publications Office of the European Union.

Farahat, A. (2022). Human rights and the political: Assessing the allegation of human rights overreach in migration matters. *Netherlands Quarterly of Human Rights*, *40*(2), 180–201. https://doi.org/10.1177/09240519221092631

Farahat, A., & Leijten, I. (2022). Human rights overreach? *Netherlands Quarterly of Human Rights*, *40*(2), 83–97. https://doi.org/10.1177/09240519221099814
Fernhout, R., & Groenendijk, C. A. (2010). Vrij verkeer, Europa route en omgekeerde discriminatie: Wie houdt wie voor de gek? *Asiel en Migrantenrecht*, *1*, 4-16.
Fischer, A. (2022). Colonialism, context and critical thinking: First steps toward decolonizing the Dutch legal curriculum. *Utrecht Law Review*, *18*(1). https://doi.org/10.36633/ulr.764
Gammeltoft-Hansen, T., & Madsen, M. R. (2021). Regime entanglement in the emergence of interstitial legal fields: Denmark and the uneasy marriage of human rights and migration law. *Nordiques*, *40*. https://doi.org/10.4000/nordiques.1518
Grant, S., Kofman, E., Peel, C., & Wray, H. (2015). *Family Friendly? The Impact on Children of the Family Migration Rules: A Review of the Financial Requirements*. Children's Commissioner for England.
Griffiths, M. (2021). "My passport is just my way out of here": Mixed-immigration status families, immigration enforcement and the citizenship implications. *Identities*, *28*(1), 18–36. https://doi.org/10.1080/1070289X.2019.1625568
Groenendijk, K. (2006). Family reunification as a right under community law. *European Journal of Migration and Law*, *8*(2), 215–230. https://doi.org/10.1163/157181606777975003
Groenendijk, K. (2014). Reverse Discrimination, Family Reunification and Union Citizens of Immigrant Origin. In E. Guild (Ed.), *The Reconceptualization of European Union Citizenship* (pp. 167–188). Brill Nijhoff. https://doi.org/10.1163/9789004251526_010
Guild, E. (2016). *BREXIT and its consequences for UK and EU citizenship or monstrous citizenship*. Brill Nijhoff. https://doi.org/10.1163/9789004340893_001
Guy, D. J. (1991). *Sex and Danger in Buenos Aires: Prostitution, Family, and Nation in Argentina*. University of Nebraska Press.
Hammarberg, T. (2011). *Human Rights in Europe: No Grounds for Complacency*. Council of Europe.
Haritaworn, J. (2007). Beautiful beasts: Ambivalence and distinction in the gender identity negotiations of multiracialized women of Thai descent. *Women's Studies International Forum*, *30*, 391–403. https://doi.org/10.1016/j.wsif.2007.07.003
Heijs, E. (1991). Nederlanderschap in de Nederlandse koloniën: Regulering van immigratie vanuit de koloniën door nationaliteitsbeleid in Nederland. *Recht der Werkelijkheid*, *12*(2), 21–42.
Jones, G. (2007). *Tussen onderdanen, rijksgenoten en Nederlanders. Nederlandse politici over burgers uit Oost en West en Nederland 1945–2005*. Rozenburg Publishers.
Knop, K. (2001). Relational Nationality: On gender and Nationality in International Law. In T. A. Aleinikoff & D. Klusmeyer (Eds.), *Citizenship Today: Global Perspectives and Practices* (pp. 89–124). Carnegie Endowment for International Peace.
Kulu-Glasgow, I., & Leerkes, A. (2011). Playing hard(er) to get: The state, international couples, and the income requirement. *European Journal of Migration and Law*, *13*(1), 95–121. https://doi.org/10.1163/157181611X554267
Lambert, H. (2014). Family Unity in Migration Law: The Evolution of a More Unified Approach in Europe. In V. Chetail & C. Bauloz (Eds.), *Research Handbook on International Law and Migration*. Edward Elgar Publishing.
Lansbergen, A. (2009). Metock, implementation of the citizens' rights directive and lessons for EU citizenship. *Journal of Social Welfare and Family Law*, *31*(3), 285–297. https://doi.org/10.1080/09649060903354605
Lavanchy, A. (2014). *The circulation of people. How does "race" matter in Switzerland?* (Working Paper No. 7). Université de Neuchatel.
Lee, C. (2010). "Where the danger lies": Race, gender and Chinese and Japanese exclusion in the United States 1870–1924. *Sociological Forum*, *25*(2), 248–271. https://doi.org/10.1111/j.1573-7861.2010.01175.x
Lopez, I. H. (1997). *White by Law: The Legal Construction of Race*. New York University Press.

Lorke, C. (2019). Undesired intimacy: German–Chinese couples in Germany (1900s–1940s). *The History of the Family*, *24*(3), 560–584. https://doi.org/10.1080/1081602X.2019.1630292
Luibhéid, E. (2013). *Pregnant on Arrival: Making the Illegal Immigrant*. University of Minnesota Press.
McClintock, A. (1995). *Imperial Leather: Race, Gender, and Sexuality in the Colonial Contest*. Routledge.
Opsahl, T. (1973). The Convention and the Right to Respect for Family Life, Particularly as Regards the Unity of the Family and the Protection of the Rights of Parents and Guardians in the Education of Children. In A. H. Robertson (Ed.), *Privacy and human Rights: Reports and Communications Presented at the Third International Colloquy About the European Convention on Human Rights* (pp. 255–275). Manchester University Press.
Parker, D. (2016). Chinese People in Britain: Histories, Futures and Identities. In G. Benton & F. N. Pieke (Eds.), *The Chinese in Europe* (pp. 67–95). MacMillan Press.
Pascoe, P. (2009). *What Comes Naturally: Miscegenation Law and the Making of Race in America*. Oxford University Press.
Pellander, S. (2021). Buy me love: Entanglements of citizenship, income and emotions in regulating marriage migration. *Journal of Ethnic and Migration Studies*, *47*(2), 464–479. https://doi.org/10.1080/1369183X.2019.1625141
Quené, M. (2022). Bestaansmiddelenvereisten in het Europees migratierecht: (Sociale) uitsluiting als onbedoeld effect? In J. Coene (Ed.), *Armoede en Sociale Uitsluiting: Jaarboek* (pp. 199–212). University Press Antwerp.
Ruffer, G. B. (2011). Pushed beyond recognition? The liberality of family reunification policies in the EU. *Journal of Ethnic and Migration Studies*, *37*(6), 935–951.
Ryan, J. (1999). 'She lives with a chinaman': Orient-ing 'white' women in the courts of law. *Journal of Australian Studies*, *23*(60), 149–159.
Rygiel, P. (2015). Does international law matter? The Institut de Droit international and the regulation of migrations before the first world war. *Journal of Migration History*, *1*(1), 7–31. https://doi.org/10.1163/23519924-00101002
Scholten, P., Entzinger, H., Kofman, E., Hollomey, C., Lechner, C., Vacchelli, E., & Kraler, A. (2012). *Integration from abroad? Perception and impacts of pre-entry tests for third country nationals* (WP4 PROSINCT Comparative Reports). ICMPD.
Sirriyeh, A. (2015). "All you need is love and £18,600": Class and the new UK family migration rules. *Critical Social Policy*, *35*(2), 228–247. https://doi.org/10.1177/0261018314563039
Spijkerboer, T. (2018). The global mobility infrastructure: Reconceptualising the externalisation of migration control. *European Journal of Migration and Law*, *20*(4), 452–469. https://doi.org/10.1163/15718166-12340038
Staver, A. (2013). Free movement and the fragmentation of family reunification rights. *European Journal of Migration and Law*, *15*(1), 69–89. https://doi.org/10.1163/15718166-12342024
Staver, A. (2015). Hard work for love: The economic drift in Norwegian family immigration and integration policies. *Journal of Family Issues*, *36*(11), 1453–1471. https://doi.org/10.1177/0192513X14557491
Stoler, A. L. (2001). Tense and tender ties: The politics of comparison in North American history and (post) colonial studies. *The Journal of American History*, *27*(3–4), 829–865. https://doi.org/10.2307/2700385
Stoler, A. L. (2002). *Carnal Knowledge and Imperial Power*. University of California Press.
Stovall, T. (1998). The color line behind the lines: Racial violence in France during the great war. *The American Historical Review*, *103*(3), 737–769. https://doi.org/10.1086/ahr/103.3.737
Swart, A. H. J. (1990). Artikel 8 van het Europees Verdrag tot bescherming van de rechten van de mens. *Handelingen Nederlandse Juristen Vereniging*, *120*(1), Tjeenk Willink.
Van Walsum, S. K. (2000). *De schaduw van de grens: Het Nederlandse vreemdelingenrecht en de sociale zekerheid van Javaanse Surinamers*. Kluwer.

Van Walsum, S. K. (2008). *The Family and the Nation: Dutch Family Migration Policies in the Context of Changing Family Norms*. Cambridge Scholars Publishing.
Volpp, L. (2005). Divesting citizenship: On Asian American history and the loss of citizenship through marriage. *University of California Law Review*, *53*, 405–483.
WODC/INDIAC. (2009). Internationale gezinsvorming begrensd? Een evaluatie van de verhoging van de inkomens- en leeftijdseis bij migratie van buitenlandse partners naar Nederland. Den Haag.
Wray, H. (2015). The "Pure" Relationship, Sham Marriages and Immigration Control. In J. Miles, R. Probert, & P. Mody (Eds.), *Marriage Rites and Rights* (pp. 141–165). Hart Publishing. https://doi.org/10.5040/9781782259664.CH-007
Wray, H. (2016). *Regulating Marriage Migration into the UK: A Stranger in the Home*. Routledge. https://doi.org/10.4324/9781315604510
Wray, H., Kofman, E., & Simic, A. (2021). Subversive citizens: Using EU free movement law to bypass the UK's rules on marriage migration. *Journal of Ethnic and Migration Studies*, *47*(2), 447–463. https://doi.org/10.1080/1369183X.2019.1625140
Yuval-Davis, N. (1997). *Gender and Nation*. Sage Publications. https://doi.org/10.1080/01419870.1993.9993800
Zolberg, A. (1997). The Great Wall Against China: Responses to the First Immigration Crisis, 1885–1925. In J. Lucassen & L. Lucassen (Eds.), *Migration, Migration History, History: Old Paradigms and New Perspectives* (pp. 291–315). Peter Lang.
Zwanepol, M., Onstenk, A., & Tazelaar, P. (2021). *Monitor basisexamen inburgering buitenland 2020*. Significant Public. https://www.tweedekamer.nl/downloads/document?id=67067909-1910-4a4f-a1eb-205eb3aa15a8&title=Monitor%20inburgeringsexamen%20buitenland%202020.pdf

7 Better off without parents?

Refugee children and family reunification: norms and ethical concerns

Irene Olivero

1. Introduction

Imagine being a child living in a country where you fear daily persecution because of your race, religion, nationality, membership in a particular social group, or political opinion. Now, suppose you discover the opportunity to escape your country and seek refuge in a different nation. In such circumstances, what should you, as a refugee minor, expect from the host country? Refugee minors, as such, have specific needs, including essential provisions like accommodation, healthcare, and psychological support. Furthermore, as minors, i.e., individuals in the process of growth and development, children have fundamental needs, such as nourishment, adequate clothing, education, protection from harm, affection, stability, emotional support, consistency, and structure.[1] It is therefore ethically desirable to draft and enforce specific laws and principles to ensure these needs are met. Moreover, these specific regulations should guarantee *all* refugee children, without distinction, equal access to the fulfilment of these needs. Divergent treatment is warranted only where significant and justified differences apply.

Now, consider the scenario where you, as a refugee minor, desire to have a family member apply for family reunification. What should you anticipate in this situation? It is reasonable to expect the right to be reunited with a family member to be based on the concept of family itself, intended as a social unit composed of individuals who share emotional bonds, mutual support, and shared responsibilities. It

Acknowledgements: I am very grateful to Annette Düfner for fruitful discussions on this topic, precious comments on earlier versions, and encouragement in pursuing this research. The same gratitude extends to Felipe G.A. Moreira. I would also like to especially thank my mother, avv. Azzurra Beddini, for crucial discussions and help to navigate the Italian legislation on the matter. A further mention goes to Sabrina Gallo for her insights as a social worker. Lastly, I am very much in debt to the editors, and to the referees for their valuable comments, which helped me a lot in improving earlier drafts.

1 While some of these needs are not exclusive to minors or refugee minors, they are universally recognised as essential for all minors. This is because minors have limited capacities to fulfil these needs independently.

DOI: 10.4324/9781003503217-9

seems fair to expect the host nation not to privilege a biological concept of family over a social or legal one.

This chapter aims to correlate some of the existing laws that pertain to safeguarding the rights of refugee children with the regulations governing their right to family reunification. The purpose is to use the analysis of these regulations to draw some ethical considerations on the concepts of family and parenthood that lie behind them and how these impact refugee children. This chapter, ultimately, emphasises the significance of relinquishing biased perspectives and unsubstantiated assumptions. It does not aim to provide technical legal analyses or specific legal solutions to the highlighted issues. Laws and regulations in place, examples, and empirical data serve to draw philosophical remarks.

I begin by introducing a few debates surrounding the underlying assumptions behind the laws at stake (Section 2). Drawing on the insights of Annette Düfner and Lars Hillmann (2019), I highlight some involuntary, indirect inequalities between the rights granted to accompanied vs unaccompanied refugee minors resulting from the current regulations on this matter (Section 3).[2] I then review the literature on the use of DNA testing in family reunification cases (Section 4). Combining these findings, I point out that the indirect, unequal treatment reserved for accompanied vs unaccompanied refugee minors and for children biologically vs children socially or legally related to their parents is neither ethically justified nor ethically desirable. I discuss how these regulations raise additional critical ethical concerns when both contexts are considered together, as they incidentally create lose-lose situations for refugee minors without a biological family connection. The laws in place seem even to lead to the (provocative) ethically challenging, indirect consequence that refugee minors may be better off without parents (Section 5). To address these issues, I advocate for a revision of the relevant laws, beginning with a critical examination of the underlying assumptions. Specifically, I argue that challenging and reevaluating the existing concept of family that grounds the right to family reunification will contribute to safeguarding the best interests of refugee minors and guaranteeing them equal access to opportunities (Section 6).

2. Minors, basic needs, and the concept of family

Is it *better* for a child to have parents? Children have specific basic needs of shelter, food, clothing, medical care, and protection from harm. Children also need love, education, stability, emotional support, consistency, and structure (e.g., rules, boundaries, and limits).[3] Parents typically provide these needs – a reason to claim

2 The laws discussed in this chapter are linked to the European Union legal system in general and some specific European countries. In particular, I will take Germany, Italy, and Finland as examples. This is because relevant analyses concerning the issues at stake have been conducted with data from these countries.

3 The ones mentioned are *basic* needs, and this list does not aim to be exhaustive. Naturally, for some children, this list may be more extensive were they to require special care and attention due to infelicitous circumstances. I will henceforth consider the basic needs that are common to children, other things being equal.

that children are better off *with* parents. This is so, naturally, in all standard models of care where parents meet the mentioned needs of their children, not in situations in which parents abuse, neglect, or mistreat their children.[4] Consequently, one may ask: is it *sufficient* for children to have parents in order to meet all their needs? The answer here seems much less straightforward and may require a case-by-case evaluation.

Given these considerations, it seems crucial to identify what grounds parenthood, i.e., what confers parental rights and/or responsibilities towards a particular child and establishes the obligations involved in fulfilling the child's needs. The so-called *geneticist account* grounds parenthood on genetic and biological connection, claiming that being related by blood is sufficient to yield parental rights and obligations (Rosenman, 1995; Shanley, 1995). *Labour-based accounts* hold that what makes someone a parent is the work they perform as a parent. According to this kind of account, people who play (or have played at a certain point) a parental role in a child's life have thereby become the parents (Archard, 2004; Millum, 2010). *Intentional* and *voluntarist accounts* claim that parenting comes with one's will and intention of being a parent. Intending to be a parent and pursuing that intention is sufficient to imply parental rights and obligations for the subject of the intention (Hill, 1991; Fuscaldo, 2006). *Causal accounts* maintain that anyone causing the existence of someone can be regarded as having parental rights and obligations towards the one whose existence they caused (Nelson, 1991; Bigelow et al., 1988; Blustein, 1997; Archard, 2010). There are also pluralist accounts on the matter, which hold that more than one of these relations can ground parental rights and responsibilities.

No agreement has been reached with respect to this matter. However, regardless of what it takes to be a parent, one may ask: is it better to have biological or social parents? *Biological parents* are those who have a genetic or biological relationship with a child. They are the individuals who have contributed their genetic material to the conception of the child, either through natural reproduction or assisted reproductive technologies. I counterpose them to *social parents*, who are individuals who have assumed the role of a parent in a child's life, regardless of any biological or genetic connection. They may be legal guardians, adoptive parents, foster parents, stepparents, or individuals who have formed a significant parental role through emotional and nurturing relationships with the child. *Social parents* is thus a broad category that covers, but is not limited to, *adoptive parents*, who are individuals or couples who legally assume the role of a parent to a child through the process of adoption.

The most popular view, especially among lay people, is that children are better off with their biological parents. People commonly appeal to the value of having biological children or parents through the genetic connection shared among the

4 For the sake of this discussion, I will not consider cases in which parents abuse, neglect, or mistreat their children, even though some may hold that children are better off with parents, even in these infelicitous cases, as long as these parents provide shelter, food, and clothing, at least to a certain extent.

relevant members of the formed family.[5] It seems that the reason for this view is that children biologically related to their parents have a similar basis of genetic identity, and many think that genes and DNA make us *who we are*. In this view, genetic similarity is intrinsically valuable, and parents and children should resemble one another in some physical aspects, for genetic resemblance brings about a greater inclination for love and attachment to family members.[6]

Some authors have defended this idea that children are better off with their biological parents, while others have questioned it. David Velleman, for instance, claims: 'other things being equal, children should be raised by their biological parents' (Velleman, 2005, p. 362, fn. 3) because the connection with one's biological parents is highly significant in forming one's identity – knowing one's biological parents is so irreplaceable in one's identity formation that it is even immoral to create children with the intention of depriving them of such connection (Velleman, 2005, 2015). In contrast, Hugh LaFollette (1980) argues that adopted children have more chances of having their needs fulfilled and respected. This comparative advantage is attributed to the rigorous evaluation that *prospective adoptive parents*, i.e., individuals or couples aiming to adopt, must undergo, as well as to the demanding criteria they must meet in order to be deemed fit for adoption. By undergoing such scrutiny, prospective parents demonstrate not only a strong will but also their capability to assume the role, along with its associated privileges and duties. LaFollette points out that, statistically speaking, adopted children are five times less likely to be abused than biological children (LaFollette, 1980, p. 194). Such an *ex-ante* screening does not standardly apply to generic social parenting. Nevertheless, as Susan Golombok and Clare Murray (1999) argue, families that lack a genetic link show more positive outcomes than families biologically connected. They ascribe this favourable outcome to the fact that individuals or couples who choose to raise a child who is not genetically related to them are often deeply committed to the responsibilities of parenthood, which leads to enhanced well-being for the children in their care. The parents' strong desire to have children often outweighs any potential drawbacks associated with the absence of a genetic bond between parents and children.

Either way, regardless of whether children are better off with biological or social parents, their basic needs are universal and independent of the conditions in which they grow up or who their caretakers are. Regulations in place to serve the rights and needs of minors ought to ensure that all children, without distinction, have these needs adequately fulfilled. In the following sections, I show that these regulations, despite aiming to protect the rights and needs of refugee minors, in fact lead to an unjustified, unequal treatment of the categories of children they affect. I then argue that such disparity in treatment seems attributable to the fact that these

5 For works raising these issues or claims, see, for instance, Velleman (2005), Hamilton et al. (2007), Kolodny (2010), Tooley (1998), and Hursthouse (1987, 1992).

6 For a discussion of these themes, see, for instance, Rulli (2014, 2016).

laws rely on assumptions about the questions posed in this section and that these assumptions, although initially plausible, do not withstand further scrutiny.

3. Refugee children: regulatory approaches for accompanied and unaccompanied refugee minors

With the help of Düfner and Hillmann's research (2019), in this section, I show how some regulatory approaches designed to define and protect the rights of refugee minors lead to indirect, ethically unjustified inequality in the support reserved for accompanied vis-à-vis unaccompanied refugee minors. I will consider as relevant examples the regulations in force in Germany and Italy.[7]

Here, I use the term 'refugee' to cover all categories of forced migrants in need of international protection as offered in the EU. The term 'minors' (or 'children') refers to *all* individuals below the legal age of 18. Refugees below the legal age of 18 are considered unaccompanied when neither their parents, legal guardians, nor any other person who is entitled to care for them resides with them. If children are accompanied by individuals other than their parents, say, by older siblings, uncles, or aunts, they count as unaccompanied as long as this other person is not declared and required by the law to care for all issues of the child at stake permanently and by explicit agreement with the parents (Kunkel, 2011). Hence, in most cases, children accompanied by older siblings, uncles, or aunts are considered unaccompanied by law, regardless of social science approaches using other definitions.[8]

In the mentioned countries, i.e., Germany and Italy, some of the rights established for refugee minors are not the same. These rights differ depending on whether the child is accompanied. In Germany, an unaccompanied minor who arrives seeking refuge is to be cared for immediately by the youth administration of the region where the child was found while waiting to be assigned a final legal guardian (Kunkel, 2011). Moreover, the unaccompanied child must be provided with temporary custody and housed in facilities specialised in caring for unaccompanied refugee minors. These facilities need to meet very high standards. For example, accommodations must include a playroom and a study room. By contrast, accommodation solutions available for accompanied refugee minors are, in fact, largely unsuitable and fail to adequately cater to the well-being of these children (Düfner & Hillmann, 2019, § 3).

Moreover, because a local legal guardian is appointed for unaccompanied children, they have somebody to help them with the local language, bureaucracy, and other day-to-day issues. In contrast, accompanied children lack access to these benefits. They can only rely on their non-native-speaking parents, who often have little to no clue

7 The choice of these countries is due, in particular, to available literature on this specific matter. Yet, as Düfner and Hillmann point out (2019, p. 332), laws regarding asylum seekers are almost entirely determined by European directives or regulations. Similarities can be found across Europe.

8 As anticipated, diving further into the legal details is not in the interest of this chapter. I am concerned here with highlighting from an ethical point of view the indirect inequality that the law in force entails for accompanied vs unaccompanied refugee minors.

about navigating the host nation's bureaucracy, culture, and other challenges, and they may be psychologically worn out. Düfner and Hillmann point out in this respect:

> staff members at youth centres for unaccompanied children are trained to support vulnerable children and possess first-hand knowledge of the local language, the local health system, as well as the education system. Many refugee parents arrive in Germany with no knowledge of the local language and may be suffering from traumatic war experiences.
>
> (Düfner & Hillmann, 2019, p. 338)

The regulations in force in Italy imply a similar outcome: the unequal treatment of accompanied vs unaccompanied refugee children.[9] To add something to the discussion, it is worth noting that unaccompanied minors have the right to be provided with accommodation and care within the country in which they are found, as established by law 47/2017 of the United Text on Immigration. This law aims to enhance the rights and protection of unaccompanied refugee children, including prohibiting rejection at the border and preventing repatriation. In contrast, these rights are not granted to accompanied minors.

In sum, in both the examined countries, the law in force generates a discrepancy between the rights granted to unaccompanied vis-à-vis accompanied refugee children. Unaccompanied refugee children are granted comparatively more rights and benefits than accompanied ones.

4. Family reunification: regulatory solutions for biological and non-biological refugee minors

Another context in which the laws that are supposed to serve the rights of all minors alike fail to do so, to a certain extent, is the one that pertains to the right to family reunification. Through the existing literature on the matter, this section aims to show how the regulatory solutions in force lead to indirect inequality in the treatment of children related to their parents via biological resemblance vis-à-vis children who are not. The indirect inequality affects several countries that allow family reunification and has been studied primarily in regard to Germany (e.g., Lemke & Heinemann, 2014), Finland (e.g., Lee & Voigt, 2020), and the United States (e.g., Farahany et al., 2019; Lee & Voigt, 2020).[10]

Family reunification is the process – and right – by which family members living abroad (beneficiaries) can be reunited with their relatives who are citizens or have long-term residence permits in a given country (sponsors). The right to family reunification comes from the protection of family life as stipulated in, amongst others, the Universal Declaration of Human Rights (Jastram & Newland, 2003). Actually –

9 See § 23, 24, d.lsg. n°.140 of 5 May 2005; § 31 of the United Text on Immigration, modified in 2016.

10 For another interesting comparative study involving data from Austria, Finland, and Germany, see Heinemann et al. (2013).

as Matthew Lister (2018) notices – because the right to family reunification derives from the right to family protection, family reunification should be considered not as the right of an outsider to enter a given country but the other way around: as the right of a citizen or long-term resident to bring in family members.

Family reunification is one of the primary means for people to move legally between states, and it is currently the most significant form of immigration to Europe (Müller, 2012), even to countries traditionally quite reluctant to receive immigrants.[11] Which family members are eligible for family reunification varies from country to country within the overall framework of the Family Reunification Directive (2003/86/EC). As a minimum, they include spouses and unmarried children (if under legal age). Minors holding a residence permit may serve as sponsors. For the purposes of the present chapter, I will only consider the perspective of these minor sponsors.

All countries' policies require proof of kinship to grant family reunification, whether the proof is biological or legal documentation (marriage, birth certificates, or adoption documentation). Since the 1990s, DNA analysis has been increasingly used to verify the authenticity of familial claims in family reunification cases.[12] In the absence of existing documentary evidence, DNA testing seems the most reliable, objective, and easy tool for establishing whether the relatedness subsists. Reliability and objectivity lie in particular in the fact that – proponents of DNA testing argue – while a person may make false statements or present false documents, DNA tests cannot lie in proving biological relatedness.[13] It is noteworthy, though, that although DNA testing is, on a theoretical level, a voluntary option used when other means of proving family ties are unavailable, in practice, immigration officials require it more often than expected (Lee & Voigt, 2020, § 2).

In Germany, evidence shows that indeed, even when legal documents proving family relations are provided, it is a common administrative practice to ask applicants for DNA proof (Kreienbrink & Rühl, 2007; German Bundestag, 2008; Frenz, 2008; UN High Commissioner for Refugees, 2008; European Migration Network, 2011a, 2011b).[14] Catherine Lee and Torsten Voigt observe: 'In practice, DNA testing is often used as an obstacle in the immigration procedures, it becomes

11 Family reunification accounts for approximately 36% of legal immigration to Germany and 29% to Italy (Lister, 2018, p. 155, fn. 8).

12 As of today, at least 20 countries worldwide, including 16 European countries, use DNA testing to settle otherwise inconclusive or doubtful cases (Taitz et al., 2002a, 2002b; Esbenshade, 2010; Heinemann et al., 2013). The countries that have included DNA testing in decision-making processes about family reunification cases include Australia, Austria, Belgium, Canada, Denmark, Estonia, Finland, France, Germany, Hungary, Italy, Lithuania, Malta, the Netherlands, New Zealand, Norway, Switzerland, Sweden, the United Kingdom, and the United States (European Migration Network 2011a, 2011b).

13 As Lynch et al. (2008) remark, DNA testing has become the new 'gold standard' for identifying people.

14 As Lemke and Heinemann point out: 'the results of our research indicate that DNA testing for family reunification is not an *ultima ratio* but a standard tool for the verification of a family relationship in immigration cases' (Lemke & Heinemann, 2014, p. 496). Lee and Voigt stress that this is proven for both EU countries and the United States (Lee & Voigt, 2020, p. 440).

a tool to exclude people on the basis of supposed biological facts' (Lee & Voigt, 2020, p. 436).

Furthermore, the German Federal Foreign Office reports a list of more than 40 countries for which official documents or other pieces of evidence will be considered invalid or extremely questionable (German Bundestag, 2008). When it comes to these 'blacklisted' countries, DNA evidence is considered the only reliable, objective, and truthful manner to discern whether certain individuals belong to the same family.[15] Applicants from these countries need therefore to resort to DNA testing to obtain permission for family reunification, a permission often denied when sponsors and beneficiaries cannot demonstrate to be biologically related (e.g., Lemke & Heinemann, 2014; Lee & Voigt, 2020). Several cases have been reported where more than ten pieces of evidence were submitted to, but rejected by, the local immigration authorities when the exam did not confirm a genetic link (Gaserow, 2007; Funk, 2008).

It falls outside the scope of this chapter to highlight *all* possible ethically challenging implications derived from using DNA testing to approve family reunification applications.[16] Here, I place particular attention on the impact of DNA analysis on creating differences in the treatment of children biologically related to their family vis-à-vis minors with adoptive or foster parents (legally declared so).[17] It emerges that, in practice, the policies discussed in this section favour minors with a DNA connection to their family members, granting them a more advantageous position compared to children without a biological connection to their family. Minors with genetic links to their family are more likely to be reunited with their family members. Additionally, refugee minors from economically disadvantaged countries face further obstacles in this regard, indicating that the policies in force create disparities based not only on a particular concept of family but also on the country of origin (e.g., Lemke & Heinemann, 2014; Lee & Voigt, 2020).[18]

Moreover, as Thomas Lemke and Torsten Heinemann point out, the use of DNA testing to determine whether there is biological kinship brings about additional disparities, for it establishes a 'double standard of family recognition for native citizens and immigrants' (Lemke & Heinemann, 2014, p. 491). While native citizens have a variety of family situations legally acknowledged, the family concept for immigrants who want to be reunited with their family members seems to be more

15 As Lemke and Heinemann remark: 'According to German immigration law, no distinction shall be made between biological children and adopted children if the applicants can prove the adoption by official documentation. However, as German authorities regard official registration systems in the blacklisted countries as insufficient, this claim is difficult to sustain in administrative practice' (Lemke & Heinemann, 2014, p. 499).

16 For a few analyses of some crucial ethical challenges brought by DNA testing for family reunification cases, see, e.g., Heinemann and Lemke (2013), Lemke and Heinemann (2014), Farahany et al. (2019), and Lee and Voigt (2020).

17 In this context, I specifically refer to parents who can provide legal proof of their relationship with their children, for the laws discussed in this section only recognise legal bonds as valid.

18 A further difference in treatment derives from the fact that the burden of the expenses for proving DNA relatedness falls entirely on the applicant. Applicants need to have financial means to provide additional proof of existing bonds and comply with what is required.

narrow and biological. As highlighted earlier, the use of this double standard also depends on the country of origin of the applicant or of the members with whom they wish to be reunited. While official documents or other pieces of evidence are rejected when the third countries involve sub-Saharan Africa or Central and South East Asia areas, this is not the case for citizens of, e.g., the United States or other developing countries, such as those in Latin America (Lemke & Heinemann, 2014, p. 495).

In sum, the law in force generates, in practice, a double discrepancy: one between refugee minors biologically related to their parents and those with social or legal caregivers, and another between citizens and refugee minors. In both cases, the former category is granted comparatively more rights in terms of the family they are entitled to. Moreover, an additional difference in treatment depends on the country of origin: minors from economically advantaged backgrounds receive more favourable treatment compared to children from certain financially disadvantaged nations.

5. Better off without parents? An ethical examination of disparities in the treatment of refugee minors and their right to family reunification

Section 3 shows that the regulations that are supposed to grant (at least in Germany and Italy) certain rights and fulfil the needs of all refugee minors, in practice, result in an involuntary unequal treatment of accompanied vs unaccompanied refugee children. Being accompanied results in fewer rights and benefits – rights and benefits that are, though, critical for the well-being of all refugee minors. Section 4 shows that some regulations for family reunification (especially in Germany, but also in other countries) lead, in practice, to the indirect unequal treatment of minors of families with DNA connections vis-à-vis minors of families with social and legal ties. The current policy for family reunification also generates a double standard in the rights and benefits granted to children who are citizens of the relevant countries vs refugee minors, especially if the latter minors cannot show proof of biological kinship to their family and come from certain disadvantaged nations. In this section, after reporting the ethical issues that arise independently in the two contexts, I emphasise that when it comes to safeguarding the best interests of refugee minors and ensuring their needs are fulfilled, the influence of the allegedly relevant unequal circumstances is not particularly significant. The policies in force are not ethically justified. I then evaluate the two situations together to show that if we sum the unequal treatment resulting from the existing regulations in both contexts, we get an even less ethically pursuable or desirable outcome.

5.1 Refugee minors: is the difference in the treatment of accompanied and unaccompanied children ethically justified?

From an ethical standpoint, treating individuals (or categories of individuals) unequally is justifiable when significant disparities exist between their circumstances.

Hence, the imbalance in the treatment of accompanied and unaccompanied refugee minors would be warranted if significantly different circumstances apply.

Prima facie, the favourable treatment of unaccompanied children can be justified as a counter-balance to the disadvantage of living without parents or other figures acting in their stead (i.e., of being accompanied).[19] However, on closer inspection, accompanied children do not have that much greater of an advantage over unaccompanied ones in the relevant respects.

These children's needs (e.g., personal space, education, psychological and language support, etc.) are similar and do not depend on them being accompanied. Having parents does not seem sufficient to fulfil these needs and to warrant the discrepancy in treatment. For example, both categories of minors would benefit from playrooms or study rooms (Düfner & Hillmann, 2019). Different circumstances do not play that of a significant role, especially if we consider that the parents of accompanied children are forced to live in assigned facilities while their asylum procedures are pending and cannot, therefore, ensure accommodations suitable to meet their children's needs.[20] One could argue that children accompanied by their parents may have an advantage in finding food or bathrooms due to parental assistance. Yet, it is hard to believe that their need for suitable living space is diminished solely because of their parents' presence.

Moreover, parents or alternative guardians of accompanied minors cannot help much with local language, bureaucracy, psychological support, and so on. As foreigners, they themselves may require assistance in these respects. Staff members at youth centres for unaccompanied children are trained and competent to support fragile children and possess first-hand knowledge of the local language, health system, and education system. But accompanied children may also require this same additional support, and they may be unable to get it from their accompanists. It is not (and cannot be) assumed that their parents have arrived in Germany with basic knowledge of the local language or have not suffered from traumatic war experiences (Düfner & Hillmann, 2019, p. 338).

Being accompanied certainly constitutes a significant advantage with respect to psychosocial well-being. Nevertheless, as highlighted, being accompanied does not seem *per se* sufficient to fulfil all the essential needs of refugee minors. The unequal treatment of accompanied vs unaccompanied refugee children is not ethically justified, for being accompanied does not constitute an advantage significant enough with respect to the relevant needs mentioned.

Additionally, the privileged treatment reserved for unaccompanied minors may lead to an undesirable side effect: knowing that your children will receive privileged care, accommodation, and educational support and will not be returned to the

19 For an interesting report on the conditions of unaccompanied migrating minors, see Menjivar and Perreira (2019).

20 Düfner and Hillmann conclude in this respect: 'As there is no difference in the accommodation needs of accompanied and unaccompanied children, housing them in such different settings therefore violates the principle of equality before the law' (Düfner & Hillmann, 2019, p. 336).

country of origin if sent away by themselves, may represent a significant pull factor. Not just that: once in the host country, parents may feel somewhat incentivised to deny a relationship with their children (Düfner & Hillmann, 2019, p. 338).

5.2 Family reunification: is the difference in the treatment of biological vs non-biological families ethically justified?

By the same ethical principle, it does not seem that the indirect, unequal treatment reserved for minors who are biologically related vis-à-vis minors who are non-DNA connected to their family is justified. In this context, the unjustifiability appears even more evident. There are no significant differences in circumstances between minors biologically related to their family and those who are not. Both categories of minors appear to be on equal footing in terms of needs. There seems to be no good reason to grant family reunification only upon the possibility of proving DNA connections and discard even legal documents that establish relationships among relevant family members. Additionally, considering the economic disadvantage of the countries where children originate from as a justification for their unfavourable treatment vis-à-vis minors from a more economically privileged background does not appear defensible. On the contrary, it suggests the need for equal treatment regardless of economic circumstances. The practice of enforcing DNA testing in such cases and overturning family reunification decisions on that basis is not ethically pursuable.

It may be argued that the use of DNA testing prevents fraudulent family reunification claims (European Commission, 2011; Müller, 2012; Lee & Voigt, 2020) and child trafficking. However, in practice, DNA testing targets and discriminates against particular groups of applicants (Lemke & Heinemann, 2014; Fitzgerald & Cook-Martìn, 2014) and does not prevent criminal uses of family reunification, as biological relatives traffic minors too (Farahany et al., 2019, p. 5).

Moreover, this policy's outcome is normatively undesirable, as it may challenge the ethical and legal principle of preserving the child's best interests. Testing for biological relationships may reveal hidden social adoptions, misattributed parenting (e.g., Farahany et al., 2019; Lee & Voigt, 2020), or other unwanted genetic information. The new evidence may lead to the minor's abandonment, mistreatment, or neglect.[21]

5.3 Refugee minors and family reunification: is the difference in treatment of the relevant categories of minors ethically desirable?

The combination of indirect, involuntary inequalities resulting from the existing regulations serving to protect the rights of refugee minors and their right to family reunification leads to an additional undesirable outcome that lacks ethical

21 For some interesting examples, see, for instance, Lemke and Heinemann (2014) and Lee and Voigt (2020).

justification. The regulations at stake in the two examined contexts inadvertently put refugee minors who do not share biological relationships with their family members in lose-lose situations. If they migrate as accompanied minors, they cannot gain the same rights and benefits granted to unaccompanied children, and they face a higher risk of being expelled along with their accompanying relatives. On the other hand, if they attempt to benefit from the privileges afforded to unaccompanied minors, they have fewer chances of being reunited with their family members. By contrast, their peers who can prove biological kinship with their family are in a slightly more privileged position. Given the examined policies, they can seek asylum as unaccompanied minors and be awarded the rights and benefits associated with that category and will be more likely to be reconnected with their family members, as they can provide evidence of genetic ties to them. To this extent, one may draw the provocative conclusion that refugee minors with social and legal bonds to their families are better off without parents (or accompanists).

Needless to say, my aim is not to imply that lacking parents is desirable. Rather, this admittedly provocative conclusion is to raise attention to two crucial aspects. Firstly, the ethically unjustified consequences appear to stem from unsubstantiated assumptions underlying the regulations purported to protect the rights of refugee minors seeking family reunification. Secondly, a critical examination and revisitation of these assumptions may help with aligning these regulations more effectively with their intended purpose. As an initial step, it is essential to reevaluate the significance attributed to biological ties in parenthood and the concept of family.

6. Regulations, refugee minors, and the concept of family

Section 3 highlights the indirect, unequal treatment of accompanied vs unaccompanied refugee minors that comes from the formulations of specific laws purported to guarantee and protect the rights and needs of refugee children. Certain fundamental rights common to all refugee minors seem better respected in the case of unaccompanied children, while the ones of accompanied refugee children remain comparatively unguarded.

The highlighted imbalance results from the assumption that children are better off with parents or alternative guardians. As pointed out in Sections 2 and 4, this is generally true; therefore, *prima facie* justifies the mentioned disparity and the specific favourable treatment of unaccompanied refugee minors. However, a second unfounded assumption is behind the laws at stake. It is taken for granted that having parents or other figures who act in their stead is *per se* sufficient to have these rights and needs ensured. As highlighted in Sections 2 and 5.1, this is not the case. Thus, the unequal treatment of accompanied vs unaccompanied refugee children is ethically unjustified, for being accompanied does not constitute an advantage significant enough with respect to the relevant needs mentioned.

Consequently, it is ethically desirable to adjust the relevant regulations so that accompanied children also get their basic needs met. Given the needs and vulnerability of children, both categories of refugee minors should get the benefits that are currently reserved for unaccompanied minors. Additional psychological and financial assistance should be provided to the unaccompanied minors to compensate for the absence of parental care.

Section 4 highlights the discrepancy in the rights reserved for biological vs non-biological families concerning family reunification. The resulting imbalance seems to be the outcome of an assumption underlying granting family reunification: children are better off with their biological parents. Under these policies, the primary concept of family is and *should* be based on DNA kinship. Lee and Voigt support this thesis when they point out: 'The official policies of the countries in our study see in DNA testing a tool that can establish the correct form of familial tie – that is, biological – when other forms of evidence cannot' (Lee & Voigt, 2020, p. 441). Similarly, Lemke and Heinemann claim: 'The establishment of DNA testing in administrative decision-making on family reunification reduces the already narrow definition of the family in German immigration law to biological ancestry' (Lemke & Heinemann, 2014, p. 498). DNA testing is used to reinforce the assumption that biological bonds are more fundamental than social or even legal relations. This idea perfectly matches the so-called *geneticist account* that grounds parenthood based on genetic and biological connection and statements such as the ones of Velleman, which endorse that children are better off raised by their biological parents (Velleman, 2005 §2).

However, this conception has been questioned and is increasingly inadequate from both a practical and a theoretical standpoint. Endorsing this narrow conception of the family seems 'a vivid example of unhelpful armchair philosophy' (Roache, 2016, p. 755). Moreover, on a practical basis, 'the biological concept of family seems increasingly inadequate to account for the complex dynamics of contemporary family relations' (Lemke & Heinemann, 2014, p. 499). It also leads to unjustified, challenging ethical consequences. The genetic concept of family leads to stigmatising families established non-biologically (Farahany et al., 2019). In this respect, DNA testing does not and *should not* define what a family or a parent is.[22]

As pointed out in Section 2, the underlying reason for thinking that genetic ties are and should be prioritised seems to lie in the assumption (or bias) that biological parents are naturally driven to love their offspring. Nevertheless, as Tina Rulli highlights, 'why this is so is typically left unexplained; perhaps it is self-evident to most people' (Rulli, 2014, p. 118). No scientific or substantial efforts have been made to support the belief that biological parents are inherently better for children than social parents. Merely assuming such a thesis does not serve as a valid justification, particularly from an ethical standpoint. Furthermore, available data contradict this assumption. As discussed in the previous section, biological parents are also involved in child trafficking, highlighting that this assumption is unfounded (Farahany et al., 2019, p. 5). As mentioned in Section 2, instances of abuse, mistreatment, and neglect are more prevalent in biological households, while statistics show that adopted children are comparatively less exposed to these

22 As Farahany et al. remark: 'A DNA test cannot verify family relationships; it can confirm only biological ones' (Farahany et al., 2019, p. 5).

risks (LaFollette, 1980, p. 194). The idea that children are only safe with their biological family is misleading.

Moreover, there have been no attempts to discover how people raised in non-biological families actually conceive themselves in relation to their biological vs adoptive or social parents. Existing observations simply indicate that adoptees generally express curiosity about their biological origins (Roache, 2016). Merely assuming the moral superiority of the traditional biological notion of family, without substantial evidence or supporting arguments, is insufficient to justify its adoption over alternative concepts. The conventional understanding of the family, based solely on biological connections, lacks ethical and empirical foundations. Such a concept is increasingly outdated and necessitates revision to encompass broader social and legal bonds.[23] Revisiting this concept constitutes a crucial initial step towards formulating more equitable regulations concerning family reunification.

7. Conclusion

This chapter has examined the existing laws pertaining to the rights of refugee children and their access to family reunification. From the analysis, it emerged that some specific current regulations fail to adequately serve their purpose and safeguard the rights and needs of all the refugee minors concerned. The laws in place lead to an ethically unjustified treatment of some categories of refugee children. In particular, it appears that the ones who pay the highest price are minors accompanied by non-biological parents. I showed that these involuntary inequalities stem from underlying assumptions in these laws that lack justification. These laws seem to take for granted certain answers to the questions posed in Section 2. Is it sufficient for the overall well-being of a child to have parents? Specific regulations supposed to serve the rights of refugee children assume the answer to be yes, independently of the particular circumstances affecting these minors. Is it better for a child to have biological or social parents? Specific laws in the matter of family reunification favour DNA relationships. I thus advocated for the need to discard the unjustified assumptions underlying these regulations. Specifically, I argued that reevaluating the concept of family and parenthood to embrace social and legal relationships is pivotal in safeguarding the best interests of all refugee minors and ensuring equal opportunities for all of them. The existing regulations require an unbiased reevaluation that takes into account the ethical concerns and consequences arising from the current treatment of refugee children. This way, we can work towards a more equitable system that genuinely serves the rights and well-being of all refugee minors.

References

Archard, D. (2004). *Children: Rights and Childhood* (2nd ed.). Routledge.
Archard, D. (2010). The Obligations and Responsibilities of Parenthood. In D. Archard & D. Benatar (Eds.), *Procreation and Parenthood* (pp. 103–127). Oxford University Press. https://doi.org/10.1093/acprof:oso/9780199590704.003.0005

23 On concept revision, see, for instance, Haslanger (2009, 2012, 2016) and Thomasson (2020).

Bigelow, J., Campbell, J., Dodds, S., Pargetter, R., Prior, E., & Young, R. (1988). Parental autonomy. *Journal of Applied Philosophy*, *5*, 3–16.

Blustein, J. (1997). Procreation and parental responsibility. *Journal of Social Philosophy*, *28*(2), 79–86. https://doi.org/10.1111/j.1467-9833.1997.tb00377.x

Düfner, A., & Hillmann, L. (2019). Better off without parents? Legal and ethical questions concerning refugee children in Germany. *Journal of Ethnic and Migration Studies*, *45*(2), 331–348. https://doi.org/10.1080/1369183X.2017.1404268

Esbenshade, J. (2010). *An Assessment of DNA Testing for African Refugees*. Immigration Policy Center.

European Commission. (2011). *Green paper on the right of family reunification of third-country nationals living in the European Union (Directive 2033/86/EC), COM* (p. 735). European Commission.

European Migration Network (EMN). (2011a). *Ad-hoc query on the concept of family member*. Retrieved October 15, 2012, from http://emn.intrasoft-intl.com/html/index.html

European Migration Network (EMN). (2011b). *Ad-hoc query on verification of legality and genuineness of marriage & validation of paternity*. Retrieved September 18, 2012, from http://emn.intrasoft- intl.com/html/index.html

Farahany, N., Chodavadia, S., & Katsanis, S. H. (2019). Ethical guidelines for DNA testing in migrant family reunification. *American Journal of Bioethics*, *19*(2), 4–7. https://doi.org/10.1080/15265161.2018.1556514

Fitzgerald, D., & Cook-Martín, D. (2014). *Culling the Masses: The Democratic Origins of Racist Immigration Policy in the Americas*. Harvard University Press.

Frenz, W. (2008). Begrenzung ausländerrechtlicher Maßnahmen durch europäische Grundrechte. *ZAR*, *28*(11–12), 385–388.

Funk, V. (2008). Mal DNA-test, mal Familienfoto. *Frankfurter Rundschau*, *30*.

Fuscaldo, G. (2006). Genetic ties: Are they morally binding? *Bioethics*, *20*(2), 64–76. https://doi.org/10.1111/j.1467-8519.2006.00478.x

Gaserow, V. (2007). Grenzen dicht für Birmaner: Anwälte: Zwang zum Gentest bei Familiennachzug ist unüberwindbare Hürde. *Frankfurter Rundschau*, *22*.

German Bundenstag. (2008). DNS-Abstammungsgutachten im Rahmen von aufenthaltsrechtlichen Identitätsfeststellungen. Antwort auf die Kleine Anfrage der Abgeordneten Ulla Jelpke, Sevim Dagdelen, Jan Korte und der Fraktion DIE LINKE. *Drucksache*, *16*(7698), 1–5.

Golombok, S., & Murray, C. (1999). Social versus biological parenting: Family functioning and the socioemotional development of children conceived by egg or sperm donation. *The Journal of Child Psychology and Psychiatry and Allied Disciplines*, *40*(4), 519–527. https://doi.org/10.1111/1469-7610.00470

Hamilton, L., Cheng, S., & Powell, B. (2007). Adoptive parents, adaptive parents: Evaluating the importance of biological ties for parental investment. *American Sociological Review*, *72*(1), 95–116. https://doi.org/10.1177/000312240707200105

Haslanger, S. (2009). Family, ancestry and self: What is the moral significance of biological ties? *Adoption & Culture*, *2*, 91–122.

Haslanger, S. (2012). *Resisting Reality: Social Construction and Social Critique*. Oxford University Press. https://doi.org/10.1093/acprof:oso/9780199892631.001.0001

Haslanger, S. (2016). Theorising with a Purpose: The Many Kinds of Sex. In C. Kendig (Ed.), *Natural Kinds and Classification in Scientific Practice* (pp. 129–144). Routledge.

Heinemann, T. & Lemke, T. (2013). Suspect families: DNA kinship testing in German immigration policy. *Sociology*, *47*(4), 810–826.

Heinemann, T., Naue, U., & Tapaninen, A. (2013). Verifying the family? A comparison of DNA analysis for family reunification in three European countries (Austria, Finland and Germany). *European Journal of Migration and Law*, *15*(2), 183–202. https://doi.org/10.1163/15718166-12342030

Hill, J. L. (1991). What does it mean to be a "parent"? The claims of biology as a basis for parental rights. *New York University Law Review*, *66*, 353–420.

Hursthouse, R. (1987). *Beginning Lives*. Blackwell.

Hursthouse, R. (1992). Beginning lives. *Noûs*, *26*(1), 134–137.
Jastram, K., & Newland, K. (2003). Family Unity and Refugee Protection. In E. Feller, V. Türk, & F. Nicholson (Eds.), *Refugee Protection in International Law: UNHCR's Global Consultations on International Protection* (pp. 555–603). Cambridge University Press. https://doi.org/10.1017/CBO9780511493973.029
Kolodny, N. (2010). Which relationships justify partiality? The case of parents and children. *Philosophy and Public Affairs*, *38*(1), 37–75. https://doi.org/10.1111/j.1088-4963.2009.01173.x
Kreienbrink, A., & Rühl, S. (2007). *Family Reunification in Germany: Small Scale Study IV in the Framework of the European Migration Network*. Federal Office for Migration and Refugees.
Kunkel, P. (2011). Comments on § 7 Social Code VIII. In P. Kunkel, J. Kepert, & A. K. Pattar (Eds.), *Sozialgesetzbuch VIII: Kinder- und Jugendhilfe* (4th ed.). Nomos.
LaFollette, H. (1980). Licensing parents. *Philosophy and Public Affairs*, *9*, 182–197.
Lee, C., & Voigt, T. H. (2020). DNA testing for family reunification and the limits of biological truth. *Science, Technology, and Human Values*, *45*(3), 430–454. https://doi.org/10.1177/0162243919862870
Lemke, T., & Heinemann, T. (2014). Biological citizenship reconsidered: The use of DNA analysis by immigration authorities in Germany. *Science, Technology, and Human Values*, *39*(4), 488–510. https://doi.org/10.1177/0162243913509414
Lister, M. (2018). The Rights of Families and Children at the Border. In E. Brake & L. Ferguson (Eds.), *Philosophical Foundations of Children's and Family Law* (pp. 153–70). Oxford University Press.
Lynch, M., Cole, S. A., McNally, R., & Jordan, K. (2008). *Truth Machine: The Contentious History of DNA Fingerprinting*. University of Chicago Press.
Menjívar, C., & Perreira, K. M. (2019). Undocumented and unaccompanied: Children of migration in the European Union and the United States. *Journal of Ethnic and Migration Studies*, *45*(2), 197–217. https://doi.org/10.1080/1369183X.2017.1404255
Millum, J. (2010). How do we acquire parental rights? *Social Theory and Practice*, *36*(1), 112–132. https://doi.org/10.5840/soctheorpract20103615
Müller, A. (2012). *Misuse of the Right to Family Reunification: Marriages of Convenience and False Declarations of Parenthood*. Federal Office for Migration and Refugees.
Nelson, J. L. (1991). Parental obligations and the ethics of surrogacy: A causal perspective. *Public Affairs Quarterly*, *5*, 49–61.
Roache, R. (2016). The value of being biologically related to one's family. *Journal of Medical Ethics*, *42*(12), 755–756. http://dx.doi.org/10.1136/medethics-2016-104049
Rosenman, A. S. (1995). Babies Jessica, Richard and Emily: The need for legislative reform of adoption laws. *Chicago Kent Law Review*, *70*, 1851–1895.
Rulli, T. (2014). The Unique Value of Adoption. In F. Baylis & C. McLeod (Eds.), *Family-Making: Contemporary Ethical Challenges* (pp. 109–128). Oxford University Press. https://doi.org/10.1093/acprof:oso/9780199656066.003.0007
Rulli, T. (2016). Preferring a genetically-related child. *Journal of Moral Philosophy*, *13*(6), 669–698.
Shanley, M. L. (1995). Fathers' rights, mothers' wrongs? Reflections on unwed fathers' rights and sex equality. *Hypatia*, *10*(1), 74–103. https://doi.org/10.1111/j.1527-2001.1995.tb01354.x
Taitz, J., Weekers, J. E., & Mosca, D. T. (2002a). DNA and immigration: The ethical ramifications. *The Lancet*, *359*(9308), 794. https://doi.org/10.1016/S0140-6736(02)07889-3
Taitz, J., Weekers, J. E., & Mosca, D. T. (2002b). The last resort: Exploring the use of DNA testing for family reunification. *Health and Human Rights*, *6*(1), 20–32. https://doi.org/10.2307/4065312
Thomasson, A. L. (2020). A Pragmatic Method for Normative Conceptual Work. In H. Capellen, D. Plunkett, & A. Burgess (Eds.), *Conceptual Engineering and Conceptual Ethics* (pp. 435–458). Oxford University Press. https://doi.org/10.1093/oso/9780198801856.003.0021

Tooley, M. (1998). Personhood. In P. Singer & H. Kuhse (Eds.), *A Companion to Bioethics* (pp. 117–126). Blackwell Publishers. https://doi.org/10.1002/9781444307818.ch13
UN High Commissioner for Refugees. (2008). *UNHCR note on DNA testing to establish family relationships in the refugee context*. Retrieved January 15, 2012, from www.unhcr.org/refworld/docid/48620c2d2.html
Velleman, J. D. (2005). Family history. *Philosophical Papers*, *34*(3), 357–378. https://doi.org/10.1080/05568640509485163
Velleman, J. D. (2015). *Beyond Price: Essays on Birth and Death*. Open Book Publishers.

Part III

Accessing family reunification

8 Moving in circles

The beginning and end of exercising free movement rights

Hester Kroeze

1. Introduction

1.1 Exercising free movement rights

One of the greatest benefits of being an EU citizen is the enjoyment of the right to move freely between the Member States.[1] The exercise of these free movement rights is subjected to the conditions and limitations in the Citizens Directive (2004/38/EC). Residence in another Member State requires that an EU citizen is either economically active or economically self-sufficient. When EU citizens meet these requirements they can derive family reunification rights from EU law.[2] Upon return to their home Member State, EU law allows EU citizens' family members to retain residence rights they obtained in another Member State (Spaventa, 2015; Schoenmaekers & Hoogenboom, 2014).[3] In these *return situations*, EU law continues to be applicable. The situation of returning EU citizens must therefore be distinguished from the situation of so-called static nationals of the home Member State who did not exercise free movement rights and to whom the relevant provisions of EU law do not apply.

If national rules for family reunification are more stringent than those in EU law, returning EU citizens and their family members find themselves in a more beneficial position than EU citizens who stayed at home (Tryfonidou, 2009; Verbist, 2017; Van Elsuwege, 2014; Hanf, 2011). This opens up the possibility that nationals of that Member State circumvent stringent immigration measures of their Member State. If they are unable to comply with these conditions, they could temporarily move to another Member State, obtain a derived residence right for family members there, and then return with those family members to their home Member State (Costello, 2009; Guild, 2019; Kroeze, 2020). This raises the question of how much exercise of free movement rights is needed to obtain family reunification

1 Article 21 TFEU.
2 Articles 2, 3 and 7 Citizens Directive.
3 CJEU, 7 July 1992, C-370/90, *Surinder Singh*, ECLI:EU:C:1992:296, §§ 19–20; CJEU, 11 December 2007, C-291/05, *Eind*, EU:C:2007:771, §§ 35–36; CJEU, 12 March 2014, C-456/12, *O. and B.*, EU:C:2014:135, §§ 47–49; CJEU, 5 June 2018, C-673/16, *Coman*, EU:C:2018:385, §§ 24–25.

DOI: 10.4324/9781003503217-11

rights in the host Member State and retain them upon return.[4] Is it sufficient to move for a short stay of less than three months by crossing a border for a cup of coffee or a (short) holiday in another Member State? If the answer is affirmative, this would render the national rules on family reunification of their own nationals meaningless. Ensuring the effectiveness of Article 21 TFEU on free movement of persons and simultaneously respecting the Member States' competence to regulate family reunification rights of static EU citizens therefore requires clarity on the conditions that EU citizens must fulfill in the host Member State before they can return to their home Member State while retaining their family members' residence rights acquired under the Directive.

1.2 Terminating the exercise of free movement rights

An EU citizen's residence in another Member State can be terminated on grounds of public policy, public security or public health.[5] It can also be terminated when the EU citizen does not or no longer fulfills the substantive requirements for legal residence in that Member State.[6] In that situation, a Member State may require the EU citizen to leave or even expel the person from its territory.[7] It is, however, then not allowed to impose an entry ban on the EU citizen whose residence has ended.[8] Visits up to three months or permanent residence after five years cannot be subjected to substantive requirements.[9] The termination of residence for other reasons than public policy, public security or public health is therefore only relevant for residence of three months to five years.[10]

In practice, the possibility to expel EU citizens who no longer fulfill the economic requirements under Article 7 of the Citizens Directive is used for 'footloose' EU citizens, often without proper housing, who get involved in low-level criminality. The severity of their crimes does not reach the threshold of becoming a threat to public order or public security, but as habitual offenders they do disturb public order and disproportionately burden (local) enforcement officers and the criminal justice system. When these people are not economically active and do not dispose of sufficient resources, their residence is terminated on the basis of Articles 15 and 30 of the Citizens Directive, followed by their expulsion (Kramer, 2021; Ristuccia, 2022). Since, however, Member States are not allowed to impose an entry ban in this situation, EU citizens retain all rights under the directive, even after their expulsion. This means that as soon as they leave the host Member State they could, in principle, turn around and immediately re-enter that Member State and claim a new residence right for less than three months under Article 6 of the Citizens Directive.

4 Opinion of Advocate General Sharpston in CJEU, 30 September 2010, C-34/09, *Ruiz Zambrano*, ECLI:EU:C:2010:560, § 86.
5 Articles 27–28 Citizens Directive.
6 Articles 15 and 30 Citizens Directive.
7 CJEU, 14 September 2017, C-184/16, *Petrea*, ECLI:EU:C:2017:684.
8 Article 15(3) Citizens Directive.
9 Articles 6 and 16 Citizens Directive.
10 Article 7 Citizens Directive.

At first sight, this seems a logical consequence of free movement of persons in an area without internal borders which prevails over protective measures of the Member States. At the same time, the effectiveness of EU rights does not only relate to the conferral thereof, but also to the possibility to terminate these rights when the requirements are no longer fulfilled. If an EU citizen could indeed comply with an expulsion order by stepping across the border and then turn around and re-enter, this would circumvent the effects of the expulsion order and undermine the effectiveness of the earlier termination of residence.[11] A proper functioning of the Citizens Directive therefore not only requires clarity on the conditions to terminate an EU citizen's residence right under Article 7, but also on the requirements that an EU citizen must fulfill to *complete an expulsion order* and re-enter the host Member State. This raises the question of how EU citizens can effectively end their residence in the host Member State and under which circumstances they are allowed to return again under Article 6 of the Citizens Directive.[12]

A clear parallel can be drawn between the effective exercise of free movement rights that allows an EU citizen to return to his home Member State with the retention of family members' residence rights, on the one hand, and the completion of an expulsion order that was issued because the EU citizen no longer fulfills the requirements for legal residence in another Member State, on the other. In both scenarios, the relative ease of crossing a border allows for strategic use of free movement rights, either to obtain and retain family reunification rights or to circumvent an expulsion order. In both scenarios, the question is raised regarding how much time across the border – in opposite directions – is needed to begin or end the exercise of free movement rights. This chapter explores the case law of the Court of Justice of the European Union (CJEU) on this topic, as well as possible parameters to determine whether the exercise of free movement rights has effectively started or has been terminated.

The next section (2) focuses on the retention of family reunification rights in a return situation. The subsequent section (3) focuses on the completion of an expulsion order. The next section (4) further analyzes the two situations and draws some conclusions from the comparison between them. The chapter ends with a few concluding remarks (5).

2. Retention of family reunification rights in return situations

2.1 Introduction and development of the return situation

Shortly before the adoption of the Maastricht Treaty, the CJEU issued its judgment in the *Surinder Singh* case,[13] which introduced the return situation in EU law. The follow-up case of *Eind* confirmed the *Surinder Singh* return rule and extended

11 Opinion of Advocate General Rantos in CJEU, 10 February 2021, C-719/19, *FS*, ECLI:EU:C:2021:104, §§ 73–77.

12 Dutch Council of State, 25 September 2019, ECLI:NL:RVS:2019:3262, § 11.

13 CJEU, 7 July 1992, C-370/90, *Surinder Singh*, ECLI:EU:C:1992:296.

it to the situation where the EU citizen is not economically active or economically self-sufficient upon return to his home Member State.[14] The CJEU justified the retention of rights with the notion that the prospect of losing residence rights obtained by family members upon return to an EU citizen's home Member State could discourage the EU citizen to exercise free movement rights under Article 21 TFEU.[15] In both cases, the involved EU citizens had resided for several years in the host Member State, so there was no question of (evidently) circumventing national law. The CJEU therefore did not need to instruct the Member States on how much movement would be necessary to retain family members' residence rights upon return. The Member States therefore developed divergent approaches and criteria for EU citizens to benefit from this case law. Austria and Germany, for instance, only required a short period of employment or residence in another Member State before family reunification rights could be retained upon return, whereas the Netherlands required a minimum period of six months of residence (Guild, 2019, pp. 365–366). This six-month period was not substantiated and challenged before the national court. The most important follow-up questions therefore came from the highest administrative court of the Netherlands, the Council of State, in two cases where the duration of residence abroad was difficult to demarcate: *O. and B.* (Spaventa, 2015; Schoenmaekers & Hoogenboom, 2014).[16]

The first case (*O.*) was about a Nigerian national and his Dutch wife. They both registered in Spain and stayed there for a couple of months. When the Dutch woman could not find employment, she returned to the Netherlands. Her Nigerian husband remained in Spain, where his wife frequently visited him on weekends and holidays. The second case (*B.*) was about a Moroccan national and his Dutch wife. The man resided in Belgium, where his wife rented an apartment. She remained in the Netherlands but spent all her weekends in Belgium with him. The question before the CJEU was whether the exercise of free movement rights by the women in these two cases was sufficient to bring their husbands to the Netherlands and retain the residence rights they obtained under EU law in Spain and Belgium, respectively. The CJEU reiterated that the acknowledgment of a residence right to a family member of an EU citizen in a return situation is justified because the refusal thereof could discourage the EU citizen from exercising free movement rights (§§ 45–46). Such discouragement only occurs when residence of the EU citizen in the host Member State 'has been sufficiently genuine so as to enable that citizen to create or strengthen family life in that Member State' (§ 51). The preservation of family life is thus key, both in the host Member State *and* upon return to the home Member State. Nevertheless, the Court's clarification does not quite solve the issue, because the logical follow-up question is, how much 'creation or

14 CJEU, 11 December 2007, C-291/05, *Eind*, EU:C:2007:771, § 38.

15 CJEU, 7 July 1992, C-370/90, *Surinder Singh*, ECLI:EU:C:1992:296, §§ 19–20; CJEU, 11 December 2007, C-291/05, *Eind*, EU:C:2007:771, §§ 35–36; CJEU, 12 March 2014, C-456/12, *O. and B.*, EU:C:2014:135, §§ 47–49; CJEU, 5 June 2018, C-673/16, *Coman*, EU:C:2018:385, §§ 24–25.

16 CJEU, 12 March 2014, C-456/12, *O. and B.*, EU:C:2014:135, §§ 52–53.

strengthening of family life' is sufficient to retain a residence right upon return to the home Member State? The CJEU does not elaborate on this question, but considers that:

> Residence in the host Member State *pursuant to and in conformity with the conditions set out in Article 7(1)* of that directive is, in principle, evidence of settling there and therefore of the Union citizen's *genuine residence in the host Member State and goes hand in hand with creating and strengthening family life* in that Member State.[17]

Although the Court's clarification is helpful to some extent, it does not answer the question of what the decisive criterion is to retain an EU citizen's family member's residence right that was obtained in another Member State in a return situation. Is it decisive to comply with the criteria in Article 7(1) of the Citizens Directive, or to genuinely reside in another Member State, or to create or strengthen family life in that Member State? And how do these elements relate to each other? Is residence in accordance with Article 7(1) of the Citizens Directive automatically sufficient to fulfill the requirements of genuine residence, or is it a precondition? Is the classification of residence as genuine sufficient to evidence that family life was created or strengthened, or is it a prerequisite? And are the requirements for the retention of a residence right in a return situation limited to the EU citizen's residence in another Member State, or are there additional requirements that must be fulfilled by the family member(s)?

There seems to be a difference between short-term travel on the basis of Article 6 of the Citizens Directive and long-term settling in the host Member State in accordance with Article 7 of the Citizens Directive. *O. and B.* was therefore understood as the introduction of a requirement of three months of residence in the host Member State before a family member's residence right can be retained upon return to the EU citizen's home Member State (Guild et al., 2019, p. 303; Verbist, 2017, p. 110; Barnard, 2019, p. 209). In the final judgments that followed the preliminary reference in *O. and B.*, the Dutch Council of State also came to that conclusion. It ruled that the visits of the two women to Spain and Belgium, respectively, never surpassed three months of residence and were therefore insufficient to acknowledge a residence right to their husbands in the Netherlands.[18]

The CJEU, however, did not actually designate the duration of residence in another Member State to be the decisive criterion to retain family members' residence rights in return situations. Instead it referred to the nature of the EU citizen's residence in another Member State and attached importance to the question of whether the exercise of rights is based on Article 6 of the Citizens Directive

17 Ibid., §§ 52–53, italics added.

18 Dutch Council of State, 20 August 2014, ECLI:NL:RVS:2014:3179, § 4.3 and ECLI:NL:RVS:2014:3184, § 5.3.

alone or also in conformity with the requirements of Article 7 of that directive.[19] Residence in another Member State for more than three months should indeed be in accordance with Article 7 of the Citizens Directive, but there is no three-month waiting period to be economically active or economically self-sufficient and thus comply with the conditions in Article 7. Therefore, residence for a period of less than three months *can* be in accordance with the requirements in this provision as well. This makes it difficult to uphold that duration of residence in another Member State is the decisive criterion to determine whether the exercise of free movement rights was genuine and effective and warrants the retention of family reunification rights upon return to the home Member State (Kroeze, 2020). The case of *Altiner and Ravn*[20] confirms this understanding of *O. and B.* The case concerned the third-country national stepson of a Danish citizen who resided first one and then two months with her in Sweden. For the CJEU, this was still sufficient for the stepson to be eligible for a residence right upon her return to Denmark.

What about the other elements the CJEU mentioned in *O. and B.* – genuine residence that goes hand in hand with creating and strengthening family life? The phrase 'goes hand in hand' could imply (1) that family life is decisive and genuine residence is evidence thereof, or (2) that genuine residence is decisive and family life is evidence thereof, or (3) that the combination of genuine residence and the creation or strengthening of family life is needed to retain family members' residence rights in a return situation. Either way, residence in conformity with the requirements of Article 7 of the Citizens Directive would be but one way to prove that these criteria are fulfilled. Similarly, the duration of residence can be relevant to assess genuine residence in another Member State, but Member States should involve other qualitative elements of genuine residence and family life as well. Residence in another Member State for less than three months thus does not automatically justify the conclusion that the exercise of EU rights was not sufficient, if there are other circumstances that indicate genuine residence and/or the creation or strengthening of family life. Vice versa, residence in another Member State for more than three months does not automatically lead to the retention of rights upon return to the EU citizen's home Member State, if there are no other circumstances that support genuine residence or indicate the creation or strengthening of family life. Considering the Court's established case law that the existence of EU rights should be assessed on a case-by-case basis and that beneficiaries can submit all types of evidence, this reading of *O. and B.* (in both directions) makes perfect sense.[21]

2.2 Identifying qualitative criteria for retention of rights in a return situation

The proposed reading of *O. and B.* raises the question of what qualitative elements should be taken into account to evaluate genuine residence and/or the

19 CJEU, 12 March 2014, C-456/12, *O. and B.*, EU:C:2014:135, §§ 52–53.
20 CJEU, 27 June 2018, C-230/17, *Altiner and Ravn*, ECLI:EU:C:2018:497.
21 CJEU, 17 February 2005, C-215/03, *Oulane*, ECLI:EU:C:2005:95, § 53; CJEU, 9 January 2007, C-1/05, *Jia*, ECLI:EU:C:2007:1, § 41.

creation and strengthening of family life to such an extent that it warrants the retention of family members' rights in a return situation. Neither the Citizens Directive nor the case of *O. and B.* elaborate on that question. The first clarification came from the European Commission, which issued a Communication to offer guidance to determine whether the exercise of EU rights is genuine and effective in 2009.[22] To distinguish between legitimate use of free movement and family reunification rights and (abusive) circumvention of national migration law, the Communication provides a list of criteria to take into account. These criteria include (1) the circumstances under which an EU citizen moves to another Member State, including his economic status and possible previous family reunification attempts; (2) the degree of effectiveness and genuineness of residence in the host Member State, including the fulfillment of registration formalities, securing accommodation and enrolling children at an educational establishment; and (3) circumstances of the EU citizen's return to his home Member State, including the duration of residence in the host Member State before his return. Circumstances which indicate a lack of genuine residence in the host Member State could, according to the Communication, be a trigger for the possibility of abuse of rights, which precludes the retention of family reunification rights upon return to the EU citizen's home Member State. Relevant circumstances in this respect could be a (very) short duration of residence in the host Member State, a failure to demonstrate sufficient efforts that were undertaken to establish oneself in the host Member State, or frequent returns to the home Member State. It can, however, not 'be inferred that the residence in the host Member State is not genuine and effective only because an EU citizen maintains some ties to the home Member State'.[23]

The mentioned criteria can be an aid in assessing genuine residence and the creation or strengthening of family life in another Member State, although the Court's judgment in *O. and B.* did cause the Commission Communication to become outdated to some extent. The judgment confirmed that circumstances such as the fulfillment of registration formalities, securing accommodation and enrolling children at an educational establishment in the host Member State are relevant indications of genuine residence and/or genuine family life. Factors such as economic status, previous failed family reunification attempts or continuing work in the home Member State, on the other hand, cannot actually play a role in the assessment of genuine residence and/or genuine family life in another Member State. *O. and B.* thus partly confirms the Commission's guidelines and partly renders them obsolete.

22 European Commission, Communication from the Commission to the European Parliament and the Council on guidance for better transposition and application of Directive 2004/38/EC on the right of citizens of the Union and their family members to move and reside freely within the territory of the Member States, 2 July 2009, COM (2009) 313 final.

23 Ibid., § 4.3.

3. Completion of an expulsion order

3.1 The necessity of completing an expulsion order

The case law on expulsion of EU citizens because they no longer fulfill the requirements to reside in another Member State and on the completion of their expulsion order is more recent than the case law on return situations. The ascertainment that these EU citizens no longer fulfill the criteria for legal residence in the host Member State is often a derivative from the lack of formal employment and the apparent need to foresee in their primary needs in an irregular manner. Their residence right is terminated on the basis of Articles 15 and 30 of the Citizens Directive, followed by their expulsion from the Member State's territory (Kramer, 2021; Ristuccia, 2022).

The question on completion of an expulsion order that is issued because an EU citizen no longer fulfills the requirements for residence in another Member State for more than three months[24] was brought before the CJEU in the *FS* case.[25] FS was a Polish national who resided in the Netherlands as a worker but then lost his employment and did not show any efforts to find a new job, nor did he have sufficient means to meet his needs. The Dutch authorities found that he no longer met the requirements for lawful residence under Article 7 of the Citizens Directive and decided that he had to leave the country or be expelled. FS eventually complied with the decision and moved to Germany but stayed near the border and frequently travelled to the Netherlands to purchase marihuana. On one of his visits to the Netherlands, he was arrested on suspicion of theft and placed in administrative detention to await his expulsion to Poland (Neier, 2021). To answer the question whether the administrative detention was in accordance with the law, it was necessary to know whether the expulsion order against FS continued to have legal effect at the moment he was arrested. If his departure from the Netherlands was sufficient to comply with the expulsion order, which would then have expired, the continued enjoyment of Articles 5 and 6 of the Citizens Directive would have allowed him to regain access to the Netherlands on the basis of these articles and render the detention unlawful. If his temporal departure had not (immediately) altered his lack of a residence status in the Netherlands, the expulsion order would continue to resort legal effect, and this would justify the placement in detention to effectuate the decision to expel FS.[26] The CJEU aptly summarized the preliminary question as being asked to rule 'on the circumstances in which a Union citizen who has been the subject of an expulsion decision, pursuant to Article 15(1) of Directive 2004/38, may [obtain] a new right of residence, under Article 6(1) of that directive, in the host Member State' (§ 62).

Referring to its earlier case law, the CJEU first reiterated that the Citizens Directive governs the conferral as well as the loss of EU rights (§§ 64–67). It proceeded

24 Article 7 Citizens Directive.

25 CJEU, 22 June 2021, C-719/19, *FS*, ECLI:EU:C:2021:506, §§ 33–34; CJEU, 2 September 2021, C-718/19 *Ordre des barreaux francophones et germanophone*, ECLI:EU:C:2021:662.

26 CJEU, 22 June 2021, C-719/19, *FS*, ECLI:EU:C:2021:506, §§ 51–52; Dutch Council of State, 25 September 2019, ECLI:NL:RVS:2019:3262, § 10.

to consider the possibility that the mere physical departure of an EU citizen would be sufficient to comply with an expulsion decision and would then allow that EU citizen to immediately return to the territory of the Member State by which he had been expelled. 'Acting repeatedly in that way, that Union citizen could be granted numerous rights of residence successively . . . even though, in reality, those various rights would be granted for the purposes of the same single actual residence'[27] (Ristuccia, 2022). If such an interpretation were accepted, that EU citizen would effectively enjoy a residence right of unlimited duration without fulfilling the requirements in Article 7 of the Citizens Directive to reside for longer than three months in the host Member State. This residence right would be authorized by a successive reliance on Article 6 of that directive, even though this provision is only meant to reside in a Member State for less than three months (§ 74). The CJEU considered this interpretation to be inconsistent with the gradual system of residence rights which the directive has introduced (§ 78). It therefore ruled that complying with an expulsion order requires that EU citizens not only physically cross the border but also genuinely and effectively terminate their residence in the host Member State so that upon return 'his or her residence cannot be regarded as constituting in fact a continuation of his or her preceding residence on that territory' (§§ 80–81). It is for the referring court to ascertain whether the EU citizen has complied with this obligation in such a way that the expulsion decision has expired, or not (§ 82).

3.2 Identifying qualitative criteria for the completion of an expulsion order from the host Member State

The follow-up question is how national courts must determine whether an EU citizen has genuinely and effectively terminated residence in the host Member State. Following the Opinion of the Advocate-General, the CJEU first clarified that Member States cannot require a minimum period of absence from the host Member State, because this would introduce a limitation to the exercise of the fundamental right of free movement in the Member States that is not foreseen in EU law.[28] Member States are allowed to take the duration of residence outside of their territory into account as one of the elements in the overall assessment of the termination of residence. The longer the absence, 'the more that absence attests to the genuine and effective nature of the end of [the EU citizen's] residence'. A very brief absence, on the other hand, can be indicative of a continuation of an earlier period of residence in the host Member State (§ 90).

The CJEU continued to deem of relevance all factors that evidence 'a break in the links between the Union citizen concerned and the host Member State', such as deregistration from the population register, leaving housing arrangements and

27 CJEU, 22 June 2021, C-719/19, *FS*, ECLI:EU:C:2021:506, § 73; Opinion of Advocate General Rantos in CJEU, 10 February 2021, C-719/19, *FS*, ECLI:EU:C:2021:104, §§ 73–77.

28 CJEU, 22 June 2021, C-719/19, *FS*, ECLI:EU:C:2021:506, §§ 83–89; Opinion of Advocate General Rantos in CJEU, 10 February 2021, C-719/19, *FS*, ECLI:EU:C:2021:104, §§ 91–93.

ending (public service) contracts in the host Member State (§ 91). These elements must be evaluated in light of the specific circumstances of the EU citizen who is being expelled, including the extent of integration, the duration of residence in the host Member State and the family and economic situation of the EU citizen.[29] The host Member State may also consider the relevant circumstances during the EU citizen's absence from its territory, including evidence that the EU citizen 'moved the center of his or her personal, occupational or family interests to another State'[30] (Ristuccia, 2022). The assessment can be foregone if there is a material change in the circumstances which enables the EU citizen to fulfill the requirements for lawful residence in another Member State under Article 7 of the Citizens Directive. In that case, the expulsion decision loses its rationale and its effects and expires.[31] Furthermore, due to the prohibition to impose an entry ban, the expulsion decision cannot be enforced if the EU citizen's presence in the host Member State is justified under Article 5 of the Citizens Directive, which regulates the entry of an EU citizen to a Member State, for instance to attend a hearing in court.[32]

In its final decision, the Dutch Council of State ruled that FS did not complete his expulsion order, so he could not reobtain a right to stay in the Netherlands on the basis of Article 6 of the Citizens Directive. His re-entry into the Netherlands was thus unlawful, so the arrest and administrative detention were legitimate. In reaching this decision, the Council took into account that after his departure from Dutch territory, FS stayed close to the border at a friend's house and frequently travelled to the Netherlands to purchase marihuana. This means that the duration of his absence from the Netherlands was always very short, no more than a month, with the exception of three months of detention in Germany. FS himself submitted that he had stayed in Germany and Poland, but he was not able to substantiate this with factual evidence. The Council of State thus deemed it unlikely that he moved the center of his personal, occupational or family interests to another state.[33]

4. Moving in circles: some observations

Considering the similarities between the retention of family members' residence rights in a return situation and the completion of an expulsion order, it is no surprise that the respective assessment criteria overlap. This calls for a few general observations about the beginning and end of exercising free movement rights. The first

29 CJEU, 22 June 2021, C-719/19, *FS*, ECLI:EU:C:2021:506, §§ 91–92; Opinion of Advocate General Rantos in CJEU, 10 February 2021, C-719/19, *FS*, ECLI:EU:C:2021:104, § 100.

30 CJEU, 22 June 2021, C-719/19, *FS*, ECLI:EU:C:2021:506, § 93; Opinion of Advocate General Rantos in CJEU, 10 February 2021, C-719/19, *FS*, ECLI:EU:C:2021:104, § 99.

31 CJEU, 22 June 2021, C-719/19, *FS*, ECLI:EU:C:2021:506, § 95; Opinion of Advocate General Rantos in CJEU, 10 February 2021, C-719/19, *FS*, ECLI:EU:C:2021:104, § 84; Dutch Council of State, 30 May 2022, ECLI:NL:RVS:2022:1510, §§ 6–6.1.

32 CJEU, 22 June 2021, C-719/19, *FS*, ECLI:EU:C:2021:506, §§ 101–103; Dutch Council of State, 23 February 2022, ECLI:NL:RVS:2022:562, § 11.1.

33 Dutch Council of State, 23 February 2022, ECLI:NL:RVS:2022:562, §§ 11–12.

observation is that the mere crossing of a border between Member States is neither sufficient to effectively exercise free movement rights that warrant the retention of family members' residence rights in a return situation nor to complete an expulsion order. To obtain family reunification rights, an EU citizen must effectively and genuinely exercise EU rights in another Member State. In a return situation, they must prove the genuine exercise of EU rights by providing evidence of genuine residence and the creation or strengthening of family life in another Member State. To complete an expulsion order, an EU citizen must effectively and genuinely terminate residence in the host Member State.[34]

The CJEU connects its assessment of initiating or terminating the exercise of EU rights to the progressive ratio of the Citizens Directive, which presumes that lengthier residence implies further integration in the host Member State's society and warrants more extensive protection against expulsion.[35] Residence in accordance with the requirements in Article 7 of the Citizens Directive is indicative of genuine residence and the creation or strengthening of family life that is necessary to retain family members' residence rights upon return to the EU citizen's home Member State. A short visit to another Member State on the basis of Article 6 of the Citizens Directive, on the other hand, is insufficient. Similarly, residence based on Article 7 of the Citizens Directive in another Member State than the Member State that issued the expulsion order is indicative of the completion thereof. If the expulsion order is completed, the EU citizen reobtains the right to enter the Member State that issued the order for a short stay of less than three months.[36] For the completion of an expulsion order, it is not sufficient to enter another Member State for only a short visit and then return to the expelling Member State without effectively terminating residence in service of completing the expulsion order.

Despite the connection of the exercise of free movement rights and the completion of an expulsion order to the progressive ratio of the Citizens Directive, this chapter has argued that the duration of residence in another Member State cannot in itself be sufficient to determine the effective beginning or ending of the exercise of free movement rights. Indicative thereof in the case of the return situation is that although residence in another Member State for more than three months *must* be in accordance with Article 7 of the Citizens Directive, the EU citizen *can* already comply with the requirements in this provision from the first day of entry. The case

34 In English and French, the criteria for genuinely and effectively exercising and terminating the exercise of free movement rights are identical ('réel et effectif' in French). In other languages, this is not the case. In Dutch, exercise of EU rights must be 'reëel en daadwerkelijk' versus 'daadwerkelijke en effectieve beëindiging' (termination) of residence. In German, the criteria are 'tatsächlich und effectiv' versus 'tatsächlich und wirksam'. In Spanish, the criteria are 'auténtico y efectivo' versus 'real y efectiva'.

35 CJEU, 14 November 2017, C-165/16, *Toufik Lounes*, ECLI:EU:C:2017:862; CJEU, 17 April 2018, C-316/16 and C-424/16, *B. and Franco Vomero*, ECLI:EU:C:2018:256.

36 If the requirements for durable residence for more than three months under Article 7 of the Citizens Directive are fulfilled, the EU citizen may re-enter immediately, even if the expulsion order has not been completed yet.

of *Altiner and Ravn* is also indicative, where the CJEU deemed the stepson of a Danish national eligible for a residence right in Denmark, even though his residence with her in Sweden had been less than three months.[37] For the completion of an expulsion order, the CJEU even explicitly considered that Member States cannot require a minimum period of absence from the host Member State before an EU citizen becomes eligible to reobtain a residence right on its territory.[38] Member States should, instead, take account of all relevant circumstances that indicate a break in the links between the EU citizen and the host Member State. Sections 2 and 3 of this chapter discussed some of the qualitative elements that can be considered when evaluating a return situation or the completion of an expulsion. These sections also demonstrated that Member States may require EU citizens to submit sufficient administrative as well as factual evidence of presence in or absence from the host Member State, respectively.

After evaluating the most important similarities between the doctrines on return situations and the completion of an expulsion order, it is relevant to flag an important difference. In *FS*, the CJEU considered that the relevant circumstances that must be weighed in the evaluation of the completion of an expulsion order, must evidence 'a break in the links between the Union citizen concerned and the host Member State'.[39] It may, furthermore, be considered whether the EU citizen 'moved the center of his or her personal, occupational or family interests to another State'.[40] These considerations constitute new elements in the case law of the CJEU. For the assessment of a return situation, the Commission Communication even expressed the opposite view that it cannot be inferred that 'residence in the host Member State is not genuine and effective only because an EU citizen maintains some ties to the home Member State'.[41] Should the relevance of 'breaking links' with the host Member State for the case of *FS* be considered an override of the Commission Communication perspective that maintaining ties with a Member State does not preclude genuine residence in another Member State? Or is this requirement exclusively applicable to expulsion without being equally relevant for return situations?

Similarly, in the case law on return situations, the possibility to assess evidence that the EU citizen 'moved the center of his or her personal, occupational or family interests to another State' has not been part of assessing effective and genuine exercise of free movement rights as a precondition to retain family reunification rights. Must this criterion, due to *FS*, be added to the evaluation of effective and genuine exercise of EU citizens' free movement rights in another Member State? Or must it be concluded that there is a substantive difference between genuine

37 CJEU, 27 June 2018, C-230/17, *Altiner and Ravn*, ECLI:EU:C:2018:497.

38 CJEU, 22 June 2021, C-719/19, *FS*, ECLI:EU:C:2021:506, §§ 83–89.

39 CJEU, 22 June 2021, C-719/19, *FS*, ECLI:EU:C:2021:506, § 91.

40 CJEU, 22 June 2021, C-719/19, *FS*, ECLI:EU:C:2021:506, § 93.

41 European Commission, Communication from the Commission to the European Parliament and the Council on guidance for better transposition and application of Directive 2004/38/EC on the right of citizens of the Union and their family members to move and reside freely within the territory of the Member States, 2 July 2009, COM (2009) 313 final, § 4.3.

exercise of free movement rights in another Member State and effectively terminating residence in that Member State for the purpose of completing an expulsion order? The criteria for retaining rights in a return situation would then simply be more lenient than the criteria for completing an expulsion order. This outcome is very well possible, because despite the comparability of the return situation and the completion of an expulsion, there is an important difference as well. Exercising free movement rights in another Member State to obtain family reunification rights is a voluntary movement that is not forced upon an EU citizen as a consequence of being an unreasonable burden on the social assistance system of a Member State, whereas an expulsion order is exactly that and thus involuntary. This difference could justify that the criteria to complete an expulsion order are stricter than the requirements for genuine and effective exercise of free movement rights in another Member State that warrants the retention of family reunification rights upon return to the home Member State.

5. Concluding remarks

The developments that were discussed in this chapter demonstrate that the understanding of free movement of persons is never finished. Each judgment lightens up another shadow in the landscape of EU law, but also reveals new blind spots, possible inconsistencies and new questions. The complexity that results thereof can be confusing, even troublesome. At the same time, this chapter is a reminder that EU law, despite its complexity, rests on principles and assumptions whose relevance is not confined to each individual case before the CJEU and can be relied on to discern parallels that bring the sometimes seemingly divergent cases back together. These parallels can reveal differences, even inconsistencies, in the Court's reasoning, which could call into question the soundness of the presumptions and logic of EU law. Simultaneously, however, they provide internal quality safeguards that allow to review a measure or interpretation of EU law in light of its own system, which – in the long term – benefits cross-fertilization and coherence within that system. The possibility of such internal review does not take away the need to also evaluate the interpretation of EU rights on the basis of norms external to the EU framework and overall fairness, but it does benefit the development, soundness and coherence of EU law as a whole.

References

Barnard, C. (2019). *The Substantive Law of the EU: The Four Freedoms*. Oxford University Press.

Costello, C. (2009). Metock: Free movement and "normal family life" in the Union. *Common Market Law Review*, *46*, 587. https://doi.org/10.54648/cola2009024

Guild, E. (2019). EU citizens, foreign family members and European Union Law. *European Journal of Migration and Law*, *21*(3), 358–373. https://doi.org/10.1163/15718166-12340055

Guild, E., Peers, S., & Tomkin, J. (2019). *The EU Citizenship Directive: A Commentary*. Oxford University Press. https://doi.org/10.1093/oso/9780198849384.001.0001

Hanf, D. (2011). Reverse discrimination in EU law: Constitutional aberration, constitutional necessity, or judicial choice? *Maastricht Journal of European and Comparative Law*, *18*, 29–61. https://doi.org/10.1177/1023263X1101800103

Kramer, D. (2021). On the futility of expelling poor union citizens in an open border Europe. *European Papers*, *1*, 155–165. https://doi.org/10.15166/2499-8249/459

Kroeze, H. (2020). Distinguishing Between Use and Abuse of EU Free Movement Law: Evaluating Use of the "Europe-Route" for Family Reunification to Overcome Reverse Discrimination. In N. Cambien, D. Kochenov, & E. Muir (Eds.), *European Citizenship Under Stress* (pp. 222–270). Brill Nijhoff. https://doi.org/10.15166/2499-8249/267

Neier, C. (2021). New clarifications on ending the union citizen's right of residence: The grand chamber decisions of the European court of justice of June 22, 2021 in C-718/19 and C-719/19. *European Papers*, *2*, 941–954. https://doi.org/10.15166/2499–8249/507

Ristuccia, F. (2022). "Cause tramps like us, baby we were born to run": Untangling the effects of the expulsion of "undesired" Union citizens: FS. *Common Market Law Review*, *59*, 889–914. https://doi.org/10.54648/cola2022056

Schoenmaekers, S., & Hoogenboom, A. (2014). Singh and Carpenter revisited: Some progress but no final clarity. *Maastricht Journal of European and Comparative Law*, *21*, 494.

Spaventa, E. (2015). Family rights for circular migrants and frontier workers: O. and B. (C-456/12) and S and G (Case C-457/12). *Common Market Law Review*, *52*, 753–777. http://dx.doi.org/10.2139/ssrn.2573688

Tryfonidou, A. (2009). *Reverse Discrimination in EC Law* (Vol. 64). Kluwer Law International BV.

Van Elsuwege, P. (2014). The Phenomenon of Reverse Discrimination: An Anomaly in the European Constitutional Order? In L. S. Rossi & F. Casolari (Eds.), *The EU After Lisbon, Amending or Coping with the Existing Treaties?* (pp. 161–176). Springer. https://doi.org/10.1007/978-3-319-04591-7_7

Verbist, V. (2017). *Reverse Discrimination in the European Union: A Recurring Balancing Act*. Intersentia.

9 Relationship triangle and the Citizens Directive

Does subsisting marriage exclude the access to derived residence of durable partners?

*Nicole Štýbnarová**

1 Introduction

The provisions allowing mobile EU citizens to be joined by their third-country national (TCN) or EU family members[1] are harmonized in the Citizens Directive (2004/38/EC). These provisions[2] extend the right to accompany a mobile EU citizen to their 'family members' spouses, registered partners (as defined in national provisions), children, and dependent parents' (Guild et al., 2019, p. 81). Additionally, the Directive's Article 3(2)b binds states to 'facilitate' in accordance with their national legislation the entry and residence of the 'partner with whom the Union citizen has a durable relationship, duly attested'.[3] These informal, durable partners are a sub-group of 'extended family members'.[4] As opposed to 'family members' (under Article 2(2)) whose stay must be allowed, member states possess considerable discretion in conditioning the stay of 'extended family members' (under Article 3(2)).[5] This discretion is reflected in the term 'facilitate' employed by the Directive in regard to extended family members, including informal partners. The meaning of 'facilitate' under the Directive was notably explained in the seminal *Rahman* case: member states should confer a certain advantage in entry and residence to informal partners of residing EU citizens over residing TCNs and their family members.[6]

This chapter turns to an under-analysed interpretative puzzle that the Citizens Directive does not address (Guild et al., 2019, p. 76): can TCNs claim to be in a 'durable relationship, duly attested' with an EU citizen, and qualify thus for derived residence rights, if they are formally married to someone else? This effectively

* I would like to thank Helena Wray, Saskia Bonjour, and Sanna Mustasaari for their incredibly helpful comments. All errors are my own.

1 While the Directive provides for derived residence rights of family members who are both third-country nationals and EU citizens, in practice EU citizens rarely use these provisions, due to the strong residence rights they possess by virtue of being EU citizens (Boeles et al., 2014, p. 74).

2 Article 2(2) Citizens Directive.

3 Article 3(2)b Citizens Directive.

4 Article 3(2) Citizens Directive.

5 The chapter will refer to persons under Article 3(2)b as durable or informal partners.

6 CJEU, 5 September 2012, C-83/11, *Rahman and Others*, ECLI:EU:C:2012:519.

DOI: 10.4324/9781003503217-12

is a question of how law can reflect (or refuse to reflect) situations which are not uncommon in social reality.

The Citizens Directive, as opposed to the Family Reunification Directive (2003/86/EC), does not explicitly authorize states to reject the stay of spouses in polygamous marriages[7] or to reject reunification of a couple in an informal durable relationship when one of them is married.[8] Although the European Commission advised in a guideline for the Citizens Directive that states might not recognize polygamous marriages,[9] the text of this Directive solely provides that both spouses and long-term partners are eligible for derived residence right and does not give a clear response to the situation where both (informal and matrimonial) relationships exist simultaneously (Guild et al., 2019, p. 36; Rogers et al., 2012, pp. 9–30). This chapter characterizes these situations as 'relationship triangles'. The term stands for all situations where a TCN has a durable relationship to an EU citizen which qualitatively belongs under Article 3(2) of the Citizens Directive, but at the same is married to someone else. In practice, this happens when the TCN has been cohabiting with a mobile EU citizen in an EU country and is meeting all other criteria of 'durable relationship' as articulated by case law of the Court of Justice of the European Union, and simultaneously is married in a third country.[10] The intensity of the marriage abroad can vary; this marriage can only exist on paper, or it can also be still functional in some ways.

The Citizens Directive foresees limitations to derived residence rights of durable partners on the bases of public policy, security, and health.[11] These must be invoked in response to individual conduct of the applicant which threatens one of these fundamental interests of the host society.[12] It is questionable whether these could extend to the 'relationship triangle' situations. The absence of an explicit rule gives potential flexibility to national courts adjudicating such cases.

This chapter thus discusses how the varying factual circumstances of the durable partnership and of the marriage can affect the assessment of claims for derived right of residence by these TCNs. The chapter proceeds as follows. Section 2 reviews systematically relevant case law of the European Court of Human Rights (ECtHR) and the Court of Justice of the European Union (CJEU) addressing cross-border legal protection of durable informal relationships, marriages, and family reunifications. Here the chapter teleologically revisits the Citizens Directive and concludes that durable couples receive discretionary access to derived residence

7 Article 4(4) Family Reunification Directive.

8 Article 16(1)c Family Reunification Directive.

9 European Commission, Communication from the Commission to the European Parliament and the Council on guidance for better transposition and application of Directive 2004/38/EC on the right of citizens of the Union and their family members to move and reside freely within the territory of the Member States, 2 July 2009, COM (2009) 313 final, p. 4.

10 It can also happen the other way around, when an EU citizen is formally married and cohabiting with a durable TCN partner, but the principles of assessment may differ from those discussed in this chapter.

11 Article 27 Citizens Directive.

12 Ibid.

in order to: 1) give a maximum deference to freedom of movement of EU citizens and 2) to respect family life in a broad sense. Section 3 then introduces different national transpositions (Feldman & Mazzechi, 2018) of the Directive in 12 EU countries and discusses the impact of the form of transposition on the possible assessment of access to derived residence by TCNs simultaneously married and in a durable relationship. This is followed by a review of cases of 'relationship triangle' adjudicated in the UK and Czechia. The overview focuses on two variables affecting the assessment of a 'relationship triangle': 1) the explicit definition of durable partner in the national transpositions as unmarried and 2) the status of EU citizen (acting as a sponsor) as mobile or static. Section 4 then summarizes that the national discretion in allowing residence of durable partners has limits linked to the twofold objective of the Citizens Directive and the established meaning of the term 'facilitation' as articulated in the relevant regulatory materials and CJEU case law.

The chapter argues that the national assessment of derived residence rights of durable partners should primarily focus on the length of cohabitation and intention to live together permanently (Peers et al., 2014, p. 209), rather than the formal impediment of ongoing marriage, and supports this substance-oriented approach by national case law.

Previous research argued that the marriage-based 'nuclear family' is understood to be a prime relationship qualifiable under the Citizens Directive for derived residence (Agoston et al., 2014, p. 7; Mustasaari, 2015, pp. 359–372) and that spouses, partners in informal relationships (McGlynn, 2005, p. 161; Staver, 2013, p. 73), and same-sex partnerships (Kochenov & Belavusau, 2019) are all subjected to different treatment under the Directive. Despite this evidenced effect, the chapter argues that neither the regulatory intention nor the subsequent interpretation by the CJEU point towards the primacy of marriage over informal relationships. Therefore, in 'relationship triangles' the two forms of family union should be arguably regarded as parallel rather than mutually exclusive. This argument also contributes to debates about the evidentiary weight of the form of the relationship and its substance in EU family reunification law (Mustasaari, 2015, p. 364). To this point, the chapter argues that the regulatory objective of the Citizens Directive can be applied to justify a substantive or a formal approach in different contexts. Finally, the chapter discusses whether this open-ended assessment of rights of durable partners leads to a diminished national migration control and explains how evidentiary requirements can be implemented to alleviate this concern.

2 Marriages and durable relationships in European case law and the Citizens Directive

The primary reason for the duty of states to 'facilitate' the stay of durable partners is to remove obstacles from EU citizens' freedom of movement.[13] Additionally,

13 Article 7(2) Citizens Directive; European Commission, Communication from the Commission to the European Parliament and the Council on guidance for better transposition and application of Directive 2004/38/EC on the right of citizens of the Union and their family members to move and reside freely within the territory of the Member States, 2 July 2009, COM (2009) 313 final, pp. 3–4.

durable partners were afforded a discretionary derived residence to maintain the unity of the family in a broad sense,[14] as required by the EU Charter of Fundamental Rights and the European Convention on Human Rights (ECHR).[15] The ECHR protects informal and de-facto family life under the rights to family life in its Article 8.

The CJEU repeatedly referred to the ECHR and the ECtHR's interpretation thereof as guiding in interpreting relevant provisions of EU law dealing with family life. For example, in *Home Department v. Rozanne Banger*,[16] the CJEU followed the ECtHR decision in *Schalk and Kopf v. Austria* to elaborate the scope of the term 'family'. According to the ECtHR the term 'is not confined to marriage-based relationships and may encompass other de-facto "family" ties where the parties are living together out of wedlock' in situations where children were born out of wedlock.[17] Protection under Article 8 of the ECHR thus extends to marriage and other genuine relationships irrespective of the lack of formalization.[18] Crucially, the Court asserted that, in the absence of legal recognition of family ties, long-term cohabitation can establish family life worth protection under the ECHR.[19]

As much as family life can exist even without formalization of the family bond and still require protection, the ECtHR argued that formal marriage without a 'fully developed' family life also deserves effective protection. For example, in the reunification case of *Abdulaziz and others v. the UK*, the ECtHR ruled that the term 'family' 'must at any rate include the relationship that arises from a lawful and genuine marriage . . . even if a family life of the kind referred to by the Government has not yet been fully established'.[20]

The ECtHR thus extended family life protection to informal relationships if they demonstrate the practice of close personal ties (measured by cohabitation, length of relationship, or demonstration of commitment to each other[21]), as well as to marriage without this substance, if concluded with genuine intentions. This extensive understanding should be appreciated all the more, given that Article 8 of the ECHR generally affords states a wide margin of appreciation,[22] especially in migration-related areas.[23]

14 Ibid., p. 4.
15 Ibid., p. 3.
16 Opinion of Advocate General Bobek in CJEU, 12 July 2018, C-89/17, *Rozanne Banger*, EU:C:2018:225, § 37.
17 ECtHR, 24 June 2010, *Schalk and Kopf v. Austria*, No. 30141/04, § 91 cited in Opinion of Advocate General Bobek in CJEU, 12 July 2018, C-89/17, *Rozanne Banger*, EU:C:2018:225, § 37.
18 ECtHR, 24 January 2017, *Paradiso and Campanelli v. Italy*, No. 25358/12.
19 ECtHR, 18 December 1986, *Johnston and Others v. Ireland*, No. 9697/82.
20 ECtHR, 24 April 1985, *Abdulaziz, Cabales and Balkandali v. The United Kingdom*, Nos. 9214/80, 9473/81 and 9474/81.
21 ECtHR, Guide on Article 8 of the European Convention on Human Rights, version of 31 December 2019, p. 58.
22 ECtHR, 15 December 2009, *Babiarz v. Poland*, No. 1955/10.
23 ECtHR, Guide on Article 8 of the European Convention on Human Rights, version of 31 December 2019, p. 49; ECtHR, 28 May 1985, *Abdulaziz, Cabales and Balkandali v. The United Kingdom* No. 9214/80, 9473/81 and 9474/81.

The CJEU's adjudication strikes some similarities in navigation between the evidentiary weight of form and substance of a relationship. For example, the *Diatta* case dealt with separated marriage of a TCN spouse with a mobile EU citizen. Because of this separation, the national authorities refused to extend Mrs Diatta's residence and her status of a family member of an EU worker. The CJEU argued that since spouses are allowed to join mobile EU citizens to allow their exercise of free movement, the provision cannot be interpreted restrictively, and therefore 'marital relationship cannot be regarded as dissolved so long as it has not been terminated by the competent authority' even if the spouses live separately and intend to divorce at a later date.[24] In this ruling, the CJEU found that even if the emotional ties and other durability elements of the marriage have diminished, the subsisting legal form can lead to a derived residence right. This broad understanding of reunification rights was linked to maximization of the facilitation of freedom of movement of working EU nationals[25] (Goldner Lang, 2008, p. 5; Weiler, 1992, p. 90), although the CJEU might also have chosen this interpretation to address the precariousness of the spouses' legal status under EU law (O'Leary & Iglesias Sánchez, 2021, p. 511).

The *Diatta* case tells that in observing the fundamental principle of free movement, both the form and the substance of a relationship have legal relevance. While this case focused on the weight of the form, another case, *Rozanne Banger*, dealt with the weight of the substance. Either is relevant under the logic of limiting dissuasion, meaning that the EU citizen would be discouraged from moving if those who are personally close to her were barred from joining her.[26] The deterrent might be sometimes stronger for a partner in a durable relationship than for a partner in marriage as 'with regard to who is effectively "close" to a person, formal box-based generalisations are hardly appropriate'.[27]

The CJEU also extended the objective to strengthen the right of freedom of movement to cases of EU citizens returning to their home state from another EU state (see also Kroeze, this volume). As such, national rejections of EU citizens' partners' residence based on the incompatibility of national and foreign legal provisions for forming the given relationship were quashed.[28] Rejections of a derived residence of informal partners of EU citizens must instead be based on an extensive examination of their personal circumstances, including the extent of economic or physical dependence and the degree of relationship between them.[29] These rejections must also respect the fundamental nature of freedom of movement of persons

24 Ibid., § 20.

25 CJEU, 13 February 1985, C-267/83, *Aissatou Diatta*, ECLI:EU:C:1985:67, §§ 15, 17 and 21.

26 Opinion of Advocate General Bobek in CJEU, 10 April 2018, C-89/17, *Rozanne Banger*, ECLI:EU:C:2018:225, § 37.

27 Ibid.

28 CJEU, 12 July 2018, C-89/17, *Rozanne Banger*, ECLI:EU:C:2018:570, § 29; CJEU, 5 June 2018, C-673/16, *Coman and Others*, ECLI:EU:C:2018:385.

29 CJEU, 5 September 2012, C-83/11, *Rahman and others*, ECLI:EU:C:2012:519, §§ 22–23; Opinion of Advocate General Bobek in CJEU, 10 April 2018, C-89/17, *Rozanne Banger*, ECLI:EU:C:2018:225, § 64.

within EU law.[30] While matters of public policy, safety, and health can under the Directive preclude derived residence rights of (extended) family members, these are under EU law conceptualized as impediments to freedom of movement rather than impediments to family unity[31] and must, therefore, be interpreted strictly.[32] This was argued by the CJEU in the *Coman* case preventing Romania to invoke public policy to reject recognition of a same-sex marriage formed during a freedom of movement–based stay in another member state.[33]

In the case of *Rozanne Banger*, the legal question was not the interpretation of public policy but of the term 'facilitate'. The UK legislation applied in this case (transposing the Citizens Directive) provided that UK citizens might reunify with spouses or registered partners[34] and did not mention durable partners at all. The CJEU ruled that even if, under the Citizens Directive, the obligation of states to facilitate reunification of informal partners is subject to discretion,[35] states cannot decide not to facilitate due to Article 21 TFEU, providing for freedom of movement of EU citizens. Because derived residence of informal partners can only be rejected based on 'an extensive examination of the applicant's personal circumstances and be justified by reasons',[36] states cannot reject it due to lacking formalization.[37] At further occasions, the CJEU asserted that the 'personal circumstances' to be examined are those of the informal relationship between the applicant and the sponsor.[38]

Although neither the ECtHR nor the CJEU directly addressed the implications of a subsisting marriage for the derived residence right of an informal partner, some principles inferred earlier in this chapter could be extended to such cases. First, both formal and informal family ties are worth legal protection. Second, marriage can, by the weight of its status, lead to derived residence rights of formal spouses even in the absence of a durable family life between them.[39] Notably, both courts

30 European Commission, Communication from the Commission to the European Parliament and the Council on guidance for better transposition and application of Directive 2004/38/EC on the right of citizens of the Union and their family members to move and reside freely within the territory of the Member States, 2 July 2009, COM (2009) 313 final, p. 3.

31 Article 27 Citizens Directive.

32 European Commission, Communication from the Commission to the European Parliament and the Council on guidance for better transposition and application of Directive 2004/38/EC on the right of citizens of the Union and their family members to move and reside freely within the territory of the Member States, 2 July 2009, COM (2009) 313 final, p. 3.

33 CJEU, 5 June 2018, C-673/16, *Coman and Others*, ECLI:EU:C:2018:385.

34 CJEU, 12 July 2018, C-89/17, *Rozanne Banger*, ECLI:EU:C:2018:570, § 12.

35 Article 3(2)b) Citizens Directive.

36 CJEU, 12 July 2018, C-89/17, *Rozanne Banger*, ECLI:EU:C:2018:570, § 41.

37 Ibid., §§ 27 and 41.

38 Opinion of Advocate General Bobek in CJEU, 12 July 2018, C-89/17, *Rozanne Banger*, EU:C:2018:225, § 66; CJEU, 5 September 2012, C-83/11, *Rahman and Others*, ECLI:EU:C:2012:519, § 23; European Commission, Communication from the Commission to the European Parliament and the Council on guidance for better transposition and application of Directive 2004/38/EC on the right of citizens of the Union and their family members to move and reside freely within the territory of the Member States, 2 July 2009, COM (2009) 313 final, p. 4.

39 This shall be distinguished from ingenuine marriage or marriage of convenience: Article 35 Citizens Directive.

argued this for different reasons. In *Abdulaziz and others* (ECtHR), the reasons were to fully respect the right for private and family life, considered together with the principle of non-discrimination. In the case of *Diatta* (CJEU), the reasons were to facilitate freedom of movement of workers in the EEC. This perceived evidentiary weight of formal status, however, does not automatically mean that the formal status of marriage can override existing aspects of durability and family life in other relationships, for example to exclude the latter from family reunification. This leads to the third principle, in the absence of formalization, de-facto family ties accordingly amount to what is required to protect family life (ECtHR)[40] and to what is required to prevent obstacles to freedom of movement and within that objective 'facilitate' residence of extended family members of EU citizens (CJEU).[41]

EU law further conditions these principles. As ruled in the cases of *Rozanne Banger* and *Coman*, the derived residence rights cannot be rejected with a mere reference to national provisions about the form of the relationship. Similarly, the invocation of public policy by national authorities in the *Coman* case[42] was dismissed by the CJEU,[43] as states are arguably not allowed to define public policy unilaterally, and any definition of public policy requires a genuine and sufficiently serious threat to a fundamental interest of society.[44]

These principles broadly apply to the 'relationship triangle' subject of this chapter. When national authorities assess if a TCN partner who is married and at the same time in a durable relationship with a mobile EU citizen can receive a derived residence right, they are limited by the aforementioned principles. The most salient limitation arguably arises from the meaning of 'duty to facilitate', which includes a duty to 1) assess the circumstances of the informal relationship and to 2) only reject derived residence rights upon 'an extensive examination of the applicant's personal circumstances'. If the national authority wished to reject derived residence for public policy reasons, it would have to demonstrate serious threat to fundamental interests of the society beyond incompatibility with national family law.

These are limits articulated by the CJEU and applicable to mobile EU citizens. Since multiple states (Guild, 2019, pp. 369–372) (as detailed in Section 3) extended their transposition of the Citizens Directive to static nationals (i.e. persons who have not made use of the freedom of movement), it is worthwhile to consider which of the listed principles apply when interpreting the transposed Directive's provisions in regard to them. Even where freedom of movement does not apply, state authorities must nevertheless adhere to the principle of respecting family life in a

40 ECtHR, 24 January 2017, *Paradiso and Campanelli v. Italy*, No. 25358/12, § 140.

41 CJEU, 12 July 2018, C-89/17, *Rozanne Banger*, ECLI:EU:C:2018:570, §§ 27 and 41.

42 CJEU, 5 June 2018, C-673/16, *Coman and Others*, ECLI:EU:C:2018:385, § 14.

43 A similar line of reasoning was earlier adopted by the ECtHR See ECtHR, 21 July 2015, *Oliari and others v. Italy*, Nos 18766/11 and 36030/11; ECtHR, 30 June 2016, *Taddeucci and McCall v. Italy*, No. 51362/09; ECtHR, 23 February 2016, *Pajić v. Croatia*, No. 68453/13.

44 CJEU, 5 June 2018, C-673/16, *Coman and Others*, ECLI:EU:C:2018:385, § 44.

broad sense, or de-facto family life as articulated by the ECtHR.[45] In such cases, the authorities can, in principle, attach more weight to the objective of effective control of migration in interpreting the applicability of public order, within the limits of ECtHR case law (Guild et al., 2019, p. 18). The following section shows that some national courts did not wish to use this enlarged leverage. This was not strictly due to human rights considerations, but rather due to a national internalization of the EU legal reasons behind including informal partners among beneficiaries of a derived residence rights and its implication for the evaluation of provided evidence.

3 National transposition and case law

As member states define and regulate informal partnerships differently in their domestic law (Boele-Woelki et al., 2015), the national transpositions of provisions on access to a derived residence right of durable partners under the Directive also vary (Wray et al., 2014; Feldman & Mazzechi, 2018). This section argues that the national transposition can make a difference in assessing the implications of formal marriage of TCNs for their derived residence rights as durable partners.[46] Where the transposition directly provides that the durable partner must be unmarried, no case law emerges to dispute the application of the law to 'relationship triangles'. When national transpositions extend to static nationals as well, then identical provisions as those in the Directive apply in these strictly domestic situations. However, since no use of the freedom of movement was made, the interpretative imperative of freedom of movement does logically not apply.

This section considers transpositions in several member states. Additionally, it considers case law on 'relationship triangles' from the UK and Czechia. These states did not directly specify in their transposition that a durable partner under Article 3(2)b of the Directive must generally be unmarried. The case law was selected to include a state with a definition of the term 'durable partner' which indirectly addresses possible co-existence with marriage (the UK) and a state with a less explicit definition (Czechia). Further, cases from these states were selected to combine 'relationship triangles' of static and mobile citizens to compare if these cases were evaluated differently when freedom of movement was technically at stake and when it was not.

To date, seven member states extended the personal scope of the transposed Directive to static citizens (Guild, 2019, pp. 369–372): Czechia, Spain, Estonia, Croatia, Italy, Sweden, and Slovenia. Other member states such as Belgium, Denmark, Poland, and the Netherlands treat their static nationals differently (and

45 ECtHR, Guide on Article 8 of the European Convention on Human Rights, version of 31 December 2019, §§ 171, 267.

46 Another comparison of the different transpositions could focus for example on the varying strength of the access right of durable partners. For example, in Belgian transposition, informal partners have the same right of access as spouses (Van den Bogaard et al., 2021, p. 93).

often less favourably) than mobile EU citizens (Guild, 2019, pp. 370–371). In spite of a formal extension to static nationals, the specificity of purely internal situations (D'Aoust, 2018, p. 181) implies that the original text of the Directive (including the regulatory intent to facilitate free movement) and case law of the CJEU (limiting the states' discretion) do not have to be considered when national courts assess static citizens' partners' claims. Nonetheless, even in cases of static nationals, courts must consider the other objective on which the Directive builds: the broad conception of respect for family life as arising from the ECtHR case law.

In transposition, states shall specify the national criteria for 'facilitation' of derived residence rights of durable partners.[47] As such, they can define durable partners in the national transposition legislation. When the national transposition provides that the partner or an EU citizen must be unmarried, it makes an important difference for adjudicating cases of 'relationship triangle'. For example, the Swedish transposition defines the durable (cohabiting) partner as someone unmarried.[48] In practice, this specification limits the ability of courts to reject derived residence rights of a durable partner based on individual circumstances of each relationship which, as elaborated earlier, is an interpretative principle put forward by the CJEU and the EU Commission. Cases of 'relationship triangles' would be automatically rejected in such legal frameworks.

Some other states enacted a mitigated version of this condition which balances the EU interest to facilitate residence of informal partners and the national interest to control migration. For example, the UK excluded access to derived residence by durable partners when a spouse, registered partner, or durable partner of the EU citizen or applicant is already residing in the UK and simultaneously that marriage, registered partnership, or durable partnership is subsisting.[49] Even though the UK's transposition addressed the matter of coexistence of a durable relationship and other forms of recognized partnership (typically marriage), it did not clarify whether a marriage of a durable partner with a spouse *not* residing in the territory precludes by its mere existence access to a derived residence right. The Home Department in the Upper Tribunal Case No. *IA/47006/2013* interpreted the provision strictly: 'this office will not accept that there is a durable relationship when any previous marriage has not broken down',[50] suggesting that derived residence of a formally married durable partner is not possible.

The case concerned a TCN residing in England as a durable partner of a mobile EU citizen. During the residence period at the occasion of airport immigration check, he disclosed to immigration officers that he visited his wife and children abroad. This information was then taken up later during his application for permanent residence after five years of residing as a durable partner of an EU citizen. The

47 Opinion of Advocate General Bobek in CJEU, 12 July 2018, C-89/17, ECLI:EU:C:2018:225, § 53.

48 European Parliament, Obstacles to the Right of Free Movement and Residence for EU Citizens: Country Report for Sweden, 2016, p. 21; Sambolag (2003, p. 376) in wording according to SFS 2011: 493, Section 1, 3 st.

49 The Immigration (European Economic Area) Regulations 2016, Regulation 2(1).

50 Upper Tribunal (Immigration and Asylum Chamber) Appeal Number: IA/47006/2013, § 2.

authorities alleged that the applicant was involved in polygamy and that residence which would effectively legitimize polygamy must be seen as illegitimate. However, the reviewing tribunal was less rigid in this case. It suggested that the religious marriage abroad would not have been recognized in the UK, and accordingly that the applicant did not marry the EU citizen, therefore equating the current situation to polygamy was erroneous.[51] The tribunal also clearly distinguished between assessing the durability of the relationship with the EU citizen and demanding that the previous marriage end in divorce:

> Judge erred in alighting on the issue of whether the Appellant had a divorce from his Pakistani wife but failed to address the more fundamental issue which is whether a religious marriage in Pakistan would have been recognised as a marriage in the UK and should have focused on the durability of the relationship [with the durable partner].[52]

The tribunal thus did not assume the question of divorce and of durability of the informal relationship to be mutually dependent, but rather it implied that while divorce from a previous marriage is not irrelevant, the question of durability of the present relationship is separate and a 'more fundamental issue'.

A similar approach was adopted by some Czech courts when assessing whether an ongoing marriage disqualifies a TCN from the status of durable partner according to Article 3(2)b of the Citizens Directive. The Czech transposition[53] of the Directive states that a family member of an EU citizen is a person that can prove that they have a durable partner relationship with an EU citizen other than marriage and that they share a common household; additionally, character, steadiness, and intensity of the relationship should be considered.[54] This provision thus reflects the authoritative interpretation of the term 'facilitate', as elaborated earlier.

However, it does not specify if the durable partner must be unmarried. Perhaps for that reason, there is a large volume of cases defined here as a 'relationship triangle' in Czechia. The large volume of cases also helps portray the possible variations of 'relationship triangles'. In some cases, the married partner's divorce was already pending and the informal relationship subject to the decision was well documented.[55] In other cases the informal relationship was less evident and the applicant's unwillingness to file for divorce was unexplained.[56] In one case, the divorce

51 Ibid., § 5, § 9.
52 Ibid., § 9.
53 Translations of Czech laws and arguments in case law in this chapter are the author's own.
54 Act No. 326/1999 Coll. on residence of foreigners in Czech Republic (Zákon č. 326/1999 Sb. O pobytu cizinců na území ČR), § 15a (2)b).
55 Cases No. 62 A 145/2015-59 (Regional Court in Brno); 9 A 22/2016–41 (Municipal Court in Prague).
56 Cases No. 10 A 43/2012-61 (Municipal Court in Prague); 4 Azs 151/2015–35 (Supreme Administrative Court).

abroad was legally impossible.[57] In another case, the applicant's first application for derived residence based on a marriage with a Czech citizen was dismissed since they were found to be separated; the applicant thus resubmitted his application to derived residence based on his new informal partnership with another Czech citizen (before filing for divorce).[58] In all the reviewed cases, the EU citizen was static but, as will be shown, the adjudication of Czech courts aligned with the reasoning of the English court applied to a mobile EU citizen.

In earlier cases of 'relationship triangles', Czech courts tended to understand the two relationships in the framework of the transposed Directive as mutually exclusive. The key argument was that if an ongoing marriage did not prevent getting residence as a durable partner, the public interest in effective exercise of migration control would be diminished and, therefore, this would threaten the public order.[59] These courts did not deal in depth with human rights' aspects, such as private and family life.[60]

A breakthrough decision came in 2015, when the Czech Supreme Administrative Court ruled that the sole existence of marriage cannot be seen as an absolute impediment to become a durable partner in the sense of the Directive.[61] Although this case also concerned a static EU citizen, the court referred to previous case law of the CJEU and the original text of the Citizens Directive to argue that the meaning of the term 'facilitate' (used in the transposed version accordingly) obliges national authorities to decide based on the personal circumstances of the couple.[62] The court continued that these criteria must be considered before the claim can be dismissed due to the formal impediment of an ongoing marriage with another person. It found that the previous case law which rejected durable partners' residence applications only because they were married erred by not addressing other relevant circumstances of the relationship between the EU citizen and the durable partner. Without considering the imperative of freedom of movement, the court thus interpreted the term 'facilitate' and its implications for relevant evidence similarly as the CJEU.

In later Czech cases, courts were presented with situations of applicants who had their reunification applications rejected based on the impediment of ongoing marriage, and this effectively meant that they could not claim reunification or derived residence at all, anywhere else. To illustrate, in one case, the TCN was married to a Czech citizen and resided as in Czechia as family member of this citizen. Later, he applied for extension of his residence; however, the application was rejected since they no longer shared a household. Consequently, he applied for a derived residence based on a new relationship formed in the previous year with

57 Case No. 15 A 135/2013-62 (Regional Court in Ústí nad Labem).

58 Case No. 15 A 32/2016-38 (Regional Court in Ústí nad Labem).

59 Case No. 62 A 145/2015-59 (Regional Court in Brno) § 27.

60 Ibid., § 32.

61 Case No. 4 Azs 151/2015-35 (Supreme Administrative Court).

62 Ibid., § 39.

his informal Czech partner while the applicant's marriage was subsisting. This was also rejected.

The reviewing court then argued that the sole existence of a marriage does not exclude the possibility of forming a durable relationship under Article 3(2)b of the Citizens Directive.[63] The evaluation of durable partnerships should arguably examine whether the relationship is actual (not just pro forma), regardless of its legal or formal status.[64] In this way, the court emphasized the Directive's objective of maintaining family unity in a broad sense (or de-facto family ties) and pushed for an independent position of informal partnerships in the portfolio of derived residence rights under the Directive. The informal relationship between the applicant and the EU partner was due to be evaluated regardless of the subsisting marriage.[65] Accordingly, the reasons why this marriage had not ended in divorce were important for the assessment of the durable relationship but should not be seen as impediments to its effectivity.[66] Similar principles were articulated by another court reviewing an administrative rejection of derived residence application by a TCN who could not end his subsisting marriage in his country of origin because this was legally impossible.[67]

Interestingly, neither the UK nor the Czech courts used the argument of free movement. This signals that both countries' courts understood informal durable couples' derived residence as separate from and parallel to derived residence of spouses, regardless of the migratory context. Informal partners' derived residence is arguably effective if their relationship is strong and committed, where formal ties with other persons are less important.

The UK residence rules for EU nationals ceased to function after Brexit. Nevertheless, for the present analysis, the argumentation of the English court provides a valuable perspective. This is precisely because the English court did not support its argumentation with freedom of movement (even though it could have) and instead argued based on its conceptual understanding of possible mutual exclusivity of marriage and durable relationship in the framework of derived residence rights under the Directive. This demonstrates that various national courts, regardless of freedom of movement, independently arrived at an interpretation of Article 3(2)b of the Directive (as transposed) in which marital status should not a priori exclude the possibility for durable partners of EU citizens to claim derived residence.

4 Synthesis of European principles and national approaches

As has been explained in Section 2, two important objectives determine the position of informal couples claiming access to derived residence under the Citizens Directive: not impeding free movement and maintaining family in a broad sense.

63 Case No. 15 A 32/2016-38 (Regional Court in Ústí nad Labem), § 22.
64 Ibid.
65 Ibid., § 24.
66 Ibid., § 12.
67 Case No. 15 A 135/2013-62 (Regional Court in Ústí nad Labem), § 2.

Doctrinal legal perspective to 'relationship triangle' situations would have one expect that these objectives have different relevance in adjudication involving static or mobile EU citizens. However, as shown earlier, national judicial approaches seem to accept the rationale behind strengthening residence rights of durable partners leading to separation of form from substance in 'relationship triangle' cases, irrespective if those are linked to freedom of movement.

In the logic of the CJEU, the emphasis on formal or substantial truth was fleeting, depending on which could in the given case pose an obstacle to freedom of movement (as shown in *Diatta, Coman,* and *Rozanne Banger*). The overarching principle of freedom of movement, which is understood as a fundamental right,[68] then explained why the Court sometimes emphasizes substantive (*Rozanne Banger*),[69] and other times formal (*Diatta*),[70] truth.[71]

In assessing a 'relationship triangle' involving a mobile EU citizen, the objective of facilitating free movement would accordingly be the key interpretative criterion. This, however, can fuel worries of diminishing migration control among the member states, as the CJEU case law would support applications of individuals in informal durable relationships as well as in separated marriages. However, as will be demonstrated later in this chapter, in such cases, states would not be forced to authorize residence of both durable partners and their legally subsisting spouses.

The situation which would worry states would be the following: TCN applicant A is a durable partner of mobile EU citizen B and simultaneously is formally married to C in a third country. The interpretative principles by the CJEU would give support to centralizing the aspect of 'closeness'[72] with its potential to defer free movement, and thus favour authorizing of A's residence as a durable partner. However, what could subsequently happen is that A's TCN spouse C could apply for reunification with A based on the principle articulated in *Diatta,* centring form over diminished substance. However, such a case would not anymore concern reunification with a mobile EU citizen, and the *Diatta* principle would no longer apply (instead this would be regulated by the Family Reunification Directive). In another situation, mobile EU citizens could theoretically serve as 'sponsors' to both TCN durable partners and TCN (separated) spouses. This, however, is slightly beyond the scope of this chapter, which focuses on the definition of durable partners with regard to their possible formal marriage (as opposed to co-existing durable relationship and marriage of EU citizen). Notably, in this later case, the CJEU's conflicting adjudication based on form and substance could lead to effectively diminishing states' migration control. This is, however, not the case if we apply principles based on form and substance jointly to interpret the definition of TCN durable partners.

68 CJEU, 13 February 1985, C-267/83, *Aissatou Diatta,* ECLI:EU:C:1985:67, § 13.

69 CJEU, 12 July 2018, C-89/17, *Rozanne Banger,* ECLI:EU:C:2018:570, § 41; Opinion of Advocate General Bobek in CJEU, 12 July 2018, C-89/17, *Rozanne Banger,* ECLI:EU:C:2018:570, § 37.

70 CJEU, 13 February 1985, C-267/83, *Aissatou Diatta,* ECLI:EU:C:1985:67, §§ 15, 18, 19 and 20.

71 For theoretical division of adjudicating based on form or substance, see, e.g., Kennedy (1976, p. 1777).

72 Opinion of Advocate General Bobek in CJEU, 12 July 2018, C-89/17, *Rozanne Banger,* ECLI:EU:C:2018:570, § 37.

A further principle identified in Section 2 is the limited discretion of member states in 'facilitating' the residence of durable partners. The national versions of 'facilitation', as argued earlier, should be based on the assessment of personal circumstances of the informal partnership. The case law, however, leaves the scope of 'personal circumstances' open to member states' discretion.[73] At the same time, the EU Commission constantly interprets 'personal circumstances' as factors of the relationship between the applicant and the sponsor, not factors of their relationships with other people. These include, for example, the length of relationship or joint mortgage[74] as well as economic and physical dependency.[75]

This does not mean that the marriage of the durable partner cannot be included among relevant 'personal circumstances', although it is a factor of relationship of one of the applicants with a third person. When the spouses are separated and the marriage exists only on paper, it will more likely present a circumstance in favour of facilitating the derived residence right of the TCN durable partner. Additionally, the CJEU continuously stresses that the evaluation of personal circumstances of the durable partnership must be 'extensive', and therefore, 'it is incumbent upon the competent authority to take into account various factors that may be relevant in the particular case'.[76] In this interpretation, the marriage of the applicant cannot, as a sole factor, automatically overrule other relevant factors, or even prevent those from being evaluated. This was accordingly understood in the reviewed national cases.

The condition that personal circumstances must be evaluated also delimits the discretion of the member states in defining the scope of facilitation. National transposition legislation automatically excluding married durable partners (such as in Sweden) might not comply with the CJEU's interpretation of the term 'facilitation' if challenged by a mobile EU citizen. In light of the prime interpretative principle to strengthen freedom of movement, such transposition might prove incompliant, especially in cases when divorce is impossible, as discussed in Section 3.

This defined scope of evaluation of personal circumstances has procedural implications on the applicants' burden of proof and the duty to duly attest the durable relationship.[77] Accordingly, the EU Commission in listing possible evidentiary requirements to attest durable relationships asserted that the couple can be asked to present documents attesting that they are partners and that their partnership is

73 CJEU, 5 September 2012, C-83/11, *Rahman and Others*, ECLI:EU:C:2012:519, § 24; CJEU, 12 July 2018, C-89/17, *Rozanne Banger*, ECLI:EU:C:2018:570, § 40.

74 European Commission, Communication from the Commission to the European Parliament and the Council on guidance for better transposition and application of Directive 2004/38/EC on the right of citizens of the Union and their family members to move and reside freely within the territory of the Member States, 2 July 2009, COM(2009) 313 final, p. 4.

75 CJEU, 5 September 2012, C-83/11, *Rahman and Others*, ECLI:EU:C:2012:519, § 23.

76 CJEU, 12 July 2018, C-89/17, *Rozanne Banger*, ECLI:EU:C:2018:570, §39; CJEU, 5 September 2012, C-83/11, *Rahman and Others*, ECLI:EU:C:2012:519, § 23.

77 Article 3(2)b) Citizens Directive.

durable.[78] It did not suggest that the couple should be asked to disprove their relationships with others, as their sole burden of proof relates to the durability of the relationship between themselves. This does not mean that they cannot be asked to present documents relating to their relationships with third parties; however, if they fail to disprove other relationships, this should not bear more relevance than their evidencing of the durable relationship at stake. This interpretation, ensuing from the text of the Directive and the subsequent guidelines, was formulated by the Czech courts in cases of static citizens.[79] In simple words, the biggest evidentiary weight shall not be attached to evidence which is at the penumbra of the applicants' evidentiary duty.

Finally, a decision arguing that ongoing marriage impedes the possibility of the formation of a durable relationship for the purpose of residence might draw from a perceived legal superiority of marriage over informal relationship. This might be understood based on the differentiation in the Directive itself (formulation that 'the right to exercise free movement is granted' in Article 2(2) v. 'facilitate' in Article 3(2)). The *travaux préparatoires*, however, suggest that establishing a hierarchy of reunification entitlements of EU citizens was not the objective behind the different formulations. The documents mention that the sole objective was to give informal partners access to reunification without imposing changes in national legislations.[80] This is supported further by the CJEU's interpretation in the *Rahman* case, stating that 'facilitation' should not be read as implying the inferiority of EU citizens' informal relationships to marriages, but rather it should be understood as establishing the superiority of informal relationships of EU citizens to those of TCNs.[81]

Therefore, there is no evidence for such teleological interpretation. On the contrary, the relationship between marriage and durable partnership under the Citizens Directive is parallel. The AG in *Rozanne Banger* explicitly noted that preceding case law strengthening the position of married couples in situations of returning EU citizens should not automatically be 'interpreted as an intention to limit that case-law solely to "family members"' and that 'the considerations that led the court to an application by analogy of the rights of entry and residence of family

78 European Commission, Communication from the Commission to the European Parliament and the Council on guidance for better transposition and application of Directive 2004/38/EC on the right of citizens of the Union and their family members to move and reside freely within the territory of the Member States, 2 July 2009, COM(2009) 313 final, p. 4.

79 Case No. 15 A 32/2016-38 (Regional Court in Ústí nad Labem), § 22; 4 Azs 151/2015-35 (Supreme Administrative Court).

80 European Commission, Communication from the Commission to the European Parliament pursuant to the second subparagraph of Article 251 (2) of the EC Treaty concerning the common position of the Council on the adoption of a European Parliament and Council Directive on the right of citizens of the Union and their family members to move and reside freely within the territory of the Member States, 30 December 2003, SEC(2003) 1293 final- COD 2001/0111, p. 9.

81 CJEU, 5 September 2012, C-83/11, *Rahman and Others*, ECLI:EU:C:2012:519, § 21.

members under Article 2(2) of the Directive . . . are equally applicable to "extended family members" under Article 3(2)'.[82]

This circles back to the overarching interpretative principle of strengthening the right to free movement, which rests on the potential of a relationship to deter free movement and, as such, relativizes the status of marriage in relation to informal partnerships. In the words of the AG the main aspect of the assessed relationship is closeness, which 'might in reality be stronger with regard to a partner under Article 3(2) of the Directive . . . than it is perhaps with regard to some of the categories listed in Article 2(2)'.[83] Thus, the assessment of a durable partnership–derived residence, when marriage of the TCN subsists, should not be limited to finding a formal legal incompatibility, and arguing that valid marriage abroad excludes the possibility of becoming a durable partner under Article 3(2)b of the Directive.

In the cases of static EU citizens, domestic courts do not have to consider the teleology of EU legal instruments, nor the associated interpretation of EU institutions. It would thus be doctrinally expected that in cases of mobile citizens, courts will use freedom of movement as an argument, and that in cases of static citizens courts will rely on human rights principles and relevant ECHR case law. As demonstrated, none of the reviewed courts followed these expectations.[84] The argumentation of Czech courts centred on the understanding of the applicants' burden of proof and the corresponding hierarchy of evidence based on the transposed provisions of the Directive. Since none of the courts referred to freedom of movement in their interpretation, they regarded the derived residence of durable partners to depend essentially on the durability of the relationship, rather than on the subsisting formal status of a simultaneous marriage.

5 Conclusions

The 'relationship triangle' cases are not addressed in the Citizens Directive, which is perhaps why such cases appear before domestic courts. One of the general principles, inferred from the case law of the ECtHR and the CJEU, is that both formal and informal family ties require respect from the state. Both the CJEU and the ECtHR held that even when the marriage lacks durability, it can by the weight of its status effectuate family reunification or a derived residence right. The access to residence of a married TCN in a durable informal relationship with an EU citizen might at first sight, therefore, appear to be weakened by the valid marital status.

However, the term 'facilitation' in the Citizens Directive binds states to assess the residence rights of durable partners of mobile EU citizens based primarily on the circumstances of the durable partnership (as opposed to the circumstances of their relationships with other people). This evaluation, according to the CJEU, must

82 Opinion of Advocate General Bobek in CJEU, 12 July 2018, C-89/17, *Rozanne Banger*, ECLI:EU:C:2018:570, §§ 35 and 46.

83 Ibid., § 37.

84 4 Azs 151/2015-35 (Supreme Administrative Court); Upper Tribunal, (Immigration and Asylum Chamber) Appeal Number: IA/47006/2013, § 9.

be extensive and consider various factors. It thus cannot depend on one aspect only, the formal status. This meaning of 'facilitation' implies that the formal marriage of the TCN can be considered as one aspect in the evaluation but is less fundamental and should not automatically trump other aspects of the relationship between the durable partners. This understanding might even suggest that national transpositions defining durable partners as unmarried (e.g., in Sweden) might transgress the discretion afforded by the Directive, since they impose an a priori condition, allowing the authorities to reject residence of married durable partners without investigating the circumstances of the durable relationship.

The aspect of durability should thus bear the most weight in the assessment of the residence of durable partners of mobile EU citizens. This does not conflict with the principles articulated in the CJEU's case of *Diatta*, emphasizing the effects of a formal marriage, as both approaches stem from the same objective: to provide a maximum deference to free movement. As demonstrated in Section 4, accentuating formal aspects in cases of marriage and substantive aspects in cases of durable relationship will not reduce the national powers of migration control.

According to the doctrine, whether the EU citizen acting as a sponsor is mobile or static matters for the assessment of the TCN's derived residence right. However, the review of national case law showed that irrespective of the relevance of freedom of movement, the courts' decisions hinged primarily on the durability of the relationship. This is because the national courts understood that both the Directive and its national transpositions constitute durable partners' residence right as autonomous and dependent dominantly on due attestation of the relationship. The courts thus understood the durable partners' duty to 'duly attest' to extend primarily to the relationship subject to the derived residence right, rather than other coexisting relationships. Evidence pertaining to the coexisting formal relationship is not irrelevant and may help or impair the assessment. At the same time, these aspects are not central to the assessment, and the national courts agreed that their impact is somewhat limited if the durable relationship itself can be duly attested.

References

Boeles, P., den Heijer, M., Lodder, G., & Wouters, K. (2014). *European Migration Law*. Intersentia.

Boele-Woelki, K., Mol, C., & van Gelder, E. (Eds.). (2015). *European Family Law in Action. Vol. V: Informal Relationships*. Intersentia.

D'Aoust, A. M. (2018). Family Migration and Membership. In A. Weinar, S. Bonjour, & L. Zhyznomirska (Eds.), *The Routledge Handbook of the Politics of Migration in Europe* (pp. 179–189). Routledge.

Feldman, T., & Mazzechi, M. (2018). Durable relationship and family members by analogy in the European Union. *Review of European Studies*, *10*(4), 175–182. https://doi.org/10.5539/res.v10n4p175

Goldner Lang, I. (2008). Family reunification of European community nationals. *Croatian Yearbook of European Law and Policy*, *1*, 163–202. www.cyelp.com/index.php/cyelp/article/view/6

Guild, E. (2019). EU citizens, foreign family members and European Union law. *European Journal of Migration and Law*, *21*(3), 358–373. https://doi.org/10.1163/15718166-12340055

Guild, E., Peers, S., & Tomkin, J. (2019). General Provisions. In E. Guild, S. Peers, & J. Tomkin (Eds.), *The EU Citizenship Directive: A Commentary* (2nd ed., pp. 18–86). Oxford University Press. https://doi.org/10.1093/oso/9780198849384.001.0001

Kennedy, D. (1976). Form and substance in private law adjudication. *Harvard Law Review*, *89*(8), 1685–1778. https://doi.org/10.2307/1340104

Kochenov, D., & Belavusau, U. (2019). *Same-sex spouses in the EU after Coman: More free movement, but what about marriage?* (EUI Working Paper Law, 2019/03, pp. 1–18). https://hdl.handle.net/1814/64525

McGlynn, C. (2005). Family reunion and the free movement of persons in European Union law. *International Law FORUM Du Droit International*, *7*(3), 159–166. https://doi.org/10.1163/157180405774579974

Mustasaari, S. (2015). The "nuclear family paradigm" as a marker of rights and belonging in transnational families. *Social Identities*, *21*(14), 359–372. https://doi.org/10.1080/13504630.2015.1071699

O'Leary, S., & Iglesias Sánchez, S. (2021). Free Movement of Persons and Services. In P. Craig & G. de Búrca (Eds.), *The Evolution of EU Law* (3rd ed., pp. 506–545). Oxford University Press. https://doi.org/10.1093/oso/9780192846556.003.0016

Peers, S., Hervey, T., Kenner, J., & Ward, A. (2014). *The EU Charter of Fundamental Rights: A Commentary*. Hart Publishing.

Rogers, N., Scannell, R., & Walsh, J. (2012). *Free Movement of Persons in the Enlarged European Union*. Sweet & Maxwell.

Sambolag. (2003). Wording according to SFS 2011.

Staver, A. (2013). Free movement and the fragmentation of family reunification rights. *European Journal of Migration and Law*, *15*(1), 69–89. https://doi.org/10.1163/15718166-12342024

Van den Bogaard, R. et al. (2021). *Moving to Belgium as an EU citizen: Registration formalities for EU workers, self-employed persons, jobseekers and their family members in Belgium, with a comparative outlook*. Myria.

Weiler, J. (1992). Thou shalt not oppress a stranger: On the judicial protection of the human rights of non-EC nationals – a critique. *European Journal of International Law*, *3*(1), 65–91. https://doi.org/10.1093/oxfordjournals.ejil.a035808

Wray, H., Agoston, A., & Hutton, J. (2014). A family resemblance? The regulation of marriage migration in Europe. *European Journal of Migration and Law*, *16*(4), 209–247. https://doi.org/10.1163/15718166-12342054

10 The 'humanitarian' clause of the Dublin III Regulation

Limiting entrance, gatekeeping values

Ifigeneia Intzipeoglou and Maria Nefeli Skotori

1. Dublin design and development: Dublin III, the instrument

1.1 Introduction

Family is at the heart of personal and social life. Family serves as the foundation upon which human beings depend for their emotional, social and financial needs; its importance is recognised under international law as a human right. Unsurprisingly, the forced separation of family members – frequent in a refugee context – has a detrimental impact on the mental and physical health of those affected. In Europe, Article 8 of the European Convention on Human Rights (ECHR) and Article 7 of the European Union's Charter of Fundamental Rights (Charter) dictate the respect for private and family life. EU countries not only have the negative obligation not to separate families but they may, in specific circumstances, further have a positive obligation to allow family reunification in their territory.[1] The Dublin III Regulation (2013/604/EU) reflects this positive obligation for applicants for international protection within Europe (Guild et al., 2014, p. 14). Equally, it is one of the very few existing legal pathways for asylum seekers to move from one EU Member State to another.

In this chapter, we will engage with Article 17(2) that enshrines humanitarian and cultural considerations in the Dublin III Regulation. We will explore the manner that this so-called humanitarian clause has been applied to cases of family reunification with extended family members, relatives suffering from serious health issues and families separated after their arrival on EU soil. Admittedly, Article 17(2) is part of a discretionary clause allowing the Member States of the EU the choice of acceptance in take-charge requests under this provision. Subsequently, we will comment that according to multiple actors, including the United Nations High Commissioner for Refugees (UNHCR), this Article has received a very limited application, with countries like Germany and the United Kingdom rejecting almost the totality of the take charge requests made through Article 17(2). In line with other institutional accounts (Peers, 2012) reviewing the limited application

1 CJEU, 27 June 2006, C-540/03, *Parliament v. Council*, ECLI:EU:C:2006:429, § 54.

DOI: 10.4324/9781003503217-13

of Article 17(2) as a 'missed opportunity', we argue that the rejection of Article 17(2) claims reflects States' attitudes towards mutual 'burden-sharing'. Further, we propose that Article 17(2) case law mirrors institutional *juris-inertive* Western attempts to insulate the cultural coherence (Engelbert, 2019, p. 139) of the 'Euro-fortress' (Kincheloe & Steinberg, 1997, p. 6) against 'foreign', Other familial values and relational practices (Meissner & Heil, 2021).

1.1.1 Dublin III: general mechanisms

The Dublin III Regulation is not an instrument of family reunification per se. Instead, it determines which EU Member State is responsible for assessing an applicant's asylum claim (Garlick, 2016). Chapter III of the Regulation provides the criteria for a Member State to become responsible for examining the application for international protection of an asylum seeker anywhere in the Union when they have family legally residing in that Member State. In case the applicant is an adult, only spouses and minor children are considered family members. When the applicant is an unaccompanied minor, given their vulnerability, the family circle is widened to include parents, siblings, aunts, uncles and grandparents (Article 2, points g–h and Article 8). Family members need to be recognised beneficiaries of international protection or applicants for international protection to benefit from the binding Dublin family reunification procedure according to Chapter III (Articles 9 and 10).

The regular procedure for family reunification under the Dublin III Regulation can be summarised as follows: If a Member State, the 'requesting Member State', where an applicant has lodged their asylum claim finds out that they have family members within the notion of the Dublin III Regulation as outlined earlier, it has three months to submit a *take-charge* request to the Member State where this family member resides under Articles 8–10 of the Regulation. The 'receiving Member State' has to examine if the criteria of the Regulation are met in the next two months, and if so, it is bound to accept the request. Then, the asylum seeker should be transferred to the Member State where their family member resides to have their asylum application assessed there. The Dublin system was designed to be a quick, straightforward process, adhering to strict timelines and reuniting family members before the applicant's asylum claim is assessed. However, it is widely accepted that in practice, it is riddled with complications: disregard for time limits, lack of access to legal aid, and triggering rebuttals for safety and compliance presumptions in Member States deemed unsafe for asylum applicants upon reception (see, for example, the *N.S.* judgement of 2011;[2] see also Schmalz, 2021, p. 363).

2 CJEU, 21 December 2011, C-411/10 and C-493/10, *N.S. and M.E. and Others*, ECLI:EU:C:2011:865, §§ 77–86.

1.1.2 The Article 17(2) mechanism: explaining and chronicling Article 17(2)

As part of the sovereignty and humanitarian discretionary clauses of Chapter IV, Article 17(2) of the Dublin Regulation allows EU Member States to choose to derogate from the binding rules of responsibility determination enshrined in Chapter III and reunite applicants that hold any kind of familial or communal relations. This derogation is possible 'on humanitarian grounds based in particular on family or cultural considerations'; these terms are not defined in the Regulation, leaving a wide margin of appreciation when the EU Member States examine this clause. In addition, Article 17(2) is provided with a longer time frame for its realisation than the other Dublin procedures in an attempt to balance its optional character. A *take-charge* request during the family reunification procedure on this basis can be sent 'at any time before a first decision regarding the substance is taken' contrary to the three-month limit applied to family reunification procedures based on the binding articles in Chapter III.

The derogation being possible 'on humanitarian grounds based in particular on family or cultural considerations' has straightforwardly been the case since its predecessor, Article 9 of the Dublin I Regulation[3] ('for humanitarian reasons, based in particular on family or cultural grounds'), carrying on to Dublin II[4] Article 15. While Dublin I presents the case for a rather short humanitarian clause, Dublin II presents an extended model, including considerations 'on account of pregnancy or a newborn child, serious illness, severe handicap or old age', as well as for unaccompanied minors in paragraphs 2 and 3. These considerations identify the need for the asylum seeker in the aforementioned circumstances to be reunited 'with another relative present in the territory of one of the Member States' (para. 2), under the condition that the family ties were pre-existing in the country of origin. In the case of unaccompanied minors, such reunification was additionally conditional to the 'best interests of the minor' (para. 3). However, it is worth noting that even in Dublin III, the characteristic terms ('humanitarian grounds', 'family or cultural considerations') are not defined within the Regulation, allowing for a wide margin of appreciation for the EU Member States examining the clause.

An interesting feature that exhibits significant development is the provisions in case of request refusal: Dublin I Article 9 did not provide a specific procedure for such a case. Dublin II Article 15(5) provided that 'conciliation mechanisms for settling differences between Member States concerning the need to unite the persons in question or the place where this should be done, shall be adopted in accordance with the procedure', presumably in the case of examining the grounds for refusal or

3 Convention Determining the State Responsible for Examining Applications for Asylum lodged in one of the Member States of the European Communities ('Dublin Convention'), 15 June 1990, OJ C 254.

4 Council Regulation (EC) No. 343/2003 establishing the criteria and mechanisms for determining the Member State responsible for examining an asylum application lodged in one of the Member States by a third-country national, 18 February 2003, OJ L 50/1-50/10.

deciding based on the applicant's best interests. The 'procedure' referenced earlier is the regulatory and safeguard procedure set out by Articles 5 and 7 of the 1999 Comitology Decision.[5] Article 17(2) of Dublin III presumably abandons its predecessor's conciliatory nature and specifies that 'a reply refusing the request shall state the reasons on which the refusal is based', in favour of receiving clear grounds that could be potentially useful for judicial review.

2. The use of Article 17(2): the numbers

2.1 Article 17(2) requests

In its conception, Article 17(2) was welcomed by the UNHCR and civil society organisations as a way for EU Member States to mitigate some of the injustices of the Regulation as applied and to facilitate the reunification of families and communities (UNHCR, 2017, p. 129). Unfortunately, in practice, Article 17(2) has been rarely used by EU Member States. For example, according to Eurostat data, in 2018, a total of 1,060 take-charge requests were issued on the basis of Article 17(2) of the Regulation, which accounted for no more than 0.7% of all Dublin procedures initiated that year (European Parliament Research Service, 2020, p. 64). Over 75% of those emanated from Greece, far ahead of other countries. Its limited use continued well into the next years, always championed by Greece, followed by Malta.

Take-charge requests on the basis of Article 17(2) have often been issued on the following occasions:

1 Materiality: Primarily, for cases of vulnerable family members who fall outside the family criteria of Chapter III (European Parliament Research Service, 2020, p. 52). Non-refugee sponsors: in cases when the sponsors hold a status outside international protection rules. Since the Dublin III Regulation is a legal instrument designed to allocate the responsibility for examining applications for international protection among EU Member States, priority is given to family reunification of asylum seekers and recognised refugees of Chapter III, as mentioned earlier. Thus, reuniting asylum seekers with members of their families that hold subsidiary protection status, migratory residence permits or even citizenship fall outside of the Regulation's scope; therefore, it is left to the discretion of EU Member States to accept them.

2 Temporality:

   a. A large number of requests to take charge are taking place when the three-month deadline for sending a take-charge request has expired for familial relationships that would otherwise fall under one of the non-discretionary articles

5 Council Decision laying down the procedures for the exercise of implementing powers conferred on the Commission, 28 June 1999, 1999/468/EC. This Decision disabled the Council from dismissing a proposal by simple majority (Article 5) and increased transparency for Commission activities (Article 7); this era of EU reforms brought about attempts at achieving a power shift between the Commission and Council implementing powers and implementation of legislation in specific cases.

of the Regulation. This scenario entails the failure of the competent asylum authorities of the requesting Member State to send the take-charge request on time. Recent practice of the authorities of certain receiving Member States, especially Germany, have posed an added burden to meet the time limit criterion for outgoing family reunification requests. Following the publication of the decision in *Tsegezab Mengesteab* in 2017,[6] the Dublin Units in receiving Member States adopted an interpretation that all outgoing requests should be made within the three-month deadline counting from the moment an applicant expressed their intention to seek international protection before any authority of the requesting Member State. The novelty of the interpretation was that until then the three-month time limit started counting from the moment of the lodging of the application for international protection before the competent national authorities of the requesting Member States which were linked with the national Dublin Units. In Greece, this led asylum seekers with close family members in Germany to miss the relevant time limit since the wish to apply for international protection is expressed before the police. Hence, it can take several months or up to a year for the application to be fully registered by the Asylum Service and be brought to the attention of the competent Dublin Unit, all while the time limit has been surpassed and the discretionary article of the Regulation should be employed (AIDA, 2022, p. 73).

b. Article 17(2) has been widely used for cases of subsequent separation, i.e., when members of nuclear families travel together into the soil of the EU and then some family members decide to continue their journey to other European countries either before or after the family has lodged their application for international protection (AIDA, 2023, p. 76).

3 Special cases: in extremely rare circumstances, Article 17(2) was used to request the reunification of members of minorities with their communities in other Member States, as in the case of the Mandean people in Spain who rejoined their larger community present in Germany (UNHCR, 2017, p. 130). Recently, the discretionary clause in Article 17(2) was used as the legal basis for ad hoc voluntary relocation schemes of migrants saved at sea to other EU countries, following their disembarkation in Italy and Malta, the so-called Messina model supported by the then European Asylum Support Office (EASO, 2019). Last but not least, it is also reported that during the pandemic, the humanitarian provision was used as an additional basis for accepted take-charge requests that have missed the six-month transfer deadline due to Covid-19 travel restrictions in order for the procedure to be re-activated again (AIDA, 2021, p. 80).

2.2 The outcomes of Article 17(2) requests

If the number of cases requesting reunification based on Article 17(2) is very low, then the rate of acceptance of these claims seems even more disheartening. According to civil society organisations from Greece – the country in which, as already

6 CJEU, 26 July 2017, C-670/16, *Tsegezab Mengesteab*, ECLI:EU:C:2017:587.

mentioned, the humanitarian clause is employed most frequently – in the period 2020–2021, 80% of Article 17(2) cases were rejected contrary to 20% of cases rejected when submitted on the bases of the binding articles of the Regulation (FENIX, 2021, p. 6). These data seem to coincide with the ones published by the Greek Asylum Service for 2020, where from the 3,740 relevant cases, only 683 were accepted, a percentage of roughly 18% (AIDA, 2021, p. 80). No official data specifically for Article 17(2) procedures have been provided from the Greek Asylum Service in the following years, but since the application of the Article has remained the same no significant changes can be expected (AIDA, 2023, p. 72).

There are certain factors frequently reasoned when deciding upon rejecting an Article 17(2) take-charge request. The main reason why requests for applying the humanitarian clause are refused is reportedly linked to the different evidentiary requirements among Member States to establish family links or a relationship of dependency. According to Article 16 of the Dublin III Regulation, pregnant women, newborn children, elderly people and sufferers of serious illness and severe disability that are dependent on their children, siblings or parents shall be brought together by Member States provided that family ties existed in the country of origin and the family members are able to take care of the dependent person. It should be noted, though, that a relationship of dependency is not a requirement for the application of Article 17(2) under the Dublin Regulation. Nevertheless, the majority of Member States arbitrarily use it as an additional prerequisite for applying it (UNHCR, 2017, p. 131).

Another usual justification for the rejection of these cases is that 'there are not enough humanitarian grounds', a verbatim quote from rejections received by the Greek Dublin Unit (FENIX, 2021, pp. 19–20). In these cases, following a rejection, there is little more that can be presented beyond re-emphasising the extent of the dependency or providing further arguments to justify the gravity of the humanitarian situation of the applicants during a re-examination request. As a result, disputes regarding the applicability of the humanitarian clause can at times lead to lengthy negotiations between the Dublin Units of different Member States concerned before a conclusion is reached, contrary to the spirit of the Regulation.

The common requests for re-examination of cases of Article 17(2) of the Regulation have caused the Dublin Units of certain Member States to adopt a new practice in order to reject these cases more swiftly, citing an interpretation of judgement *X and X*.[7] In these cases, the Court of Justice of the European Union (CJEU) ruled through the preliminary question procedure that requested Member States should answer re-examinations of take-charge requests within two weeks, otherwise the requesting Member States become responsible for the applicants. The Court noted that this strict time limit is compatible with the objective of the Dublin III Regulation for rapidly processing applications for international protection when the same applicant has applied in more than one Member State and encouraged them to engage in sincere cooperation by promptly re-examining such requests.

7 CJEU, 13 November 2018, C-47/17 and C-48/17, *X and X*, ECLI:EU:C:2018:900.

However, according to information provided by the Greek Dublin Unit, the authorities of many receiving Member States implemented this ruling to mean that only one re-examination request for each case is accepted starting in 2020, even though this is not mentioned anywhere in the CJEU's judgement and, on the whole, it concerned a different Dublin procedure than family reunification. It has been observed that many re-examination requests concerning cases under Article 17(2) remain intentionally unanswered by receiving Member States for a period exceeding the two-week time limit, and a final response rejecting any further examination usually comes only after a reminder is sent by the Greek authorities (AIDA, 2021, p. 76, 2023, p. 72).

3. The use of Article 17(2): jurisprudence

3.1 Supranational courts

It goes without saying that given the limited use that the humanitarian clause has received from Member States, there is not an extensive jurisprudence from supranational courts handling its application. The European Court of Human Rights (ECtHR) has not yet dealt with a case that explicitly concerns family reunification on humanitarian grounds as contained in Article 17(2) of the Dublin III Regulation. When it comes to the CJEU, two cases are worth noting, in our opinion. Although they do not deal directly with Article 17(2) of the Regulation, they provide useful conclusions for its application. Recently, in the decision *M.A & others* of 2019,[8] the Court reiterated that the wording of Article 17 of the Dublin III Regulation generally supports an approach that the exercise of the discretionary clause is entirely optional for Member States.

In a previous decision concerning Dublin II known as *K. v. Bundesasylamt* (2012),[9] the notion of humanitarian grounds was examined based on Article 15 of the Dublin II Regulation, which provided that only dependent people could be reunited with family members based on humanitarian grounds and cultural considerations, contrary to the current form of Article 17(2) of the Dublin III Regulation. In its ruling, the EU Court interpreted, inter alia, that family reunification on humanitarian grounds can include the reunification of a grandmother with her daughter-in-law and grandchildren in the notion of relatives and noted that the person who is found in a difficult humanitarian situation can be the one in the receiving state. The Court underlined that given the possibility for Member States to derogate from the binding articles of the Regulation, such a derogation can be justified only if an exceptional humanitarian situation has arisen. In the present case, it did find that the sickness and disability of the daughter-in-law and her inability to care for her minor children constituted an exception that could justify the presence of her mother-in-law in the same Member State to support her. Nevertheless, it was a very

8 CJEU, 23 January 2019, C-661/17, *M.A & others*, ECLI:EU:C:2019:53.
9 CJEU, 6 November 2012, C-245/11, *K.*, ECLI:EU:C:2012:685.

narrow interpretation which did not allow room for replication in other cases and the Court did not provide additional criteria or examples as to which circumstances create adequate humanitarian grounds for discretionary family reunification. Given that Article 17(2) of the Dublin III Regulation no longer calls for the dependency of family members who wish to be reunited, the notion of humanitarian grounds still remains largely undefined by the CJEU.

3.2 Domestic courts

National court decisions in receiving Member States have produced mixed results when dealing with family reunification cases based on the humanitarian clause in the Dublin III Regulation. As mentioned earlier, the majority of take-charge requests were sent to Germany and the United Kingdom before departing from the European Union, and for this reason relevant case law from these countries is of particular interest (RSAegean, 2019, pp. 16–18). In Germany, there have been some cases where national courts have overruled negative decisions of the national Asylum Service rejecting family reunification based on Article 17(2) of the Dublin III Regulation for nuclear families who had voluntarily separated after entering EU soil. For instance, the Administrative Courts of Wiesbaden and Lüneburg ruled that the German authorities' discretion assessing humanitarian reasons had to be reduced to zero when it comes to single parents and their unaccompanied minor children.[10] Likewise, the Administrative Court of Frankfurt ruled that an Afghan family had humanitarian reasons within the meaning of Article 17(2) to be reunited, because members of a nuclear family are concerned, taking into account the high importance of the right to family unity and the best interests of the children.[11]

In a recent 2019 case,[12] the Berlin Administrative Court adjudicated that the responsibility of Germany to examine applications for international protection did not cease because of the expiry of a deadline, because the humanitarian grounds of Article 17(2) were confirmed due to the closeness of the familial relation. Although the deadline for responsibility had expired, the court found that Germany was still responsible for examining the applicants' asylum applications due to the close familial relationship between the applicants and their family members in Germany. This decision sets an important national precedent for prioritising the objective of family reunification under Article 17(2). It is crucial to note that the court's decision aligns with the human right to respect family life, as protected by Article 7 of the Charter and Article 8 of the ECHR. Furthermore, the court's reasoning highlights that the mere expiry of a deadline cannot be used to deny family reunification, as this would violate the interests of the applicants and their fundamental rights. The court also recognises that allowing Member States to reject their responsibility by simply ignoring the two-week deadline would undermine the Dublin regime's

10 VG Wiesbaden, 25 April 2019, Az. 4 L 478/19.WI.A; VG Lüneburg, 8 June 2019, Az. 8 B 111/19.
11 VG Frankfurt a. M., 27 May 2019, Az. 10 L 34/19.F.A.
12 Administrative Court Berlin, 15 March 2019, VG 23 L 706.18 AF.

purpose of promoting family reunification and protection of asylum seekers' rights. While positive in their outcomes, these decisions do not shed much light on the issue of family reunification with extended family members as defined in the Dublin III Regulation since they all dealt with nuclear family relationships that would fall under the binding articles of the Regulation, had the three-month deadline been respected.

Another decision from the United Kingdom could be more useful in this regard.[13] The case concerned a Syrian national who was an unaccompanied minor residing alone in Greece, where he made an application for international protection. The Greek authorities submitted a request for the United Kingdom to take charge of the asylum request so that he may be reunified with his cousin pursuant to Article 17(2) of the Dublin III Regulation. This request was refused by the British authorities on the basis that, inter alia, the family relationship was not within the scope of Article 2 of the Dublin III Regulation. Indeed, as mentioned earlier, under Article 2 of the Dublin III Regulation, family members and relatives of an unaccompanied child are spouses, parents, grandparents, aunts, uncles or another adult responsible for the applicant according to the law or practice of the state concerned. The Upper Tribunal overturned the decision of the national authorities and noted that there was sufficient evidence to show that family life between the applicant and his cousin exists, based on extreme emotional dependency between the applicant and his cousin, and evidence that the applicant's cousin assumes a position of a father figure.

4. A heterotopic analysis of Article 17(2): mirroring containment, scattering people

4.1 Sharing 'burdens' and 'relieving' definitions in the European asylum regime

Where does that practice – that *legal politic* – leave us? The blind spots and omissions of the European asylum and immigration regime are just as systemic as voluntary, as it is increasingly recognised (Bhartia, 2010, p. 331) through the cumulative challenges presented by the refugee crises of the 21st century (Nascimbene, 2016, p. 101). Refugee law is thought to be one of the rights-informed areas of law whose regime, statutes and adjudication centre on an individual-based, rather than a state-based focus; its schemes regard protection of the individual instead of protection of the sovereign state or more 'traditional' socially contracted rights (Schmalz, 2021, p. 363).

However, the concept of 'burden-sharing' (or 'responsibility-sharing') gathers its specific interest in the state body (Schuck, 1997, pp. 247–248; Zolberg, 1994, p. 162) – a state body whose internal point of view (Hart, 1994, pp. 89–91) lays

13 UK Upper Tribunal, 23 June 2020, *BAA & Anor, R (on the application of) v. Secretary of State for the Home Department*, 227 (IAC).

in constructing legal strategies of elimination and containment (Aleinikoff, 1992). That is to say, states' behaviour and systems of international protection regulate in feedback loops – responding, challenging and synergistically progressing their law-making to effectively adapt the 'normative world' to serve the material needs of the 'real world' (Schewel, 2019). In burden-sharing terms, this translates to restrictions legislated to comprehensively contain the refugee *spatially* in territory, *temporally* in procedure, and *competently* in termed and definitive 'entitled' protection (Noll, 2000, p. 41).

The structural principle of 'burden-sharing' – self-regulated by implication as well as by design (Thielemann et al., 2010, pp. 137–143) – leads to numerous interlinked results. The overwhelmed systems of the countries of first entry render burden-sharing a stranding mechanism for asylum seekers: through its delineation of normative protective, procedural and settlement limits, burden-sharing designates itself as a dually purposed referee in immiseration. 'Dually purposed' since it is, firstly, spatially containing and, secondly, wait-prolonging for asylum applicants (Human Rights Watch, 2017). The second end of that dual function gives rise to a tier of States unable to effectively regulate individual entrance to their choosing – compared to those able to do so more successfully – thus, corroding these States' internal point of view as law-making actors and enforcing an external point of view upon them by means of the wider institutional design in the EU asylum scheme. The generalised state of containment is produced at the first stage of the asylum-seeking process, wherein refugee existence – within or away from a refugee camp, detention centre, ghetto or specific facility – becomes a special, liminal heterotopia in space and time – therefore, a *chronotope* (Valverde, 2015) – under international human rights law (Giesen, 2015). Thus, using Nimführ and Sesay's definition of the reception conditions in requesting Member States as a transinsular 'island' (Nimführ & Sesay, 2019), we identify two State-sanctioned components: a spatial one – *containment* – and a temporal one – *indefinability*. These meanings may not consciously inform the direct normative reasoning of the Dublin Regulations or the European domestic and supranational courts in question, yet their instruments and resulting domestic cases are still seized as an opportunity to extend an apologetic response (Koskenniemi, 2006, § 254; see also Mouzourakis, 2014, p. 13) towards Member States 'burdened' by current crises.

Thus, *burden-sharing* is to mean *definition-relieving*, as well: to leave the interpretation of such breaches open is to ease standards and severity of criticism, wherein a separate status for refugee cases is created. For example, in the sharp observations of Marie-Bénédicte Dembour, the ECtHR is inclined to 'condone rightlessness' through cases such as *Bonger v. The Netherlands* (2005),[14] rendering the applicant unable to access Dutch social services and work while unlikely to return to his country of origin; the other non-rights in question include the negative definitions of settlement and family association (Dembour, 2015, pp. 442–481). In this example, the treatment a State reserves for its citizens and non-aliens is

14 ECtHR, 15 September 2005, *Bonger v. The Netherlands*, No. 10154/04.

prioritised by the Court, whereas the legal space reserved for asylum applicants becomes a Foucauldian *heterotopia*.

4.2 Heterotopia in the European asylum regime: an ECtHR perspective

Utopia is described as 'the perfected form of society' as it is; a mirror that allows society to see itself in a placeless, yet tangibly descriptive, reflection (Foucault, 1984, p. 3). A heterotopia, on the other hand, is a real place. It is where the Other inhabits, in crisis and deviance (Foucault, 1984, p. 4) or even a constant state of in-between (Holzer, 2013, p. 837) – arguably, a state in which asylum applicants are both experiencing as well as being labelled with (Lee & Nerghes, 2018). Yet, asylum applicants' existence is not the sole heterotopia depicted in the 'real world'. The ideal utopic of the European domestic and supranational courts as mechanisms interpreting the Convention unwavered by political considerations lay in stark contrast of their heterotopic functions: firstly, by creating judicial spaces of rightlessness and, secondly, by juris-inertively evading definition-making (see Section 4.3). Similarly, at the basis of this chapter: the utopic European Union, and its heterotopic legal and tangible spaces. Examples from a slightly different European jurisprudence to the one summarised in previous sections – now taking into consideration the ECtHR instead of the CJEU – showcase the liminal legal and 'real world' heterotopia asylum-seekers jurisprudentially inhabit. The liminal legal heterotopias occur as courts function juris-inertively when faced with international protection cases; and 'real-world' heterotopias occur in terms of the judicial treatment of the actual space (Witteborn, 2011, p. 1149) and mobility (Lafazani, 2013) asylum seekers occupy. The following ECtHR cases help demonstrate these two heterotopias.

In *J.R. and others v. Greece* (2018),[15] the Strasbourg court concluded that Article 3 of the ECtHR was not violated in a Greek hotspot where asylum seekers were detained; while the conditions at the hotspot were deemed potentially inhumane or degrading, it was semi-open and the applicants' occasional capacity to leave the premises eclipsed the severity of the actual conditions of containment. Similarly, in *Saadi v. The United Kingdom* (2008)[16] the dissenting judges considered the majority reflection of § 64 endorsing the Article 5 § 1(f) exception upholding the State's 'undeniable sovereign right to control aliens' entry into and residence in their territory' to be in stark contrast with viewing asylum seekers to be '*ipso facto* lawfully within the territory of a State'. They heavily criticised the measures justified as proportional as 'substantially weakening the scrutiny' exercised by the ECtHR. Hence, in *J.R.* the occasional capacity to leave the premises was enough to qualitatively eclipse the severity of the actual conditions of containment, while in *Saadi* State protection is similarly delimitated as non-obligated by way of detention. Through such precedent, a liminal status is created wherein asylum seekers

15 ECtHR, 25 January 2018, *J.R. and others v. Greece*, No. 22696/16.

16 ECtHR, 29 January 2008, *Saadi v. The United Kingdom*, No. 13229/03.

are deposited in a legally alienating heterotopia that is actively justified in its role as such, enabling 'containing' States to resume their practices unpurposed by considerations for international protection and almost burdening the applicant with responsibility for their rights.

4.3 Juris-generative and juris-inertive recognitions: two sides of the same coin?

But what do the aforementioned ECtHR decisions of *J.R.* and *Saadi* have in common with Article 17(2) jurisprudence? In contrast to applicants whose human rights infringements compelled the court to generate a declaratory jurisprudence stating negative (non-)rights, courts engaging with Dublin jurisprudence are compelled to engage with the regulation derivatively, stating positive yet modest and predictable rights in relation to state obligations. Such judicial approaches frame a specific heterotopia which asylum applicants are expected to occupy. In the way of Pierre Bourdieu's 'fossilised' social space (Bourdieu, 2020, pp. 26, 250–251) – whose immutable and inert nature renders its function irrelevant to the 'real world' – as far removed as Luxemburg or Strasbourg may be from the refugee camp of Lampedusa and the Controlled Access Centre of Samos, their courts help draw the borders of asylum seekers' existence within, and even beyond, those very spaces. These juris-generative mechanics reveal the double consequence upon applicants and the Dublin system alike.

Firstly, the judicial expectations of standards of living, procedural adherence and State practice – whether it is that of a benevolent 'mutual coercion' or a 'race to the bottom' (Thielemann et al., 2010, p. 33) – towards asylum seekers are of legal consequence even if spatially and temporally out of touch in the first place, thus 'fossilising' themselves. Even though these conditions are already imposed upon all applications for international protection, applicants expected to meet the added material criteria present for the special considerations of family reunification applications become a factor that accumulates complexity. Said material complexity becomes void of meaning and rarely applied according to the spirit of the Regulation – translating to uncontroversially enforcing nuclear family relations where deadlines have unjustly affected an application, as shown earlier. Thus, the meaning and utility of Article 17(2) becomes 'fossilised' in its own right on the level of assessing individual cases, while maintaining its ambiguous and opaque character.

Secondly, the derivative and unsurprising applications of Article 17(2) give rise to the term *juris-inertive*. 'Derivative and unsurprising' since, in another CJEU-ECtHR parallel, enforcing an Article 17(2)–related State obligation whose highest threshold had reasonably been met by applicant need and relation (see, e.g., *K v. Bundesasylamt*)[17] starkly resonates with the juris-generative negation of State obligation seen in the ECtHR cases *J.R.* and *Saadi*. 'Juris-inertive' because adjudicatory

17 CJEU, 6 November, 2012, C-245/11, *K.*, ECLI:EU:C:2012:685.

inertia in applying Article 17(2) to cases matching its character and purpose for the sake of more unconventional familial relations leads to the humanitarian clause being left unexplored, blurry and critically opaque.

Tribunals wilfully neglecting to apply a clause in its full capacity due to potential political unease amongst Member States sheds light on two instrumental points. Firstly, that judicial inertia can form results just as restrictive as judicial generation and, secondly, that judicial inertia in fully exploring the potential applications of a critical clause relieves the burden of devising clear or practical definitions for its future use, thus relieving State obligation to abide by such termed standards, too. These standards are absorbed by affected States through ECtHR judicial behaviour, even if they result in circumstances that are liminal and increasingly difficult to navigate for protected individuals (Dembour, 2015, pp. 442–481).

4.4 Family (?) anxieties

4.4.1 Othering and heterotopic approaches

In the case of family reunification on humanitarian grounds, the heterotopia does not merely concern different approaches towards the specific cluster of caseloads regarding asylum seekers, but also towards family forms deviating from the Western European standard. We have identified two layers in the lack of either proof of dependency or 'humanitarian grounds' when it comes to court reasonings and Dublin III cases' negotiations between States. Firstly, the functional, legal-pragmatist layer embodies the concept of *necessity*: wherein *who* is familially dependent, redundant and necessary is being interrogated while the grounds claimed for reunification are placed under considerable scrutiny. Then, the second layer responds to what is being sought out by relevant judicial authorities when examining the application of Article 17(2): *resemblance*, the material proof of dependency and exhibits of the legal or biological closeness of someone whose relationship to the applicant best resembles that of a Western European family-relational ideal. Thus, even if the goal of the humanitarian clause is not explicitly such, the precedent categorically constructed in the case law reviewed has by now rendered Article 17(2) a strict threshold for family reunification. The European West is the enforcer of liminal circumstances and simultaneous arbiter of other(ed) relationships – hence, instrumentalising Article 17(2) as another tool of 'burden-sharing' denialism among Member States.

It would, of course, be naïve to posit that this vein only runs through family reunification on humanitarian grounds: such considerations are constantly applied to binding provisions in the Dublin III Regulation, often enacting an underlying purposed attitude in the general regime of family reunification: clauses (9) and (10) of the 2003 Family Reunification Directive (2003/86/EC) mark an explicit preference for prioritising the nuclear family ('that is to say the spouse and the minor children'), while extended family and polygamous marriages were left to State discretion without regard for 'making family life possible'. Different political, legislative and judicial institutions arrive at the same point through varied means: for example, the 2014 Proposal for establishing a Union Resettlement Framework[18] nearly commanded the character of such "heterotopic" criteria. Article 10(1)(b) states that 'Member States may give preference inter alia to third-country nationals or stateless persons with . . . social or cultural links, or other characteristics that can facilitate integration in the participating Member State,' deftly underlining the 'integration potential' of the applicant(s) as possible substantive criteria for resettlement (Bamberg, 2018, p. 8). Similarly, reducing the scope of dependency clauses 'as a quid pro quo for the increased scope of the family reunification clauses' (ECRE, 2021, p. 32) in the Commission Proposal for Regulation on Asylum and Migration Management is symptomatic of that transactional and protectionist approach. The juris-generative text relating to Article 17(2) of the Dublin III Regulation arranges the various representations of familial bonds and dependency through an intentional lens of necessity and redundancy, proximity and 'otherness', facilitating an agenda of legal and political conservatism gatekeeping putative European values. The very recent rejection by Member States of the Commission's proposal to include a wider family definition to the improved rules of responsibility, a proposed instrument comparable to the Dublin III Regulation under the new Migration Pact Agreement show that Europe is not ready to abandon this position (ECRE, 2023).

4.4.2 Why this family?

> 'Their' good, re-invigorative communities also look like fragmentary ethnic enclaves. 'Their' traditional family values threaten to overturn our still new and fragile gains in gender equality.
>
> (Honig, 2001)

Member States themselves provide excellent examples of this European value-integrationist model: in recently independent, late 19th-century Greece, the concept of 'civilisation' and the 'civilised life' was imported by Western Europe through a newly founded bourgeois class recognised by historians Cassia and Bada to encompass three fundamental elements; firstly, a preference towards an urban way of living and 'professional class' conduct; secondly, an insistence on continuous schooling and higher education for the offspring of the higher classes; and third, a focus on patrilineal nuclear family rather than extended, 'anarchic' lineage ties (Cassia & Bada, 1992, p. 18). To be civilised was to ensure an order of priority for affluent dowry arrangements, providing a resource baseline of both material and social capital for immediate offspring, securing an advantageous union in the future. Henceforth, living with extended family, endorsing traditional practices of

18 Proposal for a Regulation of the European Parliament and of the Council establishing a Union Resettlement Framework and amending Regulation (EU) No 516/2014 of the European Parliament and the Council, 13 July 2016, COM/2016/0468 final.

fostering or adopting children of relatives, and polygamy, were deemed 'uncivilised' (Cassia & Bada, 1992, pp. 15–27). This is only but one example of how European dynamics of cultural hegemony lent their paradigms to idealised occidental representations of what it takes to be 'civilised', 'not-backward', and 'modern'. Of course, these Western European ideas about kinship, lineage and familial ties were not limited to newly independent 19th-century Greece, but have formed a standard intricately intertwined with the concept of 'quality of living' that lives on in the 21st century (Hareven, 1991). Hence, the category of family deemed 'necessary' and 'dependent' has been constricted by laws and policies in a way that is rigidly stratified and highly interiorised, to the extent it renders those who do not abide by it socially and culturally different (Vertovec, 2011).

The media often overlooks migration for the purposes of family ties and needs (Blinder & Allen, 2016). Instead, opinions about migration and asylum tend to be based on fears of the replacement of the 'rightful citizen' by the expansive (Mudde, 2009), larger families fostered by the 'other' culture (Müller, 2016). State sovereignty has long been linked to controlling populations (Agamben, 2016), with contemporary conservatism often viewing exerting this control as a goal in itself, as a cultural politic driven by anxieties about cultural loss (Vertovec, 2011). The extended family has taken on a political-cultural role, symbolising the rejection of progress and modernity in Europe (Vertovec, 2011) – similar to how the headscarf has been used in France to represent the rejection of sexual liberty and consumer values. These representational cultural tropes transform the rightful access to extended familial ties into a stand-in for suspicion, backwardness, ambiguity and deception.

5. Conclusion

This chapter has analysed the application of the humanitarian clause in Article 17(2) of the Dublin III Regulation. Commencing by explaining the creation and development of this article, it presented its limited use in the administrative procedures of the Dublin Units of the Member States, followed by its equally limited engagement with the jurisprudence of national and European courts. The interpretative tactics of European courts (the CJEU and ECtHR) in cases reasoning with State obligations regarding the spatial, temporal, as well as competent containment imposed on asylum seekers and in cases regarding family reunification under the humanitarian clause mirrors each other. Through high-threshold considerations of ECHR Article 3 and derivative, unimaginative applications of Dublin III Article 17(2), these mirror images both manage to ease 'responsibility-sharing' among Member States – while safeguarding occidental ideas of social order regarding individuals othered by citizenship, their containment and the structure of the family. Thus, familial relations meant to be taken into account in the spirit of the humanitarian clause yet evading the 'Western' mould are deposited to the very same legal heterotopic category as other facets of the refugee condition (reviewing as such the more obvious legal heterotopia of containment in the ECtHR cases of *J.R.* and *Saadi*), essentially being assigned a similarly liminal status by being left juridically untreated.

References

Agamben, G. (2016). *The Use of Bodies*. Stanford University Press.
Aleinikoff, T. A. (1992). State-centered refugee law: From resettlement to containment. *Michigan Journal of International Law*, *14*(1), 120–138. https://doi.org/10.1525/9780520341234-016
Asylum Information Database (AIDA). (2021). *Country report: Greece*. https://asylumineurope.org/reports/country/greece/
Asylum Information Database (AIDA). (2022). *Country report: Greece*. https://asylumineurope.org/wp-content/uploads/2022/05/AIDA-GR_2021update.pdf
Asylum Information Database (AIDA). (2023). *Country report: Greece*. https://asylumineurope.org/reports/country/greece/asylum-procedure/procedures/dublin/
Bamberg, K. (2018). *The EU resettlement framework: From a humanitarian pathway to a migration management tool?* (EPC Discussion Paper). EPC.
Bhartia, A. (2010). Fictions of Law: The Trial of Sulaiman Oladokun, or Reading Kafka in an Immigration Court. In N. De Genova & N. Peutz (Eds.), *The Deportation Regime: Sovereignty, Space, and the Freedom of Movement* (pp. 329–350). Duke University Press. https://doi.org/10.1215/9780822391340-013
Blinder, S., & Allen, W. L. (2016). Constructing immigrants: Portrayals of migrant groups in British national newspapers, 2010–2012. *International Migration Review*, *50*(1), 3–40. https://doi.org/10.1111/imre.12206
Bourdieu, P. (2020). *Habitus and Field: Lectures at the College de France (1982–1983)* (Vol. II). Polity.
Cassia, P. S., & Bada, C. (1992). *The Making of the Modern Greek Family*. Cambridge University Press.
Dembour, M.-B. (2015). *When Humans Become Migrants: Study of the European Court of Human Rights with an Inter-American Counterpoint*. Oxford University Press. https://doi.org/10.1093/acprof:oso/9780199667833.001.0001
Engelbert, J., Awad, I., & van Sterkenburg, J. (2019). Everyday practices and the (un)making of "Fortress Europe": Introduction to the special issue. *European Journal of Cultural Studies*, *22*(2), 133–143. https://doi.org/10.1177/1367549418823055
European Asylum Support Office (EASO). (2019). *Note on the "Messina model" applied in the context of ad hoc relocation arrangements following disembarkation, Valletta Harbour* (EASO/ED/2019/403). https://reliefweb.int/sites/reliefweb.int/files/resources/Note%20on%20the%20%E2%80%98Messina%20Model%E2%80%99%20applied%20in%20the%20context%20of%20ad%20hoc%20relocation%20arrangements%20following%20disembarkation.pdf
European Council on Refugees and Exiles (ECRE). (2021, February). *ECRE comments on the commission proposal for a regulation on asylum and migration management*. ECRE.
European Council on Refugees and Exiles (ECRE). (2023, June). *Editorial: Migration pact agreement point by point*. https://ecre.org/editorial-migration-pact-agreement-point-by-point/
European Parliamentary Research Service. (2020). *Study: Dublin regulation on international protection applications*. www.europarl.europa.eu/thinktank/en/document.html?reference=EPRS_STU(2020)642813
FENIX-Humanitarian Legal Aid. (2021). *Keeping families apart: The Dublin III regulation in practice*. www.fenixaid.org/articles/the-dublin-iii-regulation-in-practice
Foucault, M. (1984). Of other spaces: Utopias and heterotopias. *Architecture/Mouvement/Continuité*, 1–9.
Garlick, M. (2016). The Dublin System, Solidarity and Individual Rights. In V. Chetail, P. D. Bruycker, & F. Maiani (Eds.), *Reforming the Common European Asylum System: The New European Refugee Law* (pp. 159–194). Brill. https://doi.org/10.1163/9789004308664_008
Giesen, B. (2015). Inbetweenness and Ambivalence. In A. Horvath, B. Thomassen, & H. Wydra (Eds.), *Breaking Boundaries: Varieties of Liminality* (pp. 61–71). Berghahn Books. https://doi.org/10.3167/9781782387664

Guild, E., Costello, C., Garlick, M., Moreno-Lax, V., & Mouzourakis, M. (2014). *New approaches, alternative avenues and means of access to asylum procedures for persons seeking international protection* (European Parliament PE 509.989). European Parliament.

Hareven, T. K. (1991). The history of the family and the complexity of social change. *The American Historical Review*, *96*(1), 95–124. https://doi.org/10.2307/2164019

Hart, H. L. A. (1994). *The Concept of Law*. Oxford University Press.

Holzer, E. (2013). What happens to law in a refugee camp? *Law & Society Review*, *47*(4), 837–872. https://doi.org/10.1111/lasr.12041, https://onlinelibrary.wiley.com/doi/abs/10.1111/lasr.12041

Honig, B. (2001). *Democracy and the Foreigner*. Princeton University Press.

Human Rights Watch. (2017). *Greece: A year of suffering for asylum seekers*. www.hrw.org/news/2017/03/15/greece-year-suffering-asylum-seekers

Kincheloe, J. L., & Steinberg, S. R. (1997). *Changing Multiculturalism*. Open University Press.

Koskenniemi, M. (2006). *Fragmentation of International Law: Difficulties Arising from the Diversification and Expansion of International Law* (Fifty-Eighth Session). International Law Commission.

Lafazani, O. (2013). A border within a border: The migrants' squatter settlement in Patras as a heterotopia. *Journal of Borderlands Studies*, *28*(1), 1–13. https://doi.org/10.1080/08865655.2012.751731

Lee, J. S., & Nerghes, A. (2018). Refugee or migrant crisis? Labels, perceived agency, and sentiment polarity in online discussions. *Social Media and Society*, *3*(4), 1–22. https://doi.org/10.1177/2056305118785638

Meissner, F., & Heil, T. (2021). Deromanticising integration: On the importance of convivial disintegration. *Migration Studies*, *9*(3), 740–758. https://doi.org/10.1093/migration/mnz056

Mouzourakis, M. (2014). *'Wrong number?': The use and misuse of asylum data in the European Union*. Centre for European Policy Studies. https://cdn.ceps.eu/wp-content/uploads/2015/01/Use%20and%20Misuse%20of%20Asylum%20Data.pdf, https://www.ceps.eu/ceps-publications/wrong-number-use-and-misuse-asylum-data-european-union/

Mudde, C. (2009). *Populist Radical Right Parties in Europe*. Cambridge University Press. https://doi.org/10.1017/CBO9780511492037

Müller, J. (2016). *What is Populism?* University of Pennsylvania Press.

Nascimbene, B. (2016). Refugees, the European Union and the "Dublin system": The reasons for a crisis. *European Papers*, *1*(1), 101–113. https://doi.org/10.15166/2499-8249/8

Nimführ, S., & Sesay, B. (2019). Navigating (im)mobilities and practices of appropriation of non-deportable refugees in the Mediterranean area. *Comparative Migration Studies*, *7*, 26–45. https://doi.org/10.1186/s40878-019-0132-8

Noll, G. (2000). *Negotiating Asylum: The EU Acquis, Extraterritorial Protection and the Common Market of Deflection*. Brill. https://brill.com/edcollbook-oa/title/10731

Peers, S. (2012). *Revising the "Dublin" rules on responsibility for asylum- seekers: Further developments*. Statewatch. www.statewatch.org/media/documents/analyses/no-186-dublin.pdf

Refugee Support Aegean. (2019). *Refugee families torn apart*. https://rsaegean.org/en/refugee-families-torn-apart/

Schewel, K. (2019). Understanding immobility: Moving beyond the mobility bias in migration studies. *International Migration Review*, *54*(2), 328–355. https://doi.org/10.1177/0197918319831952

Schmalz, D. (2021). Fences and Fictions: Lessons from Schemes of Responsibility-Sharing for Refugees in Europe. In M. Iovane, F. M. Palombino, D. Amoroso, & G. Zarra (Eds.), *The Protection of General Interests in Contemporary International Law* (pp. 363–384). Oxford University Press. https://doi.org/10.1093/oso/9780192846501.003.0016

Schuck, P. H. (1997). Refugee burden-sharing: A modest proposal. *Yale Journal of International Law*, *22*(2), 243–297. https://core.ac.uk/download/pdf/72839038.pdf

Thielemann, E., Williams, R., & Boswell, C. (2010). *What system of burden-sharing between member states for the reception of asylum seekers?* European Parliament, Directorate-General Internal Policies.

UNHCR. (2017). *Study on the implementation of the Dublin III regulation*. www.unhcr.org/protection/basic/5bd1bdfe4/left-in-limbo-full-report.html

Valverde, M. (2015). *Chronotopes of Law: Jurisdiction, Scale and Governance*. Routledge.

Vertovec, S. (2011). The cultural politics of nation and migration. *Annual Review of Anthropology*, *40*, 241–256. https://doi.org/10.1146/annurev-anthro-081309-145837

Witteborn, S. (2011). Constructing the forced migrant and the politics of space and place-making. *Journal of Communication*, *61*(6), 1142–1160. https://doi.org/10.1111/j.1460-2466.2011.01578.x

Zolberg, A. R. (1994). Changing sovereignty games and international migration. *Indiana Journal of Global Legal Studies*, *2*(1), 153–170.

11 Family reunification policies in Italy

Ambivalences, discrimination, resistance

Francesco Della Puppa

1. Introduction

The family-related dynamics of migration and the process of family reunification are becoming increasingly central to the debate on EU member states' policies on migrants' entry into and social integration within the EU (Bonizzoni & Cibea, 2009; EMN, 2008; Gil Araujo, 2008;Kraler, 2010). In fact, family reunification is currently one of the main modes of legal entry into EU member states (Tognetti Bordogna, 2004).

A certain concept of family and domestic life has always constituted a *conditio sine qua non* of the social construction of the 'good citizen', linking individual, family and state (Sayad, 2002). Migration policies are a central node in this complex relationship. The conditions that the state establishes in order to 'regulate' the entry and residence of migrants' family members reflect the family model of the state and the society of destination; that is, they reveal its conception of the family as an interdependent and hierarchically ordered compact unit with the task of mediating between the individual, the state and society.

Starting from these assumptions, this chapter will analyse how the reunited and reunitable family is constructed in a socio-legal sense in the Italian policies on the subject, in order to fully understand the effects of Italian policies on migrant family structures. In so doing, my analysis will be inserted within the strand of sociological studies aimed at investigating the policies that regulate reunification, observing them from a perspective centred on processes of stratification (Lockwood, 1996) that condition and concretely redefine the intersection between the potential enjoyment of the right to a family unit and the class position, status, nationality, gender and generation of those who exercise it (Bertolani et al., 2013; Kraler, 2010; Morris, 2003; Tognetti Bordogna, 2011). The legal framework of family reunification acts as a 'double device', shaping, on the one hand, what the (migrant) family should be and look like (that is, who is part of the family and who is excluded from it) and, on the other hand, how the migrant family is supposed/obliged to contribute to the economy of the society of destination. Thus, as will be elaborated in more detail later in this chapter, reunification policies identify some family members (formally married partners and children) as entitled to reunification and exclude others, either partially (parents) or totally (siblings, adult children, etc.). Furthermore, to obtain

DOI: 10.4324/9781003503217-14

permission for reunification, the first-migrant applicant is forced to increase their discipline and productivity at work (getting a stable job and sometimes needing to look for a higher salary) and to restrict their sociality outside of work (to save economic resources and optimise working hours).

Paradoxically, whereas these policies make the road to family reunification fraught and bumpy, Italian society fears, blames and stigmatises migrants who are on their own, that is, migrants who have not gone through the process of family reunification. However, this blame and fear, as will be shown later, are expressed in different ways based on migrants' gender and the nature of their work in Italy; that is, whether they are migrant men or migrant women and whether they are migrants who carry out a 'productive' job or their work is linked to the 'reproductive' sphere. The latter involves domestic and care work that is usually done within the domestic sphere of native Italians, as often happens in Mediterranean Europe. A male migrant who works in the primary or tertiary sector creates fear in Italian society and is perceived and represented as a threat to the social order and to a shared morality. By contrast, a migrant woman who works as care worker for an Italian family and who, therefore, must concentrate her emotional labour (Hochschild, 1979) and care work on 'our' family members, is preferable if she has not completed the family reunification process and does not live with her family in Italy. In fact, focusing on the Italian case is helpful for dealing with the central question of how family reunification policies construct a specific type of migrant family and migrant labour. Italy is a Mediterranean country characterised, on the one hand, by a 'Mediterranean model of migration' (King & De Bono, 2013; Pugliese, 2011), the structural presence of a shadow economy and the inclusion of many immigrants in this segment of the labour market (*ibidem*) and, on the other hand, by a so-called Mediterranean or familist welfare regime in which the family covers many socio-economic functions that in other European nations are the responsibility of the state or the market (Esping-Andersen, 1995).

The first section of this chapter reconstructs the sociological and regulatory debate on family reunification in Italy, while the second elaborates further on the migrant family and reunification in Italian legislation, providing a sociological and historical reconstruction of Italian policies of family reunification. The third section takes up the concept of civic stratification elaborated on by DavidLockwood (1996) and adopted by Lydia Morris (2003) to show how policies of reunification in fact reproduce and strengthen this stratification. In the fourth section, the link between work and family reunification is analysed, showing how Italian policies subordinate the possibility of migrants' family life to their work – their productive and economic capacity – making the reunification process into a labour regulation device.

2. The sociological framework

For some years, the Italian sociological literature has been investigating the dynamics of migrant families through analysing the processes of migrant family reunification (Ambrosini et al., 2010; Bonizzoni, 2009; Lainati et al., 2008;

Scabini & Rossi, 2008; Tognetti Bordogna, 2011). These studies have described the changes in generational and gender roles that occur within the migrant family before and after migration and reunification (Tognetti Bordogna, 2005). The family reunification process has also been studied in its different experiential forms and modalities (carried out by first-migrant applicant men or first-migrant applicant women, for a spouse, children, parents, etc.) and in relation to the various difficulties and repercussions that it can have for the families involved (Ambrosini, 2014; Bonizzoni, 2009; Lainati et al., 2008). The reunification process has been understood as a migratory strategy enacted by whole households (Tognetti Bordogna, 2011) and as a fundamental step in the social construction of male migrants' adult masculinity:Della Puppa (2014) shows how Bangladeshi migrant men use family reunification to rebuild their image, perception and self-representation as responsible adults and family men in their country of destination. These studies have also highlighted the emancipatory acts of many of the women who have been reunited with their husbands – freeing themselves from the subordination of an unwelcoming family environment (*ibidem*) or escaping unsatisfactory marriages and family relationships (Ambrosini, 2014; Banfi & Boccagni, 2009) – as well as the suffering and frustration experienced by those who are reunited against their will (Della Puppa, 2014). Other topics explored include long-distance motherhood and reunification (Ambrosini, 2014; Bonizzoni, 2009); the different migratory paths related to family or care work, marked by the different gender styles of men and women (Ambrosini, 2014; Bonizzoni & Boccagni, 2013); and the obstacles encountered by and support given to migrant care workers in reunification processes (Ambrosini, 2014; Della Puppa, 2012).

In European countries with a longer history of immigration, the debate includes a discussion of 'second-level' or 'newly formed' reunifications (Tognetti Bordogna, 2005; Kofman, 2004). These definitions refer to the situation in which, once they have created the necessary conditions for doing so, the first migrant (in this case usually a man) returns to his country of origin to get married – usually an arranged marriage – with a woman who joins him in the country of destination immediately afterwards. These studies emphasise the role that the family plays in reproducing assumed practices as an obstacle to social integration in the country of destination. Such practices include forced marriages (Grillo, 2008; Kofman et al., 2011; Kraler, 2010), the self-segregation of national migrant communities (Strasser et al., 2009) and the role the family plays in favouring the entry of third-country nationals within the national borders of EU countries through an 'instrumental' use of the institution of family reunification (*ibidem*).

From the point of view of the political debate on reunification, the focus has shifted from safeguarding the *minimum threshold* of migrants' 'human rights' to the *maximum defence* of the EU territory from the threat of 'undesirables'. There is thus a dual and contradictory thrust in the norms and practices of EU states regarding the enlargement of citizenship rights: while European democracies declare their commitment to guaranteeing the human rights enshrined in the universal conventions to which they are signatories – including the right to respect for family life – they also claim autonomy in determining who is allowed to enter the state's borders and how (Benhabib, 2003), consequently toughening up their policies in relation to migration, particularly in the context of the global economic crisis (Basso, 2010).

3. The legal framework

The fundamental legislation on family reunification in Italy is found in both Law 40/1998, known as the 'Turco-Napolitano' law, and the current Law 189/2002, known as the 'Bossi-Fini' law (which inherited the former's basic structure). These laws introduced partial limitations on family reunification through an increase in the socio-material parameters required to obtain a *nulla osta* (that is to say, the permission to reunite with family members), a restriction on the family members who could be admitted (or, better, excluding some family members), and a shortening in duration of the residence rights related to it. These aspects will be addressed in this section. In fact, to be granted the *nulla osta* for family reunification, the applicant must have a sufficient income and suitable accommodation (which was already the case under the Martelli Law of 1990 and the Dini Decree of 1996) to reunite with their family members (Morozzo della Rocca, 2008).

In relation to economic requirements, the '*Testo Unico delle disposizioni concernenti la disciplina dell'immigrazione e norme sulla condizione dello straniero*' (Consolidated Act of provisions concerning the discipline of immigration and regulations on the status of foreigners), implemented by Law 40/1998 and modified by Law 189/2002, refers to 'a minimum annual income from lawful sources that is not less than the annual amount of social allowance, increased by half of that amount for each family member to be reunited', and in relation to housing requirements refers to 'accommodation that falls within the minimum parameters set by the regional law for public residential housing'.[1] The intertwining of these parameters with the segmentation of the national labour market along 'ethno-national' lines – that is, certain nationalities or social groups with certain somatic characteristics are channelled towards menial and more badly paid jobs in some sectors of the labour market (Perocco, 2012; Zanfrini, 2010) – subjects the first-migrant applicant to a social and labour *discipline* aimed at maximising their ability to produce income.

The family members[2] eligible for reunification are a spouse who is not legally separated and is not less than 18 years old; minor children, including those of the

1 These parameters were introduced as a guarantee of the minimum housing standards to which families given public residential housing are entitled. When a migrant citizen applies for family reunification, this form of social, housing and welfare protection for the (Italian) family is transformed into a requirement. Whereas for families with Italian citizenship the relationship between housing conditions and family size marks the limit below which they are entitled to benefits (to access public housing), for families from third countries it constitutes the minimum threshold to be reached in order to demonstrate their capacity for self-reliance necessary for reunification. The state thus establishes a boundary that acts simultaneously in an inclusive sense for its nationals and in an exclusive sense for migrants, assigning different sets of rights and different possibilities for access to welfare. Failure to meet the same housing standards implies the provision of welfare state benefits for the former and a lack of access to the institution of family reunification for the latter.

2 This refers only to families exclusively made up of third-country nationals.

spouse or those who were born out of wedlock, provided that if there is another parent they have given their consent; dependent children aged 18 or over, if for 'objective reasons' they are unable to provide for their essential living needs, such as for health reasons that result in total disability; dependent parents, if they have no other children in their country of origin or provenance, or parents aged 65 or over, if their other children are unable to support them for documented serious health reasons.[3] For the children of migrant families, this can mean having no grandparents in the country they live in if they have a healthy uncle or aunt in their parents' country of origin who are able to support the grandparents; for migrant parents, this can mean not having the support of the older generation in reproductive and care work if they have a healthy brother or sister in their country of origin. So, there is a clear process of *legislative nuclearisation of the migrant family*. In fact, the policies of family reunification construct the migrant and reunited family as a nuclear family, a family model imagined by the destination society which reveals how the destination society thinks about the family and about itself. That is, it demonstrates that

> discourses and policies on family reunification participate in the politics of belonging, and that gender and family norms play a crucial role in this production of collective identities, i.e. in defining who 'we' are and what distinguishes 'us' from 'the others'. . . . These practices of 'othering' legitimize restrictive reforms of marriage migration policies. Also, and no less importantly, they serve the symbolic function of defining ['our'] identity, and show that the government protects this identity.
>
> (Bonjour & de Hart, 2013, p. 61)

This process of nuclearisation severely limits the possibility of reuniting with older generations, especially in emigration contexts in which the family is often composed of a high number of descendants. Precisely due to the large size of families, it is the emigrated members who live in Italy who economically support both their ascendants who are to reunite with them and their 'other children in the country of origin or provenance' whose 'sustenance' is entrusted to them (according to Law 189/2002). That is, ascendants can only be reunited if there are no children in the country of origin who can support them.

Thus, the regulation is constructed as a selective 'filter' on immigration, making it possible for young people who can access the labour market to enter the country and inhibiting the entrance of those who – even if they are family members of legally resident workers who reach the (economic and housing) requirements for family reunification – represent a cost to the society of destination within a context of cuts in social spending and welfare resources.[4]

3 Article 23 Law 189/2002.

4 However, I should note the radically different approach by the legislation in the case of the – albeit severely restricted – entry of children over the age of 18, who are eligible for reunification only in the event that they can prove they are unable to work and, therefore, lack economic autonomy in their country of origin.

In the national context, marriage emerges as a fundamental element in the rhetoric on the migrant family and reunification policies. Italian policies create a relationship of *dependence* on the first-migrant applicant who is responsible for the welfare and socio-economic and administrative status of the reunited family nucleus. This takes the form of an *economic dependence* between the family member and the first migrant, in that the latter is pushed to play the role of *sponsor*; and an *administrative dependence*, in the sense that the family member's residence document is subordinate to that of the first migrant applicant and, above all, to their employment status, since the latter's residence document is linked to their work contract.

With regard to this last point, at least for those who hold resident permits for subordinate work – which is the case in the majority of family reunifications in Italy – the Italian law subordinates the modalities and duration of the reunited family member's stay to that of the sponsor, whose regular residence permit in turn depends on their contractual relationship with their employer. The law binds the duration of the residence permit of the reunified family member to that of the residence permit of the 'foreign family member who meets the requirements for reunification'[5] and states that the spouse's residence permit for family reasons is renewable in the event of divorce only on condition that the document is converted into a residence permit for subordinate work or autonomous work or study and meets the other necessary requirements for obtaining the document. However, the conversion of a residence permit does not guarantee a break in the dependency link.

The same conditions for the residence permit conversion apply to the descendants of the first-migrant applicant in the event that, upon reaching 18 years of age, they are unable to obtain one. Articles 30 and 29 of Law 189/2002 specify that 'in the case of legal separation or dissolution of marriage or for a child who cannot obtain a residence permit, upon reaching eighteen years of age, the residence permit may be converted into a permit for employment, self-employment or study'. Therefore, in cases where first-migrant applicants are unable to give their reunited children an EU long-term residence permit, or where the reunited children are registered on the parent's residence permit until they are 14 and are subsequently granted a residence permit for family reasons until they reach the age of majority, those children will have to enter the labour market or continue their studies when they become 18 in order to continue to reside legally in Italy.[6] These regulations are very strict, for there is no guarantee that on reaching the age of majority, the reunified child will continue their studies beyond secondary school or find a job and maintain it without significant periods of unemployment.[7]

5 Article 30 Law 189/2002.

6 However, I should point out that several rulings of the Constitutional Court have also legitimised the renewal of residence permits for family reasons for children who are over 18 in educational and working conditions that diverge from those indicated by the regulations.

7 The difficulties that migrants' children have obtaining Italian citizenship should also be mentioned. If they are born in Italy to migrant parents without Italian citizenship, migrant children can apply for citizenship at the age of 18, which can be either granted or denied, with the processing of the

These regulations could also have repercussions on the educational and training choices of young people who entered Italy through family reunification, being one of the factors – alongside the hierarchical nature of Italian schools (Perocco, 2012) – that pushes them towards short-term vocational courses. It can get them into the labour market more quickly (even if in the lowest and worst-paid positions) so that they can easily renew their residence permit or at least reproduce the work-oriented *habitus* developed by their parents. Thus, 'ethno-national' social inequalities are passed down and reinforced. The institution of family reunification constructs the reunified family member as a weak subject from the point of view of citizenship rights, making it more difficult for them to engage in a process of integration that is autonomous from that of their first-migrant applicant family member.

Under current legislation it is not possible to deviate from the *nuclear family model based on marriage* (Bonjour & de Hart, 2013), neither with regard to the *family members admitted for reunification* nor with regard to those recognised to be legitimately financially supporting the first-migrant applicant to meet their material requirements. The legal framework institutionally weakens the migrant reunited family and defines the 'roles' and 'functions' that each figure in the reunification should assume. Thus, migration policies establish *who* is part of the family and who is excluded from it; *what* the family is; and, consequently, what social and economic *performance* it should enact.

4. A civic stratification device

For some migrants coming from specific national and socio-cultural contexts, the family reunification process may include the idea of reconstructing their family of origin as extensively as possible, or at least the reunification of their siblings, nephews, nieces, cousins and sisters- and brothers-in-law. Reuniting the spouse and their children born in the country of origin is one step, and not necessarily the first, of a wider and slower process of reunification implemented through exploiting the various possibilities offered by the legislation (Bertolani, 2011). Thus, in Italy, in the context of migrant family reunification, members of the same family can possess *different* civic statuses according to the different moments in their lives in which the reunification took place or depending on their various entry channels (through 'amnesty', immigration quota laws, etc.), and thus can have different residence titles and heterogeneous and stratified possibilities for inclusion and integration in their country of destination (Bonizzoni, 2012). Again, within the same family, some might have a European long-term residence permit and others a

application sometimes taking over two years. If they are not born in Italy, they have to apply in the same way as all third-country national migrants, after ten years of continuous residence and regular presence in Italy, and they must have no criminal record and access to sufficient economic capital. This is specific to Italy and further exacerbates the dependence and problems of reunited family members in this country.

temporary residence permit as a result of a series of variables, including whether or not they have sufficient income and/or housing, their knowledge of *written* Italian (which is often related to their degree of literacy and thus to their generational and regional belonging in their specific context of origin), and thus whether or not they have passed a language test, and so on.

The residency requirements and citizenship rights of the reunited family members are therefore *stratified* in various ways: by the administrative position of the first-migrant applicant on which they depend (e.g., whether the latter has a residence permit for one year, two years or four years, or a European long-term residence permit, etc.); by their own mode of entry into Europe and Italy (as asylum seekers, employee workers, self-employed, etc.); and by their possession of different forms of capital (e.g., material and cultural).

The *stratification* of the residence status – and of the corresponding citizenship rights – of the first-migrant applicants, which, depending on the type and duration of their residence documents, leads to differentiated access to the institution of reunification and reverberates onto the family members reunited with them. The law states that the first residence document for family reasons obtained after reunification can last a maximum of two years, except in cases where the reuniting person is in possession of the EU Long Term Residence Permit, which they can 'pass on'. In any case, its duration is never longer than that of the first-migrant applicant's residence permit.

Some authors (Kraler, 2010; Morris, 2003) use the lens of civic stratification (Lockwood, 1996) to analyse the growing system of inequalities, based on the relationship between different categories of individuals and the state.

David Lockwood (1996) formulated the concept of civic stratification in order to describe the different ways in which the institutionalisation of citizenship directly or indirectly structures life opportunities and social identities under conditions of social and economic inequality, ultimately demonstrating not only how a subject's positioning in the social class hierarchy acts on the process of social integration, but also how social integration acts on class structure. Bearing in mind that the device of stratification acts on all the different actors variously placed in the field of citizenship definitions, it is important to investigate how it acts in relation to the first-migrant applicant, both in regard to the distinction between 'useful citizens' and 'less useful citizens' and in relation to the acceptance of the procedural principles that underlie them. The heterogeneity of the system for obtaining the *nulla osta* for family reunification is a product of 1) different formal citizenship statuses (national, from an EU member state, or from a 'third country'); 2) different types of residence permits (residence permits for family reasons, for subordinate work, for self-employment, for seasonal work, for study, for job seeking or for political asylum, or the EU Long Term Residence Permit); 3) different lengths of resident permits (from a few months to permanent); 4) competition between differently located institutional subjects (from local to supranational levels) and 5) the multiple administrative regulations and consequent discretion used in their application (Bertolani et al., 2013; Della Puppa & Salvador, 2015; Schweitzer, 2015). Thus, different types of citizenship and different sets of rights correspond to the different *statuses* of migrant workers (long term, short term or 'irregular'), and access to family reunification can only take place if certain status requirements are met.

The diverse types of residence permits for reunifications differently regulate the holders' possibility of accessing the labour market and establish constraints and time limits on reunified subjects' stay in the territory. 'Third-country' nationals, identified on the basis of a hierarchisation of citizenship statuses, then undergo another stratification determined by their reasons for and modes of entry into the country, to which is added the further category of citizenship constituted by an 'irregular' status, resulting from entering the country without a visa or from the expiry of a residence permit. Three socio-legal statuses – long-term residency status, short-term residency status and irregular status – constitute the pivot of the civic stratification system (Kofman, 2005).

The achievement of a certain degree of (legal) stability in the territory depends on 1) the type and duration of the subject's residence permit; 2) the local administration of the municipality where the first migrant has the residence;[8] and 3) the first migrant's national citizenship, that is, the first-migrant applicant's country of origin (i.e., whether an EU country or a third country and, in the case of the latter, whether a Global North nation upon which there are no particular legislative restrictions – such as Canada, the USA, Norway, Switzerland, etc. – or a Global South nation whose citizens have great difficulty obtaining a visa).

Moreover, migrants' insertion into the labour market in Italy is characterised by 1) the 'ethno-national' segmentation of the labour market; 2) the segregation of the migrant labour force into specific jobs, with women channelled into specific sectors (which are often directly related to their living conditions, as in the case of care workers); 3) high job insecurity and 4) a significantly lower wage compared to that of native workers (Perocco, 2012; Zanfrini, 2010).

The aforementioned material requirements and definitions of the family thus have different effects on the various subjects involved: there is a *stratification* of their biographical trajectories, family trajectory and social insertion according to their citizenship/residence status. This position is in turn determined by an *intersection* between the multiple dimensions that construct the social, civic and political identity of these subjects (Anthias, 2005; Crenshaw, 1991).

If, on the one hand, the adoption of the analytical construct of *civic stratification* allows us to highlight the differentiated (and unequal) distribution of constraints and opportunities offered by the normative superstructure, on the other hand it risks overshadowing individual and collective *agency* and emphasising the heteronomous character of the reunification process in an excessively deterministic sense. I do not want to deny the ability of migrants to put strategies and practices into action in the field of family reunification and to find spaces of possibility in it, but I also want to understand the decision-making processes of these subjects in

8 It is responsible (in terms of modalities and requirements) for issuing residence permits and often also for declaring the suitability of housing and the number of people that can be accommodated (Della Puppa, 2014; Della Puppa & Gelati, 2015).

a way that is inevitably interdependent with the normative superstructure and the structural context. Thus, in the planning and implementation of reunification, the first-migrant applicant has to take into account the regulation and its requirements, as well as the system of civic stratification.

5. Work and family reunification

Sayad (2002, pp. 94–95) states: 'every instance of labour immigration contains at bottom the population immigration that will prolong it; conversely, it can be said that there is no family immigration . . . that did not begin with labour immigration'. Eric Fassin (2009, p. 22), taking up Sayad's argument, points out that

> the opposition between the two [between labour immigration and family immigration] dissolves as soon as the reality is examined. On the one hand, workers are inclined to have families: their behaviour is not dictated by economic interests alone. On the other hand, families are inclined to be job-seekers: human ties do not impede economic logic. It is not only a matter of humanitarianism, but also of rationality: it is absurd to act as if family and work were two parallel worlds, with no relationship between them.

Moreover, often the reproductive work of the reunified family member is incorporated into the first migrant's work for the market. It should also be emphasised that, especially in the current economic situation, the reunified family member is frequently required to enter the labour market to support the reunified nucleus, particularly if the first-migrant applicant becomes unemployed. This is due both to their material needs and to immigration law, which links their residence document, work contract and income. In fact, work is central in legitimising the presence of migrants and their reunified family members in Italy: not only is the reunification document already strictly linked to a work contract, but Article 26 of the Law 189/2002 states that 'the right to maintain or regain family unity with foreign family members is recognised . . . for foreigners holding a long term residence permit or short term residence permit of no less than one year's duration'.

Italian policies on migrants' entry into and regular stay in the Italian territory closely link the residence permit to migrants' employment contract: a migrant cannot obtain or keep a residence permit without an employment contract and, at the same time, cannot get an employment contract without a residence permit. This strict bond – introduced by the so-called Turco-Napolitano (Law 40/1998) and strengthened by the so-called Bossi-Fini (Law 189/2002) – became 'a model for Europe' (Basso & Perocco, 2003). It ensures that in the event of dismissal and unemployment, the migrant also becomes undocumented, placing migrant workers in a condition of permanent social and material blackmail in relation to their work. It is important to stress that this also affects and applies to reunited family members: in order to obtain the no impediment document for family reunification, the first-migrant applicant must have a job that guarantees them a salary and thus a certain income, and so, if they become unemployed, it is not only *they* who become undocumented, *but also* their united family members. Therefore, a migrant's work (specifically, first migrants who complete the reunification process with their family members) is closely connected to their family life in the destination country, and, in turn, their family life in the destination country depends on their labour.

Article 5 of the Law 189/2002 establishes that

> the residence permit for work reasons is issued following the stipulation of the job contract. . . . The duration of the relative residence permit . . . cannot exceed, in relation to a fixed-term employment contract, the duration of one year; in relation to a permanent employment contract, the duration of two years.

It goes on: 'The residence permit or its renewal are refused when the requisites required for entry and residence in the territory of the State are missing or no longer exist [for example, if the migrant worker is made redundant and loses their job]'. Moreover, given that the duration of the residence permit is directly proportional to the duration of the employment contract, a permanent employment contract entitles the holder to a two-year residence permit; a temporary employment contract longer than one year entitles the holder to a 12-month residence permit; while an employment contract lasting less than 12 months does not allow the holder to obtain an annual residence permit and consequently excludes them from the possibility of family reunification.

The possibility of the reunification of some of the subject's family members is understood as an 'awarding' application (Sirianni, 2006), in the sense that it is *discretionary* and *revocable* (Bertolani et al., 2013) as it is based on the requirement that the subject constantly demonstrates they fulfil the conditions required to access it, conditions that are interpreted arbitrarily by different institutional actors in different territorial contexts (Della Puppa & Salvador, 2015). For example, even two municipalities that are located next to one another could apply different parameters to determine the suitability of accommodation and thus whether to grant residency to the applicant. Of course, this may influence family reunification (Della Puppa, 2017; Della Puppa & Gelati, 2015; Manconi & Resta, 2010).

Work is thus the *premise* that makes reunification possible, and the migrant's family life is a *result* of their having work. Those who wish to reunite with their families must therefore subject themselves to forms of social and labour discipline in order to scrape together the overtime and the square metres of living space needed to meet the requirements of the legislation.

As Abdelmalek Sayad (2002) reminds us, from the point of view of the immigration society, unemployed migrants constitute an unacceptable paradox and a 'social scandal': any aspect of their existence – including their right to a family and emotional life of their own – is granted to them only when they put their bodies, hearts and brains to work.

At the same time, the failure to meet these conditions not only means the legal impossibility of a life with their family (or some of their family) in the country of destination, but also creates the *stigma* of the 'amoral deviant' with which the immigration society implicitly labels resident migrants 'without families'.

In fact, migrant men without families are considered to constitute a *threat* to the social, moral, sexual and value order of the 'host' society: deprived of the containment offered by the family and domesticity, they are seen as engaging in deviant and potentially hostile behaviour. Reunited family members perform a *containment function* for the first-migrant applicant, thus giving *reassurance* to society as a whole.

But precisely as a result of their condition, migrants without families are more immediately able to meet the requirement that legitimises their presence in the social context and the destination country: their complete and unreserved provision of the labour power they embody. Their reunited family members would thus represent a potential form of 'unwanted immigration' (since they are not completely adapted to the needs of the national labour market) and a 'distraction' from the work of the first migrant.

The process of family reunification and the presence of reunited family members also result in a continuous reshaping of the social fabric and its problems, a significant increase in the demand for services and a clear unravelling of the contradictions and inadequacies of the society of destination (Ambrosini, 2005).

For migrant women, on the other hand, it is the lone migrant – without reunited family members – who is the 'ideal migrant' for the society of destination, especially when she is employed as a home carer. The migrant care worker with no family of her own can devote herself unreservedly to caring for elderly and dependent people in the domestic contexts of her employers. This is part of a shared system of family values in which reproductive work is socially declined in the feminine and women are constructed as the 'traditional dispensers' of unpaid care work for the family. The care worker solves the problems of the workload of Italian families, allowing for the perpetuation of life practices and cultural models established along the gender axis, obscuring the care work carried out in the domestic context and contributing – through a system of reciprocal conveniences – to 'hidden' welfare (Bimbi, 2007; Chiaretti, 2007). Family members reunited with care workers would thus waste the labour power of the latter, absorbing some of the attention and emotional work that the immigration society expects them to dedicate to the families of their clients – in the concealment of the economic-salary exchange, since such work must be carried out 'as if you wanted and desire to do it' (Della Puppa, 2012). This is an important dimension in the Italian context, characterised by a 'Mediterranean' or 'familist' welfare regime (Esping-Andersen, 1995) in which the care work of migrant women is of structural importance. This aspect also emerges from the repeated amnesties that are issued periodically to regularise the administrative position of many care workers engaged in the homes of Italian families (Ambrosini, 2018).

6. Paradoxes, ambivalences, contradictions?

EU member states, including Italy, have always represented the family and the right to family life as a constituent element of their political, social and national identities and have defined the right to family unity as a fundamental and subjective right, to be recognised (at least formally) so as not to contradict and deny the self-representation the society tries to construct. In practice, however, this right is threatened, is difficult to obtain and is differentially granted.

The logic that has always guided immigration management policies – i.e. contingent quotas for the entry of 'third-country nationals' according to the *needs of the national labour market* – comes into contradiction both with the recognition of the subjective and fundamental right to family unity and with the idea that the nuclear family will contribute to migrants' 'social integration' in the social fabric and containment in the domestic-family sphere.

Alongside the issues of labour immigration and its regulation through quotas, there are also discussions about family reunification in the debate on EU and national migration policies. While family reunification is understood as 'imposed' immigration that is not immediately functional to the economic needs of the society of destination and is a distraction for the first-migrant worker, at the same time it is seen as fostering those workers' 'assimilability' and 'normalisation' within the social fabric.

The presence of the reunited family leads to a division between 'good' and 'bad' migrants, a division that is functional to the same system that denies many of them the possibility of reuniting with their families. The implicit selection that the society of destination makes through its cultural and normative constructions, defining 'good migrants' and, by contrast, giving 'family-less' migrants the stigma of being 'amoral migrants', reveals a paradox: the 'labour' immigration pursued by the society of destination – i.e. made up of working men and women without families – would be made up of subjects who are suspicious of the society of destination, of domestic morals and its values (Sayad, 2002). At the same time, the presumed desire to 'favour the integration process' would make it necessary to contradict the paradigm of the migrant's usefulness as embodied labour power and to put into practice policies aimed at favouring the entry of family members, whose presence alongside the first migrant would be a sign of 'civilisation', an 'assimilatory' will and a willingness to share 'our own values' (*ibidem*).

Seyla Benhabib (2003, p. 449) writes: 'While the theorists do not preclude immigration, they tend to favour the incorporation of those foreigners who "are like us" and who can become the model citizen'. To be 'like us' the 'foreigner' must show a determination to reconstruct some of their domestic and family relationships in the new context of settlement through the acceptance of the social and labour discipline imposed by national and EU policies.

7. Conclusion

This chapter has examined family reunification policies in Italy and analysed the ways in which the migrant family is constructed in political and administrative discourse at a national level, in order to understand the effect of family reunification policies on family structures and their material conditions and social life.

The first migrant's labour contract guarantees (if it is 'good' enough) their access to the institution of family reunification and also binds the reunified family member: it is not only a labour contract but also a gender and generational contract that sanctions particular roles and functions that each family member involved in the reunification must assume. Policies on reunification subordinate the family reunification of migrants to the achievement of material requirements that the first-migrant applicant must achieve through work.

The close interconnection between work and reunification allows us to grasp the permanent tension between the market, the state and (migrant) families: the *market* increasingly needs cheap labour power free from (affective) bonds and (family) ties; the state (and the aggregation of states at the EU level) is engaged in governing immigration and regulating the entry of 'foreign' citizens but also in showing that it wants to defend, at least formally, the right to family unity; and *families* are certain to claim the right to a life together and to resist their reduction to the mere embodied labour power of the first-migrant family member.

The state tries to dissolve the irreconcilable contradictions of its ambivalent interests – played out in the conflictual dialectic between families and the market – by simultaneously denying and granting family reunification, resulting in the collision of the symbolic (including self-representation) with economic (and demographic) needs.

This simultaneous concession-negation creates a dual *device*. It is a *device of social and labour discipline* that imposes on those who wish to recompose part of their family life in the context of destination both the maximisation of their working capacity and the restriction of their extended sociality. It is also a *device of civic stratification*, which differentiates the possibilities of enjoying the right to family life for first-migrant applicants and their family members; hierarchises the social, biographical, administrative, educational and work trajectories of reunified family members; and stratifies the paths and citizenship rights of migrant families. In fact, Italian policies on family reunification not only link the type and duration of the residence permit of reunited family members to that of the first-migrant applicant, but also structure and stratify the possibilities of reunification of the first-migrant applicant according to their position within the intersection of different axes of identity ('ethnicity', gender, social class, country of origin, etc.).

Furthermore, these same policies define what the immigrant family is and of whom it is or can be composed. It creates it as a nuclear structure which, in addition to not describing the majority of native Italian families, almost never reflects the family as it is experienced by migrants. At the same time, it reveals the distorted ways in which Italian society thinks about the family and itself.

References

Ambrosini, M. (2005). *Sociologia delle migrazioni*. Il Mulino.

Ambrosini, M. (2014). Parenting from a distance and processes of family reunification: A research on the Italian case. *Ethnicities*, *8*, 1–20. https://doi.org/10.1177/1468796814547059

Ambrosini, M. (2018). *Irregular Immigration in Southern Europe: Actors, Dynamics and Governance*. Palgrave Macmillan. https://dx.doi.org/10.1007/978-3-319-70518-7

Ambrosini, M., Bonizzoni, P., & Caneva, E. (2010). *Ritrovarsi altrove. Famiglie ricongiunte e adolescenti di origine immigrata*. Fondazione Ismu.

Anthias, F. (2005). Social Stratification and Social Inequality: Models of Intersectionality and Identity. In R. Crompton, F. Devine, J. Scott, & M. Savage (Eds.), *Rethinking Class: Culture, Identities, and Lifestyle* (pp. 24–45). Palgrave Macmillan. https://doi.org/10.1007/978-0-230-21454-5

Banfi, L., & Boccagni, P. (2009). Transnational Family Life: One Pattern or Many, and Why? A Comparative Study on Female Migration. In E. Kofman, A. Kohli, A. Kraler, & C. Schmoll (Eds.), *Gender, Generations and the Family in International Migration* (pp. 14–16). Amsterdam University Press. https://doi.org/10.26530/OAPEN_418151

Basso, P. (Ed.). (2010). *Razzismo di stato: Stati Uniti, Europa, Italia*. Franco Angeli.

Basso, P. & Perocco, F. (Eds.). (2003). *Gli immigrati in Europa. Diseguaglianze, razzismo, lotte*. Franco Angeli.

Benhabib, S. (2003). Transformations of citizenship: The case of contemporary Europe. Government and opposition. *International Journal of Comparative Politics*, *4*, 439–465. https://doi.org/10.1111/1477-7053.00110

Bertolani, B. (2011). Networking, transnazionalismo e famiglia. In M. Tognetti Bordogna (Ed.), *Famiglie ricongiunte: Esperienze di ricongiungimento di famiglie del Marocco, Pakistan, India* (pp. 41–62). Utet.

Bertolani, B., Rinaldini, M., & Tognetti Bordogna, M. (2013). Combining civic stratification and transnational approaches for reunited families: The case of Moroccans, Indians and Pakistanis in Reggio Emilia. *Journal of Ethnic and Migration Studies*, *40*, 1470–1487. https://doi.org/10.1080/1369183X.2013.868302

Bimbi, F. (2007). Famiglia e famiglie: Transizioni demografiche, migrazioni culturali, nodi delle politiche. *Italiani Europei*, *3*, 35–50.

Bonizzoni, P. (2009). *Famiglie globali. Le frontiere della maternità*. Utet.

Bonizzoni, P. (2012). Civic Stratification, Stratified Reproduction and Family Solidarity: Strategies of Latino Families in Milan. In A. Kraler, M. Kohli, & C. Schmoll (Eds.), *Gender, Generations and the Family in International Migration* (pp. 311–335). Amsterdam University Press. https://doi.org/10.26530/OAPEN_418151

Bonizzoni, P., & Boccagni, P. (2013). Care and Circulation Revisited: A Conceptual Map of Diversity in Transnational Parenting. In L. Baldassar & L. Merla (Eds.), *Transnational Families, Migration and the Circulation of Care* (pp. 78–93). Routledge.

Bonizzoni, P., & Cibea, A. (2009). *Family migration policies in Italy, NODE policy report*. International Centre for Migration Policy Development.

Bonjour, S., & de Hart, B. (2013). A proper wife, a proper marriage: Constructions of 'us' and 'them' in Dutch family migration policy. *European Journal of Women's Studies*, *20*, 61–76. https://doi.org/10.1177/1350506812456459

Chiaretti, G. (2007). La catena globale del lavoro di cura. In L. Corradi & F. Perocco (Eds.), *Sociologia e globalizzazione* (pp. 59–95). Mimesis.

Crenshaw, K. W. (1991). Mapping the margins: Intersectionality, identity politics, and violence against women of colour. *Stanford Law Review*, *43*, 1241–1299. https://doi.org/10.2307/1229039

Della Puppa, F. (2012). Being part of the family: Social and working conditions of female migrant care workers in Italy. *NORA – Nordic Journal of Feminist and Gender Research*, *20*, 182–198. https://doi.org/10.1080/08038740.2012.685494

Della Puppa, F. (2014). *Uomini in movimento: Il lavoro della maschilità fra Bangladesh e Italia*. Rosemberg & Sellier.

Della Puppa, F. (2017). Politiche escludenti e associazionismo immigrato in una "*banglatown*" del Nordest: Il caso di Alte Ceccato. *Mondi Migranti*, *1*, 57–76. https://doi.org/10.3280/MM2017-001004

Della Puppa, F., & Gelati, E. (2015). *Alte Ceccato: Una banglatown nel nordest*. Professional Dreammers.

Della Puppa, F., & Salvador, O. (2015). Ricongiungere la famiglia in tempo di crisi: Strategie per ricostruire e difendere l'unità familiare a inizio millennio. *Mondi Migranti*, *2*, 169–196. https://doi.org/10.3280/MM2015-002007
EMN (European Migration Network). (2008). *Family reunification* (Working Paper). EMN.
Esping-Andersen, G. (1995). Il Welfare State senza il lavoro: L'ascesa del familismo nelle politiche sociali dell'Europa continentale. *Stato e Mercato*, *3*(45), 347–380.
Fassin, E. (2009, November). L'immigration, un "problème" si commode. *Le Monde Diplomatique*, p. 22.
Gil Araujo, S. (2008). *Civic Stratification, Gender and Family Migration Policies: An Exploratory Investigation of Migrants Involved in Family Migration in Spain*. International Centre for Migration Policy Development.
Grillo, R. (Ed.). (2008). *The Family in Question: Immigrant and Ethnic Minorities in Multicultural Europe*. Amsterdam University Press. https://doi.org/10.5117/9789053568699
Hochschild, A. R. (1979). Emotion work, feeling rules and social structure. *American Journal of Sociology*, *85*, 551–575. https://doi.org/10.1086/227049
King, R., & De Bono, D. (2013). Irregular migration and the "Southern European model of migration". *Journal of Mediterranean Studies*, *22*, 1–31.
Kofman, E. (2004). Family-related migration: A critical review of European studies. *Journal of Ethnic and Migration Studies*, *30*, 243–262. https://doi.org/10.1080/1369183042000200687
Kofman, E. (2005). Citizenship, migration and reassertion of national identity. *Citizenship Studies*, *9*, 125–147. https://doi.org/10.1080/13621020500301221
Kofman, E., Kraler, A., Kohli, M., & Schmoll, C. (2011). Introduction Issue and Debates on Family Related Migration and the Migrant Family: An European Perspective (pp. 13–54). In A. Kraler, E. Kofman, M. Kohli, & C. Schmoll (Eds.), *Gender, Generations and the Family in International Migration*. Amsterdam University Press.
Kraler, A. (2010). *Civic Stratification, Gender and Family Migration Policies in Europe*. International Centre for Migration Policy Development.
Lainati, C., Grandi, F., & Oberbacher, M. (2008). *Famiglie ricongiunte in Alto Adige*. Praxis 3.
Lockwood, D. (1996). Civic integration and class formation. *British Journal of Sociology*, *47*, 531–550. https://doi.org/10.2307/591369
Manconi, L., & Resta, F. (2010). La xenofobia municipale. *Mondi Migranti*, *2*, 321–331. https://doi.org/10.3280/MM2010-002014
Morozzo della Rocca, P. (2008). *Immigrazione e cittadinanza: Profili normativi e ngiurisprudenziali*. Utet.
Morris, L. (2003). Managing contradiction: Civic stratification and migrants' right. *International Migration Review*, *37*, 74–100. https://doi.org/10.1111/j.1747-7379.2003.tb00130.x
Perocco, F. (2012). *Trasformazioni globali e nuove disuguaglianze*. Franco Angeli.
Pugliese, E. (2011). The Mediterranean model of immigration. *Academicus International Scientific Journal*, *3*, 96–107. https://doi.org/10.7336/academicus.2011.03.06
Sayad, A. (2002). *La doppia assenza: Dalle illusioni dell'emigrato alle sofferenze dell'immigrato*. Cortina.
Scabini, E., & Rossi, G. (2008). *La migrazione come evento familiare*. Vita e Pensiero.
Schweitzer, R. (2015). A stratified right to family life? On the logic(s) and legitimacy of granting differential access to family reunification for third-country nationals living within the EU. *Journal of Ethnic and Migration Studies*, *41*, 2130–2148. https://doi.org/10.1080/1369183X.2015.1037256
Sirianni, G. (2006). *Il diritto degli stranieri alla unità familiare*. Giuffrè.
Strasser, E., Kraler, A., Bonjour, S., & Bilger, V. (2009). Doing family: Responses to the construction of "the migrant family" across Europe. *History of the Family*, *14*, 165–176. https://doi.org/10.1016/j.hisfam.2009.02.005

Tognetti Bordogna, M. (2004). *Ricongiungere la famiglia altrove: Strategie, percorsi, modelli e forme del ricongiungimento familiare*. Franco Angeli.
Tognetti Bordogna, M. (2005). Struttura e strategie della famiglia immigrata. *La Rivista delle Politiche Sociali*, *4*, 171–197.
Tognetti Bordogna, M. (2011). *Esperienze di ricongiungimento di famiglie del Marocco, Pakistan, India*. Utet.
Zanfrini, L. (2010). *Il lavoro, in Fondazione ISMU, Quindicesimo rapporto sulle migrazioni 2009*. Franco Angeli.

Part IV

Proving family ties

12 Family reunification for "paperless" Eritrean refugees

A pie in the sky or a realisable right?

Sara Arapiles and Daniel Mekonnen

1. Introduction

Reunifying separated refugee families was a primary concern for the drafters of the 1951 Refugee Convention relating to the Status of Refugees, which recommended state parties to take the necessary measures for the protection of the refugee's family with a view to 'ensuring that the unity of the refugee's family is maintained'. The fundamental importance of state positive actions to maintain or re-establish refugee family unity has been reiterated by various official documents of the United Nations High Commissioner for Refugees (UNHCR).[1] Further, within the context of the European Union (EU), the Family Reunification Directive (2003/86/EC) establishes a right to family reunification. In the words of the Directive, family reunification is a 'necessary way of making family life possible'.[2] The Directive lays down the conditions for the exercise of this right by third-country nationals who are lawfully resident in the territory of the EU Member States,[3] providing some more favourable provisions for the exercise of *refugees*' right to family reunification.[4] As stipulated by the Directive, measures concerning family reunification 'should be adopted in conformity with the obligation to protect the family and respect family life enshrined in many instruments of international law', in particular the European Convention for the Protection of Human Rights and Fundamental Freedoms (ECHR) and the Charter of Fundamental Rights of the European Union (Charter).[5] The Court of Justice of the European Union (CJEU) has interpreted the latter requirement strictly, ruling that the provisions of the Family Reunification Directive '*must* be interpreted in the light of the fundamental rights and, more particularly, in the light of the right to respect for family life enshrined in both the ECHR and the [Charter]'.[6]

1 See, e.g., UNHCR, Executive Committee, Conclusion No. 1 (XXVI) Establishment of the Sub-Committee and General, 1975, para. (f).
2 Recital 4 Family Reunification Directive.
3 Article 1 Family Reunification Directive.
4 Recital 8 and Chapter V Family Reunification Directive.
5 Recital 2 Family Reunification Directive.
6 CJEU, 4 March 2010, C-578/08, *Chakroun*, ECLI:EU:C:2010:117, § 44 [emphasis added].

DOI: 10.4324/9781003503217-16

In practice, however, there exist legal and practical barriers that hinder refugees' enjoyment and exercise of their rights to family life and family reunification (EMN, 2017; Council of Europe, 2017; UNHCR, 2012). This chapter focuses on strict documentary requirements for establishing family ties and identity. The discussion is based on the specific experience of Eritrean refugees and asylum seekers in Europe. The strict requirement of documentary evidence, as will be shown, is one of the major obstacles that impedes Eritrean refugees, who are oftentimes "paperless", to realise their right to family reunification. The term "paperless" in this chapter refers to the situation in which a refugee lacks documentary evidence from their own country of origin to prove one's national identity or certain aspects of vital events of their lives, such as incidents of birth or marriage. As will be apparent, due to lack of a well-functioning documentation system in Eritrea regarding the issuance of records of vital events, Eritrean refugees often lack official documentation and, therefore, are unable to meet the documentary requirements demanded by some EU Member States during family reunification procedures. The right to family reunification thus becomes an unrealisable right for many Eritrean refugees, notwithstanding Article 11(2) of the Family Reunification Directive provides that '[a] decision rejecting an application [for family reunification] may not be based solely on the fact that documentary evidence is lacking'. While the CJEU has been asked to interpret the Directive on various occasions (Friedery, 2019), so far only one case[7] has been directly based on the provision in Article 11(2). In this case, which arose from the rejection of an application for family reunification by an Eritrean citizen and beneficiary of subsidiary protection in the Netherlands, the CJEU cautioned EU Member States to take into account other considerations when documentary evidence is lacking or cannot be obtained. This chapter will examine this ruling of the CJEU, which, despite its relevance, has not attracted scholarly attention to date.

This chapter has five major sections. Following the present introductory section, Section 2 explains the methodological approach of the research. Section 3 takes the plight of Eritrean refugees as a pertinent case study to contextualise the obstacles that "paperless" refugees face in seeking to realise their right to family reunification. Section 3 further highlights the problem of lack of official documentation that many Eritrean refugees experience in their application for family reunification, including the obligation to appear in person at Eritrean diplomatic missions, which poses serious risks to Eritrean refugees and their relatives in Eritrea. Section 4 briefly discusses legal developments at the European and international levels dealing with "paperless" refugees' right to family reunification, including contributions from UNHCR. Section 5 turns to examine the ruling of the CJEU in *E. v. Staatssecretaris van Veiligheid en Justitie*. The fact that this case arose from a rejection of an Eritrean application for family reunification on the basis of lack of evidentiary documentation, further underpins the choice of the case study. Section 6 presents concluding remarks.

7 CJEU, 13 March 2019, C-635/17, *E.*, ECLI:EU:C:2019:192.

2. A note on methodology

This chapter, especially Section 3, builds on an Expert Report co-authored by the present authors (Mekonnen & Arapiles, 2021), in which the authors discussed at length the (non-)possibilities for Eritrean refugees to access official documents from Eritrea or via Eritrean diplomatic missions. The main findings of that report were also shared in various expert meetings organised by UNHCR and other actors. The research relied on primary data gathered by the authors through semi-structured interviews, with a total of 39 interlocutors located in the following countries: Canada, Egypt, Ethiopia, Germany, Kenya, the Netherlands, Norway, Sudan, Sweden, Switzerland, the United Kingdom (UK), the United States of America (USA), and Uganda. The interviewees included Eritrean asylum seekers and refugees in cross-border situations, Eritrean legal professionals, former diplomats, asylum lawyers from various jurisdictions in Europe, academics, and staff members and representatives of independent organisations working for the protection of refugee rights. The Expert Report also drew on Eritrean legal sources as well as other secondary data, including academic and institutional sources, especially the two major reports of the United Nations Commission of Inquiry on Human Rights in Eritrea (UN Human Rights Council, 2015, 2016). Drawing on the primary data included in the aforementioned Expert Report, Section 4 of this chapter provides context to the obstacles that "paperless" refugees face in family reunification procedures, in a manner that contributes to scholarly debates on this specific challenge.

3. Contextualising the obstacles faced by "paperless" Eritrean refugees in family reunification procedures[8]

In a joint report by UNHCR and the Refugee Council (2018, p. 27) arising from a participatory study with newly recognised Eritrean refugees in the UK, it was stated that:

> UNHCR recognises the difficulties that some refugee populations can have in providing documentary evidence for the existence of their family relationships and encourages the UK and other States to ensure that such legal requirements to family reunion do not present insurmountable obstacles to refugee applicants. Similarly, a report by the Independent Chief Inspector of Borders and Immigration on family reunion applications found that, for a range of reasons, 'applicants from conflict areas or fragile states, such as Somalia and Eritrea, or those who are displaced and residing in a third country or in a refugee camp, may struggle to provide documentary evidence of identity or relationships'.

The aforementioned observations highlight critical challenges that Eritrean refugees experience in Europe in family reunification procedures. In several EU

8 This section heavily relies on Section 3 of Mekonnen and Arapiles (2021).

Member States, and most notably in Germany, Eritrean refugees have been persistently asked by local authorities to adduce passports, ID cards, and birth or marriage certificates (or similar documents) in order to process an application for family reunification. This, as will be shown, has been done in a manner that undermines fundamental rights of refugees as protected by international and EU law. This issue was one of the main reasons that gave rise to the Expert Report cited earlier, which makes the departure point for some of the assertions made in this section.

3.1 Lack of official identity and family relationships documentation

Eritrea has a poorly institutionalised history of the issuance of official documents, particularly those related to records of vital events. This is true even though the country has a fairly sufficient body of laws related to the issuance of identity-proving documents and records of vital events. The problem lies in the lack of the necessary institutional infrastructure at the ground level. Moreover, as a matter of general practice, the issuance of some of the most important records of vital events (e.g., birth and marriage certificates) is not very common in the country. When issued, such documents are issued by various entities (public and semi-private entities). For instance, in the highlands of Eritrea, where Orthodox Christianity is most dominant, a religious baptism certificate is commonly used as a proof of birth date in lieu of a formal birth certificate. A typical baptism certificate issued by the Eritrean Orthodox Tewahedo Church contains the most essential details of the baptised child, namely, the full name of the father, the date and place of birth, as well as the date and place of baptism. Municipalities in major towns of Eritrea can issue official birth certificates based on details that have been captured in religious baptism certificates. Marriage certificates can also be issued by the Eritrean Orthodox Tewahedo Church in the same way as birth certificates. In some cases, vaccination cards are also used as proof of the age of children, as those documents contain vital information about children.

In the Eritrean Muslim communities, which constitute roughly half of the total population of Eritrea, the issuance of baptism certificates is not common. This is 'partly explained by the fact that the very concept of baptism, with which [religious] birth certificates are inherently related in the Christian communities, is non-existent in Islam' (Mekonnen & Arapiles, 2021, p. 24). To our knowledge, there are no 'equivalent' religious substitutes in the Muslim communities of Eritrea that may serve as proof of birth certificates (for example, as in the case of a baptism certificate of the Eritrean Orthodox Tewahedo Church). However, the issuance of vaccination cards for children, which is now a very common practice, can serve as a means of proving a birth date. The issuance of marriage certificates is common also in the Muslim communities. It is done by a religious leader who officiates the religious ceremony of marriage. Within Eritrea, such documents can have a probative value in terms of proving the vital events they purport to record. As will be shown later in this chapter, these documents may have less probatory value outside Eritrea.

Of particular importance about the issuance of birth and marriage certificates in Eritrea is the following observation by Mekonnen and Arapiles (2021, p. 24):

> It is also not uncommon to see birth certificates or other records of vital events written with spelling errors, because standardisation is a very common problem in Eritrea. In a typical (Western) European context, a spelling error may indicate some sort of forgery in relation to the document in which the error occurs. In an Eritrean case, this is not always true; misspellings are common and do not necessarily come as indicators of forgery. Therefore, the divergence in the physical features of such documents need not be taken as a potential sign of forgery, as it is sometimes presumed by certain national authorities in Europe. The very issuance of such certificates differs from place to place.

When these documents are sent to foreign countries, for example, in the context of family reunification processes, their validity is challenged. In order to overcome this, individuals have to authenticate these documents before they are sent to foreign countries. In most cases, the authentication process involves having those documents officially converted to, or replaced by, municipal documents, which must be eventually authenticated by the Department of Consular Affairs of the Ministry of Foreign Affairs in Eritrea (before they are sent to third countries).

3.2 The difficulty of re-establishing contacts with Eritrean authorities

In most cases refugees leave their country of origin without having the most essential documents they need in order to prove some vital events of their lives (birth and marriage in particular). The abrupt nature of forced displacement means that people flee their country of origin suddenly and they only try to obtain these documents (if ever possible) once they have fled their country. In an Eritrean context, flight or forced displacement happens in a context where the intention of seeking asylum in a foreign country is rendered a criminal offence which is often punished by arbitrary and extrajudicial forms of punishment, often of a life-threatening nature. Therefore, for Eritrean refugees and asylum seekers, obtaining official records of vital events or identity-proving documents can only be done by visiting Eritrean diplomatic missions, which are persistently accused of abusive practices, as shown by various sources (e.g., DSP-Group & Tilburg University, 2017).

Approaching Eritrean diplomatic missions for purposes of obtaining official documents poses serious risks to both Eritrean applicants and their relatives (in third countries and in Eritrea). The procedure entails, among other things, the signature of a so-called regret form (DSP-Group & Tilburg University, 2017; Riggan, 2016, p. 207) in which Eritreans are compelled to make written self-incriminating statements with far-fetching implications on their fundamental rights. Without this, no consular service can be offered to them. In the self-incriminating statement, individuals are compelled to admit that by leaving Eritrea 'illegally', mainly to seek asylum and potentially also by avoiding the country's controversial National/

Military Service Programme (NMSP) they are liable for criminal accountability. This may also entail other far-fetching consequences to relatives in Eritrea, such as reprisals on the basis of imputed political opinion of a relative abroad (UN Human Rights Council, 2015, 2016; Bozzini, 2015).

There is a need here to briefly explain the NMSP of the country. The Eritrean government continues to implement this programme, which is indefinite and non-paid by nature. The practice affects people between the ages of 18 and 50, but the maximum age limit at times stretches even beyond 50. Most of the country's gross human rights violations are committed in the context of the government's controversial NMSP (UN Human Rights Council, 2015, 2016; Kibreab, 2017; Van Reisen et al., 2019). Escape from this programme is the main reason that causes many Eritreans to flee the country (Kibreab, 2009; Arapiles, 2023a, 2022, 2015). It is because of this reason that the very act of escaping the country and seeking asylum in a foreign country is regarded by the Eritrean government as a treasonous act, necessitating on the part of Eritrean diplomatic missions the practice of coerced signature of the so-called regret form (see, e.g., Riggan, 2016).

Eritrean refugees and asylum seekers are expected by some EU countries (particularly Germany, as noted earlier) to fulfil a high threshold evidentiary requirement in their family reunification applications. It is in this context that individuals (asylum seekers and refugees in particular) may visit Eritrean diplomatic missions, seeking official consular services related to records of vital events, ID card, passport, or other official documents. It is also in this context that they are compelled to confess (by signing the regret form) that they have committed a crime for which they will be held accountable whenever they return to Eritrea (Mekonnen & Arapiles, 2021). This is in addition to the payment of a so-called 2% diaspora income tax, which must be paid from any income, including money received in the form social welfare assistance (DSP-Group & Tilburg University, 2017; Mekonnen & Arapiles, 2021). These two preconditions are implemented in tandem, exposing many Eritrean asylum seekers and refugees to an additional layer of abuse in the hands of the diplomatic missions (ibid.). The very act of compelling Eritreans (directly or indirectly) to report to the diplomatic missions of Eritrea, in order to obtain official documents, is also fundamentally opposed to the underlying ground of their asylum claim, which is that of seeking protection from abuses committed by the Government of Eritrea, potentially also by its diplomatic missions.

Due to severe restrictions related to obtaining services from Eritrean diplomatic missions, most Eritreans submit alternate evidentiary documents, such as religious baptism certificates, which then may not be taken as sufficient by some EU countries. That is why it becomes imperative to consider 'other' evidentiary standards for family reunification applications. This is the option recommended by *E. v. Staatssecretaris van Veiligheid en Justitie*, as will be further discussed in the next section. Practice that is not compliant with this requirement hinders the realisation of the right to family reunification, resulting in the violation of the right to family unity and family life.

4. The right to family reunification in the absence of documentary evidence

Article 16(3) of the Universal Declaration of Human Rights (UDHR) provides that 'the family is the natural and fundamental group unit of society and is entitled to protection by society and the State'. Although the UDHR does not have the force of law, the protection of the unit of a family has been codified into international human rights instruments that have binding effect on EU Member States, namely, the International Covenant on Civil and Political Rights (ICCPR), the Convention on the Right of the Child (CRC), the ECHR, and the Charter. The 1951 Refugee Convention, for its part, while it does not address family unity specifically, it provides protection for the refugee family in a few provisions.[9]

Article 23 of the ICCPR recognises the protection of the family unity. The UN Human Rights Committee (HRC) has affirmed that the provision in Article 23 of the ICCPR 'guarantees the protection of family life including the interest in family reunification', noting that the right to protection of family life is not 'necessarily displaced by geographical separation' nor obviated 'by the absence of formal marriage bonds, especially where there is a local practice of customary or common law marriage'.[10] Article 16 of the ICCPR also provides that '[e]veryone shall have the right to recognition everywhere as a person before the law'. It is also important to note that the UN has a target to provide a legal identity to all by 2030 in the context of the UN Sustainable Development Goals (SDGs) (Corneloup & Verhellen, 2021). To the authors' knowledge, the previously cited provision of the ICCPR has not received enough attention by refugee law scholarship notwithstanding refugees were in the minds of its drafters (Arapiles, 2023b; Rodrik, 2022). The provision in Article 16 of the ICCPR was drafted parallel to its counterpart in Article 6 of the UDHR. In the discussions leading to the latter provision, the French representative, Cassin, recalled that before World War II,

> there were instances when the right to marry was refused to refugees under the pretext that they did not have all the necessary papers and documents, that they did not have an authorization of residence, an official permit, and so forth, although they might have been living in a particular country for several years.
>
> (Schabas, 2013, p. 805)

He further observed that 'the most fundamental human rights were denied' upon refugees, emphasising that Article 6 was aimed to allow refugees and other people

9 Article 4 refers to refugees' right to respect for their 'freedom as regards the religious education of their children'; Article 12(2) provides that 'rights attaching to marriage, shall be respected by Contracting States'; Article 22 concerns the public education of children in elementary school and beyond; paragraph 2 of the annexed schedule states that 'children may be included in the travel document of a parent or, in exceptional circumstances, of another adult refugee'.

10 UN Human Rights Committee, 16 July 2004, *Ngambi and Nébol v. France*, UN Doc. CCPR/C/81/D/1179/2003, para. 6.4.

in a similar fate, 'regardless of whether or not [they are] citizen[s]', to exercise their fundamental rights in a 'most concrete and practical manner' (Schabas, 2013, p. 805). Later in the discussions, the representative of Chile agreed with the point of view expressed by the French representative. He observed that 'the aim of the provision in question was to avoid the discrimination toward foreigners which might be exercised in certain countries' (Schabas, 2013, p. 1550). This underscored the obstacles that refugees faced in realising their rights. As Cassin put it, through 'small detailed regulations the most fundamental human rights were denied' to refugees (Schabas, 2013, p. 805). Article 6 of the UDHR and Article 16 of the ICCPR sought to solve that problem by obliging states to recognise 'everyone' as a person before the law so that they can enjoy other rights that require specific documentation for their realisation. Likewise, Article 25 of the Refugee Convention, more specifically, provides for the administrative assistance to refugees.

Besides the ICCPR, the CRC also protects family reunification under various provisions (in Articles 9, 10, 16, and 22(2)). Article 10 of the CRC specifically provides that 'applications by a child or his or her parents to enter or leave a State Party for the purpose of family reunification shall be dealt with by States Parties in a positive, humane and expeditious manner'. The CRC Committee has criticised the procedures on family reunification that impose excessively demanding documentary requirements and recommends to take 'all necessary measures to safeguard the principle of family unity for refugees and their children, including by making administrative requirements for family unification more flexible and affordable'.[11] Article 10 of the CRC also enjoins States parties to ensure that the submission of requests for family reunification by children 'shall entail no adverse consequences for the applicants and for the members of their family'.

For the purposes of this chapter, it is important to highlight *Mugenzi v. France*,[12] in which the European Court of Human Rights (ECtHR) reiterated that family unity was an essential right for refugees and that family reunification was a fundamental element in enabling persons who had fled persecution to resume a normal life. It emphasised that the applicant's refugee status meant that their application for family reunification should be dealt with 'speedily, attentively and with especial care, considering that the acquisition of an international protection status is proof that the person concerned is in a vulnerable position' (Council of Europe, 2017, p. 2; Hathaway, 2021). In particular, the ECtHR urged the national authorities to take into consideration 'other evidence' of the existence of family ties where the refugee is unable to provide official supporting documents.[13]

UNHCR (2001, para. 1) agrees that the right to family unity also applies in the refugee context. In the European context, in particular, UNHCR (2015) advocates for family reunification 'mechanisms that are swift and efficient' and consequently

11 It did so in its Concluding Observation to Poland in 2015, as cited in Council of Europe (2017, p. 19).

12 ECtHR, 10 July 2014, *Mugenzi v. France*, No. 52701/09.

13 ibid.

calls on Member States to facilitate family reunification by 'simplifying and expediting the family reunification process'. The UNHCR's ExCom Conclusion No. 24 (1981) more specifically remarks that, '[w]hen deciding on family reunification, the absence of documentary proof of the formal validity of a marriage or of the filiation of children should not *per se* be considered as an impediment'.[14] A 2018 judgement[15] rendered by the Swedish Migration Court of Appeal (the highest judicial organ in Sweden for matters of asylum and immigration) is instructive in this regard.

The Swedish case concerned an Eritrean woman and her child, both registered as refugees in Ethiopia and who applied for family reunification to join the woman's husband (and father of the child) and her other child, both residing in Sweden. The documents she had submitted and the information she and her husband had provided could not confirm her identity, nor she had submitted documentary evidence showing she was the mother of the children. The Swedish Migration Court of Appeal found that it was disproportionate to require the Eritrean applicants to obtain Eritrean passports from an Eritrean embassy abroad given the risks this would pose to them and their relatives in Eritrea (para. 4). It thus emphasised the need to consider 'alternative' proof of identity for Eritrean refugees in the context of family reunification applications. Accordingly, the Swedish Migration Court of Appeal held that the applicants would enjoy an alleviation of evidentiary burden with regard to their identities and that it would fall upon the Swedish Migration Agency to complete a DNA test on the family's affiliation. In ruling so, the Court relied on *Mugenzi v. France*, referred to earlier, and the Family Reunification Directive, underlining that both the ECtHR and EU law require domestic authorities to take into account 'other evidence' of the existence of family ties, where the refugee is not able to present official documents (para. 2.2).

As of 11 October 2022, there is a new court ruling[16] rendered by the Federal Administrative Court in Germany, which is the county's highest administrative court. This judgment is expected to unease several of the challenges experienced by "paperless" Eritrean refugees. The appellant, a beneficiary of subsidiary protection in Germany, had been denied the issuance of a travel document on the basis that he could reasonably be expected to apply for a passport at the Eritrean embassy. The Federal Administrative Court ruled that the appellant could not be expected to submit the regret form required to obtain a national passport. The Court saw in this form not only an expression of regret but also the self-accusation of a criminal offence, namely, illegal exit, which, as the Court noted, is a punishable offence under Eritrean law. The Court referred to Article 1(1) of the German Basic Law, which protects against being forced to accuse oneself (para. 19). It went on to say that the protection of this provision extends to cases where the individual is

14 UNHCR, Executive Committee, Conclusion No. 24 (XXXII) Family Reunification, 1981, para. 6.

15 Migration Court of Appeal (Sweden), 5 March 2018, UM 2630–17.

16 Federal Administrative Court (Germany), 11 October 2022, BVerwG, 1 C 9.21.

asked to succumb to self-incrimination in order to obtain a state benefit to which the person is fundamentally entitled (para. 20). The Court further noted that the regret form is not regulated by Eritrean law (para. 26) and that, in contrast to a 'voluntary declaration', Eritrean nationals are 'compelled to declare their loyalty to their country of origin' by signing it (para. 27). The Court continued: 'In view of the serious human rights violations and the arbitrary penalties . . . an Eritrean sign such a self-accusation against his will with unconditional acceptance of any kind of punitive measure' (para. 28). Ruling in favour of refugee rights comes as a promising development that may waive documentary requirements for "paperless" Eritrean refugees in family reunification procedures in Germany.

5. The CJEU's interpretation of Article 11(2) of the Family Reunification Directive

Article 11(2) of the Family Reunification Directive provides that '[a] decision rejecting an application may not be based solely on the fact that documentary evidence is lacking'. According to the CJEU in *E. v. Staatssecretaris van Veiligheid en Justitie*, that provision

> is explicit, without leaving a margin of appreciation in that regard, in stating that the fact that documentary evidence is lacking cannot be the sole reason for rejecting an application and in obliging Member States, in such cases, to take into account other evidence of the existence of the family relationship.[17]

This consideration, as explicitly noted by the CJEU, is compliant with the European Commission's Guidelines for the application of the Family Reunification Directive, which will be discussed shortly.[18]

The foregoing was determined by the CJEU upon the request for a preliminary ruling from a District Court in Haarlem, the Netherlands. The request arose from the rejection of an application for family reunification lodged by an Eritrean beneficiary of subsidiary protection in the Netherlands. The applicant affirmed to be the aunt and the guardian, since the death of the biological parents, of an Eritrea minor (at the time of the application) residing in Sudan. The application for family reunification was rejected by the competent authorities in the Netherlands on the grounds of (i) lack of official documentary evidence of the family relationship and (ii) the sponsor's inability to explain the absence of such evidence. The Court in Haarlem tasked with deciding on the rejection of the family reunification application asked for a preliminary ruling to the CJEU prior to ruling itself on the matter.

17 CJEU, 13 March 2019, C-635/17, *E.*, ECLI:EU:C:2019:192, para. 69.

18 European Commission, Communication from the Commission to the Council and the European Parliament on guidance for the application of Directive 2003/86 on the right to family reunification, 3 April 2014, COM(2014) 210 final.

The referring court raised two questions before the CJEU. The first question concerned Article 3(2)(c) of the Family Reunification Directive, which states that the Directive does not apply where the sponsor is a third-country national authorised to reside in an EU Member State on the basis of a subsidiary form of protection. Considering this provision, the referring court asked the CJEU whether it had jurisdiction to interpret Article 11(2) of the said Directive in a situation where an application for family reunification is lodged by a beneficiary of subsidiary protection (paras. 32–33). In essence, the assumption appeared to be that to the extent that the facts of the case do not fall within the Family Reunification Directive directly, the CJEU may not have jurisdiction to pronounce on the matter. The CJEU, however, rejected it. The CJEU first referred to its settled case law that the CJEU has jurisdiction to give a preliminary ruling on questions concerning provisions of EU law when such provisions have been made applicable by domestic law directly so that situations not falling within the scope of the EU law and situations that do fall under EU law are 'interpreted uniformly' and 'treated in the same way' (paras. 35–37). The CJEU then recalled that the Dutch law applies the rules applicable to refugees under the Family Reunification Directive to beneficiaries of subsidiary protection (paras. 38–39). In light of the foregoing, the CJEU concluded that it had jurisdiction to interpret Article 11(2) of the Directive insofar as that provision was made 'directly and unconditionally applicable' to situations such as that of the case at hand under national law (para. 43). The second question concerned Article 11(2) of the Family Reunification Directive. The referring court asked whether such provision must be interpreted as precluding an application for family reunification 'from being rejected solely on the ground that the sponsor has not provided official documentary evidence', which in the present case was evidence of the death of the minor's biological parents and, consequently, that the sponsor had an actual family relationship with him (para. 44).

In its analysis of the applicable EU law, the CJEU started off with Recital 8 of the Family Reunification Directive, which states:

> Special attention *should* be paid to the situation of refugees on account of the reasons which obliged them to flee their country and prevent them from leading a normal family life there. More favourable conditions should therefore be laid down for the exercise of their right to family reunification.
>
> (para. 3 [emphasis added])

The CJEU interpreted the aforementioned requirement strictly, as, in its ruling, it used the word 'must' instead of 'should': '[S]pecial attention *must* be paid to the situation of refugees' (para. 66 [emphasis added]). The CJEU then added that, according to the European Commission's Guidelines, this implies that it is 'often impossible or dangerous for refugees or their family members to produce official documents, or to get in touch with diplomatic or consular authorities of their country of origin' (para. 66).

Proceeding with its analysis of the applicable EU law, the CJEU, after referring to various provisions of the Family Reunification Directive, consulted the

European Commission's Guidelines. While Guidance documents issued by the European Commission are not binding and do not create new legal obligations, the CJEU attached significance to the Guidelines for the application of the Family Reunification Directive. As will be shown next, these Guidelines greatly featured in the CJEU's interpretation and application of Article 11(2) of the Family Reunification Directive. It specifically replicated a passage from the Guidelines that states that in accordance with Article 5(2) of the Directive, an application for family reunification shall be accompanied by 'documentary evidence to prove the family relationship' and that interviews and other investigations, including DNA testing, may be carried out if appropriate and necessary (para. 13). It then reproduced another passage in which the European Commission had underlined that:

> [W]hen examining applications for family reunification by refugees, Member States must make a balanced and reasonable assessment in every individual case of all the interests at play, while having due regard to the best interests of minor children. . . . No factor taken separately may automatically lead to a decision; each must enter the equation only as one of the relevant factors. (para. 13)

The CJEU subsequently reproduced various excerpts from the European Commission's Guidelines dealing with the absence of official documentary evidence. One of them pertains to the obligation posed by Article 11(2) of the Family Reunification Directive to 'take into account other evidence' when documentary evidence is lacking. As prefaced earlier, this obligation leaves no margin of appreciation according to the European Commission's Guidelines. Insomuch as such 'other evidence' is to be assessed in accordance with domestic law, these Guidelines state, as reproduced by the CJEU, that 'Member States have a certain margin of appreciation, yet they should adopt clear rules governing these evidentiary requirements' (para. 13). The CJEU then replicated the examples of 'other evidence' to establish family links given by the Guidelines, which *may* include:

> [W]ritten and/or oral statements from the applicants, interviews with family members, or investigations carried out on the situation abroad. These statements can then, for instance, be corroborated by supporting evidence such as documents, audio-visual materials, any documents or physical exhibits (e.g. diplomas, proof of money transfers. . .) or knowledge of specific facts. (para. 13)

Lastly, the CJEU replicated the following excerpt from the European Commission's Guidelines, which states that Article 17 of the Family Reunification Directive:

> [R]equires that Member States take all relevant factors into account while examining the evidence provided by the applicant, including age, gender, education, background and social status as well as specific cultural aspects. The Commission considers that where serious doubts remain after other

> types of proof have been examined, or where there are strong indications of fraudulent intent, DNA testing can be used as a last resort.
>
> (para. 13)

Having referred, at the outset, to the applicable EU law, the CJEU proceeded with its own analysis. It first observed that national authorities have a margin of discretion when examining whether there is a family relationship (para. 52). However, the CJEU held that such margin of discretion afforded to the EU Member States 'must not be used by them in a manner which would undermine the objective of Directive' (para. 53), which in the CJEU's words is 'to promote family reunification' (para. 45) or its effectiveness. The CJEU added that when interpreting their national law, EU Member States must do it 'in a manner consistent with EU law' and in compliance with the 'fundamental rights protected by the legal order of the [EU]' (para. 54), in particular Article 7 of the Charter, which recognises the right to respect for private or family life, and the child's best interests recognised in Article 24(2) of the Charter (paras. 55–57). This, as the CJEU noted, requires 'a case-by-case assessment which takes account of all the relevant aspects of the particular case' (para. 59), including the children's age, the circumstances in the country of origin, and the other relevant aspects mentioned in the foregoing excerpt from the European Commission's Guidelines (paras. 59 and 63). Referring back to these Guidelines, the CJEU recalled that 'no factor taken separately may automatically lead to a decision' (para. 59).

In relation to the country of origin information, the CJEU specifically held that consideration must be taken to the 'state of the legislation and the way in which it is applied, the functioning of the administrative services and, where appropriate, the existence of deficiencies affecting certain regions or certain groups of people of that country' (para. 64). Regarding the applicants' situation, the CJEU ruled that the national authorities

> must also take account of the personality of the sponsor or the member of his family concerned by the application for family reunification, the specific situation in which they find themselves and the particular difficulties they are facing, with the result that the requirements which may be set . . . for the purpose of establishing that it is not possible to provide official documentary evidence of the family relationship, must be proportionate and depend on the nature and level of the difficulties they are facing.
>
> (para. 65)

It followed that national authorities 'must' also pay special attention to the situation of refugees as discussed earlier (para. 66). Lastly the CJEU ruled that, except for the cases in which the sponsor flagrantly fails to fulfil his obligation to cooperate,

> the lack of official documentary evidence of the family relationship and the potential implausibility of the explanations provided in that regard must be regarded as *mere elements* to be taken into account in the case-by-case

> assessment of all the relevant elements of the specific case and do not free the competent national authorities from the obligation laid down by Article 11(2) of [Directive 2003/86/EC] to take other evidence into account.
>
> (para. 68 [emphasis added])

This consideration, according to the CJEU, does not exclude the national authorities from complying with their obligations laid down in Article 11(2) of the Family Reunification Directive to take 'other evidence into account' (para. 68), which, as discussed at the beginning of this section, leaves no margin of appreciation in that regard (para. 69).

Based on the foregoing analysis, first, the CJEU held that the sponsor in the case at hand did not have the official documents she was asked to provide by the respective national authorities in the Netherlands (namely, the death certificates of the applicant's parents) because she came from a small village in Eritrea where the possession of specific official certificates was unusual (para. 75). Further, the CJEU observed that 'it would be impossible to obtain those certificates today' since the Eritrean minor left the country illegally, and in such circumstances, requesting official documents by means of local acquaintances 'would have exposed them to potential "dealings with the diaspora" and would have engendered dangers for their family residing in Eritrea and a risk of having to pay a "diaspora tax"' (para. 75).

Second, the CJEU acknowledged that, for the purpose of examining the plausibility of the explanations provided by the sponsor (in relation to the lack of and impossibility to obtain death certificates), the concerned authorities had considered country of origin information. However, the CJEU observed that it was 'not readily apparent' that they had taken into account the manner in which relevant Eritrean legislation is applied or that the issuing procedure of official documents varies strongly by region (being more limited in rural areas). The CJEU further stated that the evidence did not make it possible to verify whether and to what extent the Dutch authorities had considered the 'personality and specific circumstances' of the sponsor and the applicant and the particular difficulties they have encountered before and after fleeing Eritrea (para. 76).

Third, the CJEU held that the concerned national authorities did not consider the applicant's age, his situation both as a refugee in Sudan and before, in Eritrea, nor the child's best interests (para. 77). Here, the CJEU added that if the sponsor's account held true, granting the application for family reunification 'could be the only means of ensuring that [the applicant] has the opportunity to grow up in a family environment' (para. 77).

In the light of the aforementioned considerations, the CJEU concluded that the answer to the second question is that Article 11(2) of the Family Reunification Directive must be interpreted as precluding, in circumstances such as those in the case at hand, the concerned application for family reunification 'from being rejected solely on the ground that the sponsor has not provided official documentary evidence of the death of the minor's biological parents' (para. 81).

6. Conclusion

As this chapter has discussed, strict official documentary requirements are one of the major obstacles that impede Eritrean refugees, who are oftentimes "paperless", to realise their right to family reunification, and ultimately enjoy family life. It was shown that Eritrean asylum seekers and refugees experience difficulties in obtaining identity-proving documents and records of vital events due to some abusive practices related to Eritrean diplomatic missions around the world. This chapter has argued that EU law, in particular Article 11(2) of the Family Reunification Directive, requires national authorities to consider 'other' evidentiary documents where "paperless" refugees are unable to provide official documents to establish the existence of family ties. At the core of this chapter is the analysis of *E. v. Staatssecretaris van Veiligheid en Justitie*, a preliminary ruling by the CJEU that arose from a rejection of an Eritrean application for family reunification due to lack of evidentiary documentation. In this ruling, the CJEU made it clear that the obligation posed by Article 11(2) leaves no margin of appreciation in obliging EU Member States, in cases where documentary evidence is lacking, to take into account 'other evidence of the existence of the family relationship'. Drawing on guidelines on the Family Reunification Directive issued by the European Commission, the CJEU held that national authorities must undergo a case-by-case analysis that takes into consideration country of origin information, the applicant's personal circumstances, and in the case of minors, their best interests. The CJEU emphasised that it must be a holistic assessment, meaning that 'no factor taken separately', including the lack of official documentation, may automatically lead to a rejection of the family reunification application.

References

Bozzini, D. (2015). The fines and the spies: Fears of state surveillance in Eritrea and in the diaspora. *Social Analysis*, *59*(4), 32–49. https://doi.org/10.3167/sa.2015.590403

Corneloup, S., & Verhellen, J. (2021). SDG 16: Peace, Justice and Strong Institutions. In R. Michaels, V. Ruiz Abou-Nigm, & H. van Loon (Eds.), *The Private Side of Transforming Our World: UN Sustainable Development Goals 2030 and the Role of Private International Law* (pp. 505–540). Intersentia.

Council of Europe Commissioner for Human Rights. (2017). *Realising the right to family reunification of refugees in Europe*. Council of Europe. www.refworld.org/docid/5a0d5eae4.html

DSP-Group & Tilburg University. (2017, July). *The 2% tax for Eritreans in the diaspora: Facts, figures and experiences in seven European countries*. DSP-Group & Tilburg University.

EMN. (2017, April). *EMN synthesis report for the EMN focussed study 2016. Family reunification of third-country nationals in the EU plus Norway: National practices*. https://ec.europa.eu/home-affairs/sites/homeaffairs/files/00_family_reunification_synthesis_report_final_en_print_ready_0.pdf

Friedery, R. (2019.) Developments in family reunification cases before the CJEU. *Bratislava Law Review*, *3*(2), 6–17. https://doi.org/10.46282/blr.2019.3.2.142

Hathaway, J. C. (2021). *The Rights of Refugees Under International Law*. Cambridge University Press. https://doi.org/10.1017/9781108863537.004

Kibreab, G. (2009). Forced labour in Eritrea. *Journal of Modern African Studies*, *47*(1), 41–72. https://doi.org/10.1017/S0022278X08003650

Kibreab, G. (2017). *The Eritrean National Service: Servitude for "the Common Good" and the Youth Exodus*. James Currey.

Mekonnen, D., & Palacios-Arapiles, S. (2021, April). *Access to official documents by Eritrean refugees in the context of family reunification procedures: Legal framework, practical realities and obstacles, expert report*. https://equal-rights.org/site/assets/files/1287/report_access_to_official_documents_eritrea_equalrights_irap_may-2021.pdf

Palacios-Arapiles, S. (2015, July). The true human rights situation in Eritrea: The new UK home office guidance as a political instrument for the prevention of migration (RLI Working Paper No. 14). https://sas-space.sas.ac.uk/6097/

Palacios-Arapiles, S. (2022). European divergent approaches to protection claims based on the Eritrean military/national service programme. *International Community Law Review*, *24*, 335–357. https://doi.org/10.1163/18719732-bja10089

Palacios-Arapiles, S. (2023). Enslaved by Their Own Government: Indefinite National Service in Eritrea. In M. Van Reisen, M. Mawere, K. Smits, & M. Wirtz (Eds.), *Enslaved Trapped and Trafficked in Digital Black Holes: Human Trafficking Trajectories to Libya* (pp. 195–254). Langaa RPCIG. http://dx.doi.org/10.2139/ssrn.4335096

Riggan, J. (2016). *The Struggling State: Nationalism, Mass Militarization, and the Education of Eritrea*. Temple University Press.

Rodrik, D. (2022). Rights not recognized: Applying the right to recognition as a person before the law to pushbacks at international borders. *International Journal of Refugee Law*, *33*(4), 541–580. https://doi.org/10.1093/ijrl/eeac013

Schabas, W. (2013). *The Universal Declaration of Human Rights: The Travaux Préparatoires*. Cambridge University Press.

UN Human Rights Council. (2015, June 4). *Report of the commission of inquiry on human rights in Eritrea (first report)* (UN Doc. A/HRC/29/42). UN Human Rights Council.

UN Human Rights Council. (2016, June 8). *Report of the commission of inquiry on human rights in Eritrea (second report)* (UN Doc. A/HRC/32/47). UN Human Rights Council/

UNHCR. (2001, November 8–9). *Summary conclusions: Family unity, expert roundtable organized by UNHCR and the graduate institute of international studies*. www.unhcr.org/419dbfaf4.pdf

UNHCR. (2012, December). *Access to family reunification for beneficiaries of international protection in Central Europe: Research and report by Jadwiga Maczynska*. www.unhcr.org/ro/wp-content/uploads/sites/23/2016/12/Family_Reunification.pdf

UNHCR. (2015, October). *Family reunification in Europe*. www.unhcr.org/56fa38fb6.pdf.

UNHCR and Scottish Refugee Council. (2018, September). *A journey towards safety: A report on the experiences of Eritrean refugees in the UK*. www.unhcr.org/uk/protection/integration/5b8fe8694/a-journey-towards-safety-a-report-on-the-experiences-of-eritrean-refugees.html

Van Reisen, M., Saba, M., & Smits, K. (2019). "Sons of Isaias": Slavery and Indefinite National Service in Eritrea. In M. Van Reisen, M. Mawere, M. Stokmans, & K. A. Gebre-Egziabher (Eds.), *Connected and Mobile: Human Trafficking and the Digital Divide*. Langaa Research & Publishing CIG.

13 The recognition of child and polygamous marriages in Belgium

Alignment between private international law and migration law?

Leontine Bruijnen

1. Introduction

Although the number of child and polygamous marriages has generally decreased in the last decade, their existence cannot be ignored. According to UNICEF (2022), 19% of women aged between 20 and 24 years are married before the age of 18. Child marriages occur mainly in Africa (excluding North Africa) and South Asia. Polygamous marriages, on the other hand, occur mainly in West Africa. About 11% of the population in sub-Saharan Africa lives in a polygamous household (Kramer, 2020). When a spouse in a child or polygamous marriage migrates from a third State to a European Union (EU) Member State, the question arises whether and how EU Member States recognise these marriages. This recognition is important for family law purposes such as parenthood, where private international law (PIL) is relevant,[1] on the one hand, and for migration law purposes, such as family reunification, on the other.

No harmonisation of the recognition of foreign marriages (including child and polygamous marriages) has taken place at the EU level so far. PIL that regulates the recognition of foreign marriages is largely made by the national legislature. By contrast, some harmonisation has taken place in the field of migration law, which is regulated both by the national legislature of the Member States and the EU legislature.[2]

The absence of harmonisation in PIL combined with the existence of some harmonisation in migration law create tensions. The two areas of law overlap but sometimes also collide. The aim of this chapter is to investigate which role PIL plays in the recognition of marriages for migration law purposes, more precisely for family reunification. Child and polygamous marriages will be used as case studies. Their recognition in the Belgian legal system is discussed with reference to case law. Before addressing the legal framework, the definitions of child and polygamous marriage for the purpose of this contribution will be given. Hereafter, the Belgian PIL rules regarding the recognition of child and polygamous marriages will

1 On the role of private international law, see Den Haese and Verhellen (this volume).

2 According to Article 79 TFEU, the EU shall develop a *common* immigration policy. It is thus not the sole competence of the EU (Thym, 2016).

DOI: 10.4324/9781003503217-17

be discussed. Subsequently, the European and Belgian legal framework regarding family reunification will be addressed. Given the limited scope of this contribution, the focus will be on family reunification on the basis of the Family Reunification Directive (2003/86/EC).

2. Definitions

In this contribution, *child marriage* refers to a marriage where one of the parties was not 18 years old at the moment of the conclusion of the marriage. This age limit corresponds to the definition of a child in Article 1 of the UN Convention on the Rights of the Child (UNCRC). Under Belgian family law, marriages are in principle not permitted before the age of 18. Only in exceptional cases, this ban can be lifted by the family court.[3]

A *polygamous marriage* is a marriage between more than two persons. Technical and effective polygamous marriages are discussed. An effective polygamous marriage refers to the situation where a polygamous marriage is entered into intentionally. A technically polygamous marriage is caused by differences in legal systems. This includes the situations where a person cannot divorce or the divorce is not recognised (e.g. because it is a repudiation) and remarries.

Under Belgian family law, the conclusion of a second marriage before the dissolution of the first marriage is not permitted.[4]

3. PIL and the relevance of public policy

3.1 Recognition of foreign marriages

Since no international instrument on the recognition of foreign marriages[5] applies in Belgium and there is no EU instrument on the matter, the rules laid down in the Belgian Code of Private International Law (hereinafter: Code PIL) apply. Pursuant to Article 27, a foreign authentic instrument, such as a foreign marriage certificate, is recognised in Belgium by all authorities without any procedure. However, a number of conditions apply.

Firstly, the validity of the marriage must be established in accordance with the law applicable by virtue of the Code PIL. For this purpose, Articles 46 and 47 Code PIL are relevant. Article 46 determines the law applicable to the valid celebration of the marriage. This includes the question whether the spouses have reached the minimum age to marry. The conditions for the validity of the marriage are governed by the law of the State of which the concerning spouse is a national at the time of the marriage celebration. Article 47 determines the applicable law to the

3 Articles 144–148 Old Civil Code.

4 Article 147 Old Civil Code.

5 The 1902 Hague Marriage Convention and 1978 Hague Convention on Celebration and Recognition of the Validity of Marriages are only in force in a few States. Belgium is not included.

formal validity of the marriage. This includes the question whether the marriage can only be performed in a religious institution. The formal validity of the marriage is governed by the law of the State where the marriage is celebrated.

Secondly, there should be no evasion of the law. According to Article 18, facts and acts committed with the sole purpose to evade the application of the law designated by the Code PIL are not taken into account.

The third condition concerns the public policy exception of Article 21. The application of (a provision of) foreign law must be refused if it would lead to a result which is manifestly incompatible with public policy. The public policy exception cannot be invoked lightly; it must be used with restraint. In addition, an assessment of the specific circumstances of the case is necessary. Two factors must be taken into account. Firstly, the degree to which the situation is connected with the Belgian legal order. Secondly, the significance of the consequences produced by the application of the foreign law.[6]

The Belgian Code PIL does not contain a definition of public policy. The characteristics of public policy are that it is topical, relative and national. Topical refers to the fact that the interpretation of public policy depends on society's view at the time the public policy is invoked. Relativity refers to the degree to which the situation is connected to the Belgian legal order. The closer the connection with the Belgian legal order, for example by Belgian nationality or residence, the stricter the public policy exception will be applied. Lastly, national refers to the fact that public policy is determined by fundamental values of Belgian society and human rights (Traest, 2006). The content of public policy is derived from Belgian substantive law, which also includes international treaties. Consequently, the best interests of the child, enshrined in Article 22bis of the Belgian Constitution and the UNCRC, influence the interpretation of the public policy exception in PIL. The case law of the European Court of Human Rights (ECtHR) also shows that the margin of appreciation that States have in shaping their national public policy is constrained by the principle of the best interests of the child (Baratta, 2019).[7]

Pursuant to Article 27 Code PIL, every Belgian authority, including the migration authorities and civil registrars, is competent to decide on the recognition of a foreign marriage certificate. Each authority examines the recognition of the marriage in the context of the application before them, whether it is for family reunification or for other reasons, for example, establishing parentage. As a result, these authorities may recognise marriages differently.[8] If an authority refuses to recognise the marriage certificate, whether it is child or a polygamous marriage, an appeal may be lodged before the court of first instance.[9] The court's decision

6 This relates to the consequences of (not) applying foreign law. As discussed later in the context of polygamous and child marriages, some consequences may be accepted in the Belgian legal order while others are not.

7 ECtHR, 28 June 2007, *Wagner and J.M.W.L. v. Luxembourg*, No. 7624/01.

8 See for a discussion on the contradictory decisions of Belgian authorities, Vanvoorden (2008).

9 Article 27 in conjunction with Article 23 Code PIL.

on the (non-)recognition of the marriage is decisive and must be respected by all Belgian authorities.

3.2 Polygamous marriage

Application of the public policy exception may result in the non-recognition of a foreign marriage. It is also possible that only some consequences of the marriage are recognised. This is called the attenuated effect of the public policy exception. In Belgium, polygamous marriages are considered to be contrary to public policy. Nevertheless, some consequences of a polygamous marriage can be recognised. The judgement of the Court of Charleroi of 11 December 2008 illustrates this. This case concerns the request for recognition of a Moroccan birth certificate of a child born from a polygamous marriage. The filiation tie between the father and the child was established by marriage. The marriage is not recognised in Belgium because it is a polygamous marriage and thus contrary to public policy. The Court explains that the fact that the marriage is valid under Moroccan law is sufficient to recognise the filiation link between the father and child. The recognition of the birth certificate does not lead to a result that is contrary to public policy. The Court further states that Belgian law, based on its fundamental principles, prohibits discrimination between children born within and outside wedlock.[10]

Another judgement that illustrates the attenuated effect is the judgement of the Brussels Court of 8 June 2010. This concerns a request to grant Belgian nationality to two children on the basis of the father's Belgian nationality. The Belgian authorities refused this because they do not recognise the father's polygamous marriage and, consequently, the filiation link between the children and their father. The Court clarifies that this case is only about the recognition of the filiation link. Nevertheless, the Court indicates that the marriage is not recognised in Belgium due to its violation of the public policy. The Court also states that the non-recognition of the filiation links would have consequences contrary to the best interests of the children who, under Belgian law, would be deprived of civil status documents indicating the filiation links. The recognition of the filiation link can thus not be refused on the basis of the non-recognition of the polygamous marriage.[11]

These judgements demonstrate that a distinction can be made between the recognition of the polygamous marriage, on the one hand, and the recognition of the filiation ties of the children born from the polygamous marriage on the other. Furthermore, the courts seem to place an emphasis on the situation of the child (Verhellen & Wautelet, 2022). The distinction between non-recognition of the polygamous marriage and recognition of a consequence of the marriage is important not only

10 Court of First Instance Charleroi, 11 December 2008, *Revue du droit étrangers* 2009, 730–732.

11 Court of First Instance Brussels, 8 June 2010, *Tijdschrift voor Vreemdelingenrecht* 2011, 17–19. See for a similar judgement, Court of First Instance Liège, 18 October 2014, *Revue du droit étrangers* 2014, 265–266.

for civil law purposes, but also for family reunification (Wautelet, 2009).[12] This will be addressed in Section 4.

3.3 Child marriage

As said earlier, the public policy refusal ground requires an assessment of the specific circumstances of the case. The judgements of the Court of Liège from 25 May 2018 and 17 May 2019 show this.[13] The latter case concerns the recognition of a marriage concluded in Somalia in 2007. The wife was 17 years at the time; the husband was 22. The first case concerns the request for recognition of a marriage concluded in 2010. The wife was 14 years old at the time; the husband was 18. The Court's reasoning and decision in these cases are similar. Since in the first case recognition of the marriage was relevant for family reunification and in the second case recognition was relevant for establishing affiliation, I will focus on the first case. In this case, the husband fled Somalia and arrived in Belgium in 2015. He was recognised as a refugee. The wife applied for a family reunification visa in 2017, but this was denied by the Immigration Office. The reasons for the rejection were doubts about the authenticity of the marriage certificate and the fact that the marriage was contrary to Belgian public policy, since the wife was 14 years old at the time of the marriage.

The couple requests the Court to recognise their marriage. The Court refers to the relevant rules on recognition of foreign marriages in the Code PIL. Since both spouses were Somali nationals at the time of the marriage, Somali law applies to the substantive validity of the marriage. Somali law also applies to the formal validity of the marriage because the couple married in Somalia.

The Court examines whether the marriage is contrary to Belgian public policy because of the minority of the wife at the time of the marriage. The Court states that the connection of the situation with the Belgian legal order is limited since the recognition is requested five years after the marriage. Moreover, the significance of the consequences arising from the application of the foreign law is limited. The wife was 20 years old when she applied for the visa and is now 22. Her husband is only three years and three months older than her. Given the current age of the wife, the recognition in Belgium of the Somali marriage does not violate Belgian fundamental values. The Court concludes that the marriage is recognised in Belgium.

The Liège Court's judgements of 25 May 2018 and 17 May 2019 demonstrate firstly the importance of the timing of the request for recognition. The Court examines the violation of public policy at the time of the request for the recognition. The passage of time influences the degree in which the situation is connected

12 Belgian case law shows that polygamous marriages can have certain legal consequences for pensions rights. See, for example, Family Court Brussels, 24 October 2019, Tijdschrift@ipr.be 2019, 53–56. See for a discussion of the case law on pension rights, Verhellen and Wautelet (2022).

13 Family Court Liège, 25 May 2018, Tijdschrift@ipr.be 2018, 94–98 and Family Court Liège, 17 May 2019, Tijdschrift@ipr.be 2019, 165–171.

with the Belgian legal order and the significance of the consequences produced by the application of the foreign law. Moreover, the scope and content of the public policy exception are based on society's view at the time of the judgement. Hence, when recognition is sought of a child marriage concluded in 1970, it is not decisive what the view of Belgian society on child marriages was in 1970. What matters is the view of Belgian society at the time of the request for recognition (Wautelet, 2018).

Secondly, the judgement shows the importance of the age of the spouses at the time of the recognition request in determining whether the child marriage is considered to be contrary to public policy. If both spouses are adults at the time of the request for recognition, there does not seem to be an immediate violation of public policy. Furthermore, the Court pays attention to the age difference between the spouses when determining whether there is a violation of public policy.[14]

3.4 Scope of public policy

The influence of the principle of the best interests of the child on the public policy exception is visible in the case law on polygamous marriages. As mentioned in Section 3.2, a polygamous marriage violates the Belgian public policy. However, certain consequences of the marriage can be recognised in the Belgian legal order. This includes the recognition of a filiation link that arises from the polygamous marriage. The recognition of this filiation link can be in the best interests of the child. The best interests of the child can thus give substance to the (attenuated effect of) the public policy exception.

Unlike in the case law on polygamous marriage, the attenuated effect of the public policy exception and the influence of the best interests of the child are not (yet) visible in the published Belgian case law on the recognition of child marriages. The lack of an explicit reference to the best interests of the child can be explained by the fact that child marriages, unlike polygamous marriages, are not automatically contrary to public policy and can be recognised. The recognition of a child marriage depends on the specific circumstances of the case. The best interest of the child may already be taken into account when assessing the specific circumstances of the case, even when no explicit reference is made to this principle.

4. Migration law: towards a European definition of 'spouse'?

This section discusses one component of the harmonisation of migration law at the EU level, namely, the Family Reunification Directive, with references being made to its implementation in Belgian legislation. In addition, the focus is on the general rules and not on the specific rules for refugees.

14 These findings are based on two judgements, as there are no more published judgements. Therefore, these conclusions should be interpreted cautiously.

4.1 Definition of 'spouse' in the Family Reunification Directive

The Family Reunification Directive governs family reunification of a third-country national residing lawfully in the territory of a Member State, also referred to as the sponsor, with their third-country family members.[15] The aim of family reunification is to preserve the family unit.[16]

Article 4 determines with whom family reunification can take place. It distinguishes between, on the one hand, family members who must be granted entry and residence and, on the other hand, family members in respect of whom Member States may authorise entry and residence. This contribution focuses on the first category, which concerns the nuclear family.[17] Pursuant to Article 4(1), entry and residence must be granted to 'the sponsor's spouse' and children. The term children in Article 4(1) includes children born in and out of wedlock, born out of earlier marriages and adopted children.[18]

The question arises how the term 'spouse' should be interpreted, whether this is done on the basis of a Member State's PIL or whether it has an autonomous interpretation. Neither the proposal, nor the guidance for application, nor the report on the implementation of the Directive provides an answer.[19] In addition, Article 5 does not seem to provide an answer either. This article states that when a sponsor or their family apply for family reunification, they must provide documentary evidence of the family relationship and certified copies of their family member(s)' travel documents. The Directive does not specify which documents are required and whether they should be legalised. There is no clear link to the (private international) law of the Member State concerned, which does not mean that this PIL will not interfere.

Based on the case law of the Court of Justice of the European Union (CJEU), it can be stated that when there is no reference to national law, a concept receives an autonomous interpretation. In the past, the Court has received questions about the interpretation of other concepts in the Family Reunification Directive,[20] including the definition of 'minor child' in Article 4(1)(c). With reference to the *Ouhrami* case the Court answered:

> It must be recalled that, in accordance with the need for a uniform application of EU law and the principle of equality, a provision of EU law which makes

15 Article 1 Family Reunification Directive.

16 Article 2(d) Family Reunification Directive.

17 Recital 9 Family Reunification Directive.

18 European Commission, Proposal for a Council Directive on the right to family reunification, 1 December 1999, COM (1999) 638 final.

19 European Commission, Proposal for a Council Directive on the right to family reunification, 1 December 1999, COM (1999) 638 final; European Commission, Communication from the Commission to the European Parliament and the Council on guidance for application of Directive 2003/86/EC on the right to family reunification, 3 April 2014, COM(2014) 210 final; European Commission, Report from the Commission to the European Parliament and the Council on the Implementation of Directive 2003/86/EC on the right to family reunification, 29 March 2019, COM(2019) 162 final.

20 CJEU, 12 December 2009, C-519/18, *Bevándorlási és Menekültügyi Hivatali*, ECLI:EU:C:2019:1070 and CJEU, 12 April 2018, C-550/16, *A and S*, ECLI:EU:C:2018:248.

> no express reference to the law of the Member States for the purpose of determining its meaning and scope must normally be given an autonomous and uniform interpretation throughout the European Union, and that interpretation must take into account, inter alia, the context of the provision and the objective pursued by the legislation in question.[21]

Based on this reasoning and the fact that Article 4(1)(a) does not refer to the national law of the Member States, it can be argued that 'spouse' receives an autonomous interpretation. The importance of the aforementioned reasoning also follows from the fact that the Court applies it to other EU instruments.[22]

Assuming that there is an autonomous interpretation of 'spouse', the question arises whether only the autonomous interpretation must be complied with in order to be considered a spouse under the Directive or whether national law, including PIL, must also be taken into account.[23] In both scenarios there is a chance of a legal limping situation. This means that the same relationship is lawful and valid in one legal order or area of law but not in another (Verhellen, 2018). It is possible that a marriage is recognised on the basis of PIL but does not fall under the autonomous definition of the Directive. This relates to the situation that the marriage is recognised for purposes such as inheritance, but does not entitle a spouse to family reunification. If a marriage falls within the autonomous definition of the Directive and thus entitles to family reunification, it is also possible that the marriage is not recognised on the basis of PIL for family law purposes, such as establishing parentage. The existence of such legal limping situations is not desirable and demonstrates the importance of the alignment between the recognition for migration and family law purposes. One way to achieve this is to use PIL as a guiding instrument in both areas.

Article 4(1) of the Family Reunification Directive has been implemented in Article 10 §1, paragraph 1, 4° of the Belgian Aliens Act. The latter article refers to

21 CJEU, 16 July 2020, C-133/19, *B.M.M.*, ECLI:EU:C:2020:577 and CJEU, 26 July 2017, C-225/16, *Ouhrami*, ECLI:EU:C:2017:590. The latter did not concern the Family Reunification Directive.

22 See, e.g., CJEU, 18 January 1984, C-327/82, *Ekro*, ECLI:EU:C:1984:11; CJEU, 6 March 2008, C-98/07, *Nordania Finans and BG Factoring*, ECLI:EU:C:2008:144 *and CJEU, 2 April 2009, C-523/07, A.*, ECLI:EU:C:2009:225. The latter judgement shows that the same reasoning has been used to determine the scope of 'habitual residence' under Article 8(1) Brussels IIa Regulation, which is a PIL instrument. By contrast, an example of an explicit reference to the (private international) law of the Member State to determine the existence of a marriage can be found in recital 10 Rome III Regulation. Another example, but for determining majority, is Article 4(1)(d) Family Reunification Directive. It states that majority is determined based on '*the law of the Member State concerned*'.

23 The *Coman* judgement, which addressed the gender-neutral interpretation of 'spouse' under the Citizens Directive (2004/38/EC), does not provide any clarification. Unlike the Advocate General, the Court did not explicitly state that this concept has an autonomous interpretation. CJEU, 5 June 2018, C-673/16, *Coman and Others*, ECLI:EU:C:2018:385. If an autonomous interpretation is assumed, this means that although the marriage is not recognised pursuant to national PIL and therefore has no family law consequences, it is still recognised for migration law purposes. In this situation, the application of PIL may conflict with the autonomous definition of spouse.

'the foreign spouse'. There is no reference to the Code PIL in this provision, which does not exclude the interference of PIL rules. Denys (2019) states that the status of spouse must be proved according to the law of the nationality of the person concerned, which is a reference to PIL. The recognition of the marriage certificate, which is done according to the Code PIL, is important (Denys, 2019). The Circular of 17 June 2009 refers to Article 12bis Aliens Act and clarifies that the family tie is determined by official documents proving this tie, drawn up in accordance with the rules of PIL, both as regards the substantive and formal conditions and the legalisation. This supports the view that PIL is the tool to determine the scope of the concept 'spouse' in the context of family reunification. This approach is also reflected in Belgian case law.[24] Unlike the Directive, the Belgian implementation is clearer and does not support an autonomous interpretation.

4.2 Polygamous marriage

Article 4(4) Family Reunification Directive states that if the sponsor already has a spouse living with him in the Member State, family reunification of a further spouse should not be allowed. Article 4(4) is a mandatory provision; in case of a polygamous marriage, Member States are prohibited to authorise family reunification with a further spouse.

According to Article 4(4), family reunification is not allowed 'in the event of a polygamous marriage, where the sponsor already has a spouse living with him in the territory of a Member State'. The last part of this sentence can be seen as an autonomous definition of polygamous marriage. However, if the approach is followed that PIL determines the scope of (polygamous) marriage, then this can be seen as a condition in addition to the recognition based on PIL. Strictly speaking, the Directive does not prohibit family reunification because of the mere existence of a polygamous marriage. In theory, family reunification with a further spouse is allowed if the sponsor does not live with his first spouse. An explanation for this can be found in recital 11. This prescribes that the right to family reunification should be in line with the values and principles recognised by the Member States, in particular with respect to the rights of women and children. This justifies restrictive measures against polygamous *households* (Hailbronner et al., 2016).[25]

The Explanatory Memorandum to the Directive's proposal justifies the restriction with the fact that polygamous marriages are not in line with the fundamental principles of Member States' legal orders. However, when a polygamous marriage

24 See, e.g., Council for Alien Law Litigation, 7 October 2021, No. 261 826; Council for Alien Law Litigation, 4 April 2019, No. 219 450 and Council for Alien Law Litigation, 21 September 2018, No. 209 795. The decision of the Council for Alien Law Litigation of 23 October 2007 discusses the division of competences of the civil courts and administrative courts concerning the appeal against the refusal of recognition of a foreign marriage for the purpose of family reunification. Council for Alien Law Litigation, 23 October 2007, No. 2970.

25 Recital 11 Family Reunification Directive. This justification can be questioned, see Štýbnarová (2020).

has been legally concluded in a non-EU State, certain effects of this marriage should be taken into account. The proposal does not clarify which effects should be taken into account. Moreover, it determines that the sponsor must not be deprived from leading a normal family life. Therefore, family reunification with one spouse and her children is allowed. Family reunification with the minor children of a further spouse can only take place if the child's interests prevail over other considerations. An example of this is the situation where the biological mother of the child has died.[26] Unfortunately, this clarification is omitted in the Directive. Therefore, it is unclear, at least from the text of the Directive, whether family reunification is mandatory if it is in the best interests of the minor children of a further spouse.

Belgian law excludes family reunification of a spouse of the polygamous sponsor if another spouse already resides in Belgium. It is not important for which spouse family reunification is applied for, nor whether the spouse already residing in Belgium cohabits with the sponsor.[27] In the past, minor children of a further spouse did not receive the right to family reunification. The Belgian Constitutional Court decided that this created an unacceptable difference between children born out of a polygamous and a monogamous marriage. The children of the first and second marriage enjoy a right to family reunification based on their filiation link with their father and not based on the marriage of their parents. The Court ruled that the difference in treatment violates the principle of non-discrimination and several rights enshrined in the UNCRC, including the best interests of the child. The Belgian provision is therefore amended. The restriction concerning polygamous *spouses* is, however, based on a relevant criterion and corresponds to the purpose of the legislation and the aim of safeguarding the Belgian and European international public policy.[28] Therefore, family reunification with a further spouse is restricted.

4.3 Child marriage

In addition to hindering family reunification in the case of a polygamous marriage, the Directive hinders family reunification in the case of a child marriage. Article 4(5) entitles Member States to require that the sponsor and their spouse have a certain minimum age before the spouse is able to join the sponsor. The minimum age can be up to 21 years, which is the case in Belgium. Nonetheless, the age is 18 years if the marriage existed before the sponsor arrived in Belgium.[29] The

26 Recitals 10 and 11, Articles 4(4) and 5(5) Family Reunification Directive; European Commission, Proposal for a Council Directive on the right to family reunification, 1 December 1999, COM (1999) 638 final.

27 Belgian law is stricter than the Directive. There is discussion whether this is allowed (Denys, 2019).

28 This reasoning is similar to the recognition of polygamous marriages for establishing parentage. However, there is no reference to the (attenuated effect of the) public policy exception and recognition based on PIL in the judgement. Constitutional Court, 26 June 2008, No. 95/2008.

29 Article 10 §1, paragraph 1, 4° Aliens Act of 15 December 1980.

rationale behind a minimum age requirement is that Member States can ensure a better integration and can prevent forced marriages.[30]

In the *Marjan Noorzia* case, the CJEU ruled that Article 4(5) does not preclude Member States from requiring that the spouses must have reached the age of 21 when the application is lodged. According to the Court, compliance with the age requirement at the moment of submission neither prevents nor makes it excessively difficult to exercise the right to family reunification. Lastly, the measure does not run counter to the aim of preventing forced marriage

> since it permits the presumption that, due to greater maturity, it will be more difficult to influence the persons concerned to contract a forced marriage and accept family reunification if they must have reached the age of 21 by the date when the application is lodged than it would be if they were under 21 at that date.[31]

Advocate General Mengozzi points out that it is questioned what the effect of this minimum age requirement is on the prevention of forced marriages. Furthermore, he states that the age requirement prevents young spouses whose marriage is genuine and not forced to exercise their right to family reunification. The objective of restricting forced marriages must therefore be weighed against the right of genuinely married couples to exercise their right to family reunification, which is based on the right to respect of family life laid down in Article 8 of the European Convention on Human Rights and Article 7 of the Charter of Fundamental Rights of the European Union. Unlike the Court, the Advocate General concludes that the age requirement must be satisfied at the moment when the decision on family reunification is taken, and not at the moment of submission.[32]

Strictly speaking, Article 4(5) does not prohibit family reunification in case of child marriages. It is aimed at preventing forced marriages but, as the Advocate General correctly points out, the age requirement does not do justice to the spouses who have entered into a consensual marriage and have not yet reached the age of 21 years.[33] Consequently, the Directive hinders family reunification with a minor spouse. Nevertheless, the Directive does not prevent a couple who married as minors from waiting until they meet the age requirement before applying for family reunification. The age requirement concerns the time of application or time of effective reunification and not the time of celebration of the marriage.

30 Article 4(5) Aliens Act.

31 CJEU, 17 July 2014, C-338/13, *Marjan Noorzia*, ECLI:EU:C:2014:2092.

32 Opinion of Advocate General Mengozzi in CJEU, 30 April 2014, C-338/13, *Marjan Noorzia*, ECLI:EU:C:2014:2092 and Milios (2015).

33 Given the limited scope of this chapter, I will not elaborate on the issue that not all child marriages are forced marriages.

4.4 Public policy in the family reunification directive

Article 6(1) determines that an application for entry and residence of family members may be rejected on grounds of public policy, public security or public health. Furthermore, an application for family reunification may be withdrawn or refused to be renewed on these grounds.

Although the proposal states that public policy must be properly defined, it does not specify by whom and how this should be done.[34] Apparently, this can largely be determined by the Member States, taking into account the relevant case law of the CJEU and the ECtHR. Furthermore, recital 14 clarifies that a person should not constitute a *threat* to public policy and that a conviction for committing a serious crime falls within the scope of public policy. The situations where the third-country national belongs to an association which supports terrorism, supports such an association or has extremist aspirations fall within the scope of public policy and public security.[35] In the *G.S.* judgement, the Court further clarified the public policy of Article 6: it applies if the offence which warranted the criminal conviction is sufficiently serious to establish that it is necessary to rule out residence of the applicant. In addition, the individual assessment of Article 17 must be carried out.[36]

Moreover, the Court explained that in order to determine the scope of the public policy of Article 6, account must be taken of the wording of the provision, the context and the objective of the Directive. Hence, the scope of public policy under the Directive is more limited than in the situation where the right to free movement has been exercised. In order to be considered a threat to public policy, it is not necessarily required that the personal conduct of the applicant represents a genuine, present and sufficiently serious threat affecting one of the fundamental interests of society. The public policy in Article 6 must be interpreted strictly.[37]

The Belgian Aliens Act also seems to give a limited definition of public policy and refers in Article 11 §1, 3° to the cases of Articles 3, 5° to 8°. Consequently, a residence permit can be refused, for example, if there is a danger for international relations or a danger for the public policy, peace and security.

As previously discussed, the restriction on family reunification in the case of a polygamous marriage is laid down in Article 4(4). The provisions on public policy (Article 6 and recital 14) do not refer to this provision. Neither the proposal, nor the guidance for application or the report on the implementation of the Directive mention that Article 4(4) is part of the public policy grounds. The proposal only states that polygamous marriages are contrary to the fundamental principles of the Member States. It is therefore debatable whether Article 4(4) is a *lex specialis* of

34 European Commission, Proposal for a Council Directive on the right to family reunification, 1 December 1999, COM (1999) 638 final.

35 European Commission, Communication from the Commission to the European Parliament and the Council on guidance for application of Directive 2003/86/EC on the right to family reunification, 3 April 2014, COM(2014) 210 final.

36 CJEU, 12 December 2019, C-381/18, *G.S*, ECLI:EU:C:2019:1072.

37 CJEU, 12 December 2019, C-381/18, *G.S*, ECLI:EU:C:2019:1072.

Article 6 and whether the restriction of family reunification in the case of polygamous marriage, falls within the definition of public policy of Article 6. Thus, the public policy grounds in Article 6 seems to differ from the public policy exception in PIL. This may indicate that the Directive interprets concepts such as public policy autonomously. However, this does not mean that PIL and its public policy exception cannot interfere. Belgian case law on family reunification in the case of polygamous marriages shows an example of this. Here, a marriage certificate concerning a polygamous marriage is not recognised on the basis of the public policy exception of Article 21 Code PIL. Based on this non-recognition, the family member cannot qualify as a spouse under Article 10 §1, paragraph 1, 4° Aliens Act and the application for family reunification is refused.[38] Interestingly, the application is not rejected on the basis of Article 10 §1, 7° Aliens Act, which corresponds to Article 4(4) Family Reunification Directive, but on the basis of the non-recognition of the marriage certificate according to PIL rules. Thus, there is only a reference to public policy in PIL.[39]

Based on what was just outlined, public policy seems to be interpreted differently in the Directive than in PIL. The PIL public policy requires that the individual circumstances are taken into account. Article 6 Directive does not explicitly mention this but refers to Article 17. This applies if a Member State rejects an application, withdraws or refuses to renew a residence permit or orders the removal of the sponsor or their family members. According to Article 17,

> Member States shall take due account of the nature and solidity of the person's family relationships and the duration of his residence in the Member State and of the existence of family, cultural and social ties with his/her country of origin.

Consequently, Member States have to examine each case individually and do a proportionality test.

Next to Article 17, Article 5(5) should be taken into account. This article explicitly mentions that when an application is examined, Member States shall have due regard to the best interests of minor children. The application of Article 5(5) and 17 means that if Member States require a minimum age of 21 years for spouses on the ground of Article 4(5), they have to carry out a case-by-case assessment, taking into account all personal circumstances. Based on this individual assessment, Member States should not automatically reject an application concerning a spouse who is under the age of 21. If there is no forced marriage or need for better integration, Member States should consider making an exception. In doing so,

38 Council for Alien Law Litigation, 22 March 2010, No. 40 553; Council for Alien Law Litigation, 3 April 2009, No. 25623 and Council for Alien Law Litigation, 4 May 2009, No. 26914.

39 Hailbronner et al. (2016) have a different view than the Belgian Council. They argue that the non-recognition of polygamous marriages under the Directive is independent from the recognition in PIL.

they should assess the situation individually. An example of such an exception is the situation where one of the spouses is under the age of 21 years and the spouses have a common child.[40] In this situation, an exception must be made based on the best interests of the couple's child. It is not clear to what extent the best interests of the child can be used to make an exception to the minimum age requirement for the spouses. After all, it can be argued that it is in the interests of a minor spouse, whose interests as a child should be taken into account pursuant to Article 5(5), to be reunited with their spouse.[41]

5. Conclusion

This contribution demonstrated that PIL and migration law are not always aligned. The central question was: which role does PIL play in the recognition of child and polygamous marriages for migration law purposes, more precisely for family reunification? To examine the role of PIL in family reunification, the recognition of child and polygamous marriages under Belgian PIL was first described.

Hereafter, analysis of the Family Reunification Directive revealed that it does not assign an explicit role to PIL, in particular to determine who can be considered a spouse for the purpose of family reunification. The Directive does not clarify whether PIL rules on recognition of foreign marriages should be used. Rather, the Directive contains its own provisions that affect applications for family reunification in the case of a child or polygamous marriage. Applying these provisions does not always lead to the same result as if only PIL had been applied.

Application of Article 4(5) Directive means that family reunification with a spouse who is under the age requirement is not possible. It was argued that maintaining this age requirement and not allowing family reunification with a minor spouse, could be contrary to the best interests of the child. Pursuant to Article 5(5), these interests should be taken into account when Member States examine an application. Article 4(5) affects the way child marriages are treated within the framework of an application for family reunification. If Belgian PIL had been applied, the result could be similar. A child marriage is not automatically contrary to the public policy exception of Article 21 Code PIL and can be recognised in Belgium. Case law seems to indicate that the circumstances of the case, including the fact that the spouses are no longer minors, are important. The best interests of the child can also play a role in the interpretation of the public policy exception.

Application of Article 4(4) Directive results in that family reunification with more than one spouse is not possible. Family reunification with the minor children of a further spouse may be possible. Following the judgement of the Belgian

40 European Commission, Communication from the Commission to the European Parliament and the Council on guidance for application of Directive 2003/86/EC on the right to family reunification, 3 April 2014, COM(2014) 210 final.

41 This problem also exists in Belgian law, although the minimum age can be 18 years when the marriage existed before the sponsor came to Belgium.

Constitutional Court, it can be argued that family reunification with these minor children should be allowed based on the principle of non-discrimination and the best interests of the child as stipulated in Article 5(5). If Article 4(4) is interpreted in this way, the result of applying this provision is the same as if Belgian PIL were applied. Under Belgian PIL, a polygamous marriage is not recognised, but certain legal consequences can be attached to the marriage, such as the establishment of a filiation link. The best interest of the child also plays a role in this.

The public policy grounds in the Directive do not clarify the role of PIL either. The interpretation of public policy in the Directive seems different and more limited than in PIL. The public policy exception of Article 21 Code PIL has a broad scope and refers to the fundamental values of Belgian society and human rights. Based on the *G.S.* judgement, public policy under Article 6 Directive must be interpreted strictly and not exclusively on the basis of national law. Public policy is given a specific interpretation for the Directive. Respecting human rights and the best interests of the child does not seem to be part of the public policy of Article 6, but this seems to follow from other provisions of the Directive. The public policy of Article 6 does not seem to affect an application for family reunification in the event of a child or polygamous marriage. Public policy in PIL, on the other hand, plays an important role in the recognition of polygamous and child marriages.

Thus, the role of PIL in the Family Reunification Directive is ambiguous. The case law of the CJEU points to an autonomous interpretation of 'spouse'. However, Belgian legislation and case law assign a clear role to PIL. They use PIL to determine whether someone qualifies as a spouse. This approach is also supported by the literature, which states that the application of PIL has the advantage of focusing on the individual case. In addition, PIL is a neutral instrument and does not pursue any specific objectives, such as the regulation of migration (van Loon, 2019; (Corneloup et al., 2017; Mustasaari, 2014).

Moreover, the use of PIL can ensure that child and polygamous marriages are treated in the same way within a national legal order for different purposes, such as establishing parenthood and applying for family reunification. The use of PIL as a guiding instrument, can therefore lead to alignment between different areas of law in a country. Returning to the central research question, the role of PIL in the Family Reunification Directive is not (yet) very clear. However, the role of PIL in the Belgian implementation seems clearer. This is thus food for thought for the EU legislature.

References

Baratta, R. (2019). Recognition of a Foreign Status Filii. In E. Bergamini & C. Ragni (Eds.), *Fundamental Rights and Best Interests of the Child in Transnational Families* (pp. 171–185). Intersentia.

Corneloup, S., Heiderhoff, B., Horati, C., Jault-Seseke, F., Kruger, T., Rupp, C., van Loon, H., & Verhellen, J. (2017). *Private international law in a context of increasing mobility*. www.europarl.europa.eu/thinktank/en/document/IPOL_STU(2017)583157

Denys, L. (2019). *Overzicht van het Vreemdelingenrecht*. INNI Publishers.

Hailbronner, K., Arévalo, C., & Klarmann, T. (2016). Part C. Immigration II Family Reunification Directive 2003/86/EC. In K. Hailbronner & D. Thym (Eds.), *EU Immigration and Asylum Law* (pp. 300–426). C.H. Beck/Hart/Nomos.

Kramer, S. (2020). *Polygamy is rare around the world and mostly confined to a few regions*. Pew Research Center. www.pewresearch.org/fact-tank/2020/12/07/polygamy-is-rare-around-the-world-and-mostly-confined-to-a-few-regions/

Milios, G. (2015). Family reunification for third-country nationals. *European Journal of Migration and Law*, *17*(1), 127–146. https://doi.org/10.1163/15718166-12342074

Mustasaari, S. (2014). The married child belongs to no one. *Child and Family Law Quarterly*, *26*(3), 261–282.

Stybnarova, N. (2020). Teleology behind the prohibition of recognition of polygamous marriages under the EU family reunification directive: A critique of effectiveness. *Journal of Muslim Minority Affairs*, *40*(1), 104–116. https://doi.org/10.1080/13602004.2020.1741168

Thym, D. (2016). Part C. Immigration I. Legal Framework for EU Immigration Policy. In K. Hailbronner & D. Thym (Eds.), *EU Immigration and Asylum Law* (pp. 271–299). C.H. Beck/Hart/Nomos.

Traest, M. (2006). Artikel 21 Openbare Orde-Exceptie. In J. Erauw, M. Fallon, E. Guldix, J. Meeusen, M. Pertegás Sender, H. van Houtte, M. Watté, & P. Wautelet (Eds.), *Het Wetboek internationaal privaatrecht becommentarieerd* (pp. 112–116). Intersentia.

UNICEF. (2022). *Child marriage*. https://data.unicef.org/topic/child-protection/child-marriage/

van Loon, H. (2019). De verhouding tussen internationaal privaatrecht en migratierecht in verband met de waardigheid van het kind. *Tijdschrift voor Familie- en Jeugdrecht*, *41*(7–8), 154–160.

Vanvoorden, K. (2008). De erkenning door Belgische overheden van buitenlandse akten inzake de burgerlijke staat: Tegenstrijdige beslissingen. *Tijdschrift voor Vreemdelingenrecht*, 11–18.

Verhellen, J. (2018). Balancing Migration Policy and Personal Autonomy in Private International Law. In M.-C. Foblets, M. Graziadei, & A. Renteln (Eds.), *Personal Autonomy in Plural Societies* (pp. 169–177). Routledge. https://doi.org/10.4324/9781315413617-14

Verhellen, J., & Wautelet, P. (2022). The Treatment of Diversity in Family Law in Belgium: Between Acknowledgment and Indifference. In N. Yassari & M.-C. Foblets (Eds.), *Normativity and Diversity in Family Law* (pp. 227–253). Springer. https://doi.org/10.1007/978-3-030-83106-6_10

Wautelet, P. (2009). Quelques réflexions sur le statut des enfants issues d'une union polygamique. *Revue du droit des étrangers*, *151*, 733–736.

Wautelet, P. (2018). Un mariage somalien et minorité des époux. *Revue du droit des étrangers*, *198*, 331–339.

14 Your relationship is genuine, but your marriage is not

Defining marriages of convenience in EU and UK law

Aleksandra Ancite-Jepifánova

1. Introduction

Since the inception of the European Union (EU), every Member State national has the ability to live in the host Member State with their family members, including those holding a passport of a non-EU country.[1] Already since the 1960s, the right to family reunification has been regarded an intrinsic component of free movement: it was considered that the absence of such an opportunity would prevent individuals from relocating and consequently impede the creation of the single market.[2]

The scope of the relevant provisions has been continuously broadened by both Union legislation and the Court of Justice of the European Union (CJEU) alongside the general expansion of free movement rights. Over the past decades, however, the generous family reunification rights enjoyed by mobile EU citizens[3] began to sharply contrast with domestic family reunification policies in (predominantly Western European) Member States, which were becoming increasingly restrictive. The possibility for third-country national (TCN) family members of mobile EU citizens to obtain residence rights under EU law, consequently, was increasingly perceived as a route enabling unwanted foreigners to sidestep national immigration laws.

Such practices are commonly designated by Member States as abuse of EU law and, among other things, linked with the discourse on marriages of convenience, allegedly contracted to help the non-EU national party regularise their stay in the EU.[4] Several governments have repeatedly claimed that such arrangements constitute a serious problem and called for limitations on the right to family reunification under the Citizens Directive (2004/38/EC), the key instrument in the field.[5]

1 See, e.g., CJEU, 23 November 1976, C-40/76, *Kermaschek*, ECLI:EU:C:1976:157, § 9.
2 See, e.g., the Preamble to the Regulation (EEC) No. 1612/68 of the Council of 15 October 1968 on freedom of movement for workers within the Community.
3 By 'mobile' the chapter refers to EU citizens who have exercised their free movement rights by moving to another Member State.
4 A similar discourse is also employed in relation to registered partnerships of convenience or acknowledgements of children.
5 For a discussion see Section 2.

DOI: 10.4324/9781003503217-18

From the very outset of the debate on marriages of convenience, the British authorities had been expressing particularly strong concerns about the issue, a narrative that further intensified during the pre-Brexit period. As will be shown in the subsequent sections, such anxieties have ultimately found expression in a set of legislative measures adopted in the UK in recent years. Likewise, the pressure exercised by the UK and several other Member States prompted EU institutions to develop a position on the matter and introduce soft-law instruments addressing perceived marriages of convenience at the European level.

The significance of these developments cannot be overstated. State-exercised controls aiming to determine the authenticity of marriage may significantly impact the position of EU citizens whose close ones do not possess the nationality of one of the EU Member States, potentially coming into tension with the objective of eliminating all possible obstacles to free movement.

The aim of this chapter, therefore, is to provide a critical analysis of legal grounds that are used or may be used by the state to target something as sensitive and private as marriage, notwithstanding the protection guaranteed to families under the Citizens Directive. More specifically, the chapter focuses on one of the most important and potentially problematic aspects of marriage controls – namely, the definition of marriages of convenience in EU free movement and UK law, in so far as it concerns the residence rights of mobile EU citizens and their family members. Against this background, it is important to note that the EU law provisions addressing the issue of marriages of convenience continue to be relevant in the UK post-Brexit – in particular, with respect to UK-resident EU citizens covered by the EU-UK Withdrawal Agreement of 2019.[6]

The chapter is structured in two parts. The first part provides a concise overview of the tensions between the EU and Member States and looks at the degree to which the Union's institutions and the CJEU have accommodated the governments' concerns about perceived abuse. Following that, the chapter moves on to specifically examine the definition of marriages of convenience in EU law by focusing on the Citizens Directive and the relevant soft-law measures adopted in recent years. The second part of the chapter considers how marriages of convenience are defined in UK legislation and case law and whether the British approach to the issue is compatible with EU law. In addition, it also briefly explores the relevant developments in the UK after Brexit.

2. Tensions between the EU and Member States in family reunification cases

As noted in the introduction, over the past two decades the liberal EU approach to family reunification of mobile EU citizens started to come into considerable

6 Agreement on the withdrawal of the United Kingdom of Great Britain and Northern Ireland from the European Union and the European Atomic Energy Community [2019] OJ C384/1. See Section 4 for more details.

tension with developments in domestic family reunification laws in a number of Member States.

Having adopted restrictive labour migration policies giving preference only to highly skilled non-EU national workers, the governments seek to limit the number of TCN family migrants who cannot be selected in the same way as foreign labour force. With this aim, several states made the admission of family members, including spouses, of their own nationals conditional upon the fulfilment of stringent requirements (Bonjour & Block, 2016; Bonjour & de Hart, 2013; Wray, 2013, 2015). In 2012, for instance, the UK increased the probation period before indefinite leave to remain could be granted from two to five years, introduced the requirement to demonstrate that the relationship is 'genuine and subsisting' and, most importantly, imposed onerous financial requirements on British national sponsors.[7]

At the same time, EU citizens exercising their free movement rights remained exempt from any additional requirements when it came to living with certain categories of their non-EU family members. In the context of this chapter, it is important to stress that the Citizens Directive privileges marriages and registered partnerships over unregistered relationships. While spouses and registered partners[8] of EU citizens fall within the scope of 'direct' family members protected under Article 2(2), unmarried partners are considered 'extended' family members and covered by Article 3(2). The main difference between the two articles is that Member States are obliged to admit 'direct' family members, whilst only 'facilitate' admission of 'extended' family members, which is subject to degree of their discretion. Unmarried partners are, therefore, disadvantaged in comparison to married couples – not only because national governments are not obliged to recognise such relationships, but also because these must be 'duly attested' even where they do so. Whilst the Directive does not foresee systematic checks or additional requirements with respect to married couples; unmarried partners may be required to comply with extra conditions, as well as undergo a thorough examination to convince the authorities that their relationship is of sufficient quality.

The gap between the liberal EU approach and restrictive national family reunification provisions has given rise to anxieties among several governments who started to complain about the growing numbers of non-EU nationals allegedly seeking to circumvent domestic immigration rules by marrying mobile EU citizens. Such concerns, among other things, have found reflection in CJEU case law. The principal point of friction between the EU and Member States in this context is the position of EU citizens who meet their future spouses when they are already in the host country. It is exactly this group that is typically associated with abuse of EU law via marriages of convenience, particularly where the TCN family members are overstayers or unauthorised migrants who can regularise their status by marrying an EU citizen.

7 Statement of changes to the Immigration Rules HC 194, June 2012.

8 Provided that the host Member State treats these as equivalent to marriage.

With a few exceptions, the CJEU has always strived to remove all real or potential obstacles to family reunification, which could prevent EU citizens from freely exercising their free movement rights (for an overview see Guild, 2016). The position of couples who meet already in the host Member State was explicitly clarified in its landmark ruling in *Metock and Others*,[9] delivered in 2008 and extensively discussed in the literature (see, e.g., Costello, 2009; Lansbergen, 2009; Peers, 2009). In its decision, the Court overturned its earlier controversial judgement in *Akrich*,[10] which introduced the so-called prior lawful residence rule – a significant constraint of EU citizens' right to family reunification. In the latter case, the CJEU ruled that, to fall within the scope of EU law, the non-EU national must already be 'lawfully resident' in the first Member State before moving with their EU citizen spouse to another Member State.

In two subsequent decisions, *Jia*[11] and *Eind*,[12] the CJEU sought to clarify and limit the *Akrich* ruling before ultimately reversing it completely in *Metock*. The Court sensibly reasoned that if Member States retained exclusive competence over admitting family members without a prior residence status, the EU citizen's ability to live with their families would depend on domestic family reunification provisions of each Member State. This, consequently, would result in a situation where the EU citizen could be discouraged from continuing to live in one Member State and encouraged to leave to be able to lead a family life in another Member State with more liberal rules, or in a third country. In the view of the Court, this would seriously obstruct the exercise of free movement rights, which would be incompatible with the objective of establishing the internal market. The CJEU therefore held that the TCN spouse of a mobile EU citizen benefits from the provisions of the Citizens Directive 'irrespective of when and where their marriage took place and of how the national of a non-member country entered the host Member State'.[13] In other words, the Directive applies even in cases when the couple have met already in the host Member State and the non-EU party had previously lived in that country irregularly.

The CJEU ruling in *Metock* significantly aggravated tensions between the EU and several Member States who appeared extremely unwilling to revoke the prior lawful residence rule. By July 2008, when *Metock* was delivered, the rule had already been implemented in 11 Member States (European Commission, 2008, p. 4).

The UK together with Ireland, where *Metock* originated from, were among the countries voicing the strongest concerns about perceived abuse of EU free movement law via marriages of convenience. Unlike other EU Member States, who opted for transitional restrictions, the UK and Ireland immediately opened their

9 CJEU, 25 July 2008, C-127/08, *Metock and Others*, ECLI:EU:C:2008:449.
10 CJEU, 23 September 2003, C-109/01, *Akrich*, ECLI:EU:C:2003:491.
11 CJEU, 9 January 2007, C-1/05, *Jia*, ECLI:EU:C:2007:1.
12 CJEU, 11 December 2007, C-291/05, *Eind*, ECLI:EU:C:2007:771.
13 CJEU, 25 July 2008, C-127/08, *Metock and Others*, ECLI:EU:C:2008:449, § 99.

labour markets to nationals of eight Member States that joined the EU in 2004. At the same time, the British and Irish governments had retained national control over non-EU migration by securing opt-outs from most of the EU-level measures adopted in the area of immigration, asylum and border control, including the Schengen regime and the Family Reunification Directive (2003/86/EC) regulating family reunification of lawfully resident third-country nationals.

At the centre of the UK and Irish objections related to *Metock* have been complaints about the increase in marriages between male migrants from West Africa and the Indian subcontinent and female nationals of Central and Eastern European Member States (see, e.g., Joyce, 2012; Pendry & Dowling, 2012). Yet even assuming that purely artificial arrangements contracted solely for immigration purposes do take place, such combinations of nationalities could hardly be considered unusual. Provided that after arrival, many mobile EU citizens share social, work and study spaces with non-EU nationals, it is indeed unsurprising that some of them end up forming a relationship with TCN partners who happen to possess a short-term or irregular status. The governments, however, consider these pairing patterns suspicious, focusing on the perceived large cultural differences between the partners (see, e.g., Department of Justice (Ireland), 2011; Joyce, 2012, p. 5). This discourse has been further backed up by media reports exposing 'the world of fake marriages', where poor and vulnerable Eastern European women, often guided by marriage 'fixers', marry third-country national men for financial gain or are coerced into such arrangements (for discussion on how UK media approach the issue, see Wemyss et al., 2018).

In the years following the judgement in *Metock*, the UK, together with a few other Member States, continuously attempted to persuade EU institutions to narrow down family reunification rights. The topic of abuse of free movement rules was discussed, among other fora, at Justice and Home Affairs Council meetings (Department of Justice (Ireland), 2011; Groenendijk & Fernhout, 2010, pp. 5–7) and within the Commission expert group on the right to free movement of persons (FREEMO) (see, e.g., European Commission, 2013a, 2017). In 2013, the UK, Austria, Germany and the Netherlands explicitly called for a more restrictive interpretation of the free movement provisions. In their letter to the Irish Presidency of the Council and three European Commissioners, the interior ministers of the four Member States called the Commission to 'to draw up proposals' to tackle the perceived systematic abuse through marriages of convenience, fraud or benefits tourism (letter from the Ministers of the Interior of Austria, Germany, the Netherlands and the UK to the Irish Presidency, 2013, p. 3).

The initiative of the four Member States was ultimately rejected by the Commission and the rest of the Council, not least due to the inability of the relevant governments to provide statistical evidence of the 'widespread abuse' they were referring to (European Commission, 2013b, pp. 3–9; Council of the European Union, 2013, p. 8). The UK government, in particular, failed to provide statistics of detected marriages of convenience in support of its claims and instead described several anecdotal cases illustrating the phenomenon – for instance, the story of a Church of England vicar who was found guilty of knowingly solemnising over

350 alleged 'sham marriages' (House of Commons European Scrutiny Committee, 2014, p. 43).

The Commission earlier underlined that Member States were already allowed to address individual cases of potential fraud or abuse, including marriages of convenience (European Commission, 2008, p. 9). The relevant provisions are found in Article 35 of the Directive, which stipulates that 'Member States may adopt the necessary measures to refuse, terminate or withdraw any right conferred by this Directive in the case of abuse of rights or fraud, such as marriages of convenience'. The relevant examination of marriages between mobile EU citizens and third-country nationals, however, must only be carried out on a case-by-case basis, and systematic checks are prohibited – a principle established by the CJEU[14] (see also European Commission, 2009, p. 16, 2014, p. 17).

The pressure exercised by Member States, nonetheless, prompted the Commission to adopt two soft-law instruments aimed at providing governments with guidance on how to approach potential abuse: the Guidance on the better application of the Citizens Directive (European Commission, 2009) and the Handbook specifically addressing the issue of alleged marriages of convenience (European Commission, 2014). The Handbook is the key document in this context which, among other things, deals with the scope of the definition of marriages of convenience, used for the purposes of the Directive. Section 3 of this chapter correspondingly explores how the relevant concept is defined in EU free movement law and whether its interpretation, offered by the Handbook, is compatible with the Citizens Directive.

3. Defining marriages of convenience in EU law: the 'sole purpose' test

Although the Citizens Directive does not contain a self-standing definition of 'marriages of convenience', it implies that this concept shall be understood for its purposes as marriages contracted with the only aim being to legalise the stay of a third-country national in the EU. Whilst Article 35 of the Directive entitles Member States to adopt measures to tackle marriages of convenience, the wording of its Preamble makes clear that these are marriages 'contracted for the sole purpose of enjoying the right of free movement and residence'.[15] This definition has been reproduced in the Commission Guidelines and Handbook. According to the latter, marriages of convenience are formally valid marriages 'contracted for the sole purpose of conferring a right of free movement and residence under EU law on free movement of EU citizens to a spouse who would otherwise not have such a right' (European Commission, 2014, p. 8).

It is also reiterated that marriages of convenience are regarded as a specific form of abuse where 'abusive conduct is linked to the absence of intention to create a family as a married couple and to lead a genuine marital life' (European

14 CJEU, 18 December 2014, C-202/13, *McCarthy*, ECLI:EU:C:2014:2450, §§ 50–52.

15 Recital 28 Citizens Directive.

Commission, 2014, p. 8). The Handbook further clarifies that the abusive character in this case is represented by '*mala fide* of the spouses prior to and at the moment they enter into the marriage' (European Commission, 2014, p. 8). In other words, the notion of the 'sole purpose' under the Directive shall be understood as referring to purely artificial arrangements that have no other substance apart from an immigration motive.

Such interpretation is in line with the jurisprudence of the CJEU who, when examining the general concept of abuse in EU law, gives decisive weight to the objective circumstances that demonstrate the actual exercise of EU rights, regardless of the subjective motives of the EU citizens involved.[16] In its case law, the CJEU has consistently employed the narrow 'sole purpose' test, referring to abuse as 'wholly artificial arrangements which . . . are set up with the sole aim of obtaining . . . advantage'.[17] This interpretation has also been endorsed by AG Poiares Maduro, who referred to the 'sole purpose' paradigm as excluding situations where the activity in question 'may have some explanation other than the mere attainment' of the relevant advantage.[18] In addition, it is only where the conduct concerned does not have any other motive apart from obtaining such an advantage, that the objective of the relevant EU rules is not achieved (Lyal, 2011, p. 431).

It follows, therefore, that, for a marriage to be regarded one of convenience, obtaining an immigration benefit must be its only aim, rather than one among many. Such an approach is reasonable, provided that the Citizens Directive privileges marriage over non-registered partnerships and many couples may decide to get married just to be able to live together in one country. On the first impression, this logic has also been reflected in the Handbook, which states that 'a marriage cannot be considered a marriage of convenience simply because it brings an immigration advantage' (European Commission, 2014, p. 9).

The subsequent sentence, however, contradicts the previous passage by claiming that:

> [T]he notion of 'sole purpose' should not be interpreted literally (as being the unique or exclusive purpose) but rather as meaning that the objective to obtain the right of entry and residence must be the predominant purpose of the abusive conduct.
>
> (European Commission, 2014, p. 9)

This interpretation is highly confusing and seems to suggest that the Commission seeks to arbitrarily expand the definition provided by the Citizens Directive. It is a

16 A two-limb abuse test was introduced by the CJEU in its landmark judgement *Emsland-Stärke*. CJEU, C-110/99, *Emsland-Stärke*, ECLI:EU:C:2000:695, §§ 52–53.

17 CJEU, 20 June 2013, C-653/11, *HMRC*, ECLI:EU:C:2013:409, § 46; see also CJEU, 12 September 2006, C-196/04, *Cadbury Schweppes*, ECLI:EU:C:2006:544, §§ 55, 75; CJEU, 27 October 2011, C-504/10, *Tanoarch*, ECLI:EU:C:2011:707, § 51.

18 Opinion of Advocate General Poiares Maduro in CJEU, 21 February 2006, C-255/02, *Halifax*, ECLI:EU:C:2006:121, § 89.

general principle of EU law that a soft-law act is valid as long as it does not derogate from primary or secondary law provisions of EU law or CJEU jurisprudence[19] (see also Stefan, 2012, p. 60). Going further than the Directive, therefore, constitutes a clear breach of EU law.

As a soft-law instrument, the Handbook lacks legally binding force and has been developed as a voluntary interpretative tool. Nonetheless, it may have wide-ranging implications for the individuals concerned if translated into national law or used as a reference source by the judiciary. As will be demonstrated in Section 5, this is precisely what has happened in the UK where judges relied on its most confusing passages to undermine the definition of marriages of convenience under the Citizens Directive, which has had serious implications for the couples involved.

4. UK domestic law: multiple definitions of the same concept

The control over the authenticity of marriages between mobile EU citizens and third-country nationals in the UK is exercised at two levels – before and after the marriage is entered into. As noted earlier in Section 2, those benefitting from automatic protection under the Citizens Directive are married couples and registered partners only; the admission of (yet) unmarried or unregistered partners, by contrast, is subject to the discretion of the respective Member State and is regulated by its national immigration law. Furthermore, since the substantive family law falls within the exclusive competence of Member States,[20] the Union institutions are not authorised to adopt measures regulating the conditions for entering into marriage. Accordingly, the governments are entitled to define marriages for residence purposes that are yet to be contracted without having regard to the definition provided in EU law.

Unlike the Citizens Directive, which refers to 'marriages of convenience', UK domestic immigration law employs the term 'sham marriage' to designate marriages contracted for immigration purposes. Among others, the definition of a 'sham marriage' is applicable to prospective marriages involving mobile EU citizens. It is found in Section 24(5) of the Immigration and Asylum Act 1999 and reads as follows:

> A marriage (whether or not it is void) is a "sham marriage" if—
>
> (a) either, or both, of the parties to the marriage is not a relevant national,[21]
> (b) there is no genuine relationship between the parties to the marriage, and

19 CJEU, 12 December 1973, C-149/73, *Witt*, ECLI:EU:C:1973:160, § 3; CJEU, 15 February 1996, C-226/94, *Grand Garage Albigeois*, ECLI:EU:C:1996:55, § 21.

20 Articles 3–4 TFEU *a contrario*; for an analysis, see European Parliament (2012).

21 A 'relevant national' was previously defined in Section 24(6) of the Act as a UK, EEA or Swiss citizen. Since 1 July 2021, it excludes EEA citizens (except Irish citizens and EEA citizens with a status or a pending application under the EU Settlement Scheme).

(c) either, or both, of the parties to the marriage enter into the marriage for one or more of these purposes—

  (i) avoiding the effect of one or more provisions of United Kingdom immigration law or the immigration rules;
  (ii) enabling a party to the marriage to obtain a right conferred by that law or those rules to reside in the United Kingdom.

In contrast to the Citizens Directive, the Immigration and Asylum Act definition omits the word 'sole' and only refers to the 'purpose' instead. Taken alone, such wording may cover situations where securing residence rights for the TCN spouse is not the sole but the primary purpose of the marriage. The conditions, however, are cumulative, and this flaw is somewhat mitigated by the requirement of the absence of a 'genuine relationship' between the parties. Given a wide variety of global relationship patterns, the evaluation of the 'genuineness' of the relationship is deeply subjective and open to misconceptions. Nevertheless, if the couple is in a relationship and wishes to get married to enable the TCN partner to stay in the UK, their situation, at least in theory, should not fall within the 'sham marriage' definition.

Before the end of the post-Brexit transitional period on 31 December 2020, the situation of already married couples was covered by the Citizens Directive, transposed in UK law by the Immigration (European Economic Area) Regulations of 2016.[22] When referring to marriages for immigration purposes, the EEA Regulations used different terminology from that of the Immigration and Asylum Act, designating such unions as ones 'of convenience', the term employed by the Directive.

The definition of the relevant concept in the Regulations read as follows:

> "[M]arriage of convenience" includes a marriage entered into for the purpose of using these Regulations, or any other right conferred by the EU Treaties, as a means to circumvent—
>
> (a) immigration rules applying to non-EEA nationals (such as any applicable requirement under the 1971 Act to have leave to enter or remain in the United Kingdom); or
> (b) any other criteria that the party to the marriage of convenience would otherwise have to meet in order to enjoy a right to reside under these Regulations or the EU Treaties.[23]

The absence of the word 'sole' from the Regulations was crucial. When interpreted literally, this definition could target every couple where the non-EU national would gain an immigration advantage from the marriage, including those who were in a

22 Immigration (European Economic Area) Regulations 2016, SI 2016/1052 (hereinafter: EEA Regulations).

23 Regulation 2(1) EEA Regulations.

close relationship and/or intended to lead a family life. The definition provided in the Regulations, hence, was arguably in breach of the Citizens Directive. Moreover, it was also broader than the 'sham marriage' definition found in the Immigration and Asylum Act: whilst in the latter the word 'sole' is equally omitted, it expressly provides that there should not be a genuine relationship between the parties.

The UK decision to leave the EU has profoundly transformed the position of UK-resident EU citizens and their family members. Since the end of the transition period, EU citizens are divided into two categories that are covered by separate sets of provisions. Those who have moved or will move to the UK after this date fall into the scope of British immigration law and will need to comply with UK national family reunification rules. By contrast, those who relocated to the country before 31 December 2020 and either married their TCN partners or already lived with their spouses in the UK by this date are covered by the EU-UK Withdrawal Agreement of 2019, incorporated into the British law by the European Union (Withdrawal Agreement) Act 2020. The latter group should accordingly continue to enjoy the residence rights in the UK on the same terms as under the Citizens Directive, including EU law safeguards the states must respect when targeting perceived marriages of convenience. All beneficiaries of the Withdrawal Agreement (and correspondingly the Withdrawal Agreement Act) were required to apply for a new status online under the so-called EU Settlement Scheme (EUSS), introduced as an Appendix EU to the UK Immigration Rules (2016).

Article 20(3) of the Withdrawal Agreement stipulates that the UK may adopt measures to combat fraud or abuse on the same conditions as set out in Article 35 of the Citizens Directive and with respect to the same procedural safeguards listed in this document. The UK Immigration Rules correspondingly provide that, for the purposes of family reunification under the EU Settlement Scheme, the term 'spouse' excludes marriages of convenience.

These concepts are defined there as marriages 'entered into as a means to circumvent':

(a) any criterion the party would have to meet in order to enjoy a right to enter or reside in the UK under the EEA Regulations; or
(b) any other provision of UK immigration law or any requirement of the Immigration Rules; or
(c) any criterion the party would otherwise have to meet in order to enjoy a right to enter or reside in the UK under EU law; or
(d) any criterion the party would have to meet in order to enjoy a right to enter or reside in the Islands under Islands law.[24]

Similarly to the definition of marriages of convenience found in the EEA Regulations, this definition contains neither the word 'sole' as provided under the Citizens Directive, nor the passage that there should not be a 'genuine relationship' between

24 Immigration Rules Appendix EU, Annex 1.

the parties as stipulated in the Immigration and Asylum Act. As noted earlier, this approach is arguably in breach of Article 35 of the Citizens Directive and, consequently, the Withdrawal Agreement and Agreement Act.

An accusation of being involved in a marriage for immigration purposes may have serious implications for EU citizens and their partners – both at the pre- and post-marriage stage. In the UK, unmarried partners can qualify for residence rights only where they can provide extensive evidence of living together in a relationship 'akin to marriage' for at least two years.[25] For couples who have not yet reached this threshold, marriage may often represent the only opportunity to stay together, particularly where the non-EU party has an unstable or irregular residence status.

Since pre-marriage controls escape the ambit of EU law, governments may systematically examine all intended marriages involving foreigners, a measure that cannot be applied to already existing marriages under EU law. Since 2015, the UK authorities conduct systematic checks on almost all couples involving non-EU nationals who give a marriage notice at a register office. Under the so-called 'referral and investigation scheme', civil registrars are required to refer to the Home Office[26] all prospective marriages involving non-EU nationals without indefinite leave to remain or a valid marriage visitor or fiancé(e) visa.[27] In case of suspicions, the couple may be asked to undergo an investigation.

Formally, as long as the parties comply with the investigation, they will be allowed to marry even if their marriage is believed to be a 'sham'. Yet, irrespective of whether or not the couple has complied with an investigation and if it has even been started in the first place, unauthorised migrants may be removed from the UK any time before their marriage is registered.[28] EU citizens whose TCN partners have no valid leave to remain, therefore, face a particularly high risk of being separated. The very fact of giving a marriage notice automatically means coming to the attention of the Home Office, which may eventually lead to an opposite outcome and potentially force EU citizens to relocate to be able to enjoy family life with their partners. Hence, although formally the UK pre-marriage controls did not breach the Citizens Directive, the free movement rights of EU citizens might have nonetheless been seriously obstructed.

Even if the couple manages to enter into marriage, a finding that it is not genuine may still lead to their separation. In that case, the UK authorities may refuse any subsequent residence application made by the TCN party on the basis of marriage – previously under the EEA Regulations[29] and more recently under the

25 Part 8, § 295A(i)(a)(i) Immigration Rules.

26 Ministerial department of the UK government, responsible for Home Affairs.

27 Section 28H, Marriage Act 1949. Since 1 July 2021, the scheme also includes intended marriages involving EEA citizens (except Irish citizens and EEA citizens with a status or a pending application under the EU Settlement Scheme).

28 Section 10 Immigration and Asylum Act.

29 Non-EU spouses of EU citizens whose marriage was found to be one of convenience were not considered family members for the purposes of the EEA Regulations. See Regulation 2(1) EEA Regulations.

EU Settlement Scheme.[30] Where a non-EU national has already obtained an EUSS leave on the basis of marriage that is subsequently found to be one of convenience, the leave will typically be curtailed or revoked.[31] Moreover, an accusation of being involved in a marriage of convenience may also lead to cancellation of other forms of permission to enter or stay, previously granted to a TCN party under the Immigration Rules.[32] Following that, the person can be administratively removed under Section 10(1) of the Immigration and Asylum Act.

Against this background, two different terms ('marriage of convenience' and 'sham marriage') and multiple definitions of the same concept are highly confusing and undermine legal certainty. The adverse consequences of this state of affairs have been most visible in UK domestic jurisprudence. Section 5 provides a brief overview of the most problematic rulings in this respect, as far as post-marriage situations are concerned.

5. The concept of marriages of convenience in UK case law

British courts frequently struggle with providing a correct definition of marriages of convenience in the context of EU free movement law. In a line of high-level cases, delivered over the past decade, the courts adopted a strikingly confusing approach, not least due to the apparent misinterpretation of the Commission Handbook caused by its obvious ambiguity – in particular, an attempt to arbitrarily expand the definition of marriages of convenience provided by the Directive.

The Supreme Court ruling in *Sadovska & Anor v. Secretary of State for the Home Department (SSHD)*[33] is an important case where Commission soft law became national hard law – in this particular situation, however, this has led to adverse implications for EU citizens and their TCN family members. The Court first described the phrase 'marriage of convenience' as 'a term of art' which is defined in the Citizens Directive and 2009 Guidelines as one contracted for the sole purpose of enjoying Treaty rights.[34] Yet, the judge then went on to quote a passage from the Commission Handbook which says that the notion of 'sole purpose' should not be interpreted as being the unique or exclusive purpose but the predominant purpose of the abusive conduct. The Court then suggested that the Handbook expanded the definition provided in the Directive by stating that the

30 Under § EU16(a) Immigration Rules Appendix EU, an application to the EUSS scheme may be refused on so-called suitability grounds if the applicant has submitted false or misleading information that is material to the decision to grant or refuse leave. The Home Office guidelines clarify that reliance on a marriage of convenience does fall within the scope of the relevant provision (Home Office, 2023, p. 39). See also Regulation 18(1)(e) Proposed Marriages and Civil Partnerships (Conduct of Investigations, etc.) Regulations 2015, SI 2015/397.

31 § A3.5(a) and (b) Immigration Rules Appendix EU(FP); § A3.4(a) Immigration Rules Appendix EU.

32 § 9.6.2 Immigration Rules.

33 *Sadovska & Anor v. SSHD* [2017] UKSC 54.

34 *Sadovska & Anor v. SSHD* [2017] UKSC 54, §§ 22–24.

entry and residence in the EU shall be not the only, but the predominant purpose.[35] As mentioned above, such an interpretation is deeply problematic and arguably violates the Directive.

In the same month that the decision in *Sadovska* came up, the High Court delivered its judgement in *Molina, R*.[36] This ruling further departed from EU law by rather paradoxically suggesting that a couple may enter into a marriage of convenience even if they are in an ongoing relationship. In the view of the court, there was a difference between a 'sham marriage' and a 'marriage of convenience'. The judge argued that, under the Immigration and Asylum Act, a 'sham marriage' could only be established if there was no genuine relationship between the parties, whereby a 'marriage of convenience' under the EEA Regulations was 'one that has been entered into . . . for the purpose of gaining an immigration advantage'.[37]

The court accordingly stated that:

> [A] 'marriage of convenience' may exist despite the fact that there is a genuine relationship and in the absence of any deception or fraud as to its existence. The focus is upon the intention of one or more of the parties and, in the present context, whether the sole aim is to gain an immigration advantage.[38]

The ruling in *Molina* entirely misinterpreted the 'sole purpose' or 'purely artificial arrangements' principle established for the purposes of the Directive. As noted in Section 4, it is indeed the case that the EEA Regulations do not contain the phrase 'sole purpose' and could potentially cover a broader range of situations contrary to what is envisaged under EU law. This has led to a puzzling conclusion that the definition of a marriage of convenience in EU law is somehow broader than the one found in the UK Immigration and Asylum Act, which, in reality, is not the case.

The erroneous approach established in *Sadovska* and *Molina* was further applied in later case law. For example, in an Upper Tribunal (UT) decision in *Saeed* of 2022 the judge summarised her approach as follows:

> The terms 'sham marriage' and 'marriage of convenience' are not mutually exclusive. The absence of a genuine relationship at the time of the marriage being entered into would render the marriage one of convenience (and a 'sham'); however, if there is a genuine relationship at the time of the marriage, while it could not be categorised as a 'sham' marriage, it may still amount to a marriage of convenience (depending on the predominant purpose).[39]

35 *Sadovska & Anor v. SSHD* [2017] UKSC 54, § 29.

36 *Molina, R (On the Application Of) v. SSHD* [2017] EWHC 1730 (Admin).

37 *Molina, R (On the Application Of) v. SSHD* [2017] EWHC 1730 (Admin) § 64.

38 *Molina, R (On the Application Of) v. SSHD* [2017] EWHC 1730 (Admin), § 73.

39 *Saeed (Deception, knowledge, marriage of convenience)* [2022] UKUT 00018, § 29(ii).

In a number of situations, the erroneous 'predominant purpose' approach adopted by the judges has led to particularly problematic outcomes when marriages which involved pregnancy and/or childbirth were designated ones of convenience. In *Gjura v. SSHD*, the First-Tier Tribunal (FtT)[40] went as far as to suggest that the non-EU spouse fathered a child solely to obtain an immigration status.[41] This finding seems even more disturbing, provided that the judge did accept that both parties were involved in the upbringing of the child. It nonetheless placed weight on other factors, such as 'scant evidence' of the couple living together, their perceived inability to easily communicate when they first met, and the fact that they gave different addresses to the registrar when recording the birth of their child. It is remarkable that the FtT findings were upheld by the UT, which, by reference to *Sadovska*, considered that the FtT judge was entitled to conclude that the 'sole or main' purpose of marriage, despite the child, was to obtain an immigration advantage.[42]

In a similar case of *Khan v. SSHD*, the FtT accepted that the non-EU national involved was a 'caring and loving parent' of his child, yet concluded that the marriage was one of convenience because of his 'dreadful' immigration history and several discrepancies identified in the marriage interviews.[43] The judge strikingly noted that the appellant had 'further sought to strengthen his position in the UK by conceiving a child with the sponsor' and expressed doubts that his intentions had been 'honourable or genuine'.[44] In its ruling, the Upper Tribunal also referred to *Molina* and *Sadovska* to erroneously state that a marriage of convenience is a marriage contracted for predominant purpose to gain a right of residence under EU law. The Upper Tribunal, nonetheless, ultimately concluded that the FtT did not carry out a balanced assessment of all the evidence, focusing on the negative and failing to give due weight to the positive factors, suggesting the marriage was not one of convenience. The decision was, therefore, set aside.[45]

On the other hand, there are situations when a marriage, initially contracted solely to help a non-EU citizen obtain an immigration advantage, later transforms into a real relationship. In several such cases, UK courts have interpreted the 'sole purpose' definition literally, effectively dividing established families of EU citizens. Once they had established that the original purpose of the marriage has only been an immigration advantage, the present state of the relationship was considered irrelevant.[46] In a recent Upper Tribunal ruling in *SSHD v. Nketia*, delivered in summer 2022, the judge concluded that 'since the marriage commenced life as a marriage of convenience, it will always be a marriage of convenience'.[47]

40 The court of first instance in the UK.
41 Quoted in the Upper Tribunal judgement in *Gjura v. SSHD* [2019] UKUT 07856 (IAC).
42 *Gjura v. SSHD* [2019] UKUT 07856 (IAC).
43 Quoted in the Upper Tribunal judgement in *Khan v. SSHD* [2019] UKUT 03191 (IAC), §§ 7–8.
44 *Khan v. SSHD* [2019] UKUT 03191 (IAC), § 7.
45 *Khan v. SSHD* [2019] UKUT 03191 (IAC), §§ 17–25.
46 See, e.g., *A U v. SSHD* [2017] UKUT 00052 (IAC); *Raqueeb v. SSHD* [2018] UKUT 01754 (IAC).
47 *SSHD v. Nketia* [2022] UKUT 04841 (IAC), § 47.

Such an outcome is highly problematic and was most likely unintended by the drafters of the Directive. It strikingly contradicts the overarching purpose of the right to family reunification granted to mobile EU citizens – namely, to provide them with an opportunity to live with their family members in a country of their choice, which would, in turn, facilitate free movement and their integration into the host Member State. Therefore, to achieve the aim of the Citizens Directive, the definition should not be interpreted literally, but rather as covering cases having no other substance both before and after the wedding. A literal reading of the definition, on the other hand, denies residency to non-EU nationals leading a real family life. That, in turn, would create unnecessary hardship for the EU citizen spouse and, quite possibly, prompt the couple to relocate.

Furthermore, a significant point of concern is that when examining cases involving children, the judges made no reference whatsoever to the principle of the best interests of the child. Under the UN Convention on the Rights of the Child, in all actions concerning children, undertaken by the state actors, the best interests of the child shall be a primary consideration (Article 3(1)), whereby the authorities shall ensure that children are not separated from their parents against their will (Article 9(1)). A situation where a finding that the marriage is one of convenience may result in the removal of the TCN parent is likely to come into considerable tension with these provisions. This has also been reiterated in the Commission Handbook, which underlines that, typically, it is in the child's best interests to be able to continue living in the host EU Member State with both parents, notably where the child is well integrated or is in education in this country (European Commission, 2014, p. 24).

6. Conclusion

This chapter has shown that marriages of convenience in EU free movement law are a heavily debated concept whose interpretation has appeared deeply problematic – both at the European level and in the UK. Although Article 35 of the Citizens Directive permits Member States to derogate from free movement in individual cases of abuse, such as marriages of convenience, this concept is defined narrowly, and the relevant provision is to be interpreted strictly. The principal constraint on the concept, which is imposed by both the Citizens Directive and the CJEU, is the narrow 'sole purpose' test; it implies that securing a residence status for the non-EU national party must be the only aim of the marriage, rather than one among many. This is logical, provided that the Directive continues to pursue a conservative approach by regarding marriage as a proxy for a serious long-term commitment, and privileging spouses (and registered partners) over unmarried couples. For couples involving non-EU nationals, consequently, marriage may often represent the only opportunity to stay together, particularly where the TCN party has an unstable or irregular residence status.

Over the past decade, the growing Member State anxieties about the perceived abuse of EU free movement law via marriages of convenience have prompted the Commission to adopt two soft-law instruments providing governments with guidance on how to approach the issue. The principal document issued in this context is a Handbook, entirely dedicated to marriages of convenience. The Handbook, however, provides its own interpretation of the concept, claiming that, under the Directive, the notion of the 'sole purpose' should not be understood as being the exclusive but rather the predominant purpose of the marriage. The relevant passage contradicts the wording and spirit of the Citizens Directive and hence derogates from EU hard law.

The confusion is further exacerbated by the fact that there are multiple definitions of marriages for residence purposes in UK law, none of which accurately reflects the wording of the Citizens Directive. Such an approach significantly undermines clarity and legal certainty, which is best evident in the findings of UK courts interpreting the concept. Having juxtaposed the definitions of 'sham marriages' and 'marriages of convenience' in UK domestic law, as well as referred to the problematic passage of the Handbook, the judges ultimately concluded that a marriage of convenience might be entered into by a couple in a genuine relationship, a paradoxical interpretation that is obviously inconsistent with the Directive. On the other hand, several judges have approached the 'sole purpose' definition literally, i.e., as including cases where a marriage, initially contracted only for residence purposes, later transformed into a real relationship. Such interpretation is equally inconsistent with the overarching purpose of the family reunification provisions enshrined in EU law, which aim to remove obstacles to free movement of EU citizens. Bearing this in mind, couples leading family life should still be able to benefit from Treaty provisions, irrespective of their original or concurring intentions.

As demonstrated in the chapter, the approaches described earlier result in particularly disturbing outcomes, such as cases where marriages involving children are designated as ones of convenience. This finding has serious repercussions for the non-EU national party who would not be allowed to obtain residence rights on the basis of marriage and would typically be liable for removal. This may effectively result in EU citizens being separated from their TCN spouses or, alternatively, urged to move to another country where they could live together – an outcome most likely unintended by the drafters of the Citizens Directive. Another point of significant concern is that, when dealing with the problematic category of cases involving children, the UK judges have ignored the principle of the best interests of the child, which needs to be observed at all times.

Lastly, the situation has further deteriorated after the end of the post-Brexit transition period on 31 December 2020. The UK withdrawal from the EU has significantly limited the group of EU citizens whose families continue to benefit from protection on the same terms as under the Citizens Directive. EU citizens who relocated to the UK after 31 December 2020, consequently, are equated to full-fledged foreigners and need to comply by UK domestic family reunification rules, which are much more restrictive than EU law. Among other things, this implies that married couples involving the latter group of EU citizens are now subject to more intensive scrutiny, including the systematic requirement to provide extensive evidence that their relationship is 'genuine and subsisting'.

References

Bonjour, S., & Block, L. (2016). Ethnicizing citizenship, questioning membership: Explaining the decreasing family migration rights of citizens in Europe. *Citizenship Studies*, *20*(6–7), 779–794. https://doi.org/10.1080/13621025.2016.1191429

Bonjour, S., & de Hart, B. (2013). A proper wife, a proper marriage: Constructions of "us" and "them" in Dutch family migration policy. *European Journal of Women's Studies*, *20*(1), 61–76. https://doi.org/10.1177/1350506812456459

Costello, C. (2009). *Metock*: Free movement and "normal family life" in the Union. *Common Market Law Review*, *46*(2), 587–622. https://doi.org/10.54648/cola2009024

Council of the European Union. (2013, December 5–6). *Document 17342/13 (Presse 534)*. https://data.consilium.europa.eu/doc/document/ST-17342-2013-INIT/en/pdf

Department of Justice (Ireland). (2011, June 9). *Sham marriages leading to abuses of EU freedom of movement rights* [Press release]. https://jobs.justice.ie/en/JELR/Pages/PR11000079

European Commission. (2008). *Report from the Commission to the European Parliament and the Council on the application of directive 2004/38/EC on the right of citizens of the Union and their family members to move and reside freely within the territory of the member states* (COM (2008) 840 final). https://eur-lex.europa.eu/LexUriServ/LexUriServ.do?uri=COM:2008:0840:FIN:en:PDF

European Commission. (2009). *Communication from the Commission to the European Parliament and the Council on guidance for better transposition and application of directive 2004/38/EC on the right of citizens of the Union and their family members to move and reside freely within the territory of the member states* (COM(2009) 313 final). https://eur-lex.europa.eu/LexUriServ/LexUriServ.do?uri=COM:2009:0313:FIN:EN:PDF

European Commission. (2013a, March 14). *Final minutes of the fifteenth meeting of experts on the right to free movement of persons (Directive 2004/38/EC) held on February 5, 2013*. https://ec.europa.eu/transparency/expert-groups-register/screen/expert-groups/consult?do=groupDetail.groupDetail&groupID=2397

European Commission. (2013b). *Free movement of EU citizens and their families: Five actions to make a difference* (Communication) (COM(2013) 837 final). https://eur-lex.europa.eu/legal-content/EN/TXT/PDF/?uri=CELEX:52013DC0837&from=EN

European Commission. (2014). *Staff working document – handbook on addressing the issue of alleged marriages of convenience between EU citizens and non-EU nationals in the context of EU law on free movement of EU citizens* (SWD(2014) 284 final). https://eur-lex.europa.eu/legal-content/EN/TXT/PDF/?uri=CELEX:52014SC0284%20&from=IT

European Commission. (2017, April 6). *Meeting of the expert group FREEMO on the right to free movement of persons (Directive 2004/38 EC) – Brussels, October 21, 2016*. https://ec.europa.eu/transparency/expert-groups-register/screen/expert-groups/consult?do=groupDetail.groupDetail&groupID=2397

European Parliament. (2012). *Which legal basis for family law? The way forward* (PE 462.498). www.europarl.europa.eu/RegData/etudes/note/join/2012/462498/IPOL-JURI_NT(2012)462498_EN.pdf

Groenendijk, K., & Fernhout, R. (2010). Vrij Verkeer, Europa-Route en Omgekeerde Discriminatie: Wie Houdt Wie voor de Gek? *Asiel & Migrantenrecht*, *1*, 4–16.

Guild, E. (2016). Free movement of EU citizens and their family members. *New Journal of European Criminal Law*, *7*(2), 231–249. https://doi.org/10.1177/203228441600700210

Home Office. (2023, June 22). *Marriage investigations* (Version 8.0). https://assets.publishing.service.gov.uk/media/64a3e1870ce7d4000cfccfa1/Marriage_investigations.pdf

House of Commons European Scrutiny Committee. (2014). *Thirty-first report of session 2013–14* (2013–14, HC 83-xxviii). https://publications.parliament.uk/pa/cm201314/cmselect/cmeuleg/83-xxviii/83xxviii.pdf

Joyce, C. (2012). *Misuse of the Right to Family Reunification: Ireland* (EMN Focussed Study 1). The Economic and Social Research Institute. http://aei.pitt.edu/98799/1/SUSTAT43.pdf

Lansbergen, A. (2009). Metock, implementation of the citizens' rights directive and lessons for EU citizenship. *Journal of Social Welfare and Family Law*, *31*(3), 285–297. https://doi.org/10.1080/09649060903354605
Letter from the Ministers of the Interior of Austria, Germany, the Netherlands and the UK to the Irish Presidency. (2013, April). http://docs.dpaq.de/3604-130415_letter_to_presidency_final_1_2.pdf
Lyal, R. (2011). *Cadbury Schweppes* and Abuse: Comments. In R. de la Feria & S. Vogenauer (Eds.), *Prohibition of Abuse of Law: A New General Principle of EU Law?* (pp. 427–434). Hart. https://doi.org/10.5040/9781472565570.ch-029
Peers, S. (2009). Free movement, immigration control and constitutional conflict. *European Constitutional Law Review*, *5*(2), 173–196. https://doi.org/10.1017/S1574019609001734
Pendry, E., & Dowling, S. (Eds.). (2012). *Misuse of the Right to Family Reunification: Marriages of Convenience and False Declarations of Parenthood.* Home Office.
Stefan, O. (2012). Hybridity before the court: A hard look at soft law in the EU competition and state aid case law. *European Law Review*, *37*(1), 49–69.
Wemyss, G., Yuval-Davis, N., & Cassidy, K. (2018). "Beauty and the beast": Everyday bordering and "sham marriage" discourse. *Political Geography*, *66*, 151–160. https://doi.org/10.1016/j.polgeo.2017.05.008
Wray, H. (2013). Regulating spousal migration in Denmark. *Journal of Immigration, Asylum and Nationality Law*, *27*(2), 139–161.
Wray, H. (2015). "A thing apart": Controlling male family migration to the UK. *Men and asculinities*, *18*(4), 424–447. https://doi.org/10.1177/1097184X15575108

15 Family reunification and administrative citizenship

A transnational perspective

Milena Belloni and Gert Verschraegen

1. Introduction

Amira[1] *is a 28-year-old Eritrean who has been living in Addis Ababa (Ethiopia) with her two children, Mohammed and Zuber, for the past four years. Her husband, Ahmed, fled Eritrea before the birth of their youngest child and arrived in Belgium in 2016, where he applied for asylum. He was granted international protection in 2017 and has since been working to reunite with Amira and the children.*

The challenges began when Amira submitted her application for family reunification one month past the deadline at the Belgian Embassy in Addis Ababa. This delay was due to the absence of a Belgian Embassy in Asmara, the capital of Eritrea. Family members of recognised refugees in Belgium are required to apply at the relevant Belgian Embassy within 12 months of receiving international protection to benefit from more lenient conditions.[2] *However, Amira and her two children, like many Eritrean citizens, were unable to obtain exit visas until 2018. They were only able to travel undetected to Addis Ababa after tensions over the Eritrean–Ethiopian border eased following a peace process. Unfortunately, this delay led to the denial of their family reunification application. Now, Ahmed had to demonstrate that he had sufficient income, health insurance and suitable housing to prove his eligibility to the immigration office.*

Meanwhile, Amira, as most Eritrean refugees in Ethiopia, encountered significant difficulties renewing her and her children's documentation. When her initial permission to stay in Addis expired, the Ethiopian agency responsible

1 All names used in this chapter are fictitious to protect the identity of the participants.

2 Updated information on the regulations for family reunification in Belgium can be found at https://www.vreemdelingenrecht.be/verblijfsrecht/reguliere-migratie/gezinshereniging. It is noteworthy that in August 2025 regulations became even more restrictive. This includes higher socio-economic requirements for the sponsor, the exclusion of beneficiaries of subsidiary protection from the grace period for income exemption and the shortening of the exemption period to 6 months for holders of refugee status.

DOI: 10.4324/9781003503217-19

for refugee affairs (RRS [Refugees and Returnees Service]) was closed due to the COVID-19 pandemic. As a result, she and her children were left without valid identification for over a year. Due to this lack of ID, Mohammed, the eldest child, was unable to enrol in school for two consecutive years.

During this time, Ahmed contacted a lawyer in Belgium to file an appeal on Amira's behalf. Amira was then summoned by the embassy in Ethiopia to submit marriage and birth certificates of herself and the children. However, Amira could not properly speak Amharic, and there was no Tigrinya translator when she submitted the documents. 'I gave them to the Embassy', she claimed, 'but they say they have never received them'. This resulted in a second rejection of the application. Subsequently, Amira was called again to submit the documents, but the consular official refused to accept them: the 'birth certificates', as Amira called these documents, were, in fact, vaccination booklets and on them Zuber's name was spelled as 'Aziber'. The official suggested that this was going to represent a problem because it did not correspond with the other documents they had submitted.

Meanwhile, the lawyer representing Ahmed filed three appeals to the Court of Alien Law Litigation to contest the decision of the Federal Migration Office that decides over family reunification in Belgium. Each time, the Migration Office had to reassess the decision but found new reasons to reject the application. The first time the application was rejected due to Amira's application being too late; the second time it was rejected because Ahmed was not renting a house large enough to accommodate the whole family. The migration office finally allowed Amira and the children to take a DNA test to prove their family ties (after more than six years since the beginning of the process). In April 2024 Ahmed could finally reunite with Amira and the children.

Amira and Ahmed's story is indicative of the numerous challenges faced by refugee families separated by borders. Their case, one of many similar ones encountered in our research, illustrates the multitude of institutional actors that refugees must engage with when applying for family reunification. This includes not only the diplomatic and migration offices of the country where the sponsor resides, but also the authorities of the country of origin and the country where the family is pursuing the family reunification process. The success of their application hinges on both their ability to mount successful legal appeals against the migration office and their positive interactions with street-level bureaucrats at the embassy, the counter of national refugee agencies and their municipality of birth, just to mention a few critical locations. Throughout these interactions, refugees and their families must demonstrate the extent to which they belong to various political entities, such as being citizens of their home country, registered refugees in the first transit country or asylum seekers in the destination country. The administrative documentation required for family reunification can only be obtained if individuals and families effectively establish their affiliations with different states in this intricate transnational landscape.

The literature on migrant family reunification has primarily examined the relationship between migrants and the regulatory framework of destination states, which are typically located in the Global North, where the sponsor resides and desires to reunite with their family (for a brief review, see Belloni and Cleton, this volume). In contrast, this chapter emphasises the importance of scrutinising the process of applying for family reunification by considering the multiplicity of state actors, administrative processes and subjects located in the Global South, particularly focusing on country of origin and first asylum country outside Europe. This institutional landscape becomes particularly intricate for refugees, as we argue, due to their family's dispersal across states and their status of 'outsiders'.

As demonstrated in this chapter, family members of refugees who await reunification in the first country of asylum face structural challenges in performing what we term 'administrative citizenship'. Drawing from Stevens (2017, p. 4), administrative citizenship refers to the enactment of citizenship through administrative documentation, a process that requires individuals to provide documentary evidence, such as passports, birth certificates and IDs, to prove their citizenship (or other allegiances with a state). Unlike the legal conception of citizenship in the strict sense, the concept of administrative citizenship allows scholars to delve into the intricate process by which states, along with their bureaucratic apparatus, confer legal statuses and documentation to individuals (cf. Horton & Heyman, 2020). It also explores how individuals can perform, assert and experience their membership in a nation-state through these tangible artefacts across borders. By using this concept, our chapter aims to contribute to the growing scholarship focusing on the material aspects of legal processes (Davies, 2017; Latour, 2010) and to the role of paperwork and documents in a range of seemingly neutral administrative processes surrounding migration control and asylum (Horton & Heyman, 2020; Geoffrion & Cretton, 2021).

The concept of administrative citizenship builds upon a longstanding tradition in the anthropology of citizenship (e.g., Lazar, 2013), which examines the lived experiences of political membership, its dependence on political, bureaucratic and administrative contingencies and how individuals position themselves as claim-making subjects, often independently from the legal status they possess. We argue that the notion of administrative citizenship can shed light on some of the main challenges faced in the process of refugee family reunification. It also has the potential to contribute to the research agenda on family reunification within a transnational context. Our primary focus is on the perspective of family members awaiting reunification in first countries of asylum in the Global South. We illustrate how their administrative limbo arises from gaps and communication barriers within and between the different state identification systems that refugees must navigate.

The chapter is organised as follows. After a brief review of recent studies on family reunification, we first elaborate on the significance of 'administrative citizenship' to understand the challenges of families that live across borders and interact with different state and regional administrations. We argue that identity documents and administrative identification practices are crucial for individuals' ability to exercise their right to family life outside their country of origin. Then, the chapter discusses refugees' unique position in relation to their country of origin and their often precarious status in their first countries of asylum. In the final section, we draw on our ethnographic fieldwork in Ethiopia to illustrate how the concrete difficulties faced by Eritrean refugees in the family reunification process largely stem from unequal access to the documentation required by the assessing country. This unequal access arises from refugees' limited ability to perform their 'administrative citizenship' vis-à-vis their country of origin and first asylum country as well as from the limited capacity of their bureaucratic dossier 'to travel' across borders.

This chapter provides theoretical reflections based on a multi-sited research with Somali and Eritrean refugee families living between Belgium, Italy and Ethiopia. While the empirical material will not be extensively discussed, we draw on empirical cases to illustrate key points.[3] The research has been designed to challenge Eurocentric approaches that have dominated studies on transnational families, with a few exceptions (e.g., Anschütz & Mazzucato, 2022). Leveraging personal contacts within the Eritrean community and with several lawyers and social workers in Italy and in Belgium supporting refugees in their process of family reunification, the first author (Milena Belloni, from now on indicated as MB) has collected 30 stories of refugee families. Subsequently, MB has traced the experiences of 10 of these separated families by conducting fieldwork in Ethiopia, a country where many partners (mostly wives) and children await reunification with their husbands/fathers. To gain insight into the daily lives of these separated families, the author has followed refugees in Europe over a span of time (up to two years for some cases) and conducted home visits with their families awaiting their reunification process in different areas of Addis Ababa in March 2022. Additionally, interviews were conducted with Belgian and Italian visa officials as well as the representatives from the Ethiopian Refugee Agency, IOM family reunification section and UNHCR family assistance programme. This multi-geographic focus enables us to analyse the challenges of family reunification arising not only from the progressively restrictive legislation on family migration in Europe, but also from the transnational, fragmented bureaucratic practices of different states and agencies involved.

2. The challenges of family reunification: a short review and ways ahead

Documentary requirements are at the heart of family reunification processes. Until now, however, the study of family reunification has paid limited attention to this aspect. Instead, most research on this topic has attributed challenges faced by migrant and refugee families' challenges in reuniting to the increasingly restrictive migration regulations in receiving countries. Several studies have focused, for instance, on how democratic Western states have developed migration policies to screen ethnically diverse couples, unorthodox families and immigrant families. Within the theoretical framework of civic stratification, scholars have explored how democratic states have created a hierarchy of rights based on the residence status of their subjects (Block, 2015; Schweitzer, 2015). Family reunification in Europe has thus been regulated by differentiating national and European citizens from migrants and further stratifying migrants based on their status (e.g. labour migrants, highly skilled migrants, refugees, humanitarian migrants), assigning each

3 The research was funded by the Flemish Research Foundation (2020–2023). Grant no. 12Z3719N.

group a specific set of rights and duties (Bonizzoni & Belloni, 2023). Regulations have narrowed down the definition of 'family' and have specified the criteria for a valid marital relationship, with significant discretion often left to local officials for interpretation (D'Aoust, 2018; Scheel & Gutekunst, 2019). The role of street-level bureaucrats in assessing family reunification applications has increasingly become an important focal point of research (Infantino, 2019). Given the generalised culture of suspicion (Jubany, 2017; Alpes & Spire, 2014; Borrelli et al., 2022) that surrounds asylum and migration issues, the space of discretion is often used to the detriment of refugee families, to filter out 'proper families' rather than to ensure the enjoyment of the right to family life (De Hertog & Belloni, 2023). These street-level bureaucrats' moral views about personhood, migration, marriage, intimacy, love and their perceptions of authenticity and legality have been shown to play a key role in the assessment of family applications (e.g., Wray, 2006; Vandenbroucke, 2020).

While this body of literature has shed light on how migration and family law are enacted in practice, it primarily takes a country-centric perspective, focusing on events and interactions from the point of view of the country to which the application is directed. Issues related to 'administrative citizenship', considered as a localised practice with significant transnational implications, have largely been overlooked, with only a few exceptions (Mitchell & Coutin, 2019).

3. Administrative citizenship in a transnational context

Administrative citizenship encompasses both individuals' practical capacity to be recognised administratively by their own state of nationality, access documentation to certify their legal identity and civil status, and the state's ability to establish and maintain the necessary administrative infrastructure for registering and uniquely identifying citizens. While citizens in most liberal-democratic states in the Global North can take administrative citizenship and the concomitant ability to travel across borders for granted, refugees applying for family reunification face substantial challenges in demonstrating their legal identity, including family ties.

The significance of documentary requirements for establishing identity and legal identity underscores the importance of the system of identification used by state agencies (and increasingly also commercial actors) (Caplan & Torpey, 2002; Robertson, 2010; Torpey, 2000). Modern states rely on complex administrative systems for tasks like tax collection, family ties determination, economic transaction regulation and border control. This system includes unique identification documents (e.g., passports and identity cards; birth, death and marriage certificates), as well as administrative practices for maintaining a comprehensive citizen database (Szreter & Breckenridge, 2012; Torpey, 2000).

However, many of the regions of the world lack robust registration infrastructures, leaving a substantial proportion of the global population unrecorded (Szreter & Breckenridge, 2012). Even though universal systems of civil registration have been fostered by international organisations and donor aid (the right to have a legal identity – to be registered at birth and so forth – is one of the Sustainable Development Goals 2030 of the United Nations [Corneloup & Verhellen, 2021]), many states have not developed such a bureaucratic system, with some relying on 'social and oral authorities as arbiters of identification' (Szreter & Breckenridge, 2012, p. 3). While identity cards are a relatively new technique of population management in the history of Western states (Robertson, 2010; Torpey, 2000), recently, biometric systems of identification are becoming the standard of identification which people must meet to be recognised by their own state as well as by other states when they travel (Gelb & Metz, 2018; Sullivan, 2016; Witteborn, 2022).

It is important to mention that even in well-developed state administrations, some individuals may remain unregistered, particularly marginalised groups, such as remote rural, homeless or nomadic populations (e.g., the Roma in Europe) (e.g., Bhabha, 2017). Registration systems may also reflect discriminatory practices. Studies from the Global South highlight that registration is often granted only to those subjects who are ethnically, religiously or politically affiliated with the elites in power (Hayes de Kalaf, 2021; Blitz & Lynch, 2011). Street-level bureaucrats' work may thus be functional to a specific state project which excludes certain minorities (Marko, 2016) or those subjects who are not lenient with state demands. This is specifically the case of refugees that often face challenges due to oppositional citizenship performance back home (e.g., exile due to political, ethnic and social persecution).

Internally, the administrative existence of a person is crucial, for instance, to gain access to public services, education systems or unemployment benefits. But people also need unique identification documents to be able to travel, work or live beyond the state borders. *Externally*, access to documentation proving legal identity is essential for both legal travel and residence. The study by Mitchell and Coutin (2019) on Salvadorian migrants in the US and their transnational documentary practices precisely points to the nexus between individual abilities to procure documentary evidence from their home country's local offices and their access to legal migration status in other locations. However, the global integration of identification systems has had unequal effects on mobility (Shamir, 2005; Mau, 2010). As stated by Torpey (2000: p.xiii): "Possession of the 'right' passport may help speed movement for properly preapproved passengers, whereas those who have not undergone the pre-screening of their identification documents must wend their way through long, slow lines awaiting processing at airports and other restricted zones".

Similar considerations apply to the 'right' birth certificate, marriage certificate, school degree and so forth. The study by Mitchell and Coutin (2019) on Salvadorian migrants in the US and their transnational documentary practices precisely shows the nexus between individual abilities to procure documentary evidence from their home country's local offices and their access to legal migration status in other locations. For migrants, obtaining documentation from their country of origin can be a formidable challenge. This is often the case for refugees and undocumented migrants, who may face difficulties in returning to their home country. They may have limited social networks in the area that could offer assistance (Mazzucato, 2011). In some instances, vital registries may no longer exist due to war or political instability, or they may never have existed in the first place. Even when migrants are successful in proving their legal identity and personal status, the evidence they provide might not be recognised by foreign authorities due to differing conceptions of authenticity and officialdom (Hull, 2012; Mitchell & Coutin, 2019). For instance, while registration systems in Europe emphasise official records, many non-European systems rely on oral authorities (Szreter & Breckenridge, 2012). Somali documents, for instance, are usually based on affidavits. This means that a public official certifies a marriage, an adoption or a death by using identified witnesses. Most Somali documents issued by Somali authorities in the diaspora and in the homeland, such as passports, marriage certificates and so forth, are systematically not recognised by Western authorities. This documentation is believed to be unreliable, given the widespread practice of forgery and the limited legitimacy of Somali public officials in the international arena. Belgian diplomatic officials, for instance, cannot issue visas on the basis of a Somali passport.

Drawing on the aforementioned studies, we posit that comprehending the process of family reunification for refugees requires us to consider the capabilities of both migrants and their countries of origin to produce two types of evidence: proof of citizenship of a specific state (in the sense of "being nationals" of a specific state) and proof of other aspects of one's legal identity (age, name, marriage, parenthood, etc.). While legal scholarship often treats these evidentiary requirements as separate (see Den Haese & Verhellen, this volume), they are intrinsically intertwined when examining the challenges faced by refugees and their families during the family reunification process.

4. Refugees' unique position

Administrative citizenship is key to the family reunification processes of all migrants. We argue, however, that in the case of refugees, the transnational implications of limited access to local administrative citizenship are even more pronounced. Although Ahmed's family had to comply with strict deadlines (12 months ex-gratia period) and specific requirements (such as the submission of identity papers, birth certificates and so on) imposed by Belgian administrative practices,[4] it is the combination of transnational factors that compounded their challenges. For example, Amira faced difficulties in obtaining birth and marriage certificates in Eritrea, and securing reliable IDs from the Ethiopian administration proved to be a daunting task for her and her children. These challenges stem from the fragmentation of bureaucratic and administrative state systems and often result in a kind of 'administrative limbo'.

Refugees' success in their asylum requests largely hinges on their ability to prove their nationality of a specific state (Lawrance & Stevens, 2017). Although

4 It is important to mention that there is a gap between formal regulations and practices on the ground. Both the European Family Reunification Directive and Article 12bis § 5 of the Belgian Aliens Act establish that authorities are obliged to take into account other proof when there are no official documents of pre-existing family relationships of refugees or subsidiary protection holders. However, documents are still key to understand what applications are successful (De Hertog & Belloni, 2023).

refugee conventions explicitly permit stateless persons to be recognised as refugees, those who fall in between categories are often denied protection. In the Horn of Africa, this is particularly true for the many Eritreans who lived in Ethiopia and were then expelled but never had the nationality of either of the two countries. They were systematically rejected when seeking asylum in Europe (Campbell, 2013) due to their de-facto statelessness.

While refugees and beneficiaries of subsidiary protection usually enjoy- or should enjoy- relaxed requirements in Europe (as per the Family Reunification Directive of 2003), their families, who also find themselves in challenging situations vis-à-vis their home countries, are subjected to the same conditions as other family migrants. National regulations may contain provisions allowing for more lenient ways of proving a family relationship (e.g., Article 12bis § 5 Belgian Aliens Act[5]). However, in practice, refugees and their families are still frequently required to submit birth certificates, ID cards, passports and other evidence that is often inaccessible, especially if families are in exile (e.g., Groenendijk et al., 2017; Mekonnen & Arapiles, 2021). Families fleeing from war and political upheaval may encounter even more difficulties when the registries where their identity was recorded have been destroyed or are no longer functioning.

The limited capabilities of refugees and their family members to prove their identity are largely due to their ambivalent position as outsiders in both their homeland, the first country of asylum and potential other countries of settlement. While the asylum regime assumes that refugees have no contact with the institutions of their country of origin, the implicit requirements of asylum applications, and even more of visa requests for family members, push them to contact their national embassies to provide the necessary documentation (Belloni & Cole, 2022). In other words, to exercise their right to reunification with family members, refugees are often expected to simultaneously be politically *discriminated outsiders* and *complying citizens* of their home country. These conflicting expectations create a wide range of practical obstacles for refugees themselves and their family members, who often cannot rely on the services of their own diplomatic offices, as well as for the public officials assessing their cases.

The challenges refugees face in proving their administrative identity are not solely dependent on the situation in their country of origin. Their first, second, third, etc. countries of asylum may also be hesitant to register them as refugees and issue certifications regarding their identity and life events. In these cases, other state actors (and no longer the country of origin) become responsible for certifying the refugee's identity. Since the new registration only rarely replaces the previous identification system completely, this often leads to issues of consistency and gaps between their identity documents (see Griffith, 2012; De Hertog & Belloni, 2023). Refugees we have spoken with mentioned spelling differences, inconsistencies of

5 This article states that in order to assess a pre-existing family relationship of refugee or subsidiary protection holder, the authorities are obliged to take into account other proof if official documentation is not accessible (compare to § 6 if not in relation to refugees: then the authorities can – but are not obliged to – consider other proof). The Office of the Commissioner General for Refugees and Stateless Persons in Belgium, moreover, may provide necessary documentation.

dates and civil status mistakes in their personal files. These problems of consistency arise both from the different administrative cultures of the state actors and agencies that register their identity and from the *fluidity* of personal circumstances compared to the *fixity* of papers (Mitchell & Coutin, 2019).

How refugees can prove their administrative identity is intrinsically linked to the separate system of identification and registration for refugees established in the post-war era, the so-called individual refugee status determination (RSD) procedure. As Hovy (2018) writes:

> In addition to recording individual biographical characteristics, such as name, sex, date of birth, level of education, occupation or skills, relationship to the head of household and place of previous residence, the RSD process provides for recording the results of individual interview and background notes as well as elements to confirm the identity of the applicant (photo, fingerprints, iris scan, etc.) and scanned documents. The registration system normally includes a facility to print identity documents indicating the status of the applicant (refugee status applicant, recognized refugee, type of protection accorded, expiration date, etc.).
>
> (Hovy, 2018, p. 45)

The challenges associated with RSD are essential for understanding the complexities of family reunification in the context of forced migration. Family members of recognised refugees in Europe often submit their applications for family reunification while in exile and facing similar problems of registration and recognition as other refugees in countries of first asylum, which are often located in the Global South.

> Registration procedures exist for refugees when they cross an international border, when they arrive at the place of residence, when they access services, when they apply for individual refugee status, when they seek assistance to repatriate, when they apply for resettlement in a third country, or when they aspire to obtain citizenship in the host country.
>
> (Hovy, 2018, p. 44)

The next section illustrates some of the concrete difficulties faced by refugees we have met in Addis Ababa regarding family reunification due to a) their inability to retrieve identity and personal status certification from their home country, b) difficulties in the RSD procedures in first countries of asylum and c) the challenges in transporting their 'personal dossier' across borders.

5. Country of origin: unregistered citizens

'Many people have never had marriage and birth certificates especially in rural areas', stated Tewodros, an Eritrean outreach official for Jesuit Refugee Service (JRS) in Addis Ababa. 'Even those who have an ID may lose it while crossing the border or the Ethiopian officials may take it from you at the registration centre', explained Mulaw, an Eritrean refugee assisting others with the family reunification process. 'Obtaining passports takes time, and one must also pay a 2 percent government tax [a citizen tax – 2 percent of annual income]'.

These accounts from Eritrean refugees, who have extensive experience helping others in their community navigate the administrative complexities of visa procedures (focus group, Addis Ababa, March 2022), highlight some of the primary challenges faced by Eritrean exiles. In Eritrea, as well as in Somalia and in many other states enduring long-term turmoil, it is often the case that not all citizens are registered in public systems. Traditional community-based systems of interpersonal identification systems persist, rendering state registration unnecessary until individuals require services from the state. Marriages are solemnised by religious leaders, and baptisms are recorded in local churches. Additionally, many people end up without any identification documents, as they spend most of their lives evading the state apparatus. The price of obtaining an ID and a passport, which is especially vital for potential migrants, involves compliance with state demands, including compulsory military training and indefinite national service.

As a result, most Eritreans fleeing their country have little or no documentation. Should they wish to obtain documents once they leave their home country, such as a passport, as mentioned by Mulaw, they are required to pay a citizen tax, amounting to 2 percent of their annual income. This tax varies according to the embassy and the local context. For instance, in Ethiopia the newly established Eritrean embassy demanded a fixed sum of 150 US dollars. Through this tax, and the signing of an apology letter in which the citizen acknowledges their 'crime' of leaving their home country without authorisation, the Eritrean state effectively transforms defectors and escapees into obedient and contributing citizens (Riggan, 2016; Belloni, 2019). From an administrative perspective, refugees are reintegrated into the state system as *diaspora citizens*, but politically, this practice neutralises the subversive potential of refugees and portrays them to the outside world as penitent subjects (Belloni & Cole, 2022).

However, for Eritrean refugees, this practice gives rise to several problems. From the perspective of the asylum country, having relations with the embassy of one's country of origin is seen as contradictory to one's status as a refugee. Nevertheless, refugees who seek to reunite with their families abroad have little choice but to comply with this paradoxical practice, as their documents must be legalised by their own embassy for the family reunification process. Although during fieldwork (2022) it became clear that several visa offices were increasingly aware of these difficulties and tended to accept complementary documentation, our evidence also indicates that issues of administrative acceptance persist. It was common among the families MB interviewed in Addis Ababa that the absence of legalised documents (Verhellen, 2018) significantly prolonged and complicated the process of reunification with their loved ones in Europe.

According to the UNHCR official responsible for the family reunification assistance programme in Addis Ababa, the lack of official certification is the foremost obstacle for refugees seeking family reunification:

> Refugees may have religious certificates documenting baptisms or marriages, but embassies cannot recognise this documentation. Some countries

> require original IDs/passports and other civil status certificates authenticated by the country of origin. Some countries are accepting the proof of registration [as refugees in Ethiopia] as an ID document for family procedures, but now that has stopped too.[6]

This statement was further confirmed by IOM officials. Importantly, in Ethiopia, IOM is responsible for collecting family reunification applications for Germany[7]. One of the IOM officials (Addis Ababa, March 2022) stated:

> 95 percent of Eritreans do not have these documents so we usually introduce the application with other complementary certifications such as religious baptism and marriage certificates, but these documents are considered to be easily falsifiable and thus the applicant must sign a declaration that he/she is aware that the lack of documentation may affect the result of the process.

In practice, we encountered numerous cases of couples stuck in the German reunification process due to the absence of an Eritrean passport. This once again underscores the significance of administrative citizenship between individuals and their country of origin for the successful completion of family reunification.

6. The first asylum country: an administrative limbo

The systematic difficulties Eritrean refugees face in obtaining documentation from their country of origin and applying for family reunification (Belloni & Cole, 2022) were compounded by a temporary halt in the Ethiopian administrative apparatus due to the COVID-19 pandemic and political instability. For instance, Amira's family reunification application was significantly delayed because she could not renew her refugee ID in Ethiopia, as all the relevant offices were closed for months.

In November 2020, conflict erupted between rebel forces in Tigray, the northern region of Ethiopia, and the central Ethiopian government. Eritrean refugees, living in camps in the area, as well as those who have fled Eritrea since then, were severely affected. The lives of refugees in Addis Ababa also underwent dramatic changes since the winter of 2020.[8]

The Tigray civil war not only exacerbated the most visible forms of violence suffered by refugees in camps, but also compounded some of the problems refugees typically face when in exile. Since the war's onset, newcomers have not been registered and all processes related to identification and documentation issuance have come to a halt. In the past two years, thousands of Eritreans have lived in administrative invisibility: many of them lacked refugee cards, preventing them

6 Here the official refers to the block of issuance of all identity papers in the country – see more in the next section.

7 Family reunification is a long and time-consuming process for embassies, and many countries have decided to outsource these processes to third parties, at times to private companies and at times to international organisations.

8 For more information about the war in Tigray, see https://martinplaut.com/tag/tigray-war/.

from accessing humanitarian assistance and sending their children to school. Newborn children could not be registered, and exit visas were not issued, which also impeded family reunification processes. This posed a problem because many European visas (valid for six months) expired and had to be reissued. The Ethiopian government resumed issuing exit visas in April 2022.

An official from the IOM family reunification assistance programme explained:

> As only refugees can apply through FAP (Family Assistance Programme[9]), they need the proof of registration [issued by the Ex Ethiopian Agency for Refugees and Returnees Assistance (ARRA) – now Refugees and Returnees Services (RSS)] and the United Nations High Commissioner for Refugees (UNHCR)] and the refugee ID.

A high diplomatic official of a European embassy also stressed the importance of Ethiopian documentation and how its possession is crucial to initiate a family reunification application:

> For Eritreans it used to be necessary to present UNHCR-ARRA proof of registration in refugee camps and the Ethiopian Travel Document (ETD) to introduce their application. The ETD was the most reliable identity paper we could ask. However, it is valid for only 6 months so it usually expires by the time the acceptance [of the family reunification application] arrives. Moreover, the visa cannot be placed on the ETD because it is not among the recognized documents of our state legislation. The embassy would then print a laissez-passer to put the visa sticker on it. With this and the expired ETD refugees could go to ARRA and INVEA (now ICS – Immigration and Citizenship Services) and get an exit visa from Ethiopia. In the current geopolitical scenario people cannot apply for family reunification because they have no proof of registration, and those that have that proof of registration cannot apply for the Ethiopian Travel Document.

The aforementioned circumstances currently characterise the Ethiopian context, but similar issues can be found in other asylum states located in the Global South. Problems with registering refugees are well-documented in the literature and often lead to administrative limbo (e.g., Abdi, 2005; Pittaway, 2015; Hovy, 2018). There are multiple reasons behind this. First, asylum states sometimes express security concerns that hostile nationals may change their identity, given the ethnic and language proximity between refugees and locals. Because of the common ethnicity of Eritreans and Tigrayans – that represent the ethnic group deemed responsible for the unrest in the North –, the Ethiopian government was careful in providing new identity papers, which could allow rebels to leave the country. While ethnic proximity is often analysed in research as an important condition for promoting

9 https://germany.iom.int/family-assistance-programme-fap

local refugee integration, it is also highlighted that ethnic proximity can put certain national groups on the authorities' radar in the host country due to identification issues (e.g., Polzer, 2009; Brosché & Nilsson, 2005). During the fieldwork, this argument was frequently mentioned by people working in NGOs and international organisations to explain why new refugees could not be easily registered.

Another reason states may be reluctant to register refugees is that recording and producing refugees' documentation require a significant amount of administrative and human resources, which may already be in short supply. For instance, an RRS official in Addis Ababa spoke about "the lack of human resources" needed for the identification of newcomers during the time of upheaval between 2020 and 2022.

Even when documents are issued by the host state, often with the support of the UNHCR, there may be challenges in translating and transmitting the administrative dossier across borders.

7. The country of asylum in Europe: moving dossiers, information and statuses

While migration studies traditionally focus on the movement of people, it is as relevant to consider how bureaucratic dossiers are able to cross borders. The concept of 'crossing borders', in this context takes on different meanings. As previously discussed, administrative documentation sometimes requires physical transfer from one location to another. This necessitates individuals, or people who can act as their legal proxies, to appear in person at registration offices to obtain their official files. In some instances, family members may need to travel directly from the home country, like Eritrea, to retrieve critical identity documents that are inaccessible in exile. For instance, Amira and Ahmed's case also had to do with moving information and documentation. The lawyer would explain to Ahmed the documents that Amira had to bring to the embassy and Ahmed would explain this to Amira. Moreover, it was often Ahmed who mobilised family members in Eritrea to find the right certificate and send it to Amira so that she could present it as evidence to the embassy.

Yet, even when the documents can physically travel, they may be drafted in a way that does not align with the administrative conventions of the destination country. Even when migrants manage to produce original documents, these may be considered not reliable by other national offices due to different bureaucratic cultures and conceptions of authenticity, formality and officialdom (Hull, 2012). Legalisation practices (certifying that stamps, signatures and seals are authentic) precisely aim to fill these gaps. However, these legalisation practices are limited in contexts of conflict and fragile state apparatuses. We have already mentioned the widespread suspicion over Somali documentation based on a system of personal testimonies. Similar concerns of fraud are often raised by officials when they deal with certificates issued by religious local authorities that can hardly be checked. Moreover, not all local identity documents contain very precise or consistent information, as highlighted by the case of Amira's son's name being misspelled, which was considered to be crucial by diplomatic authorities. Variable spelling practices and mistakes, errors in transcribing vital dates are common in refugees' files.Somalis' names, for instance, are written according to different orthographic systems (e.g., Somali, English, French) and they do not use 'surnames' or family names. Instead, each individual carries the name of the father and the grandfather. When Somalis move abroad, their names may be recorded with different spellings and, in some cases, be transformed into surnames, resulting in an even more inconsistent personal profile (Mansuur, 2020).

Additionally, refugees' civil status may not always align with the legal requirements of the country of asylum. Jinske Verhellen (2018) speaks about 'the (lack of) portability of refugees' personal status'. For instance, the practice of marrying below 18 contradicts legal regimes in Europe, making such marriages unrecognisable (see, however, Bruijnen, this volume) and leading to the denial of family reunification. Several Eritrean couples that MB met between Belgium and Ethiopia encountered these difficulties. Furthermore, issues related to the recognition of polygamous marriages and informal adoption practices can also pose challenges.

Finally, the portability of refugees' and migrants' personal status is intrinsically connected to distinct administrative practices and requirements across different institutions of the same state. For instance, while a DNA test is commonly used by visa officials and the Immigration Office to assess biological relationships, it is not accepted by Belgian city councils, which typically require birth certificates. These varying administrative rules, while sometimes applied with flexibility, can constrain the ability of refugees and migrants to access important services in their new country of residence.

8. Conclusion: towards an agenda for studying family reunification in a transnational context

While most current literature on family reunification focuses on laws and regulations of the country where families aim to reunify, this chapter has emphasised the importance of analysing families' experience within the complex multi-state and transnational context in which they operate. We argue that separated families must navigate a complex institutional landscape involving at least three nation-states (the country of origin, the first country of asylum and the third country where the family intends to reside), along with interactions with a wide array of local bureaucrats and diplomatic officials. We suggested that the concept of administrative citizenship provides a useful lens for understanding the multifaceted relationships of refugees and their families with these key actors throughout the family reunification process. At every step of the way, in every interaction, refugees and their families are required to prove their membership as citizens, productive migrants or registered guests through *paperwork*. While specific circumstances vary from case to case, country to country and nationality to nationality, our chapter offers an overview of the most significant administrative gaps and transmission issues that exacerbate refugees' limited capability to perform their administrative citizenship and be reunified with their families.

We believe that this research approach holds great potential for practitioners and policy makers. The coexistence of multiple systems and practices of registration and identification which we discussed in this chapter frequently results in discrepant and inconsistent bureaucratic personal dossiers. Visa and immigration officials, who are often concerned about potential fraudulent applications, may filter out inconsistent dossiers and information and equate them with fake documentation (Jubany, 2017; De Hertog & Belloni, 2023). It is therefore important to raise awareness of the intricate institutional landscape that shapes the dossiers of refugees and their families and to point out that inconsistent information may arise from different registration systems and the complexity of refugees' trajectories rather than from attempts to fraud the system.

References

Abdi, A. M. (2005). In Limbo: Dependency, insecurity, and identity amongst Somali refugees in Dadaab camps. *Refuge: Canada's Journal on Refugees, 22*(2), 6–14. https://doi.org/10.25071/1920-7336.21328

Alpes, M. J., & Spire, A. (2014). Dealing with law in migration control: The powers of street-level bureaucrats at French consulates. *Social & Legal Studies, 23*(2), 261–274. https://doi.org/10.1177/0964663913510927

Anschütz, S., & Mazzucato, V. (2022). Reconceptualizing family reunification from a youth mobilities perspective: Transnational youth between Ghana and Belgium. *Children's Geographies, 20*(2), 160–173. https://doi.org/10.1080/14733285.2021.1919998

Belloni, M. (2019). Refugees and citizens: Understanding Eritrean refugees' ambivalence towards homeland politics. *International Journal of Comparative Sociology, 60*(1–2), 55–73.

Belloni, M., & Cole, G. (2022). The right to exit as national and transnational governance: The case of Eritrea. *International Migration.* https://doi.org/10.1111/imig.13078

Bhabha, J. (2017). Realizing Roma Rights: An Introduction. In J. Bhabha, A. Mirga, & M. Matache (Eds.), *Realizing Roma Rights* (pp. 1–14). University of Pennsylvania Press. https://doi.org/10.9783/9780812293876-001

Blitz, B. K., & Lynch, M. (Eds.). (2011). *Statelessness and Citizenship: A Comparative Study on the Benefits of Nationality.* Edward Elgar Publishing. https://doi.org/10.4337/9781849808996

Block, L. (2015). Regulating membership: Explaining restriction and stratification of family migration in Europe. *Journal of Family Issues, 36*(11), 1433–1452. https://doi.org/10.1177/0192513X14557493

Bonizzoni, P., & Belloni, M. (2023). Uneven Borders: Family Reunification Regulations and their Implications in Europe. In J. Cienfuegos, R. Brandhorst, & D. Fahy Bryceson (Eds.), *Handbook of Transnational Families Around the World.* Springer. https://doi.org/10.1007/978-3-031-15278-8_15

Borrelli, M. L., Lindberg, A., & Wyss, A. (2022). States of suspicion: How institutionalised disbelief shapes migration control regimes. *Geopolitics, 27*(4), 1025–1041. https://doi.org/10.1080/14650045.2021.2005862

Brosché, J., & Nilsson, M. (2005). *Zambian refugee policy: Security, repatriation and local integration.* https://urn.kb.se/resolve?urn=urn:nbn:se:uu:diva-331624

Campbell, J. R. (2013). *Nationalism, Law and Statelessness: Grand Illusions in the Horn of Africa.* Routledge. https://doi.org/10.4324/9780203584057

Caplan, J., & Torpey, J. (Eds.). (2002). *Documenting Individual Identity: The Development of State Practices in the Modern World.* Princeton University Press.

Corneloup, S., & Verhellen, J. (2021). SDG 16: Peace, Justice and Strong Institutions. In R. Michaels, V. Ruiz Abou-Nigm, & H. van Loon (Eds.), *The Private Side of Transforming Our World – UN Sustainable Development Goals 2030 and the Role of Private International Law* (pp. 505–540). Intersentia.

D'Aoust, A. M. (2018). Family Migration and Membership. In A. Weinar, S. Bonjour, & L. Zhyznomirska (Eds.), *The Routledge Handbook of the Politics of Migration in Europe* (pp. 179–189). Routledge. https://doi.org/10.4324/9781315512853

Davies, M. (2017). *Law Unlimited.* Routledge.

De Hertog, S., & Belloni, M. (2023). Fraudulent families? Investigating the role of paperwork in the assessment of refugees' family reunification in Belgium. *Journal of Immigrant & Refugee Studies*. https://doi.org/10.1080/15562948.2023.2271864

Gelb, A., & Metz, A. D. (2018). *Identification Revolution: Can Digital ID Be Harnessed for Development?* Brookings Institution Press.

Geoffrion, K., & Cretton, V. (2021). Bureaucratic routes to migration: Migrants' lived experience of paperwork, clerks and other immigration intermediaries. *Anthropologica*, *63*(1), 1–28. https://doi.org/10.18357/anthropologica6312021184Copied

Griffiths, M. (2012). "Vile liars and truth distorters"; truth, trust and the asylum system. *Anthropology Today*, *28*(5), 8–12. https://doi.org/10.1111/j.1467-8322.2012.00896.x

Groenendijk, C. A., Costello, C., & Halleskov Storgaard, L. (2017). *Realising the right to family reunification of refugees in Europe*. https://ec.europa.eu/migrant-integration/library-document/realising-right-family-reunification-refugees-europe_en

Hayes de Kalaf, E. (2021). *Legal Identity, Race and Belonging in the Dominican Republic: From Citizen to Foreigner*. Anthem Press. https://doi.org/10.1163/22134360-09703043

Horton, S. B., & Heyman, J. (Eds.). (2020). *Paper Trails: Migrants, Documents, and Legal Insecurity*. Duke University Press.

Hovy, B. (2018). Registration – a Sine qua non for Refugee Protection. In H. Graeme, M.-J. Abbasi-Shavazi, & E. P. Kraly (Eds.), *Demography of Refugee and Forced Migration* (pp. 39–55). Springer. https://doi.org/10.1007/978-3-319-67147-5_3

Hull, M. S. (2012). Documents and bureaucracy. *Annual Review of Anthropology*, *41*, 251–267. https://doi.org/10.1146/annurev.anthro.012809.104953

Infantino, F. (2019). *Schengen Visa Implementation and Transnational Policymaking: Bordering Europe*. Springer. https://doi.org/10.1007/978-3-030-10647-8

Jubany, O. (2017). *Screening Asylum in a Culture of Disbelief: Truths, Denials and Skeptical Borders*. Palgrave Macmillan. https://doi.org/10.1007/978-3-319-40748-7

Latour, B. (2010). *The Making of Law: An Ethnography of the Conseil d'État*. Polity.

Lawrance, B. N., & Stevens, J. (2017). *Citizenship in Question: Evidentiary Birth Right and Statelessness*. Duke University Press.

Lazar, S. (2013). *The Anthropology of Citizenship: A Reader*. John Wiley & Sons.

Mansuur, C. C. (2020). Somali names and individual identity. *Journal of Somali Studies: Research on Somalia and the Greater Horn of African Countries*, *7*(1), 123–132.

Markó, F. D. (2016). "We are not a failed state, we make the best passports": South Sudan and biometric modernity. *African Studies Review*, *59*(2), 113–132.

Mau, S. (2010). Mobility citizenship, inequality and the liberal state: The case of visa policies, *International Political Sociology*, *4*(4), 339–361. https://doi.org/10.1111/j.1749-5687.2010.00110.x

Mazzucato, V. (2011). Reverse remittances in the migration – development nexus: Two-way flows between Ghana and the Netherlands. *Population, Space and Place*, *17*(5), 454–468. https://doi.org/10.1002/psp.646

Mekonnen, D., & Arapiles, S. P. (2021). *Access to documents by Eritrean refugees in the context of family reunification*. https://sas-space.sas.ac.uk/9673/1/RLC%20BP%20No.%201.pdf

Mitchell, J., & Coutin, S. B. (2019). Living documents in transnational spaces of migration between El Salvador and the United States. *Law & Social Inquiry*, *44*(4), 865–892. https://doi.org/10.1017/lsi.2018.27

Pittaway, E. (2015). Life in Limbo: Unregistered Urban Refugees on the Thai – Burma Border. In K. Koizumi & G. Hoffstaedter (Eds.), *Urban Refugees: Challenges in Protection, Services and Policy* (pp. 164–186). Routledge.
Polzer, T. (2009). Negotiating rights: The politics of local integration. *Refuge*, *26*, 92.
Riggan, J. (2016). *The Struggling State*. Temple University Press.
Robertson, C. (2010). *The Passport in America: The History of a Document*. Oxford University Press. https://doi.org/10.1093/acprof:osobl/9780199927579.001.0001
Scheel, S., & Gutekunst, M. (2019). Studying marriage migration to Europe from below: Informal practices of government, border struggles and multiple entanglements. *Gender, Place & Culture*, *26*(6), 847–867. https://doi.org/10.1080/0966369X.2018.1489375
Schweitzer, R. (2015). A stratified right to family life? On the logic (s) and legitimacy of granting differential access to family reunification for third-country nationals living within the EU. *Journal of Ethnic and Migration Studies*, *41*(13), 2130–2148. https://doi.org/10.1080/1369183X.2015.1037256
Shamir, R. (2005). Without borders? Notes on globalization as a mobility regime. *Sociological Theory*, *23*(2), 197–217. https://doi.org/10.1111/j.0735-2751.2005.00250.x
Stevens, J. (2017). Introduction. In B. N. Lawrance & J. Stevens (Eds.), *Citizenship in Question: Evidentiary Birthright and Statelessness*. Duke University Press.
Sullivan, C. (2016). Digital citizenship and the right to digital identity under international law. *Computer Law & Security Review*, *32*(3), 474–481. https://doi.org/10.1016/j.clsr.2016.02.001
Szreter, S., & Breckenridge, K. (2012). *Registration and Recognition: Documenting the Person in World History*. Oxford University Press. https://doi.org/10.5871/bacad/9780197265314.001.0001
Torpey, J. C. (2000). *The Invention of the Passport· Surveillance, Citizenship and the State*. Cambridge University Press. https://doi.org/10.1017/CBO9780511520990
Vandenbroucke, M. (2020). Legal-discursive constructions of genuine cross-border love in Belgian marriage fraud investigations. *Critical Discourse Studies*, *17*(2), 175–192. https://doi.org/10.1080/17405904.2020.1715233
Verhellen, J. (2018). Cross-border portability of refugees' personal status. *Journal of Refugee Studies*, *31*(4), 427–443. https://doi.org/10.1093/jrs/fex026
Witteborn, S. (2022). Digitalization, digitization and datafication: The "three D" transformation of forced migration management. *Communication, Culture and Critique*, *15*(2), 157–175. https://doi.org/10.1093/ccc/tcac007
Wray, H. (2006). An ideal husband? Marriages of convenience, moral gate-keeping and immigration to the UK. *European Journal of Migration and Law*, *8*(3–4), 303–320. https://doi.org/10.1163/157181606778882582

Part V

Navigating regimes

16 Enforced transnationalism

Refugees' family lives in Germany under conditions of separation and waiting

Simone Christ and Benjamin Etzold

1. Introduction

This chapter focuses on the transformations of displaced people's family lives in the context of enforced transnationalism and long-term separation. Under conditions of violent conflict, refugees often cannot flee together in their particular family constellations, be it as nuclear family or with members of the extended family. It is often only one family member, who embarks on a long-distance journey due to different reasons such as lack of financial or social capital and the high risk of such journeys. Other family members then stay behind, be it in the place of origin, as internally displaced in the same country, or in countries of first reception. Many families, yet certainly not all displaced individuals (Belloni, 2019), hope to reunite at a later point of time in the preferred country of destination, such as Germany. The intended temporary separation from family members does, however, often continue for an indefinite period, as borders, lack of financial means, visa regimes, and the overly bureaucratic regulations of family reunification hinder the reunion of family members (Damir-Geilsdorf & Sabra, 2018; Löbel & Jacobsen, 2021; Sauer et al., 2018; Tobin et al., 2022).

In this chapter, we look into different transnational family constellations, which evolved and constantly change under conditions of long-term displacement, and in particular when one or more family members have moved to another country of protection, in our case to Germany. In all family constellations presented in our chapter, separation from loved ones for an indefinite time and yet maintained family relations across two or more countries is a drastic experience. We wanted to know how family separation, prolonged waiting for a possible reunion, and the enforced transnational organisation of family life, which we understand as 'enforced transnationalism' (Al-Ali et al., 2001), is experienced by refugees. To answer this question, we bring together insights on experiences of forced migration and protracted displacement (Etzold & Fechter, 2022; Hyndman & Giles, 2016) with research on transnationally separated families (Bryceson & Vuorela, 2002; Merla et al., 2021; Silver et al., 2018) by using a figurational approach (Baur & Ernst, 2011; Bogner & Rosenthal, 2017; Castrén & Ketokivi, 2015; Elias, 1978). Our analysis is based on 73 qualitative interviews with refugees from Syria, Eritrea, and Afghanistan and experts on displacement and family reunification, which we conducted in Germany

DOI: 10.4324/9781003503217-21

in 2020 and 2021 in the frame of an EU-funded project on the 'Transnational Figurations of Displacement' (Christ, Etzold, et al., 2021).[1]

We take four steps in our analysis. At first, we introduce the conceptual perspectives of social figurations of displacement, which we see as a particularly useful research perspective for the study of displacement dynamics, and expand it with recent literature on transnational family life under the condition of enforced separation. After having presented our methodological approach, we outline the governance regimes of family reunification to Germany under conditions of displacement and its implications for separated families. At the core of this chapter, we present three distinct transnational family figurations, which evolved after some family members moved to Germany while others could not. Each family figuration is introduced by two different case studies. We close with reflections on the policy implications of our findings and the critical potential of figurational thinking.

2. Conceptual approach: transnational family figurations of displacement

This chapter brings together recent discussion on refugees' experience of displacement and lives in exile (Etzold & Fechter, 2022; Hyndman & Giles, 2016) with studies on transnational families and family separation (Bryceson & Vuorela, 2002; Merla et al., 2021). Our focus lies on the transnational family constellations that might evolve under conditions of displacement, more specifically even under conditions of long-term and enforced separation from family members. Figurational theory (Elias, 1978) helps us to bring together these perspectives.

2.1 Social figurations of displacement

Despite ongoing separations from loved ones, refugees must not be considered as isolated individuals. Their everyday lives – and more precisely their emotions, actions, and decisions – are fundamentally shaped by different 'social figurations', in which they are embedded and which often transgress international borders. The figurational approach that was developed by the German sociologist Norbert Elias (1978) tries to overcome artificial divisions between the micro, meso, and macro level in sociological studies: it can thus be usefully applied when studying individuals', for instance refugees', perceptions and practices; their social relations, e.g., within transnational families; and how both are influenced and transformed by

1 We sincerely thank all our research participants who openly shared intimate details of their family lives in and beyond Germany with us, and to the experts who provided crucial background information. Moreover, we would like to thank Gizem Güzelant, Mara Puers, David Steffens, Philipp Themann, and Maarit Thiem for their participation in the data collection and writing of interview protocols, and Rolf Alberth and Lars Wirkus for their support with data management. We acknowledge the funding of the European Union for this research that has been conducted within the frame of the Horizon 2020 research and innovation project TRAFIG (Transnational Figurations of Displacement; grant No. 822453).

broader societal structures such as border, visa, and asylum regimes. Figurations can be understood as power-laden and 'dynamic social constellations between interdependent individuals that are produced in and through interactions and transactions' (Etzold et al., 2019, p. 10). A figurational approach is particularly useful in the study of displaced and separated families because it shifts the focus from the individual displaced person to their social entanglements and the ways that ties are maintained through practices that transgress multiple places and countries (Castrén & Ketokivi, 2015). Moreover, in the context of violent conflict and displacement, individuals' positions within these webs of relations, the modes and practices of maintaining connectivity with others, and the wider political, economic, and social structures that 'normally' shape their lives are radically transformed (Bogner & Rosenthal, 2017). The figurational approach is highly sensitive to such transformations (Baur & Ernst, 2011) and can be applied to map the changes of displaced people's practices and relations over time. In addition, the approach invites reflections on the power relations between people and sees the power shifts in social relations as fundamental driver of transformations (Etzold et al., 2019; Etzold & Fechter, 2022).

2.2 *Transnational family figurations*

Individuals are embedded in multiple social figurations, such as friendships and business networks, local communities, or states. The 'family' is, however, one of the most central social constellations in people's lives. What and who constitutes a family must not be taken for granted. Rather, it is the practices of 'doing family' through which the different members of a family constantly (re)negotiate and (re)produce who belongs to the family, how family life is organised, and how the different members imagine their lives as a family (Jurczyk et al., 2014; Montero-Sieburth et al., 2021). From a figurational perspective, family relationships are conceived of as being both 'personally lived and embedded in wider webs of relationships' (Castrén & Ketokivi, 2015, p. 1). This perspective clearly contradicts the understanding of who belongs to a family and thus has a right to family reunification from a legal perspective (see Section 4). Moreover, figurational thinking helps to map the evolution of family relations – be it more subtle changes like emancipation processes, gradual power shifts, e.g., between sexes or generations, or rather radical ruptures, as is often the case when a family member dies or one, several, or all family members are forced to flee whilst others remain behind. Most displaced people experience separation from their families – be it the nuclear or the extended family – for different periods. Family separation and the resulting enforced transnationalism, if some members have crossed international borders and others have not, are the norm rather than the exception for displaced people (Damir-Geilsdorf & Sabra, 2018; Sauer et al., 2018).

2.3 *Enforced transnationalism*

Refugees' cross-border journeys often lead to a transnationalisation of their lives, which has both advantages and disadvantages for those fleeing and those who stayed behind. Transnational relations are upheld through different familial practices such as sending remittances, everyday communication by phone or through social media, care practices, as well as mobility, wherever this is possible (Christ, Etzold, et al., 2021; Merla et al., 2021; Tobin et al., 2022; Vancluysen, 2022). The hope to reunite one day – back 'home', at the place of asylum, or in another country – is a fundamental subject of discussion in transnationally dispersed families. Yet, many displaced families struggle to actually realise family reunification under conditions of ongoing violent conflict or persecution in the home country, legal insecurity in the country of protection, and bureaucratic hurdles that stand in the way of reunion (Christ & Etzold, 2022). An involuntary continuation of transnational family lives for an indefinite period is thereby enforced upon displaced people through the governance regimes of asylum and migration. According to Al-Ali et al. (2001, p. 395) 'enforced transnationalism' encompasses transnational activities that are constrained or pushed into certain directions by the combined effects of 'state policy, the context of flight, historical antecedents, or the dominance of particular ideological, moral or cultural positions'. Entrenched experiences of 'enforced transnationalism' then do not only come into being through forced migration in the wake of violent conflict and/or state persecution, but also through the 'forced immobility' (Lubkemann, 2008) of other actors. We argue that refugees' transnational practices often have to be upheld because family members cannot depart from countries of origin or countries of first arrival and cannot overcome the multiple barriers to family reunification that are arbitrarily or even strategically upheld by European nation states.

3. Methodology

The data for this chapter is based on research for the TRAFIG project, for which we conducted qualitative interviews with refugees mainly from Syria, Eritrea, and Afghanistan living in Germany (Christ, Etzold, et al., 2021). The research team consisted of seven interviewers, who engaged with 73 people by using semi-structured interviews, biographical interviews, a focus group discussion, and expert interviews. Among them, 50 interviews were conducted with refugees and their network contacts in the years 2020 and 2021. The interviews are biased with regard to the fact that we were mainly able to interview one family member; we therefore do not know the perspective of other family members, in particular the ones living in the place of origin or in countries other than Germany. We analysed our data with the software MaxQDA by coding interviews. With the aim to distinguish the different transnational family constellations that matter in the lives of refugees, we developed a code relations model that resulted in the different 'family figurations in displacement' (see Section 5). For the code relations model, we analysed all 50 interviews with refugees based on their contact persons and the kind of support they provided at the place of living, across other places within Germany, translocal, and across international borders. The family figurations in displacement are not to be mistaken with a typology characterised by clear boundaries. Rather, they are to be understood as a process modelling of the most significant social constellations of the refugees we spoke to. Persons can take part in different figurations at the same time, for example they can be part of a reunited nuclear family figuration, as they are jointly living with close family members at a place of asylum in Germany, but still be embedded in a transnational extended family figuration if they maintain contact with members of the wider family living in other countries, for example, Turkey and Sweden. Moreover, under conditions of displacement, family figurations do change substantially. For example, a married couple lives with two children, but then the 'local nuclear family figuration' becomes torn apart because the husband's life was threatened and he was forced to leave the country and fled to Germany. They then lived in an 'involuntary separated family figuration' across two countries. Later, his wife and two minor children could follow him through family reunification and were then able to live together again at one place, but now in Germany; they thereby became a 'reunited nuclear family figuration'. The figurational approach seeks to highlight such processual changes (Baur & Ernst, 2011), in our case, in family relations (Castrén & Ketokivi, 2015).

4. The governance of family reunification to Germany

For many people who are directly affected by violent conflict, and in particular for those who are continuously living under conditions of protracted displacement, family reunification is often one, if not the only, legal pathway to protection and security. What recent trends in family reunification to Germany can we observe, and how do they relate to global displacement trends? What does the governance of family reunification for refugees coming to Germany look like?

In the ten years from 2013 to 2022, almost 850,000 persons arrived in Germany with a visa issued for family reunification. Before 2014, the majority of applications were granted to Turkish citizens. From 2015 onwards there has been, however, a substantial increase in the issuance of visas for family reunification to Syrian and Iraqi nationals and to a smaller extent also to Iranian and Afghan citizens. In 2016 and 2017 the share of beneficiaries of family reunification arriving in Germany from these four displacement-affected countries was 45 per cent. In 2017 alone 29 per cent of all arrivals to Germany on the grounds of family reunification were granted to Syrians. Among the 33,400 family reunification visas that were issued for Syrians in that year, most (59 per cent) were granted to children joining their parents, almost one-third to women joining their husbands, and a smaller share (5 per cent) to parents joining one of their children (BAMF, 2019, p. 103). After 2017, the share of Syrian nationals among beneficiaries of family reunification arriving in Germany reduced to 10 per cent in 2022 (BAMF, 2023, p. 116). Besides the often-cited statistics of asylum application, these figures demonstrate the impact of the wars and humanitarian crises in the Middle East on migration to Germany and the significance of family reunification as a – if not *the* most important – legal pathway out of protracted displacement (Christ et al., 2021, p. 10).

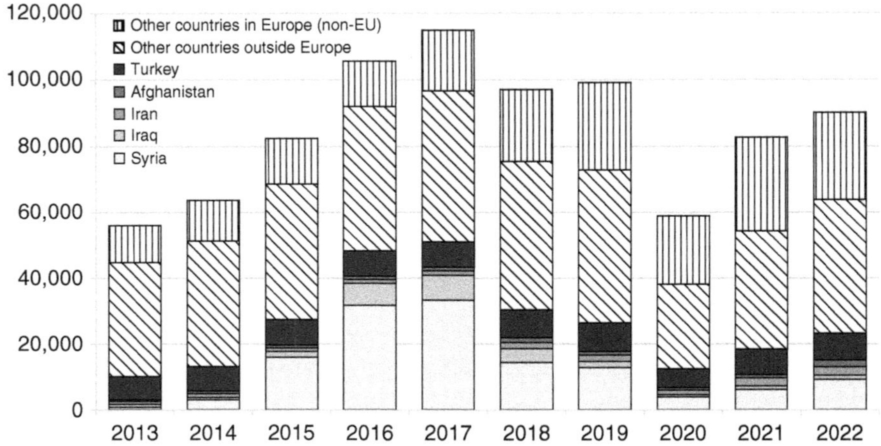

Figure 16.1 Family reunification to Germany (2013–2022), according to the top nationalities[2]

The right to family reunification is enshrined in German law, more specifically in the Residence Act (§§ 27–36). Recognised refugees who apply for family reunification within three months after the final recognition of their protection status have the right to privileged family reunification, meaning that they do not need to provide sufficient living space, healthcare insurance, or sufficient means of subsistence (Grote, 2017, p. 5).

A range of problems are, however, associated with the application and implementation procedure of family reunification to Germany, as noted by multiple scholars and human rights organisations. First, the application procedure takes too long. As the German diplomatic missions abroad are often understaffed, in particular in the Middle East, they could not handle the rapid increase in the demand for family reunification visas since 2014 (Grote, 2017, pp. 36–37). In 2016, the average waiting time for the required personal meeting at the German embassies or consulates in Turkey, Jordan, and Lebanon was 14 months (Pro Asyl, 2016) – a time in which the security and living conditions as well as the health of family members residing in countries of (first) reception often deteriorated. In this sense, the bureaucracy of the visa regime can contribute to blocking complementary pathways to protection and to protracting the affected people's displacement situation.

Second, the bureaucracy of the visa application disadvantages, and in some cases even jeopardises, people in need of protection who have been forced to flee from their homes in a hurry and who could thus not bring along all the required documents (Den Haese & Verhellen, this volume). If certain documents are missing, it is not only costly and time consuming to replace them, it is also very risky, as the displaced, their relatives, or other trusted persons have to return to war

2 © Benjamin Etzold, BICC. Source: BAMF (2019, p. 100), BAMF (2023, p. 114).

zones or interact with the officials of states from which they have fled in the first place or from which they have been persecuted. Moreover, some countries such as Eritrea do not have a harmonious official documentation (Christ, Etzold, et al., 2021; Mekonnen & Palacios Arapiles, 2021; Ton, 2018; Arapiles & Mekonnen, this volume).

Third, the narrow understanding of a 'nuclear family' who is entitled to family reunification according to the German Residence Act as the spouse and 'parent-child-relationships' (Grote, 2017, p. 18) is not necessarily in line with the reality of displaced people's family relations, in particular their sometimes complex transnational family figurations (Christ & Etzold, 2022). Parents and grandparents of recognised refugees (older than 18 years), siblings, aunts, uncles, nieces, nephews and cousins, adult children, and grandchildren are excluded from the right to family reunification. In recent years, it was particularly difficult for unaccompanied minors already residing in Germany with or without a protection status to reunite with their parents and siblings due to a lack of documentation, long times of waiting in bureaucratic procedures, no access to legal support, and inadequate guidance by the minors' legal guardian (Winzenried, 2017). The minors' right to welfare and family cohesion is often violated by the state.

Fourth, there have also been quotas to further reduce the potential and actual number of persons arriving through family reunification. Between 2016 and 2018, family reunification was suspended for two years for people with subsidiary protection. Since August 2018 it has been permitted again, but a maximum limit of 1,000 national visas for family members of beneficiaries of subsidiary protection per month was set (BAMF, 2022, p. 107). Visas are issued according to so-called humanitarian criteria, such as length of separation, age of the children, or a severe illness. Thus, for beneficiaries of subsidiary protection it was, and for some still is, a protracted process to bring family members to Germany.

5. Enforced transnationalism in family figurations of displacement

Having outlined the governance of family reunification in Germany and some of the key challenges for refugees to realise their right to family reunification, we now shed light on how family members experience separation, enforced transnational family lives, and an eventual reunion. Based on our interviews with refugees living in Germany, we identified three distinct family figurations that exemplify diverse family constellations in a transnational space: 1) the reunited nuclear family, 2) the involuntary separated family, and 3) the transnationally extended family. Each figuration is being portrayed with two different cases that differ in terms of the position of the individual within the family (child, parent, wife, husband, etc.), the order of the family members' journeys, and the different governance regimes in place (e.g. for Syrian and Eritrean refugees). The figurational approach has the potential to illuminate the dynamics between different families (e.g. Rosa and her children followed her husband/father through family reunification, whereas Dahab has been separated from her children for years) and even within a particular family (e.g. Tahir's wife followed through family reunification, whereas Tahir's elderly mother was not eligible). A successful reunion depends on may factors, such as financial and social resources, but foremost on the conditions of the governance regimes (e.g. eligible family members for reunification, (im)possibility of obtaining necessary documents).

5.1 The reunited nuclear family figuration

The reunited nuclear family figuration refers to a nuclear family that has been living together at one place that has then been separated due to conflict and displacement but finally – after an uncertain period – reunited again at one place. The following two case studies of refugees from Syria show how separation due to displacement, a life under conditions of enforced transnationalism, and eventual family reunion have been experienced.

Tahir from Syria is married – his wife lives with him in Germany now, but they did not leave Syria together. Rather, they decided that he would go there alone at first via 'irregular routes', and she should follow later via a more secure legal pathway. He had received information from contacts who came to Germany before him that family reunification would be a safe way to bring spouses or children. After his arrival, Tahir first supported his wife in Syria financially and helped his mother for her onward journey. He recalled being depressed and feeling guilty after his arrival in Germany, as he was already safe while his family remained at risk. Tahir had a strong sense of obligation to bring his family here as soon as possible. It took, however, two and a half years until Tahir was able to bring his wife to Germany through the family reunification process. Tahir had received refugee status and benefited from legal support from counselling agencies during the application procedure. Tahir's mother, however, was not eligible for family reunification, which means that she could not enter Germany legally. Therefore, she travelled irregularly from Syria to Europe – first to Turkey and then over the Aegean to Greece. His mother could not leave Greece immediately, as planned, and ended up living in a refugee shelter in Greece for a whole year before she was able to irregularly travel on to Germany. She also stayed in contact with Tahir and his other relatives in Europe, who attempted to accompany her through the process. She recalls that her time in Greece was difficult because she wanted to reunite with her children. She was also worried because she was an older woman on her own in Greece and suffered from diabetes.

Tahir's example shows the emotional burden of long-term separation. Even though he eventually succeeded in providing a safe journey for his wife through family reunification, there was no possibility to bring his mother as well, as the family reunification process is only possible for members of the nuclear family. The elderly woman thus had to risk an irregular and dangerous journey alone. Now that his wife and his mother joined him in Germany, he is still worried about his two sisters living in Syria (SsInt-BICC-GG-001-DEU).

The other example is Rosa from Syria, who told us her story as a family member following her husband through family reunification. She also experienced enforced transnational family life; however, the period of separation was much shorter compared to other refugees. Rosa's husband left Syria for Turkey to find work there.

However, as he could not find adequate work, he moved on to Europe on an irregular journey. The decision to leave was a difficult one, as Rosa recalls:

> We thought about what to do if we stay, we don't know what is coming, Aleppo was gone, half of Syria was gone, if we stay, we always discussed. When will this war end, what should we do with the children. We stay, it doesn't matter. But the children need school, need security, just need good lives.
>
> (SsInt-BICC-MT-002-DEU)

Rosa was weighing different options for the future of herself and her family, and not knowing how long the war would last, she preferred to leave for the sake of her children's future.

After Rosa's husband reached Germany, he received refugee protection and was able to apply for family reunification. In order to apply for the visa, Rosa and her children had to travel to the German consulate in Turkey, as this was the only German diplomatic representation in the region accessible to them. The irregular border crossing to Turkey was, however, very dangerous and difficult – only after the tenth attempt were they able to cross the border on foot. They knew that many people also died on the way. The family went to Istanbul, where they met Rosa's brother who had reached Istanbul one month earlier. The children were happy to be together with their cousins. After six months, the visas were processed and the family faced a difficult farewell, as they had to say goodbye to Rosa's brother and his children. When Rosa recalled this moment in the interview, she cried: '[Other] people are looking at the airport, why are these people crying all the time, it was very hard. [They do not understand that] this is not a vacation, we know we can't see each other'. When Rosa and her two daughters finally met their husband/father again after a one-year separation, they had mixed feelings. On the one hand, they were very happy to be reunited, but on the other hand, they were sad due to the separation from their other family members. Rosa explains: 'We lost each other. Family plays a big role for us' (SsInt-BICC-MT-002-DEU).

Both cases show the discrepancy between the formal eligibility for family reunification and the feeling of family members who belong to a family. Tahir wished for protection for his wife and his mother in Germany, but only his wife could travel safely through family reunification, whereas his elderly mother had to resort to an irregular journey. Rosa and her children could follow her husband through family reunification but still felt sad to separate from her brother and his children in Turkey. There was no option for them to follow to Germany through family reunification as well. Whereas the German legal system defines families as a nuclear family, our interviewees have a much broader understanding of family. Moreover, both examples demonstrate that the families experienced enforced transnationalism – at least a temporary separation from loved ones. Even though the family reunification process is a safe pathway, it often entails dangerous passages as well, as either the sponsor first travels irregularly or the beneficiaries need to move to another country in order to be able to access the visa procedure.

5.2 The involuntary separated family figuration

Most of the families we encountered in our research had endured the plights of family separation for a certain time but eventually reunited. However, there are families who are separated from their families for a very long period and are thus continuously experiencing enforced transnationalism without an end in sight. Life in such an involuntary separated family figuration places an enormous psychological burden on all members of the family. The uncertainty of family reunion forces many displaced families to organise their family lives across the distance. If a reunion is not possible, the family member in Germany tries to support the separated family members financially and emotionally. We will present two cases of protracted family separation, which differ according to who took the journey and whether it is the spouse or a child who is left without the other family members.

Omar is an unaccompanied minor from Syria who arrived in Germany with the intention to bring the other members of his nuclear family. He fled from Syria in August 2015, as his father, a medical doctor, was threatened for refusing to treat wounded IS combatants. Omar had to convince his father that it would be best if he goes to Europe alone. When he arrived in Germany in August 2015, he was still a minor. Around one year later, he was granted refugee protection. Two months later, a few days before he turned 18, he submitted the application for family reunification for his parents. The rejection on his application came some weeks after Omar had turned 18. According to a judgement by the Court of Justice of the European Union in April 2018,[3] the right to apply for family reunification cannot depend upon the speed of authorities processing an asylum procedure, stating that the date of application should be relevant, not the date of the decision (Desmet, this volume). Therefore, Omar appealed the rejection with the support of an NGO. At the time of our interview, two years had passed, but Omar had not received a decision yet. He had been separated from his parents for five years, which put a lot of stress on him: 'I was a child as I entered Germany, 15 years old. Every child needs his parents. . . . I always dreamed of them being with me in Germany . . . the same dream every day'. Omar had planned to meet his parents in Northern Iraq in July 2020. From the flat to the visa, everything was arranged when the COVID-19 pandemic made the trip impossible. Omar compared his disappointment of not meeting his parents with waking up from a nightmare. In this nightmare, he dreamt that he wanted to have a glass of water but was not able to find it and stayed thirsty forever. Omar financially supports his parents and thereby contributes crucially to financing the education of his three sisters at private universities in Syria. Omar talks to his parents twice a week. They assure each other that everything is fine, and they should not worry. Nevertheless, both sides are aware that this is not true. Whereas he upholds the transnational connectivity with his family in Syria, he has no contact with his extended family members living in Germany (SsInt-BICC-Ds-005-DEU).

3 CJEU, 12 April 2018, C-550/16, *A. and S.*, ECLI:EU:C:2018:248.

Dahab, an Eritrean woman, is a parent who went first to Germany with the intention to bring her children through family reunification. However, she has now been separated from her children for more than seven years already and still does not know how long this will last. When Dahab decided to flee Eritrea, her husband had already died. As she knew of the dangers of the journey through the Sahara Desert and the Mediterranean, she decided to bring her two minor children to her mother in Ethiopia and hoped to avail of family reunification after being recognised as a refugee in Germany. On her journey, Dahab met her current partner, Solomon, with whom she is now living in Germany. The couple has four children together; however, the two children with her deceased husband are still living in Ethiopia, as the family reunification process has failed so far. Even though Dahab was recognised as a refugee in Germany in 2016, and fulfilled all criteria for privileged family reunification, she faced manifold bureaucratic hurdles, among which the following list is non-exhaustive. Dahab's children should have registered as refugees at the Administration for Refugee and Returnee Affairs (ARRA), the Ethiopian authority cooperating with UNHCR, within the first two years after arrival in Ethiopia, of which Dahab was not aware. The non-existent registration was a big obstacle, which retarded the process of family reunification significantly (see also Belloni & Verschraegen, this volume). She tried to accelerate the process by travelling to Ethiopia, but failed. However, she finally was able to meet her children during the time of her vacation. Finally, in 2019, her children were registered as refugees with the help of the newly established Family Assistance Programme by the IOM. In spring 2020, the children had a long-awaited appointment scheduled at the German embassy, which was then cancelled due to the pandemic. Instead of a quick reunion, the waiting period continued. To make things worse, a violent conflict started in the region of Tigray in Ethiopia where the children were living. The whole region was cut off from any connections, be it flights, land transportation, or communications. Dahab did not have any information about her two sons and her mother; it was a time of anxious waiting on the whereabouts of her family. After four months, Dahab learnt that her family had been displaced, but was now in safety. A few weeks later, the children finally were able to travel to Addis Ababa for the visa interview. As the children do not have birth certificates, the children and Dahab must undertake DNA testing as proof of identity and biological kinship. The test was not a problem for Dahab in Germany; however, as of now, one and a half years after the embassy asked for this requirement, the children have not been able to do the testing due to the ongoing conflict. Moreover, Dahab was not able to be in contact with her children for the last year, as the conflict has continued and the Tigray region remains disconnected.

Both cases present separations of children from their parents – Omar from the perspective of the child, Dahab the perspective of a mother. In both cases, the children are or were minors – therefore, the narrow definition of family with the entitlement to family reunification according to the regulations apply. Nevertheless, both families experience protracted separation and an enforced transnationalisation of family lives. Bureaucratic regulations often hinder family reunification in Germany. Some requirements are impossible to meet for refugees, for example obtaining identity documents by the Eritrean state. Moreover, the procedures are lengthy and very complex, with many actors involved. In some cases, going to court and taking legal action is the last remaining option. As returning to the country of origin is often impossible – e.g. due to the revocation of the refugee status or the threat of persecution – and reunification in Germany is complicated, families consider different options to at least temporarily reunite. Omar tried to meet his parents in Iraq, and Dahab visited her children in Ethiopia. But unforeseeable external factors can hinder such family reunions. Omar's visit was impeded by the pandemic, and Dahab could not travel to Tigray due to the continuation of conflict. Years of separation make a huge difference in the eyes of children and their parents: the lost time cannot be made up again.

5.3 The transnational extended family figuration

The transnational extended family figuration refers to extended families that maintain connections across two or several states. In the case of our interviewees, it is not exceptional that the extended family is not living at the same place or even in the same country, but in very different countries. Among others, one reason why extended family members are spread across several countries is the impossibility of family reunification schemes for extended families. There is simply – with very few exceptions, such as humanitarian admission programmes (Etzold & Christ, 2021; Tometten, 2018) – no legal options for safe pathways of family members other than the nuclear family. To uphold familial connections – 'doing family' – entails different practices, such as transaction of financial resources, care practices, or communication, not only within the nuclear family but within a wider network of familial relations (Jurczyk et al., 2014), as the two following stories of Syrian women show.

Hawa from Syria and her three children arrived in Germany from Turkey in 2016, after having followed her husband through family reunification. Her husband's original plan was to go to Norway in 2015, but when he wanted to change in the Frankfurt airport, police caught him and gave him the choice to either stay in Germany or fly back to Syria. Hawa's familial network stretches across several countries. The majority of her family members have settled in different receiving countries; there is only the family of her sister who is still living in Syria in their town of origin. She is there with her husband and does not want to migrate but really would like to visit Hawa. Another sister is in Vienna; she also followed her husband via family reunification to Austria. Moreover, Hawa's parents, two brothers, and a nephew live in Vienna. Additionally, she has an uncle living in London, a friend in Paris, and aunts in Dubai and Canada. Hawa talks to her family in Syria and Austria almost every day; their communication even increased during the pandemic. She talks most with her mother and sister in Vienna. Hawa feels at home when visiting her relatives in Austria. Despite having her close relatives in Austria, she does not plan to move there. She feels obliged to stay in Germany and to give something back to the country. In Germany, Hawa's main focus is her own family with her now four children. But her example shows that her everyday life is strongly influenced by transnational family relations (SsInt-BICC-MP-007-DEU).

Asma is from Aleppo, Syria. She left Syria in 2015 together with her daughter, who still was a baby. When she arrived in Turkey, she waited for her husband to join her. Except for the beginning of their journey, the family travelled together as a nuclear family. Her case is one of the very few examples from our sample of a nuclear family that was not separated during and after the journey. From Turkey, they moved on to Greece by a rubber boat and reached Germany through the Balkan route. The flight was physically very demanding for Asma, as she was pregnant during this time. A couple of weeks after their arrival in Germany, the unborn baby died and Asma became seriously ill. She recovered and after some time got pregnant again. The baby died again. The loss of her two children was a drastic experience for Asma and her family. During the time of the interview, Asma was pregnant again. The pregnancies and the death of her two children were the prevailing topics of the interview.

Asma shared her sorrows during the new pregnancy with her mother and sisters in Syria, who are an enormous resource of emotional support. Despite the geographical distance, they are the first to know about the examination at her gynaecologist and never miss whenever she has an appointment there: 'They all have in their calendar: Asma has an appointment'. Asma, who daily chats with her mother via WhatsApp, tells the interviewer how her mother awaits her call: 'When my mother knows I have an appointment with the gynaecologist, she always waits to call me. Everything ok? She doesn't say hello. When I say everything is ok, then she says: "How are you?"' (SsInt-BICC-SC-001-DEU).

Both examples demonstrate how extended family networks stretch and are maintained across several countries whilst the nuclear family is living together at one place. Whereas Asma's family travelled together, Hawa and her children were separated from her husband but eventually reunited in Germany. For both, family is more than 'just' the nuclear family, even though there are no plans of the extended family member to reunite and move together at one particular place. They both are 'doing family' at a transnational scale, as they frequently communicate with each other and provide, among others, emotional support. While Hawa can frequently travel to Austria to see her parents and other relatives, it is impossible for Asma to visit her mother and sisters in Syria. Both expressed that they suffer from being distant to loved ones, but the means of overcoming this enforced family separation differed. After all, digital connectivity cannot fully replace personal encounters.

6. Conclusion – family separation, enforced transnationalism, and policy implications

The figurational approach offers a new perspective to displacement, as displaced people are not considered in isolation but as being part of different constellations, such as their families (Christ, Isikozlu, et al., 2021). In addition, it conceives of social relations as ever evolving; not necessarily due to individuals' own priorities and decisions but due to changing circumstances and larger structural forces over which the concerned people have no control. Violent conflict, forced migration, temporary or long-term family separation, and in some, but not all cases, family reunification have constantly transformed the family figurations of Syrian and Eritrean refugees we spoke to in Germany. This has always had long-lasting and far-reaching consequences for all family members, who more often than not live scattered across multiple places and countries: there is a change of positions, gender roles, and identities of the family members embedded in a certain figuration. All the families portrayed in this chapter have experienced separation from family members in the wake of displacement, which reflects a predominant pattern for refugees now living in Germany (Damir-Geilsdorf & Sabra, 2018; Sauer et al., 2021). The separation between the family members is not voluntarily, worse even, the duration of separation is often substantially prolonged due to the encountered barriers to family reunification. The transnational organisation of family life is then enforced upon displaced people, not only temporarily but consistently.

Policies, legal norms, and dominant discourses have tremendous influence on the family figurations of displaced people, yet their capacities to navigate the bureaucratic landscapes of family reunification are often limited. Not only due to a lack of means and legal support, but also due to very different conceptions of who 'counts' as family, many of our interviewees were deeply frustrated by the barriers to the reunification with loved ones. Conceptual discussions in anthropology and sociology (Jurczyk et al., 2014; Montero-Sieburth et al., 2021) lead us to reflect on the narrow legal definitions of family, such as in German law, which hardly correspond with people's own sense of belonging and their daily lives. After displacement and despite separation, refugees are deeply engaged in communicative practices and provide financial and emotional support to family members, also to those living in other countries. Physical distance does not mean emotional distance. Social media help family members to actively participate in each other's lives and to share personal moments across different places and borders. Social, emotional, and technological connectivity allow refugees and their kin to 'do family' in a transnational space.

Displaced people must nonetheless navigate the complex structures in the governance of family reunification in order to reunite with family members. They face numerous hurdles and obstacles: crossing the border irregularly to apply for the visa in a country of first reception, lack of legal support, issues of registration, and missing identity documents, to name just a few. That is why conditions of 'enforced transnationalism' often prevail over years and years. On the other hand, not all families would like to reunite. 'Living apart together' in a transnationally extended family seems to work well for many.

The figurational approach that we propose to study refugees' family reunification procedures helps to analyse the complexity of lived family constellations and thus also challenges a simplified legal concept of family. A figurational approach neutrally describes different actors constituting a figuration, and it sheds light on how the figuration is formed by external factors, such as the governance of family reunification. Through this description, figurational thinking has the potential to analyse the normativity of the official definition of a family and the politicisation of the family reunification process. Family reunification is usually hindered due to the legalistic framework (who is [not] eligible for family reunification) and the bureaucratic conditions (e.g. proofs of identity), which largely differ between different states. Family reunification is – in terms of numbers – the most important legal pathway for refugees to Germany. But still, the needs of displaced and separated families are only inadequately met. Not only are the procedures very lengthy and overly bureaucratic, but also is the reality and complexity of family constellations that have been torn apart by violent conflict and displacement-induced separation oftentimes not recognised. Refugees' enforced transnational lives are not only an inevitable side effect of cross-border mobility, but also an (un)intended consequence of multiple mobility barriers, in particular systematically upheld barriers to family reunification.

Acknowledgement

This contribution is based on research that has been conducted within the project 'Transnational Figurations of Displacement' (TRAFIG). We acknowledge funding for this project from the European Union's Horizon 2020 research and innovation programme under grant No 822453.

References

Al-Ali, N., Black, R., & Koser, K. (2001). The limits to "transnationalism": Bosnian and Eritrean refugees in Europe as emerging transnational communities. *Ethnic and Racial Studies*, *24*(4), 578–600. https://doi.org/10.1080/01419870120049798

BAMF. (2019). *Das Bundesamt in Zahlen 2018: Asyl, migration und integration*. BAMF – Bundesamt für Migration und Flüchtlinge. www.bamf.de/SharedDocs/Anlagen/DE/Statistik/BundesamtinZahlen/bundesamt-in-zahlen-2018.html?nn=284738

BAMF. (2023). *Das Bundesamt in Zahlen 2022: Asyl, migration und integration*. BAMF – Bundesamt für Migration und Flüchtlinge. www.bamf.de/SharedDocs/Anlagen/DE/Statistik/BundesamtinZahlen/bundesamt-in-zahlen-2022.pdf?__blob=publicationFile&v=3

Baur, N., & Ernst, S. (2011). Towards a process-oriented methodology: Modern social science research methods and Norbert Elias's figurational sociology. *The Sociological Review*, *59*(1), 119–139. https://doi.org/10.1111/j.1467-954X.2011.01981.x

Belloni, M. (2019). Family project or individual choice? Exploring agency in young Eritreans' migration. *Journal of Ethnic and Migration Studies*, *9*(2), 1–18. https://doi.org/10.1080/1369183X.2019.1584698

Bogner, A., & Rosenthal, G. (2017). Biographies – Discourses – Figurations: Methodological Considerations from the Perspectives of Social Constructivism and Figurational Sociology. In G. Rosenthal & A. Bogner (Eds.), *Biographies in the Global South: Life Stories Embedded in Figurations and Discourses* (pp. 15–49). Campus Verlag.

Bryceson, D., & Vuorela, U. (Eds.). (2002). *The Transnational Family: New European Frontiers and Global Networks*. Routledge.

Castrén, A.-M., & Ketokivi, K. (2015). Studying the complex dynamics of family relationships: A figurational approach. *Sociological Research Online*, *20*(1), 1–14. https://doi.org/10.5153/sro.3539

Christ, S., & Etzold, B. (2022). Family figurations in displacement: Entangled mobilities of refugees towards Germany and beyond. *Journal of Ethnic and Migration Studies*, *48*(18), 1–17. https://doi.org/10.1080/1369183X.2022.2090160

Christ, S., Etzold, B., Güzelant, G.G., Puers, M., Steffens, D., Themann, P., & Thiem, M. (2021). *Figurations of displacement in and beyond Germany: Empirical findings and reflections on mobility and translocal connections of refugees living in Germany* (TRAFIG Working Paper No. 10). TRAFIG. https://doi.org/10.5281/zenodo.5841892

Christ, S., Isikozlu, E., & Etzold, B. (2021). *Following their lead: Transnational connectivity and mobility along family figurations in displacement* (TRAFIG Practice Note No. 10). TRAFIG. https://doi.org/10.5281/zenodo.5845868

Damir-Geilsdorf, S., & Sabra, M. (2018). *Disrupted families: The gendered impacts of family reunification policies on Syrian refugees in Germany* (UN Women Discussion Paper No. 23). UN Women. www.unwomen.org/en/digital-library/publications/2018/4/discussion-paper-disrupted-families

Elias, N. (1978). *What is Sociology?* Columbia University Press.

Etzold, B., Belloni, M., King, R., Kraler, A., & Pastore, F. (2019). *Transnational figurations of displacement: Conceptualising protracted displacement and translocal connectivity through a process-oriented perspective* (TRAFIG Working Paper No. 1). TRAFIG. https://doi.org/10.5281/zenodo.5840818

Etzold, B., & Christ, S. (2021). Humanitarian admission programmes: How networks enable mobility in contexts of protracted displacement. *Forced Migration Review*, *68*, 63–66. www.fmreview.org/externalisation/etzold-christ

Etzold, B., & Fechter, A.-M. (2022). Unsettling protracted displacement: Connectivity and mobility beyond "Limbo". *Journal of Ethnic and Migration Studies*, *48*(18), 1–18. https://doi.org/10.1080/1369183X.2022.2090153

Grote, J. (2017). *Family reunification of third-country nationals in Germany: Focus-study by the German national contact point for the European migration network (EMN)* (Working Paper 73). www.bamf.de/SharedDocs/Anlagen/EN/Publikationen/EMN/Studien/wp73-emn-familiennachzug-drittstaatsangehoerige-deutschland.html

Hyndman, J., & Giles, W. (2016). *Refugees in Extended Exile: Living on the Edge. Interventions*. Routledge. https://doi.org/10.1017/S181638311700073X

Jurczyk, K., Lange, A., & Thiessen, B. (Eds.). (2014). *Doing Family: Warum Familienleben heute nicht mehr selbstverständlich ist.* Beltz Juventa. www.content-select.com/index.php?id=bib_view&ean=9783779943334

Löbel, L.-M., & Jacobsen, J. (2021). Waiting for kin: A longitudinal study of family reunification and refugee mental health in Germany. *Journal of Ethnic and Migration Studies*, *47*(13), 2916–2937. https://doi.org/10.1080/1369183X.2021.1884538

Lubkemann, S.C. (2008). Involuntary immobility: On a theoretical invisibility in forced migration studies. *Journal of Refugee Studies*, *21*(4), 454–475. https://doi.org/10.1093/jrs/fen043

Mekonnen, D., & Palacios Arapiles, S. (2021). *Access to documents by Eritrean refugees in the context of family reunification: Legal framework, practical realities and obstacles*. https://refugeerights.org/wp-content/uploads/2021/05/report_access_to_official_documents_eritrea_equalrights_irap.pdf

Merla, L., Kilkey, M., Wilding, R., & Baldassar, L. (2021). Key Developments and Future Prospects in the Study of Transnational Families. In N. Schneider & M. Kreyenfeld (Eds.), *Research Handbook on the Sociology of the Family* (pp. 439–451). Edward Elgar Publishing. http://dx.doi.org/10.4337/9781788975544

Montero-Sieburth, M., Mas Giralt, R., & Garcia-Arjona, N. (Eds.). (2021). *Family Practices in Migration: Everyday Lives and Relationships*. Routledge. https://doi.org/10.4324/9781003132561

Pro Asyl. (2016). *Hintergrund: Familienzusammenführung? Darauf können Sie lange warten*. https://www.proasyl.de/hintergrund/familienzusammenfuehrung-darauf-koennen-sie-lange-warten/

Sauer, L., Diabaté, S., Gabel, S., Halfar, Y., Kraus, E.K., & Wenzel, L. (2018). *Doing transnational family im Kontext von Flucht und Krisenmigration: Stand der Forschung* (BiB Working Paper 3). Bundesinstitut für Bevölkerungsforschung. www.bib.bund.de/Publikation/2018/Doing-transnational-family-im-Kontext-von-Flucht-und-Krisen migration-Stand-der-Forschung.html?nn=9859990

Sauer, L., Stichs, A., Kassam, K., Kraus, E.K., Sander, N., Schührer, S., & Siegert, M. (2021). *Migration. Familie. Soziale Beziehungen: Transnationale Familienkonstellationen und soziale Einbindung von Menschen aus Eritrea und Syrien in Deutschland.* BundesinstitutfürBevölkerungsforschung.www.bib.bund.de/Publikation/2021/Migration-Familie-Soziale-Beziehungen.html?nn=9751912

Silver, A.M., Edelblute, H., Mouw, T., & Chávez, S. (2018). Fractured families, connected community: Emotional engagement in a transnational social network. *International Migration, 56*(6), 153–168. https://doi.org/10.1111/imig.12514

Tobin, S., Etzold, B., Momani, F.A., Al Yakoub, T., AlMassad, R.F., & Shdefat, A.G. (2022). Ambivalent Entanglements: Syrian Refugees' Network Relations and (Im)mobilities in Protracted Displacement. In J. Ahrens & R. King (Eds.), *Onward Migration and Multi-sited Transnationalism: Complex Trajectories, Practices and Ties* (pp. 99–119). IMISCOE Research Series. Springer. https://doi.org/10.1007/978-3-031-12503-4_5

Tometten, C. (2018). Resettlement, humanitarian admission, and family reunion: The intricacies of Germany's legal entry regimes for Syrian refugees. *Refugee Survey Quarterly, 37*(2), 187–203. https://doi.org/10.1093/rsq/hdy002

Ton, M. (2018). Zur Anerkennung eritreischer Eheschließeungen. *Asylmagazin, 3*, 71–76.

Vancluysen, S. (2022). Deconstructing borders: Mobility strategies of South Sudanese refugees in northern Uganda. *Global Networks, 22*(1), 20–35. https://doi.org/10.1111/glob.12322

Winzenried, H. (2017). Familiennachzug zu unbegleiteten minderjährigen Flüchtlingen: Rechtliche Rahmenbedingungen und Erfahrungen aus der Beratungspraxis. *Asylmagazin, 2017*(10–11), 369–374.

17 Reassembling the right to family reunification for refugees in Belgium through social work practices of welfare bricolage

Pascal Debruyne

1. Introduction

Wars and uprisings in the Middle East, as well as the fear of persecution by authoritarian states, have led to increased numbers of refugees since 2015, posing challenges for European countries concerning asylum and integration. In Belgium, academic and political circles have mostly paid attention to policies of asylum, reception, and integration. Support for maintaining family ties across borders and during the process of family reunification has received far less attention. My research on family reunification with Syrian, Afghan, Palestinian, Eritrean, and Iraqi refugees in Belgium concentrated on the everyday practice of family reunification.

The theoretical nucleus of this qualitative research is twofold. First, it focuses on 'the policy assemblage' of family reunification (McCann & Ward, 2012; Savage, 2018, 2020) to illustrate the everyday complexity of the process of family reunification for sponsors that have received international protection. As Ghoddousi and Page (2020, p. 5) explain, '[a]ssemblage theory challenges the very concept of subjectivity: rather than an already-existing subject of study (e.g., individual humans or political entities), assemblage theory foregrounds open multiplicities of relations that constitute the subject(s)'. Or, following conceptual founders of the theory Gilles Deleuze and Felix Guattari (1987), the chapter focuses on 'becoming' more than 'being' (Bankston, 2017; Biehl & Locke, 2010). Thus, instead of considering law and procedures 'already-existing subjects of study', this chapter illustrates 'the becoming' of the policy assemblage of family reunification through the interaction of its 'components'.[1]

First, this chapter discusses the multiple political-administrative, ideological, and physical components (such as boundaries) of the assemblage of the practice of family reunification, and several 'scales' of government that it intersects. It incorporates the lifeworld dynamics of transnational families as they practise 'doing

1 According to Rabinow (2014, p. 206), an assemblage is 'not a pre-existing thing of the world with pre-given properties, but instead brings together entities in the world into a proximity in which they establish relations between and among themselves while remaining external to each other and thereby retaining their original properties'.

DOI: 10.4324/9781003503217-22

family at a distance' (Ambrosini, 2015; Rousseau et al., 2004) while experiencing the complex process of family reunification.

Second, the chapter explores the practices of 'welfare bricolage' by social professionals. Phillimore et al. (2021, p. 2) define welfare bricolage as 'the creative mobilization, use and re-use of wide-ranging resources, including multiple knowledges, ideas, materials and networks in order to address particular health concerns'. These authors focus on how individuals (citizens and social professionals) perform 'welfare bricolage' depending 'on restricted resources, and applying strategies of innovation, imagination and necessity, but also reordering, subversion, and transformation' (Phillimore et al., 2016, p. 3). Through 'welfare bricolage', civil society organisations often fill the gaps in provision and provide the social glue to connect services in the 'welfare ecosystem', for example by using their discretionary power or even bending the rules to attempt to meet their beneficiaries' needs.

This chapter examines how social professionals cope with challenges of transnational families during separation and reunification in Belgium. This focus transcends the scale of the neighbourhood, elaborating on the *transnational* and multi-scalar practices social workers put in practice to ensure the right to family reunification; this provides a transnational and multi-scalar perspective that lacks in Phillimore et al.'s (2021) use of 'welfare bricolage' (Schrooten & Raeymaeckers, 2023). This requires a set of competences and combinations of knowledge that surmount views and practices of social intervention based on 'methodological nationalism' (Schrooten, 2021).

The chapter analyses how formal (paid) and informal (voluntary) social workers deal with the complexity of the policy assemblage of family reunification, which is organised on multiple scales of government and through 'splintered' governance arrangements: embassies and private visa offices (VFS and TLS) under the Federal Ministry of Foreign Affairs; the Belgian Immigration Office, the State Secretary of Asylum and Migration, municipal civil affairs departments under the Federal Ministry of Internal Affairs; and the regional (Flemish, Walloon, and Brussels) governments for issues of welfare and care and child allowances. Consequently, 'welfare bricolage' dealing with the policy assemblage of family reunification is an example of transnational social work (Bartley et al., 2012; Boccagni et al., 2015; Negi & Furman, 2010; Schrooten, 2021).

Fieldwork for this research took place between September 2019 and March 2023 and used an open-ended qualitative research design. It included 54 semi-structured interviews with formal and informal social workers and other civil society actors ('expert interviews'), exploring their roles, social interventions, and strategies. These experts' views and experiences were juxtaposed with the lifeworld dynamics of refugee families by conducting 46 in-depth, semi-structured interviews with members of refugee families (sponsors and beneficiaries) before, during, and after their process of family reunification.

This chapter starts with an overview of how Belgian legislation on family reunification has evolved, showing how processes and practices of family reunification are an 'assemblage' wherein a heterogeneity of components intersects and interacts: social practices, things, and legal-material-social-symbolic constellations (Deleuze &

Guattari, 1987). Second, the chapter looks at how social professionals – beyond only formal social workers – expand and surmount their discretionary space to deal with the thresholds and complexity in the everyday practice of family reunification. It highlights the (widening) gap between the legal right to family reunification and its everyday practice through the lenses of 'bricolage' and 'assemblage'.

2. The policy assemblage of family reunification

2.1 What is policy assemblage?

Savage (2020) describes how policy is not achieved by a homogeneous controlled process with calibrated actors that leads to a clear outcome. Complex relationships between involved agencies shape and reshape policy, as well as a complexity of (often conflicting and abrasive) procedures. As Anderson and McFarlane (2011, p. 126) argue, assemblages are often incoherent, heterogeneous, and unstable:

> Assemblages always 'claim' a territory as heterogeneous components are gathered and hold together. But this can only ever be a provisional process: relations may change, new components may enter, alliances may be broken, new conjunctions may be fostered. Assemblages are constantly opening up to new lines of flight, new becomings.

Savage (2020) refers to three characteristics of policy, looking through the lens of 'assemblage theory'. First, there are relations of exteriority and emergence. Policies surface through the interaction between components of the assemblage but are not determined by those components only. Exterior 'events' can transform the assemblage:

> The particular ways in which components are brought together will determine the properties and effects of any given policy or agenda; and if the very same components were to be arranged differently, or new components were introduced or excluded, then different properties and effects would be produced.
>
> (Savage, 2020, p. 322)

Second, Savage points to the heterogeneity, relationality, and flux that drive everyday policy practice: the creation of policy takes place at various moments, by various actors crafting policies and circulating ideas to influence them. As Ureta (2015) argues, assemblages are the result of heterogeneous components that are brought together into particular strategic relations and with particular desired impacts. The chapter explores how policies of family reunification, assembled with an array of administrative, legal, political, ideological, and material-physical components, aim at obstructing the possibility to family reunification.

Third, Savage (2020, p. 328) argues that a policy assemblage requires attention for power, politics, and agency: 'Assemblages represent a gathering together of political imaginations, rationalities, technologies, infrastructures and agents towards steering individuals and groups in particular directions'. The next section explores the assemblage of family reunification, showing how it impacts refugee families, sponsors, and beneficiaries.

2.2 Assembling the practice of family reunification

The assemblage of family reunification as it functions today is at odds with the right to respect for family life. Family reunification policies are 'derived' from various legal sources that underpin the right to respect for family life, such as Article 16 of the Universal Declaration of Human Rights (UDHR), Article 23 of the International Covenant on Civil and Political Rights, and Article 8 of the European Convention on Human Rights (ECHR). Nevertheless, there is no human right to family reunification, only a right to respect for family life that is not absolute because it is weighed against states' rights to enforce immigration laws and maintain public order (Burchill, 2003; Desmet, this volume). This state of affairs can be traced to the colonial roots of the case law of the European Court of Human Rights (ECtHR) and states' sovereign right to decide on access to the national territory, as first set out in the *Abdulaziz* case of 1985 (De Vries & Spijkerboer, 2021, p. 299).[2]

Most people with international protection are third-country nationals, whose right to family reunification in Belgium is based on the transposition of the Family Reunification Directive (2003/86/EC). This Directive explicitly states: 'Measures concerning family reunification should be adopted in conformity with the obligation to protect the family and respect family life enshrined in many instruments of international law', family reunification being a 'necessary way of making family life possible' (Recitals 2 and 4). Although the Directive inaugurates minimal conditions to be implemented by EU Member States, Member States wishing to be less strict have room for manoeuvre (Carlier & Saroléa, 2016).

In view of the special situation of refugees, European legislation and case law of the ECtHR[3] recognise that refugee families' right to respect for family life deserves particular attention. Recital 8 of the Family Reunification Directive states:

> Special attention should be paid to the situation of refugees on account of the reasons which obliged them to flee their country and prevent them from leading a normal family life there. More favourable conditions should therefore be laid down for the exercise of their right to family reunification.

Belgium's interpretation of the Family Reunification Directive led to refugee families having a one-year period after sponsors receive international protection during

2 ECtHR, 28 May 1985, *Abdulaziz, Cabales and Balkandali v. the United Kingdom*, Nos. 9214/80, 9473/81, and 9474/81.

3 ECtHR, 10 July 2014, *Mugenzi v. France*, No. 52701/09; ECtHR, 10 July 2014, *Tanda-Muzinga v. France*, No. 2260/10.

which no socio-economic conditions are imposed (see Section 2.3.1).[4] This period is longer than the minimum of three months imposed by the Directive. Another more lenient interpretation concerns the equation in Belgium of subsidiary protection holders with refugees, whereas the former are excluded from the obligatory scope of the Directive. Nevertheless, other European countries interpret the time frame wherein refugee families must apply even more generously (Declercq, 2021).

Some provisions in the Family Reunification Directive are subject to divergent and often narrow domestic interpretations and practices, creating additional barriers for refugee families when applying for family reunification. In Belgium, this is seen in family members' obligation to apply for reunification at foreign embassies, as explained later. Additional administrative obstructions are the actual operational practices, for example those applied by the Belgian Immigration Office. During interviews, multiple social professionals complained about the office's standard rejection of applications based on missing or non-compliant documents (e.g., a registered rental agreement or a certificate of health insurance) without examining other conditions (like family ties or income). They also referred to the refusal to review the file on missing information, which forces family members to submit a new second or third application. Accordingly, Dawoud (2014, p. 287) states that the rules on family reunification in Belgium are untransparent for sponsors and beneficiaries, which does not improve legal certainty.

In a previous publication (Debruyne, 2022), I asked whether the right to family reunification is 'a Potemkin Village'[5] or an external façade, due to the complexity of the family reunification procedure in everyday practice. The Belgian federal ombudsperson refers to a violation of important ombudsnorms, such as the duty to state reasons, the principle of due diligence, and the passive provision of information (Federale Ombudsman, 2017, pp. 77–78). The Federal Migration Centre 'Myria' and the United Nations High Commissioner for Refugees (UNHCR) have also asked critical questions about obstacles in the family reunification procedure, including high costs, very narrow family definitions, and a lack of sociolegal support and support by knowledgeable lawyers (Myria, 2022; UNHCR, 2019b). These thresholds point to some components of 'the policy assemblage of family reunification'.

This assembled constellation incorporates administrative, legal, political, ideological, and material-physical components. The latter are actually existing borders and 'paper' borders interwoven in the policy assemblage as 'actants': non-human components that possess a form of agency (potential for action) within a network, as described by Latour (1996) and others involved in actor-network and assemblage theory (Anderson et al., 2012; Elder-Vass, 2015; Müller, 2015). These components have a performative effect on the everyday practice of family reunification by inducing obstacles. Or, in assemblage theory terms, new components 'emerge' through the interaction of actors (and actants).

4 Article 10, § 2, paragraph 5 Aliens Act.

5 The term comes from stories of a fake portable village built by Grigory Potemkin, former lover of Empress Catherine II, solely to impress the Empress during her journey to Crimea in 1787.

2.3 Components of the assemblage

This section explores the administrative and legal and then the political and ideological components of the assemblage, looking at how they interweave with physical and paper borders that function as 'actants' in the policy assemblage.

2.3.1 Administrative and legal components

Once again, I am confronted with the absurdity of the family reunification procedure for recognised refugees. An Afghan man would like to start the procedure for his family as soon as possible. For that start-up alone, there are insurmountable problems:

- Problem 1: wife and children do not have passports, and it is – if not impossible – anything but easy to obtain them under the new Taliban regime. But the absence of passports can possibly still be justified before the Belgian Immigration Office, something that takes a lot of time. You must be able to get into the heads of the file handlers who will decide what will or will not be accepted.
- Problem 2: even if they cannot get passports, they must still submit the application to the Belgian embassy in Islamabad, Pakistan, in another country. Apart from the possible dangers for a woman with children on the way and the costs, they must also cross the border with Pakistan without a passport. And this is only about starting the procedure, which must be done within the year after recognition to have a chance at success under flexible conditions. So, time is ticking away.

This testimony by a social worker summarises the administrative and legal complexity of the family reunification procedure. First, the Belgian legislation states that family members of recognised refugees and subsidiarily protected sponsors located abroad may submit their visa application for family reunification with the necessary documents at any Belgian embassy or consulate that can issue long-stay visas. If a person is unable to submit a particular document and has a valid reason for doing so, the embassy can send an incomplete file to the Belgian Immigration Office. This must be raised with the competent diplomatic post (Myria, 2019, p. 17). An exception to the rule of applying at a Belgian embassy exists, and circumstantial arguments on why family members cannot reach the embassy must be formally given to the Belgian Immigration Office.[6]

6 Generally, official documents should be presented, but alternative means of proof exist: if no official documents can be submitted, the Belgian government will consider 'other valid evidence' that can prove the family relationship (Article 12bis §§ 5–6 of the Belgian Aliens Act). This also applies if it is impossible to legalise the documents (following from the preparatory works of Article 12bis § 6 of the Belgian Aliens Act and the circular of 17 June 2009). In such cases, a person has to prove the impossibility – which must be 'real and objective', i.e., involuntary – by any legal means (Omzendbrief van juni 17, 2009 houdende bepaalde verduidelijkingen en wijzigings- en opheffingsbepalingen inzake de gezinshereniging, B.S., 2 July 2009).

Obviously, this obligatory travel to a Belgian embassy or consulate creates dangers for most families, for example at the border areas between Afghanistan and Pakistan. Events such as the Taliban take-over have worsened the situation. Some people cannot get visas to cross the border to Islamabad, also because they do not have a passport; this is particularly the case for women, who cannot receive papers or cross the border without a male family member. Others must pay tremendous amounts of money to obtain the obligatory Pakistani visa. According to the Belgian Office of Foreign Affairs, the border area with Pakistan is extremely dangerous (UNHCR, 2021).

In other words, these legal-administrative requirements in the assemblage of family reunification create large obstacles. Nevertheless, people cross the border multiple times to obtain the necessary documents. One Afghan family with Hazara roots testified how the husband went back and forth over the border to bring the necessary documents to the Belgian embassy, notwithstanding the danger and costs. His wife and children had been granted international protection in Belgium. The mother testified:

R: . . . Then my husband went to embassy himself. Embassy of Belgium not in Afghanistan because there it is broken, everyone is gone. Only Pakistan has and India, but India costs too much money. Pakistan is easy by car, bus, he has been there two, three times, four times.

I: Four times. Back and forth?

R: Back and forth and always with the scared days because of war. Two, three times he had been with Taliban. Taliban does not know he must go abroad. That's why he's always afraid. But anyway, fortunately everything is fine. But we pay a lot, a lot because he has little money.

This also occurs in the border area between Eritrea and Ethiopia (Belloni, 2016), with Eritreans sometimes crossing the border several times. One Eritrean family member stated:

> A lot of people can't go back to Eritrea. It's not possible for people to go back to bring back papers with them. For example, how are you going to pass? You are lucky if you can pass the first time. The second time you can come back to Eritrea. But leaving the second time, that's not possible. That's hard for people. If they catch you, you go to prison.

A recent judgement of the Court of Justice of the European Union (CJEU)[7] changes the obligation to apply for family reunification in person at a competent diplomatic post. It is a good example of the 'emergence and the relations of exteriority' that Savage (2020, p. 321) mentions as one of the characteristics of a policy assemblage. The CJEU states that there should be an exception when people cannot appear in person, especially in dangerous situations that could expose people to

7 CJEU, 18 April 2023, C-1/23, *X and Others*, ECLI:EU:C:2023:296.

inhuman or degrading treatment or even put their lives at risk. This would prevent 'perpetuating the separation of the family', the Court states in its judgement, yet 'without prejudice to the possibility for that Member State to require that those members appear in person at a later stage of the application procedure for family reunification'.[8] After this judgement, the Belgian Immigration Office changed its policy to ensure that family members unable to apply in person could still apply. Although this far from fulfils the demand by Myria and Belgian NGOs to let 'the person of reference' or 'sponsor' apply in Belgium, the change is significant for many families.

There are also difficulties with providing the necessary documents. A migration lawyer illustrated the problem:

> A first difficulty is that you often have to be able to find documents. Family reunification with refugees means that refugees often come from war countries . . . Syria, Afghanistan, Iraq, Somalia . . . these are countries that are not well structured and that hardly have a civil status. If I'm going to say, 'you have to have a marriage or birth certificate', that is a difficult task. First, because they don't exist there. Second, because you also must go get them. Should I say to an Afghan refugee or his family: 'go to Kabul to get that document'?

The administrative components that play a role in the assemblage of family reunification are often connected to the legal requirements of private international law (PIL), which determines how family situations with international components are dealt with in Belgium. PIL regulates, among other things, 'the recognition of foreign documents', a crucial element of which is the verification of the documents' authenticity, formally referred to as legalisation. The refusal of documents is often related to this (Den Haese & Verhellen, 2020).

In addition, time is of the essence during family reunification procedures. People who receive international protection have only one year in which they are exempted from demands related to income, suitable housing, and health insurance.[9] For Eritreans, Afghans, and other groups, it is close to impossible to assemble all necessary documents, obtain an appointment, and arrive at the nearest embassy within one year. As mentioned, incomplete files can be sent to the Belgian Immigration Office, accompanied by an argumentation on why families could not provide all documents in time. However, this option is often not well known and thus rarely used. Even if it is used, Myria (2019) shows that partial files are nevertheless sometimes refused. One policy advisor of an independent government service explained it as follows:

> In the beginning when I worked on the matter, I often noticed that something went wrong with that term of one year, for example. Because it was not yet

8 CJEU, 18 April 2023, C-1/23, *X and Others*, ECLI:EU:C:2023:296, § 60.

9 Article 10 § 2, paragraph 5 Aliens Act.

> so well known to care providers and to people, that submitting an incomplete file is possible. But the problem is, you really must enforce that. So, you must have a good organisation here . . . who really knows about it; okay, I must write to the embassy . . . to enforce that incomplete file. And that in the past it was more insisted on that you must first have your file in order, and then you go to the embassy, so it often went wrong.

In interviews, social professionals referred to the non-transparency and unpredictability in the assessment of foreign documents such as birth and marriage certificates, attributing it to the fact that documents can be formally assessed by different government agencies that act autonomously (Den Haese, 2022; Den Haese & Verhellen, 2020).[10] These various policy levels and administrations are not always aligned, leading to conflicting decisions, legal uncertainty, or even arbitrariness. For example, the Belgian Immigration Office is not bound by the recognition of a foreign registered partnership by the city of Ghent. Or, the embassy can recognise foreign marriage or birth certificates, and the Belgian Immigration Office will follow, but the municipality disagrees and refuses to register those involved. It is worrying that the municipal civil registry sometimes lacks the specialised expertise necessary to make informed decisions on this matter, especially in smaller municipalities (Den Haese & Verhellen, 2020, p. 212).

The complexity increases when marriage certificates are refused, which automatically pushes people into the procedure for sham marriages, sending them through a complicated maze of legal institutions. As one migration lawyer stated:

> It is true that a foreign civil status certificate can be assessed by any Belgian authority. The law says: 'in principle, everything is valid, unless you still have doubts and suspicions of falsity'. If you have a foreign marriage certificate, you can have it legalised, paid for, and presented to the Belgian embassy, then you have submitted your file. Then it may be that the Belgian Immigration Office gives a negative answer because they suspect that this is a marriage of convenience or have a suspicion that that marriage certificate is not genuine. Then you can appeal against that decision, but that is always inadvisable for two reasons. First, if your partner is still abroad, that is the lowest priority at the Council for Alien Law Litigation (CALL). That means you must wait three to four years before you get a decision. Second, the CALL says: 'it is a civil status certificate, I am not competent. The Belgian Immigration Office has its own legal authority to decide on this'.

Only the family court can ultimately judge the validity of the (marriage) document.

10 Article 27 Code of PIL.

2.3.2 Political and ideological components

What follows describes the political and ideological components of the assemblage of family reunification. It starts with how politically and ideologically steered legal transformations play a role in this assemblage. The Belgian Aliens Act of 15 December 1980 enshrines four different procedures of family reunification that lead to a set of differentiated rights, or 'civic stratification' (Morris, 2003). Article 40ter of the Belgian Aliens Act lists the legal arrangements for family reunification with Belgian citizens who have not made use of their freedom of movement ('static' Belgians), Article 40bis for mobile EU citizens, and Article 10 and 10bis for third-country nationals (those with permanent residence and temporary residence, respectively).

Definitions of which members belong to 'the family' and thus have the right to be reunited differ according to residence status. These different legal definitions of a 'family unit' often do not do justice to family realities (Saroléa & Merla, 2021), certainly not for transnational families who temporarily or permanently live apart but have cultivated family relationships across borders (Bryceson & Vuorela, 2002). The scheme for family reunification with sponsors who received international protection has the most restrictive definition of family, including parents of unaccompanied minors, the spouse or legal partner, and minor children. Other family members can request humanitarian visas (as minor siblings of unaccompanied minor sponsors often do).

The family reunification policy was tightened in 2011, with new socio-economic and age thresholds for family reunification with third-country nationals and Belgians who did not make use of their freedom of movement. Conditions such as 'sufficient housing', stable and sufficient resources, and health insurance were introduced. The sponsor must have a 'stable', 'regular', and 'sufficient' income, which prevents precarious migrant families from settling in Belgium (Saroléa, 2012). As mentioned, people with refugee or subsidiary protection status are exempted from these conditions for one year after receiving their status. These legislative changes correspond to the European trend to adopt more restrictive legislation with increasing conditionalities at the crossroads of class and race (Block, 2015; Bonjour & de Hart, 2013) that play into definitions of 'undesirable' family migrants.

The 2011 changes in the law were fundamental. Newly installed thresholds targeted certain ethno-cultural groups, with Turks and Moroccans who had acquired the Belgian nationality explicitly mentioned in the parliamentary debate (Saroléa, 2012). Civil society organisations unsuccessfully contested the amendments before the Constitutional Court (Carlier & Saroléa, 2016; Dawoud, 2014, p. 286; see also Corradi & Desmet, this volume). Next, the period during which conditions for family reunification should continue to be fulfilled was extended from three to five years for family members of Belgian nationals and EU citizens (in 2013) (European Migration Network (EMN), 2017), and family members of third-country nationals (in 2016). The Belgian Immigration Office's 'investigation period' for family reunification with third-country nationals was also extended, from six to nine months.

The most recent attempt to implement even stricter requirements for family reunification with third-country nationals is the proposition to shorten the exemption period for holders of international protection from one year to three months, equal to the minimum period determined by the Family Reunification Directive for refugees. However, the European Commission also states:

> A number of Member States do not apply the optional restrictions or are more flexible because of the particularly unfortunate situation of refugees and the difficulties they often encounter when applying for family reunification. The Commission considers this practice to be appropriate.[11]

In addition, the European Commission has specified the modalities to accompany the introduction of such a deadline. It encourages Member States that apply a time limit to 'allow the sponsor to submit the application on the territory of the Member State in order to ensure the effectiveness of the right to family reunification'. Belgian legislation currently does not allow this.

Moreover, proposals were made to increase 'the minimal reference amount' in the requirement to prove 'stable, regular and adequate resources', also for those having received international protection, if demands for family reunification are made after the one-year exemption period. A range of institutions – Myria and UNHCR (UNHCR, 2019a; Myria & UNHCR, 2018), Caritas Belgium, and Refugee Action Flanders (Vluchtelingenwerk Vlaanderen) – have expressed concern about these political proposals. This shows the dominant ideology in action, with politically fabricated increasing conditionality at work.

To understand the assemblage of family reunification processes, it is important to realise that the performance of politics is not limited to politicians alone. Civil administrations also play a role. Immigration officers at the Belgian Immigration Office interpret the law based on shared experiential knowledge 'about the law', that is 'accepted, until it will no longer be accepted' (Mascia, 2020, p. 12). As such, according to Mascia (2020), they try to decrease the chances of (successful) appeals against their refusals. In addition, a recent report of CapGemini-Invent (2022, p. 95) states:

> The Belgian Immigration Office often decides in difficult cases based on internal notes, guidelines, etc. Such internal notes and guidelines are regularly updated and communicated. . . . However, these are not made available to the wider public, so there is little transparency. It also ensures that immigration law becomes even more complicated and that the provision of advice and assistance to the citizen/migrant has become a matter for experts.

11 European Commission, Communication from the Commission to the Council and the European Parliament. Guidelines for the implementation of Directive 2003/86/EC on the right to family reunification, 3 April 2014, COM (2014) 210 final.

To summarise, the policy assemblage of family reunification is characterised by great complexity and contingency. Although it consists of a range of heterogenous components, when these interact, a power structure emerges that widens the gap between rights on paper and their accessibility in everyday practice.

3. Welfare bricolage with transnational families

It is a great challenge for social professionals to deal with the policy assemblage of family reunification for persons that have received international protection (Debruyne et al., 2002). They lack specific scripts or ready-made manuals, which forces them to act as 'bricoleurs' in their attempts to transform rights on paper into rights in practice.

3.1 What is bricolage?

Phillimore et al. (2016) refer to 'welfare bricolage' to describe interventions by social professionals (and citizens) in a superdiverse environment; they combine a wide array of instruments as well as different sets of knowledge(s) to increase well-being. Bricoleurs wish to address social needs using localised and sometimes tacit knowledge and their motivation. They lean on expertise, personal resources, and their cleverness in assembling and deploying resources. Although this sort of tacit knowledge and situated practice sound like 'powerlessness', some social professionals and organisations deploy them in a wider political strategy. In the case of family reunification, formal and informal social professionals' practices of bricolage at multiple scales 'can be understood as tactics of resistance but not of a resistance out of choice but out of necessity' (Phillimore et al., 2016, p. 17).

Why are social workers forced to act as transnational 'bricoleurs'? Apart from the legal family reunification procedure, there is no operational framework or real mandate in Belgium to deal with the needs of refugees in the process, besides support provided by UNHCR and its partner Myria. A social worker who assists unaccompanied minors described the political and ideological disinterest as follows:

> No, there is also no support for family reunification in the public opinion, so you must act and intervene a bit 'against the current'. Because there is no policy support for that. It's not that that's politically marketable either. Even more, support services that were there have also been phased out. . . . We just must start, I think, from the principle 'it's young people's right, so we have to do that'.

3.2 Practising bricolage in family reunification

The interviews with social professionals demonstrated a practice of 'welfare bricolage' that included establishing relations of trust with families; providing sociolegal support, with transnational dimensions if required; providing financial back-up and material aid at crucial moments; and taking up their political mission. These four components are discussed later. The need for (transnational) pedagogical support to address the long-term separation also emerged, but this is beyond the scope of this chapter (see Debruyne et al., 2002).

First, although establishing relations of trust is important for all social professionals dealing with family reunification, the research demonstrated that informal social professionals have more time and space to work on this. One volunteer at a solidarity citizen initiative explained his strategies:

> I know the father because he has been in the local reception initiative in X, so you then experience the period of asylum application. You know each other. So, there will be a certain bond of trust. When that man is granted international protection, then it's like 'and now you have to think about family reunification for the children'.

However, my research also indicated tensions between informal and formal social professionals. Some volunteers explained how they, contrary to formal social workers, contacted embassies (in Belgium and abroad) directly to obtain the right documents within a reasonable amount of time. They could intervene differently than their paid counterparts, according to them because the latter 'fall short', as they have limited discretionary space. A volunteer at a solidarity citizen initiative gave another example:

> I sent him to the Red Cross. And I have a file of the treatment in the Red Cross because it is not optimal. So, I had to intervene several times because the file just didn't advance. Nothing was done with it. Questions like 'what is the status of the file?', 'Do we have to hand things in, supplement them?' and so on.

These relations of trust between social professionals and refugee family members are often underestimated, but their impact on sociolegal support is fundamental. They directly affect the amount of information available about the situation and the context. The same volunteer continued:

> When the procedure takes so long, you see the person is worrying. Well, and then you start talking, 'Where and how does your family live? Are you in touch?' Yes, it turned out that he also had to send money because the children abroad had to go to school. They were in an illegal situation in Tanzania at the time. Then you learn all that. You then hear about the problems with the application of the partner of course because there is a relationship of trust. You must be able to tell someone, right?

Second, refugee families cannot deal with the complex 'assemblage of family reunification' without sociolegal and administrative support. A social worker explained:

> Yes, but . . . it's a bit strange to say because family reunification is primarily a right. So, the first thing we already do is, for example, point out in the cover

> letter that that is a right and then all the legal [stuff], where our lawyer helps us very hard. I think by listing it from, look it is a right and you can't really refuse it, because you must consider this and this jurisprudence? We write cover letters, sometimes six to seven pages long, with a lot of legal arguments. We will also read country information, for example about Eritrea . . . then we put it in there. . . . And the more you put in, the less easy it is for them to refuse.

Some formal social workers provide support outside their working hours. One social worker for unaccompanied minors testified:

> There are also guardians who either remain involved within their hours of their guidance or continue the support after their formal time of guidance. But apart from those kinds of guardians, there are mainly youth workers that support unaccompanied minors. Generally, there is a lack of support. . . . While some problems need to be tackled right away, so you don't end up in other future interventions.

Sociolegal support is unavoidably also 'transnational' in the case of family reunification. Social work practitioners that deal with the assemblage of family reunification must have a multi-scalar 'reach'. They are required to intervene across borders by, for example, 'chasing' embassies or private visa agencies (Myria, 2022). Two guardians of unaccompanied minors talked extensively about the transnational formal and informal networks they had built throughout the years. While one had established a legal network in countries like Greece and Italy, the other used informal networks of family contacts he had established in Afghanistan, Pakistan, Eritrea, and Ethiopia. As he put it: 'I just call families that I met from dealing with unaccompanied minors and ask them if they can arrange things with other families, go to the embassy or arrange documents that I need'.

These social work practices are consistent with pleas for 'transnational social work' (Schrooten, 2021), described by Negi and Furman (2010, p. 8) as 'an emerging field of practice that (a) is designed to serve transnational populations; (b) operates across nation-state boundaries, whether physically or through new technologies; and (c) is informed by and addresses complex transnational problems and dilemmas'.

Third, financial support at crucial moments throughout the process is important for many families. Family reunification comes with high costs: visas (€180/person), the translation and legalisation of documents (€20/document), bureaucratic processing costs by embassies or private visa offices, travel costs, and sometimes DNA tests, medical tests, doctors' honoraria, and humanitarian visas for other family members (€358/person). Volunteers provide most of this financial support. As one informal social professional told me about a financial donation: 'That's where we intervened. . . . We borrowed but we also gave a big gift, and it was necessary. . . . I see that this occurs in several of the volunteer associations. Another guardian uses her own network to find housing and gives (informal) loans to unaccompanied minors for plane tickets.'

A fourth and last element of this welfare bricolage is crucial to answering the question, 'What is to be done?' This is the political task of social workers (Ferguson, 2009; Gray & Webb, 2009). As illustrated, the assemblage of family reunification contains a heterogenous set of administrative, legal, political, and ideological components. But these work in strategic ways that have a political effect that steers refugee families in particular directions (Savage, 2020, p. 328; Ureta, 2015). Consequently, a political strategy surpasses interpretations of 'bricolage' as a set of creative tactics.

Paul Garrett (2021) refers to the need for 'dissenting social work'. This political task of social work goes beyond (but remains connected with) the elements of building relations of trust, providing sociolegal support and financial and material aid, and taking up a pedagogical task. My research exposed the political work organisations do, although most happens under the radar through lobbying. For example, the CAW Group, a network of local welfare organisations, sent a 'Letter to the State Secretary' on 30 May 2022 with a range of demands concerning the procedure of family reunification. They also politicised the matter more publicly, writing an op-ed on how the federal government impedes integration because of the complex procedure of family reunification (Bell, 2022). Additionally, the director of Refugee Action Flanders demanded that the right to family reunification be respected (Claus, 2022).

Organisations also take other steps, such as applying pressure through the ombudsperson. An NGO frontline worker gave the following example:

> The first step we take is to negotiate with the Belgian Immigration Office. And if they still do not give in then . . . we go to the Ombudsman. And appeal or court, that is really but the very last option, . . . that often takes a very long time, that costs a lot of money and you do not know at the end whether you will be right, so it is sometimes more interesting to just submit a new application. . . . It's not because the Belgian Immigration Office says no that they're right, right? I think if they are not right, then we will continue until we are right. And that works because we have had successes with the Ombudsman before.

But, as engaged as formal and informal social professionals are, the multi-scalar complexity of 'welfare bricolage' intervening in the assemblage of family reunification also leads to powerlessness. One social worker of a social organisation providing sociolegal support stated:

> Often, we cannot strengthen the client to take matters into their own hands because it is too unclear even for all of us. There are also no contact persons at the Belgian Immigration Office who are always approachable for care providers. And if you already ask a question, you often get the answer that a file must first be submitted before a substantive question can be answered, a

submission that often requires dangerous journeys and thousands of euros. In this way, we simply take over the powerlessness of the client, and the responsibility for whether a procedure succeeds lies entirely with a care provider, who also gets stuck.

4. Conclusion

Family reunification challenges social professionals and refugee families to the utmost extent. Foremost because the complex assemblage of family reunification produces a range of obstacles. On the level of refugee families this often leads to long-term separation in space and time. On the level of social professionals, family reunification challenges the traditional repertoire of social workers. The complexity of the everyday policy practices of family reunification pushes them to experiment and improvise; to do 'bricolage' to 'smoothen the shocks' and minimise the gap between rights on paper and rights in practice.

This chapter illustrates the importance of skilful social professionals that can practise 'welfare bricolage' in the context of family reunification. Although such practices are driven by necessity, they cannot be reduced to tactical practices in a context of powerlessness. Some organisations and social professionals also engage in 'politics', confirming the need for 'dissenting social work' that challenges systemic power that circulates in the assemblage of family reunification. By looking through the lenses of 'assemblage' and 'bricolage', the chapter offers a perspective beyond institutionalist beliefs and discourses about transparent and self-evident procedures. The wide gap between rights on paper and rights in practice is currently often only surmounted when formal and informal social workers and other social professionals deal with the transnational challenges and complexity that emerge in actual practices of family reunification.

References

Ambrosini, M. (2015). Parenting from a distance and processes of family reunification: Research on the Italian case. *Ethnicities, 15*(3), 440–459. https://doi.org/10.1177/1468796814547059

Anderson, B., Kearnes, M., McFarlane, C., & Swanton, D. (2012). On assemblages and geography. *Dialogues in Human Geography, 2*(2), 171–189. https://doi.org/10.1177/2043820612449261

Anderson, B., & McFarlane, C. (2011). Assemblage and geography. *Area, 43*(2), 124–127. https://doi.org/10.1111/j.1475-4762.2011.01004.x

Bankston, S. (2017). *Deleuze and Becoming*. Bloomsbury Publishing. https://doi.org/10.5040/9781474233583

Bartley, A., Beddoe, L., Fouché, C., & Harington, P. (2012). Transnational social workers: Making the profession a transnational professional space. *International Journal of Population Research, 2012*, 1–11. https://doi.org/10.1155/2012/527510

Bell, C. (2022). De overheid bemoeilijkt de integratie van nieuwkomers die bescherming krijgen in ons land. *Knack*. www.knack.be/nieuws/de-overheid-bemoeilijkt-de-integratie-van-nieuwkomers-die-bescherming-krijgen-in-ons-land/

Belloni, M. (2016). "My uncle cannot say 'no' if I reach Libya": Unpacking the social dynamics of border-crossing among Eritreans heading to Europe. *Human Geography, 9*(2), 47–56. https://doi.org/10.1177/194277861600900205

Biehl, J., & Locke, P. (2010). Deleuze and the anthropology of becoming. *Current Anthropology*, *51*(3), 317–351. https://doi.org/10.1086/651466
Block, L. (2015). Regulating membership: Explaining restriction and stratification of family migration in Europe. *Journal of Family*, *36*(11), 1433–1452. https://doi.org/10.1177/0192513X14557493
Boccagni, P., Righard, E., & Bolzman, C. (2015). Mapping transnationalism: Transnational social work with migrants: Introduction. *Transnational Social Review*, *5*(3), 312–319. https://doi.org/10.1080/21931674.2015.1101243
Bonjour, S., & de Hart, B. (2013). A proper wife, a proper marriage: Constructions of "us" and "them" in Dutch family migration policy. *European Journal of Women's Studies*, *20*(1), 61–76. https://doi.org/10.1177/1350506812456459
Bryceson, D. F., & Vuorela, U. (2002). Transnational Families in the Twenty-First Century. In D. F. Bryceson & U. Vuorela (Eds.), *The Transnational Family: New European Frontiers and Global Networks*. Berg.
Burchill, R. (2003). The right to live wherever you want? The right to family life following the UN Human Rights Committee's decision in Winata. *Netherlands Quarterly of Human Rights*, *21*(2), 225–245. http://doi.org/10.1177/016934410302100204
CapGemini-Invent. (2022). *Audit van de asiel- en migratiediensten voor rekening van de FOD Binnenlandse Zaken*. CapGemini-Invent.
Carlier, J. Y., & Saroléa, S. (2016). *Droit des étrangers*. Larcier.
Claus, T. (2022, June 20). Iedereen verdient het om zijn familie te kunnen zien. *Knack.Be*. www.knack.be/nieuws/iedereen-verdient-het-om-zijn-familie-te-kunnen-zien/
Dawoud, S. (2014). Gezinshereniging in België: Kan men het bos nog door de bomen zien? *Tijdschrift voor Vreemdelingenrecht*, *3*, 286–320.
Debruyne, P. (2022, January 12). Is het recht op gezinshereniging een Potemkin-dorp? "Niemand is gebaat bij gezinnen die aan hun lot worden overgelaten". *MO Magazine*. www.mo.be/opinie/niemand-gebaat-bij-gezinnen-die-aan-hun-lot-worden-overgelaten
Debruyne, P., Van Acker, K., Geldof, D., & Schrooten, M. (2002). Reassembling Social Work Within Transnational Dynamics of Family Reunification: The Case of Refugees in Belgium. In E. Gómez-Ciriano, E. J. Cabiati, & S. Dedotsi (Eds.), *Migration and Social Work: Approaches, Visions and Challenges*. Policy Press.
Declercq, A. (2021). De termijn van vrijstelling van de materiële voorwaarden bij gezinshereniging met begunstigden van internationale bescherming: Onvoldoende waarborgen voor een effectieve vrijstelling. *Tijdschrift voor Vreemdelingenrecht*, *2021*(2), 131–153.
Deleuze, G., & Guattari, F. (1987). *A Thousand Plateaus* (B. Massumi, Trans.). University of Minnesota Press.
Den Haese, S. (2022). Recognition of a status acquired abroad: Belgium. *Cuadernos Derecho Transnacional*, *14*, 1111.
Den Haese, S., & Verhellen, J. (2020). Foreign birth and marriage documents: The voice of Belgian and Dutch public servants. *Nederlands Internationaal Privaatrecht*, *2*, 195–215.
de Vries, K., & Spijkerboer, T. (2021). Race and the regulation of international migration: The ongoing impact of colonialism in the case law of the European Court of Human Rights. *Netherlands Quarterly of Human Rights*, *39*(4), 291–307. https://doi.org/10.1177/09240519211053932
Elder-Vass, D. (2015). Disassembling actor-network theory. *Philosophy of the Social Sciences*, *45*(1), 100–121. https://doi.org/10.1177/0048393114525858
European Migration Network. (2017). *Family reunification with third country national sponsors in Belgium*. https://emnbelgium.be/sites/default/files/publications/Final%20BE%20report%20on%20family%20reunification%20of%20TCN_%20July%202017.pdf
Federale Ombudsman. (2017). *Jaarverslag 2017*. www.federalombudsman.be/sites/default/files/2021-10/jaarverslag_2017_-_rapport_annuel_2017.pdf
Ferguson, I. (2009). Where's the beef? A response to Gray and Webb's "The return of the political in social work". *International Journal of Social Welfare*, *18*(2), 213–217. https://doi.org/10.1111/j.1468-2397.2009.00648.x

Garrett, P. M. (2021). "A world to win": In defence of (dissenting) social work – a response to Chris Maylea. *The British Journal of Social Work*, *51*(4), 1131–1149. https://doi.org/10.1093/bjsw/bcab009
Ghoddousi, P., & Page, S. (2020). Using ethnography and assemblage theory in political geography. *Geography Compass*, *14*(10), e12533. https://doi.org/10.1111/gec3.12533
Gray, M., & Webb, S. A. (2009). The return of the political in social work. *International Journal of Social Welfare*, *18*(1), 111–115. https://doi.org/10.1111/j.1468-2397.2008.00626.x
Latour, B. (1996). On actor-network theory: A few clarifications. *Soziale Welt*, 369–381. www.jstor.org/stable/40878163
Mascia, C. (2020). How bureaucracies shape access to rights: The implementation of family reunification in Belgium. *Journal of Ethnic and Migration Studies*, *47*(9), 2127–2143. https://doi.org/10.1080/1369183X.2020.1726734
McCann, E., & Ward, K. (2012). Policy assemblages, mobilities and mutations: Toward a multidisciplinary conversation. *Political Studies Review*, *10*(3), 325–332. https://doi.org/10.1111/j.1478-9302.2012.00276.x
Morris, L. (2003). Managing contradiction: Civic stratification and migrants' rights. *International Migration Review*, *37*(1), 74–100. https://doi.org/10.1111/j.1747-7379.2003.tb00130.x
Müller, M. (2015). Assemblages and actor-networks: Rethinking socio-material power, politics and space. *Geography Compass*, *9*(1), 27–41. https://doi.org/10.1111/gec3.12192
Myria. (2019). *Hoorzitting over wetsvoorstel 574 Gezinshereniging. Kamercommissie Binnenlandse Zaken*. www.myria.be/files/Myria_Kamercommissie_Binnenlandse_Zaken_GezinshereningingDEF_(1).pdf
Myria. (2022, June 21). *Advies: Wettelijke omkadering van het recht op een gezinsleven voor ouders van een minderjarige derdelander met verblijfsrecht*. www.myria.be/nl/publicaties/advies-een-wettelijke-omkadering-van-het-recht-op-een-gezinsleven-voor-ouders-van-een-minderjarige-derdelander-met-verblijfsrecht
Myria & United Nations High Commissioner for Refugees. (2018, June). *Gezinshereniging van begunstigden van internationale bescherming in België. Vaststellingen en aanbevelingen*, www.myria.be/nl/publicaties/gezinshereniging-van-begunstigden-van-internationale-bescherming-in-belgie
Negi, N. J., & Furman, R. (Eds.). (2010). *Transnational Social Work Practice*. Columbia University Press. https://doi.org/10.7312/negi14448
Phillimore, J., Bradby, H., Brand, T., Padilla, B., & Pemberton, S. (2021). *Exploring Welfare Bricolage in Europe's Superdiverse Neighbourhoods*. Routledge. https://doi.org/10.4324/9781003111504
Phillimore, J., Humphris, R., Klass, F., & Knecht, M. (2016). *Bricolage: Potential as a conceptual tool for understanding access to welfare in superdiverse neighbourhoods* (IRiS Working Paper Series No. 14). Institute for Research into Superdiversity.
Rabinow, P. (2014). Assembling Untimeliness: Permanently and Resistively. In J. Faubion (Ed.), *Foucault Now: Current Perspectives in Foucault Studies* (pp. 203–224). Polity Press.
Rousseau, C., Rufagari, M.-C., Bagilishya, D., & Mesham, T. (2004). Remaking family life: Strategies for re-establishing continuity among Congolese refugees during the family reunification process. *Social Science and Medicine*, *59*, 1095–1108. https://doi.org/10.1016/j.socscimed.2003.12.011
Saroléa, S. (2012). Le regroupement familial suite à la réforme de 2011. In S. Bodart (Ed.), *Droit des étrangers* (pp. 111–142). Bruyant.
Saroléa, S., & Merla, L. (2021). Migrantes et sédentaires: Des familles ontologiquement différentes? In L. Merla, S. Saroléa, & B. Schoumaker (Eds.), *Composer avec les normes. Trajectoires de vie et agentivité de migrants face au cadre légal* (pp. 259–291). Academia L'Harmattan.
Savage, G. C. (2018). Policy assemblages and human devices: A reflection on "assembling policy". *Discourse: Studies in the Cultural Politics of Education*, *39*(2), 309–321. https://doi.org/10.1080/01596306.2017.1389431

Savage, G. C. (2020). What is policy assemblage? *Territory, Politics, Governance*, *8*(3), 319–335. https://doi.org/10.1080/21622671.2018.1559760

Schrooten, M. (2021). Transnational social work: Challenging and crossing borders and boundaries. *Journal of Social Work*, *21*(5), 1163–1181. https://doi.org/10.1177/1468017320949389

Schrooten, M., & Raeymaeckers, P. (2023). Exploring welfare bricolage in Europe's super-diverse neighbourhoods. *European Journal of Social Work*, *26*(3), 602–604. https://doi.org/10.1080/13691457.2023.2178693

United Nations High Commissioner for Refugees. (2019a). *Advies betreffende wetsvoorstel n° 55 0574/001 tot wijziging van de wet van 15 december 1980 betreffende de toegang tot het grondgebied, het verblijf, de vestiging en de verwijdering van vreemdelingen wat de reglementering omtrent de gezinshereniging betreft*. https://www.unhcr.org/be/wp-content/uploads/sites/46/2019/12/UNHCR-Advies-wetsvoorstel-gezinshereniging-December-2019.pdf

United Nations High Commissioner for Refugees. (2019b). *Accompagnement juridique des demandeurs de protection internationale en Belgique*. www.unhcr.org/be/wp-content/uploads/sites/46/2019/10/UNHCR-Accompagnement-juridique-de-demandeurs-de-protection-internationale-en-Belgique-Septembre-2019.pdf

United Nations High Commissioner for Refugees. (2021). *Afghanen worstelen om veiligheid te zoeken, grenzen blijven gesloten voor de meesten*. www.unhcr.org/nl/2021/12/afghanen-worstelen-veiligheid-grenzen-blijven-gesloten/

Ureta, S. (2015). *Assembling Policy: Transantiago, Human Devices, and the Dream of a World Class Society*. MIT Press.

18 A multi-perspectivist analysis of a lived family reunification experience

At the junction of co-creative research and autoethnography

Giselle Corradi and Ellen Desmet

1. Introduction

This chapter offers an 'insider's' and 'outsider's' analysis of a fundamental and sudden legislative change in Belgium in 2011 that immediately prohibited both Belgians who had not exercised their free movement rights ('static' Belgians) and third-country nationals from being reunited with their dependent ascendants. The chapter is co-authored by a Belgian national who went through a long, expensive and emotionally exhausting process of family reunification with her Argentinean mother and who is a legal anthropologist with expertise in human rights, and a migration law scholar with expertise in legal anthropology.

The chapter starts with a description of the changes that were introduced in 2011 into the legal framework applicable to Belgian nationals who wished to pursue family reunification with an ascendant. Subsequently, it portrays how these legislative changes translated into the lived experience of family reunification of one of the authors. This chapter thus adopts a particular actor-oriented approach by zooming in on one specific person – in line with the observation that 'ordinary people' are often missing from socio-legal studies on transnational legal processes (de Hart et al., 2013).

On this basis, the next section combines expert knowledge from the legal and social sciences with experiential knowledge on family reunification at various levels of analysis. First, empirically, it uncovers some of the emotional and material effects produced by the law reform and identifies some key factors leading to the disempowerment of applicants. Second, at the theoretical level, it reflects on how intersectionality and the highly asymmetrical power relations between migration authorities and applicants play out in relation to the 'agency' of the latter. And third, methodologically, it reflects on how co-creation and autoethnography shaped the content and insights presented. The chapter is based on testimonial accounts (written in the first person) and excerpts of an interview conducted between both authors.

DOI: 10.4324/9781003503217-23

2. The law reform of 2011

The Belgian Aliens Act of 1980 provided that the lenient rules on family reunification for Union citizens and 'mobile' Belgians (who had made use of their free movement rights) were also applicable to static Belgians.[1] The law of 8 July 2011 tightened the rules for family reunification with static Belgians as well as third-country nationals. During the parliamentary debate, the stricter rules for Belgian sponsors were justified because '[m]ost cases of family reunification concern Belgians who were born in our country from migrants, or who became Belgian thanks to the *snel-Belg-wet*'. The *snel-Belg-wet* was a law of 2000 which made the acquisition of Belgian nationality faster and more flexible, hence its nickname ('fast-Belgian-act').[2] The 2011 legislative change also revealed a particular ethno-cultural bias, as evident from another intervention during the parliamentary discussion: '70 per cent of people who engage in family reunification are people who ethno-culturally belong to the Moroccan or Turkish community, but who have become Belgian through acquisition of nationality'.[3]

The equivalence of static Belgians with mobile Belgians and Union citizens in the realm of family reunification was put to an end in two major respects. First, socio-economic conditions were imposed on family reunification with static Belgians (as well as with third-country nationals). Since then, these sponsors have to prove that they have 'adequate housing', health insurance that also covers the family member as well as stable, regular and sufficient means of subsistence. Second, and crucial in the context of this chapter, the demarcation of family members entitled to family reunification was made more restrictive. As such, dependent ascendants (parents and grandparents) of adult static Belgians were excluded from the right to family reunification. The 2011 law thus introduced what has been labelled in the literature a 'reverse discrimination', in that Belgians were treated less beneficial than citizens from another EU Member State living in Belgium (Dawoud, 2014).

Various appeals for annulment of provisions of the 2011 law were submitted to the Constitutional Court. In 2013, the Court held that there was no discrimination between static Belgians and Union citizens: the right to family reunification of Union citizens aims to enable one of the fundamental objectives of the European Union, namely, free movement between EU Member States. The right to family reunification of static Belgians is governed by national law. According to the Court, the difference in treatment is justified because of the objective 'to control the migratory flows' created by family reunification, referring to the impact of the *snel-Belg-wet* mentioned earlier.[4]

The difference between Belgian minors, whose non-Belgian parents still have a right to family reunification, on the one hand, and Belgian adults, whose

1 See also Groenendijk (this volume).

2 In 2012, the options for obtaining Belgian nationality were tightened again.

3 *Parl. St.*, Chamber, 2010–2011, DOC 53-0443/018, p. 195.

4 Constitutional Court, 26 September 2013, No. 121/12, B.52.1, B.52.2; Constitutional Court, 26 September 2013, No. 123/12, B.6.1, B.6.2.

ascendants are now excluded, on the other, did not constitute a problem in the view of the Court. The right to family reunification of parents of Belgian minors takes into account the special relationship of dependency between young children and their parents. Yet, the Court held, the fact that a Belgian adult lives separately from their parents is usually the consequence of their personal choice. Moreover, Belgian adults have been able to build an affective network in Belgium. Whereas these relationships admittedly cannot be put on a par with the kinship ties with parents and grandparents, the Court considers it a fact that the permanent presence in Belgium of their third-country national parents is less necessary for the integration of Belgian adults than it is for minors. Moreover, these ascendants can apply for a residence right based on the general rules of the 1980 Belgian Aliens Act. The Court thus concluded that

> there is no disproportionate interference with the principle of equality and non-discrimination or with the right to the protection of family life in that the parents of a Belgian adult cannot be granted a residence permit for the purposes of family reunification.[5]

Another relevant issue in the framework of this chapter is that the law of 8 July 2011 did not include any transitional provisions. Consequently, when the law entered into force on 22 September 2011, it was immediately applicable on the more than 3000 family reunification files which were pending with the Belgian Immigration Office on that date. According to the federal ombudsman, the application of the new law on these files led to an unequal treatment among citizens which was 'not based on an objective criterion, but on coincidence, namely the moment at which the Immigration Office makes its decision, before or after 22 September 2011' (Federale Ombudsman, 2012, p. 135). Furthermore, the lack of transitional measures violated legal certainty and the legitimate expectation of applicants for family reunification that their file will be processed on the basis of the conditions in force at the time of filing the application. Therefore, in December 2011, the ombudsman recommended to the Chamber of Representatives to amend the Belgian Aliens Act again, by inserting transitional measures for all applications submitted before 22 September 2011 in which no final decision had been taken by this date (Federale Ombudsman, 2011, p. 5). This recommendation was not followed. In 2013, the Constitutional Court held that the immediate application of the 2011 law was not without reasonable justification, because foreigners applying for a residence right 'should bear in mind that a State's immigration laws may be amended for reasons of public interest'.[6]

5 Constitutional Court, 26 September 2013, No. 121/12, B.54.2; Constitutional Court, 26 September 2013, No. 123/12, B.7.3.

6 Constitutional Court, 26 September 2013, No. 121/12, B.66; Constitutional Court, 26 September 2013, No. 123/12, B.3.3.

The next section delves on how the previously sketched legislative reform translated into the lived experience of family reunification of one of the authors. The section offers a testimonial account, and for that reason, it switches to the first person.

3. A lived experience of family reunification in the midst of a sudden curtailment of family rights

I moved from Argentina to Belgium twenty years ago. At that time, I was in my early twenties, I was studying law in Buenos Aires and I had a good job. But then I met the love of my life and he happened to be Belgian and live on the other side of the world. After sustaining a long-distance relationship for over two years, we decided to get married and build our lives in Belgium. This was the year 2002. At that time, migration seemed to be less of a sensitive issue in Belgium than now, and as a matter of fact, my entire experience as a third-country national settling in Belgium was very positive. I remember arriving at the passport control counter at the airport and the migration officer asking me, 'Where is your ticket to travel back to Argentina?' And I replied unconcerned, 'I do not have any because I came here to get married'. And the officer answered 'Ok, that is all good, but you have to make sure that you get married within three months'. I had heard stories of couples who had been interviewed in order to verify the truthfulness of their relationship in the framework of the fight against sham relations. That never happened to us. I learnt Dutch, I finished my university studies in Ghent and I could insert myself socially and in the labour market without major difficulties.

Ten years later, in 2011, my mother's health and economic situation deteriorated, and I wanted to be able to provide her the assistance that she needed. Therefore, we initiated a procedure for family reunification. The decision to move from Argentina to Belgium was difficult for her. At sixty, leaving her roots behind was painful. But at the same time, our bonds were strong and I was planning to start a family. This gave us the energy that was necessary to embark into the – until then unknown – mess of arranging an international relocation for a person of that age.

Upon my mother's arrival in Belgium, we went to the municipal migration office to present all the paperwork that was required. Everything was in order, and we were instructed to wait as it would take about three months for the authorities to process the file. I was quite relaxed about the procedure. I saw it as a formality, and I was convinced that obtaining a residence permit for my mother would not be an issue. After all, we had complied with all the requirements. There was no reason why there should be a problem. In addition, I felt entitled to a life close to my mother. She needed my support, and I had the capacity and desire to help her. I was planning to have a child, and I wanted her to be nearby so that she could also help me. I saw no good reason why public authorities would consider it necessary to deny us this possibility.

While we were waiting for my mother's file to be processed, the aforementioned law reform took place. I recall my colleagues approaching me to express their concerns on how this would affect us. But I believed that the new law would not apply to us. Our file had been submitted before the introduction of the legislative changes, and I took for granted that the rule of law and the concomitant principle of legal certainty would apply in a 'first-world country' as Belgium.

It was to our dismay that we received a negative answer to my mother's application on the basis of the new law. I could barely believe that this was possible. And I would not accept it. So, we initiated legal proceedings to appeal. This took about five years, during which my mother was prohibited from leaving the Belgian territory. She was no longer accepted in the Dutch classes, and it became a nightmare to find health insurance services that would be willing to provide her coverage. In the meantime, my mother had to undergo a major surgery that required several months of revalidation. While she was still revalidating, we got the news that the appeal had not been successful and she received the order to leave the country within thirty days. The Immigration Office prolonged this period once, based on medical attests that we presented stating that my mother's health did not allow her to undergo a transatlantic flight, but they refused to extend more. Therefore, one early morning at 5.30 am, the police came to our house unannounced looking for my mother, while waking up my scared two-year-old child. My mother was not home and the police said that they would come back for her a week later. We quickly bought a business class ticket for her to travel to Argentina as comfortably as possible.

When I think about it, I admire how we managed to arrange and to pay for all the issues that related to my mother's resettling in Argentina. Amongst others, we had to find a furnished and equipped place to rent on a very short notice, arrange private medical insurance and get psychological support to deal with the trauma of this experience. Moreover, I had to make sure that the police believed that my mother had actually returned to Argentina. The kind of proof that I had to produce to convince the officer remained entirely within his discretion. There were no guidelines, let alone legal provisions, for me to rely upon. If unconvinced, the immigration authorities could just decide to give my mother an entry ban, which would prevent her from entering the territory of the European Union for a number of years, even to visit us as a tourist. So I had to be very careful not to upset the officer. I asked him what we needed to do, and just right then and there, out of the blue, he said: 'I have an idea, tell your mother to send her original passport with DHL so that I can see the original stamp on it proving that she entered Argentina'. So very diligently we complied with this and he seemed satisfied.

In retrospect, one of the things that I found particularly bitter was that police officers, migration authorities and even the personnel at the health insurance office treated us with suspicion, as if we were trying to do something wrong, whereas in fact we were just trying to find a way to live close to our dear ones.

When my mother was back in Argentina, we found out that she was entitled to apply for the Italian nationality. You could say that we were extremely privileged to have this option. And indeed, it gave us a lot of hope. But at the same time, this entailed another expensive, emotionally demanding and uncertain undertaking. My mother had to live in Italy on her own for about five months in order to complete the procedure. This avenue would have closed had the migration authorities decided to give my mother an entry ban. Luckily there were no problems, and upon receiving the Italian nationality, she could finally travel back to Belgium as an EU citizen.

The final 'hurdle' was dealing with the officer at the migration desk in Ghent, who demanded that my mother should provide written proof (what kind of 'proof'? and from whom?) of the reasons why she acquired a second nationality. However, there was no legal basis to request this, and after complaining about this with the officer in charge at the migration desk, my mother was finally allowed to settle in Belgium.

4. Empirical, theoretical and methodological analysis

In this section, this case of family reunification is examined at the empirical, theoretical and methodological levels.

4.1 Uncovering the emotional and material effects of the law reform

Writing on the effects of the law reform of 2011 from an insider's perspective is a way of 'claiming voice' and making visible the injustice undergone by those applicants to whom the new law was immediately applied, without transitional provisions. As an academic trained in legal anthropology, this exercise allows me to find a certain degree of solace. The legal anthropological gaze sheds light on some of the social structures that affected me personally and provides analytical tools to make sense of what happened in my life. Looking back at our trajectory of family reunification, I realise that these experiences had a profound effect on my legal consciousness as well as a negative impact on inclusion processes of both my mother and myself. Moreover, our case unveiled various legal gaps disempowering family reunification applicants and led to a cost–benefit analysis of which legal avenues to mobilise.

4.1.1 Impact on legal consciousness

Legal consciousness refers to the mutual co-constitution of actors and structures in the legal realm. On the one hand, this entails how different actors participate in the construction, reproduction and contestation of legality as a social structure, i.e., the meanings, sources of authority and cultural practices that are commonly recognised as legal. And on the other hand, it involves understanding how these meanings, sources of authority and practices in turn affect the perception that different actors have of themselves as subjects of law and their capacity to act and to mobilise the law. In other words, the concept 'legal consciousness' denotes a reciprocal process by which 'legality' emerges out of human interaction and in turn affects it (Silbey, 2005; Engel, 1998).

Until my mother's arrival in Belgium, the experiences that I had had with immigration law had been positive. This constituted an implicit point of departure when we took the decision to initiate the proceedings for family reunification of my mother. It is because Belgian immigration law had treated me fairly up until that point that I expected a fair treatment when we decided to embark on a family reunification proceeding.[7] Even after the immediate application of the new law in 2011, I still decided to mobilise Belgian law again in the appeal process. However, in time, it became clear to me that as an immigrant the possibility of being treated as a 'second-class citizen' would always be around the corner.

Legislators and judges did not consider that I was entitled to legal certainty, or, in other words, to respect for my time, energy and financial means. I was compelled to invest all of this fighting for a right to live a life close to my mother. Something that is simply a given for most people. According to the Constitutional Court, foreigners applying for a residence right 'should bear in mind that a State's immigration laws may be amended for reasons of public interest'.[8] This is true, but it does not justify the lack of transitional measures. It would have been problematic for me had I known from the outset that my mother had no right to family reunification with me. But at least, we would have known where we stood and we would have been able to make an informed decision. Yet, in one stroke, the Constitutional Court wiped out foreigners' access to the protection offered by basic legal principles, such as legal certainty, while at the same time naturalising this exclusion.

In addition to legal uncertainty, I was confronted with the distressing reality that I did not have the same rights to family life as my fellow citizens. The sheer fact of being born abroad meant that I was not entitled to share my life with a parent. I was expected to understand that this is the fair price that I needed to pay for the decision to build a stable life in the first world. In other words, there was a mismatch between my sense of entitlement to family life, and the rights that Belgian society was willing to grant me as an immigrant. These experiences have affected how I perceive my position within Belgian legal structures and society until today. Following the legal consciousness typology developed by Ewick and Silbey (1998), I would say that I moved from a 'before the law' archetype of legal consciousness, which is permeated by the ideology that the law is neutral and fair, towards an 'against the law' type of legal consciousness, which is characterised by a cynical stance towards legal institutions.[9]

In addition, this account illustrates the impact of public policies (the 2011 law) as well as relational factors (Chua & Engel, 2019) on the evolution of one's legal consciousness (Güdük & Desmet, 2022). The legal status of my mother, who became 'irregular' in the country after the rejection of her family reunification application, impacted my legal consciousness as daughter. This resonates with Abrego (2019), who showed, in relation to mixed-status families in the United States, that

7 By 'fair' and 'fairly', I mean the treatment that you may expect based on what was prescribed by the law.

8 Constitutional Court, 26 September 2013, No. 121/12, B.66 and Constitutional Court, 26 September 2013, No. 123/12, B.3.3.

9 Despite the fact that we still relied on legal procedures for my mother to acquire the Italian nationality and a residence permit as an EU citizen in Belgium, I argue that being classified as displaying a 'with the law' archetype of legal consciousness, in which the law is 'played out as a game', would not at all reflect our experience.

undocumented status does not only influence the legal consciousness of the persons concerned but also that of their family members who themselves had citizenship.

4.1.2 Impact on inclusion and social cohesion

The following testimony I gave in an interview with Ellen for a book project about lived experiences of migration law suggests that negative experiences with family reunification also negatively impact on broader processes of inclusion and social cohesion, of my mother in the first place:

> What was very difficult for my mother is that suddenly, while we were awaiting the result of the appeal procedure, she was no longer allowed to take Dutch lessons at the language school. That was actually a shame because my mother came here at a later age. She was sixty. In Argentina, as in most countries in Latin America, it is not at all common for a person of that age to know a second language. My mother knows a little bit of French because it is a language that has Latin roots and she could learn it at high school. But learning English was not common at that time, so a language such as Dutch is very unfamiliar and difficult to learn. And yet, she came to Belgium with the intention to learn Dutch. I remember that she even took private lessons. I have a good friend who is a Dutch teacher, and she followed classes with her in addition to the lessons that she followed at the language school. She needed that extra help, and she was committed to learn Dutch. But suddenly, with the negative response to the procedure of family reunification she was no longer allowed to follow Dutch classes at the language school. That was a very heavy blow for her motivation. To this day, ten years later, my mother still feels that she is not welcome in Belgium. Her migration trajectory was very traumatic and it meant 'a before and an after' for her. I think that at some point she must have thought, 'ok, if I'm not welcome here, why should I go through all the trouble of learning that difficult language?' So she never tried again.

In line with the insight that legal consciousness is relational, my story shows that inclusion processes are relational too. The negative effects on inclusion processes do not remain limited to the applicant who receives a negative decision (my mother) but extend to other parties involved as well. This is not surprising given the relational nature of family reunification processes, as is evidenced by the following interview excerpt:

> I was already ten years in Belgium. I felt well integrated, but through the whole procedure with my mother I felt that a lot of injustice was being done against me. I've always done everything in my hands to be a good citizen. I have made an effort to contribute in many ways to everything I could contribute to. And then, the moment I want to become a mother and have my mother close to me, that is not allowed. And then you suddenly feel: ok, so

> just because I was born in another country, I can't afford to have my mother near me when I need it, when it's actually in the best interests of my child to have his family close by. So where are the rights of my child, who is also Belgian by the way? He also has a right to be close to his grandmother.

Scholars have demonstrated how family reunification laws provide an insight in underlying processes of inclusion and exclusion in a given society. They unveil who are considered as 'insiders' – and should thus be allowed to be joined by their family members – in contrast to the 'outsiders', who should not benefit from such a right (Bonjour, 2007; Van Walsum, 2004). Arguably, the 2011 law has cast its net of 'outsiders' widely: aiming to restrict family reunification of 'new' Belgians, mentioning especially those with Turkish or Moroccan roots during the parliamentary debate, the affected population also included 'new' Belgians of other origins and Belgians by birth who had not made use of their right to free movement. Ironically, however, by 2011, the marriage migration of Turkish and Moroccan persons had already spontaneously declined, so the law seems to have missed its purpose in that sense (Caestecker et al., 2018).

The 2011 law negatively affected the inclusion pathways of both my mother and myself in Belgian society. Following the Constitutional Court's general endorsement of the exclusion of ascendants and the immediate application of the 2011 law, the Council for Alien Law Litigation confirmed the negative decision of the Immigration Office in my mother's case. The feelings of discrimination, injustice and arbitrariness are evident from the previous interview excerpts.

4.1.3 Legal gaps that disempower applicants

More generally, my perspective as an insider allowed me to become aware of an administrative machinery behind family reunification procedures that displays several 'ad hoc instances of legal uncertainty', which disempower applicants and act as minefields within family reunification trajectories. Examples include the arbitrariness with which medical reasons may not be accepted as valid reasons to prolong the period for voluntary departure, the wide discretionary powers of police officers who are tasked with ascertaining whether a person has left the territory, and the misplaced sense of rule-making capacity with which administrative personnel at migration front-desks demand extra paperwork, which is nowhere required by the law. These examples highlight the room for divergent interpretation and application of the law in practice by different types of street-level bureaucrats: at a distance, within the Immigration Office (see also Mascia, 2021), and in direct contact with the sponsor and family member applying for reunification, by police officers and municipal officers (see also van den Bogaard et al., 2022). This is further illustrated by the following excerpt:

> I tried to distance myself emotionally to defend myself against the brutality and violence of the whole procedure. It is not right that there is so much room for abuse of power. But that is simply the case, to your disadvantage

> of course. And at that moment I thought, okay, I just have to observe, just distance myself emotionally from this and observe like a curious researcher trying to grasp 'what is going on here?' And that's how I came to the conclusion: this is no coincidence. It is not by chance that so much discretionary space is allowed. It is the intention to generate this 'inequality of arms' that plays against the interests of migrants. What if that policeman had said: 'No, I don't believe that stamp on your mother's passport is real, and I'm giving her an entry ban'?

It is well known that street-level bureaucracy plays a central role in access to rights (Lipsky, 2010). My experience shows that legal gaps disempower applicants. This is particularly the case when it comes to valid criteria on what constitutes evidence or proof, for instance to postpone a removal from the territory, following a negative decision on a family reunification application. The 'law in the books' may have entitled my mother to a postponement on medical grounds but, 'in action', this very same law turned out to be of no value because of the lack of clear public guidelines on what migration authorities accept as valid proof of a medical condition. As a result, my mother had to take a transatlantic plane to Argentina, although this was contrary to the medical advice in the context of her revalidation.

4.1.4 Legal mobilisation

After having received a negative decision in appeal from the Council for Alien Law Litigation, we considered submitting an application before the European Court of Human Rights. However, the Court interprets the right to respect for family life (Article 8 ECHR) in a migration context in a restrictive way, only finding a positive obligation for Member States to admit family members in very specific circumstances (Dembour, 2015; Desmet, this volume). Consequently, we dismissed the mobilisation of the (Council of Europe) human rights system as a possible fruitful avenue.

Mobilising Italian nationality law as well as EU law on freedom of movement turned out to be more productive. As an Italian national, my mother also became an EU citizen. Union citizens have the right to freedom of movement within the European Union, which entails a right to stay for more than three months in Belgium on the basis of (i) work, (ii) as a holder of sufficient resources or (iii) as a student. Consequently, thanks to my income, my mother was considered as holding sufficient resources, so she could come and live in Belgium after all.

Our trajectory can be seen as an example of a 'substitution effect' (de Haas et al., 2019): a measure that aimed to limit immigration (the 2011 law) has an undesirable effect, making it less effective or even achieving the opposite result. What my mother did, with our help, constitutes a type of 'categorical substitution': because one migration channel (family reunification) became more strict, she migrated in another way (as a Union citizen).

4.2 Reflections on agency in the context of family reunification

Socio-legal studies on migration and transnational legal processes have demonstrated the importance of incorporating migrants' perspectives into research (de Hart et al., 2013) and bringing their struggles to the forefront of discussions, rather than taking the nation-state as the natural point of departure (Wyss, 2022). Actor-centred research entails a critical conceptualisation of 'agency', which in turn demands a careful assessment of power relations.

We conceptualise agency as 'the socioculturally mediated capacity to act' (Ahearn, 2001). As all laws, legal frameworks regulating migration and family reunification constitute key structures that impinge upon this capacity in enabling and constraining ways. Migration authorities and applicants mobilise these legal frameworks in their encounters, and in that sense, law opens and closes spaces of negotiation. These encounters are marked by highly unequal power relations: Wyss (2022) has shown how this plays out in the case of male migrants who have entered Europe unauthorised and who apply for asylum. She describes the stigmatising, racist and de-vulnerabilising representations that affect them and how remaining mobile, i.e., being able to quickly move from one country to another, constitutes a key tactic to escape states' control practices.[10]

For us, this tactic of mobility was out of reach. My mother had a severe impairment of her physical mobility, which required chronic medical treatment, and hence medical insurance and a stable team of doctors following up with her health. Moreover, her main motivation to migrate to Belgium was to live close to her daughter and grandson. At the same time, my life was very much locally anchored in Belgium due to personal and professional relationships that I was not willing to give up:

> I recall that when seeking legal counselling, I would hear that we 'just needed to move across the border', either to France or to the Netherlands. There, as an EU citizen who had moved to another country, my rights to family reunification with an ascendant could not be restricted. But this was so farfetched. My husband and I had successful and exigent careers in Belgium. We could not afford 'just living across the border', as if that was easy. Another 'solution' that was often proposed to me was to move with my mother back to Argentina. To me, hearing this 'solution' attested to the lack of understanding of how unstable living conditions are in my country of origin. In Belgium, it is possible to earn a respectable wage as an academic, whereas in Argentina it is a challenge to find decent work at all, even if you hold a PhD.

10 She builds on de Certeau's distinction between 'strategies' and 'tactics'. The former are located within the realm of power, whereas the latter constitute the 'art of the weak', since 'the space of a tactic is the space of the other. . . . [I]t must play on and with a terrain imposed on it and organized by the law of a foreign power' (de Certeau, 2002, p. 36).

This demonstrates the importance of intersectional perspectives on the factors that enable and constrain migrants' access to tactics to circumvent states' control practices. In our case, age, physical ability, class and race played a major role. Age and physical ability proved constraining. My mother needed to be domiciled in order to be able to access the health services that she needed. Although she was not affected in everyday life by the stigmatising, racist and de-vulnerabilising representations described by Wyss (2022), she was easy 'prey' for the police, who intended to lock her up in a detention centre and deport her if she would refuse to depart voluntarily, as if she was a dangerous criminal.

Class, being knowledgeable – to a certain extent – of the migration regulations, disposing of sufficient financial resources and being able to draw on quality legal support, enabled our deployment of tactics, such as quickly purchasing an expensive plane ticket and demanding that the head of the migration front desk explains why a certain extra document is being asked when this is not required by the law. Moreover, there was an element of ethnic origin in the mix. Being of white European descent, my mother could apply for Italian citizenship:

> For us, it worked out more or less well. But yes, we have the means to pay for a business-class ticket, to pay for those proceedings in Italy and the opportunity *tout court* to apply for Italian citizenship. Not everyone is given that.

One could say that we were privileged as compared to other applicants. But at the same time, this constellation of constraining and enabling factors resulted in constant ambivalence between strength and fragility. Socio-legal studies on migration often employ the term 'navigation' to describe the agency of migrants with a precarious legal status. 'Navigation' refers to a special form of movement that takes place when moving in a moving environment. Navigation is conceptualised as an active engagement with shaky grounds fraught with uncertainties and unpredictability (Vigh, 2009). The term captures the violent conditions and rapidly changing legal environment that characterise the migration landscape, as well as migrants' capacities to act in this context. It is true that you are not a passive victim and that you analyse what seems most convenient, assessing possible costs and benefits. But the options are very limited and the costs extremely high. I did not feel that I was 'navigating' because to me this sounds as if you are, at least to a certain extent, in control. A more appropriate term would be 'avoid drowning', which captures the survival modus in which you actually find yourself.

4.3 At the junction of co-creative research and autoethnography

Methodologically, this chapter can be situated at the crossroads of co-creative research and autoethnography. On the one hand, this chapter is the result of a co-creative process. The idea to co-write this chapter emerged following an interview that Ellen took with Giselle about Giselle's trajectory of migration and family reunification with her mother – of which excerpts have been included. Ellen was preparing a book for a broad audience about migration law on the basis of concrete cases (Desmet, 2023). It is in this context that she thought about documenting Giselle's experiences. The authors knew each other as colleagues and friends for over ten years and had co-published and co-taught on several occasions. Moreover, as a friend, Ellen had learnt about the developments in Giselle's mother's case as they unfolded, without suspecting that Giselle's accounts would one day become 'primary data'. This pre-existing connection facilitated Ellen to invite Giselle to share her views and experiences. Similarly, Giselle felt comfortable talking openly with Ellen and providing her with full access to the legal files of her mother's case. This shared history thus made it easier to conduct an interview on a sensitive issue in a climate of emotional safety and solid mutual trust and gave both authors the incentive to embark in the co-creation of an academic piece.

Ellen's expert knowledge in migration law proved complementary to Giselle's experiential knowledge on family reunification. For example, the scope of Section 2 describing the legal changes that were introduced in Belgium in 2011 resulted from a series of organic conversations amongst the authors in which they concluded that the exclusion of ascendants and the lack of interim measures needed to be the building blocks, for they were the main sources of injustice felt by Giselle.

At the same time, both authors' knowledge of academic logics, and in particular of legal anthropological discourses, provided for common ground and mutual understanding, which is a key factor in successful co-creative and collaborative research processes (Dewaele et al., 2021). Ellen's and Giselle's gaze were not exactly the same when selecting and analysing excerpts from the interview, but the shared academic background made dialogue and exchange of ideas possible. For example, as an outsider, Ellen proposed that this case displayed the operation of a 'substitution effect' (de Haas et al., 2019), to which Giselle agreed, but noticed that from an insider's perspective, her sense of 'agency' as an applicant was very limited.

On the other hand, the chapter draws on autoethnography, as it is built around the personal experiences and reflections of a legal anthropologist engaged as a sponsor in a family reunification process. Autoethnography is an approach to research in the social sciences that describes and analyses personal experience in order to understand broader societal processes (Ellis et al., 2011). It combines characteristics of autobiography and ethnography. Autobiographies are built around selected past experiences and, in particular, 'epiphanies', i.e., remembered moments that are perceived to have significantly impacted the trajectory of a person's life, whereas ethnography refers to studies of cultural practices, values, beliefs, shared experiences and systems of meaning. Autoethnographers draw on theoretical and methodological knowledge from their disciplines in order to systematically analyse what personal experiences reveal about social and cultural processes more generally. In so doing, they contrast epiphanies with existing insights and concepts from their fields.

The central epiphany in this case is the moment Giselle's mother received the first negative decision to her application for family reunification. This kicked off a five-year period of fear and uncertainty, which culminated in the confirmation of the negative decision and the order to leave the territory. If Giselle's mother would not leave of her own accord during a (prolonged) period for voluntarily departure, then she would be at risk of immigration detention in order to be forcibly removed, despite her medical condition.

Both the autoethnographic approach and the reflections on positionality that are at the core of co-creative research are based on the premise that subjectivity, emotionality and the researchers' personal backgrounds influence the research process and results. Rather than silencing these matters or assuming they don't exist, we found it useful to account for how these issues played out in the what, how and why of this piece.

5. Concluding reflections

This chapter has documented and reflected upon the lived family reunification experience of a legal anthropologist, combining an autoethnographic approach with a co-creative process with a migration law scholar. The relational nature of family reunification procedures implies that the effects of such proceedings – in terms of, for instance, legal consciousness, inclusion and social cohesion – extend beyond the applying family member to both the sponsor (i.e., the daughter) and other family members affected (e.g., a grandchild).

Within the multi-layered legal system regulating migration, several layers (Belgian family reunification provisions and Council of Europe human rights law) proved unfruitful for Giselle and her mother to realise their aspirations to live in Belgium together and support one another. Yet, other legal layers (Italian nationality law and EU law on freedom of movement) provided an unexpected yet most welcome outcome. This supports the observation of de Hart et al. (2013) in that there is no dichotomy of law providing (only) opportunities or (only) constraints, but a continuum of both opportunities and constraints.

Finally, the chapter demonstrated the importance of not over-emphasising the agency of persons 'navigating' migration systems, given the very unequal power relations within which negotiations on rights in a migration context take place, as well as the need for an intersectional perspective when assessing this capacity to act.

References

Abrego, L. (2019). Relational legal consciousness of U.S. citizenship: Privilege, responsibility, guilt, and love in Latino mixed-status families. *Law & Society Review*, *53*, 641–670. https://doi.org/10.1111/lasr.12414

Ahearn, L. M. (2001). Language and agency. *Annual Review of Anthropology*, *30*, 109–137. https://doi.org/10.1146/annurev.anthro.30.1.109

Bonjour, S. (2007). Gezin en Grens: Debat en beleidsvorming op het gebied van gezinsmigratie in Nederland sinds de jaren vijftig. *Migrantenstudies*, *1*, 2–23. https://hdl.handle.net/1887/23396

Caestecker, F., Lievens, J., Van Pottelberge, A., Dupont, E., & Vandeputte, B. (2018). Huwelijkskeuze onder inwoners van België van Marokkaanse en Turkse origine tussen 2005 en 2013, sociologische en politieke determinanten. In *Migratie in cijfers en in rechten* (pp. 118–122). Myria.

Chua, L. J., & Engel, D. M. (2019). Legal consciousness reconsidered. *Annual Review of Law and Social Science*, *15*(1), 335–353. https://doi.org/10.1146/annurev-lawsocsci-101518-042717

Dawoud, S. (2014). Gezinshereniging in België: Kan men het bos nog door de bomen zien? *Tijdschrift voor Vreemdelingenrecht*, *3*, 286–320.

De Certeau, M. (2002). *The Practice of Everyday Life* (3rd ed.). University of California Press.

de Haas, H., Czaika, M., Flahaux, M.-L., Mahendra, E., Natter, K., Vezzoli, S., & Villares-Varela, M. (2019). International migration: Trends, determinants, and policy effects. *Population and Development Review*, *45*, 885–922. https://doi.org/10.1111/padr.12291

de Hart, B., van Rossum, W., & Sportel, I. (2013). Law in the everyday lives of transnational families: An introduction. *Oñati Socio-Legal Series*, *3*(6), 991–1003.

Dembour, M. (2015). *When Humans Become Migrants: Study of the European Court of Human Rights with an Inter-American Counterpoint*. Oxford University Press.

Desmet, E. (2023). *Migratierecht: Tussen mens en staat*. Academia Press.

Dewaele, A., Meysman, S., & Buysse, A. (2021). Understanding collaborative interactions in relation to research impact in social sciences and humanities: A meta-ethnography. *Research Evaluation*, *30*(2), 179–190. https://doi.org/10.1093/reseval/rvaa033

Ellis, C., Adams, T. E., & Bochner, A. P. (2011). Autoethnography: An overview. *Historical Social Research/Historische Sozialforschung*, *36*(4), 273–290. https://doi.org/10.17169/fqs-12.1.1589

Engel, D. M. (1998). How Does Law Matter in the Constitution of Legal Consciousness? In B. G. Garth & A. Sarat (Eds.), *How Does Law Matter?* (pp. 109–144). Northwestern University Press.

Ewick, P., & Silbey, S. S. (1998). *The Common Place of Law: Stories from Everyday Life*. University of Chicago Press.

Federale Ombudsman. (2011). *Overgangsmaatregelen gezinshereniging: Tussentijds verslag 4de kwartaal 2011*. www.federaalombudsman.be

Federale Ombudsman. (2012). *Jaarverslag 2011*. www.federaalombudsman.be

Güdük, A., & Desmet, E. (2022). Legal consciousness and migration: Towards a research agenda. *International Journal of Law in Context*, *18*(2), 213–228. https://doi.org/10.1017/S1744552322000118

Lipsky, M. (2010). *Street Level Bureaucracy: Dilemmas of the Individual in Public Services* (30th anniversary expanded ed.). The Russell Sage Foundation.

Mascia, C. (2021). How bureaucracies shape access to rights: The implementation of family reunification in Belgium. *Journal of Ethnic and Migration Studies*, *47*(9), 2127–2143. https://doi.org/10.1080/1369183X.2020.1726734

Silbey, S. S. (2005). After legal consciousness. *Annual Review of Law and Social Science*, *1*(1), 323–368. https://doi.org/10.1146/annurev.lawsocsci.1.041604.115938

van den Bogaard, R.-M., Horta, A. C., Van Doren, W., Desmet, E., & Valcke, A. (2022). Procedural (in)justice for EU citizens moving to Belgium: An inquiry into municipal registration practices. *Citizenship Studies*, *26*(7), 995–1010. https://doi.org/10.1080/13621025.2022.2137944

van Walsum, S. (2004). The dynamics of emancipation and exclusion: Changing family norms and Dutch family migration policies. *IMIS Beitrage*, *24*, 119–128.

Vigh, H. (2009). Motion squared: A second look at the concept of social navigation. *Anthropological Theory*, *9*(4), 419–438. https://doi.org/10.1177/1463499609356044

Wyss, A. (2022). *Navigating the European Migration Regime*. Bristol University Press.

19 Domestic violence within the securitisation of (family and love) migration

The case of Belgium

Giacomo Orsini and Laura Merla

1. Introduction

The issue of domestic violence in the framework of migration attracts increasing academic attention (see, e.g., Williams, 2010; Raj & Silverman, 2002). Scholars from different disciplines have engaged with the seemingly frequent occurrence of abuses in migrants' households (Md Said & Emmanuel Kaka, 2023). This chapter contributes to this academic debate on the causes and dynamics of domestic violence within migrant couples and families.

In order to explore the causes of domestic violence in migration, here we purposely avoid focusing on migrants' culture/ethnicity – something rather common in the existing literature (for a review, see Rai & Choi, 2018). In fact, in the following pages we explain the occurrence of domestic violence as an outcome of key structural constraints which operate on migrants since they decide to emigrate and, even more, as they arrive in their so-called country of destination.

Specifically, the chapter discusses how migration policies relative to family reunification can impact love and family relations within migrants couples and families. It does so by focusing on a European country, that is, Belgium, whose migration policies turned increasingly restrictive and complex over the last decades. By focusing mainly on family reunification, besides looking at how policies produce the conditions for domestic violence to happen, we also discuss how these rules and procedures work to hinder migrants' ability to access protection after domestic violence has begun.

The data we present was collected primarily by Giacomo Orsini as part of an interdisciplinary research project which was co-led by Laura Merla and, between 2017 and 2020, explored how laws impact migrants' everyday life in Belgium across different domains. Empirically, we combine insights from life-history interviews with battered migrants, semi-structured interviews with experts and practitioners, and a series of observations in a family tribunal.

To understand how policies can impact so profoundly the intimate lives of migrants, we start by framing our contribution into the broader – and growing – body of literature on domestic violence within migration. Thus, we discuss the diverse datasets we rely on and how we collected information on the field – including some reflection on the key ethical and methodological considerations relative

DOI: 10.4324/9781003503217-24

to reaching this often-traumatised group of participants (Williamson et al., 2020). Next, we offer an overview of the main transformations of the policy environment regulating migrants' family and love lives in Belgium. We then describe how migration policy-driven restrictions increase the likelihood of experiencing domestic violence, thus focusing on the time preceding the occurrence of violence. Next, we present how these and other measures make it also more difficult for abused migrants to access any form of assistance from institutional or non-institutional actors operating in Belgium. We conclude with some reflections on the incompatibility of securitising migration and the effective protection of migrants from suffering domestic violence.

2. Institutional factors versus migrants' culture/ethnicity: a theoretical framing for analysing domestic violence in migration

In recent times, research on domestic violence within the context of migration has increased and attracts growing scholarly interest within the field of migration studies (see, e.g., Md Said & Emmanuel Kaka, 2023; Williams, 2010). Nevertheless, the subject remains relatively marginal within the vast literature on gender and/or migration. Dating back to the 1990s, early work was mainly concerned with mapping and thus bring to the surface the occurrence of domestic violence in migrant families: these studies focused mainly on Europe and the United States (see, e.g., Goldman, 1999; Bui & Morash, 1999).

For the apparently frequent violence occurring within migrant couples (see, e.g., De Schrijver et al., 2018; Erez, 2002), much of this research offers cultural explanations (Rai & Choi, 2018). In the words of Menjívar and Salcido (2002, p. 901) 'there [is] a common tendency [in the literature] to stereotype domestic violence in some ethnic group as an inherent part of their cultural repertoire'. From this perspective domestic violence results from the clash between patriarchal mores inherent to the migrant's culture and the personal freedoms available to women in the destination countries (see, e.g., Razack, 1998; Narayan, 1995). Others have focused on the difficulties migrant women face in freeing themselves from their abusers. Also in this case, migrant women's inability and/or unwillingness to report maltreatments and protect themselves from their partners is considered to be consequent to the patriarchal gender relations that exist within the migrant community (Sumiya, 2018).

However, as also noted by other academics, these approaches have a number of analytical limitations. First, they are rooted in monolithic – and thus possibly stereotypical (Romero, 2008) – understandings of migrants' culture. In fact, the focus on culture fails to recognise the internal diversity of migrant communities, as it overshadows differences concerning, for example, social class or education (Yick, 2007). Secondly, the lack of consideration for the context in which migration takes place has been criticised. By not accounting for factors impacting on migrants in their so-called destination countries, researchers miss taking into account the effects of cultural and non-cultural factors, such as racism, segregation or exclusion (see, e.g., Menjívar & Salcido, 2002; Ozcurumez et al., 2021).

On the basis of these criticisms, a growing number of scholars started searching for alternative explanations for domestic violence within migrants' households. For example, researchers have focused on restrictive migration policies to show how these normative frameworks can increase migrants' vulnerability and, consequently, the likelihood of domestic violence to take place. Among others, Stoyanova (2019) has demonstrated how in Europe securitised family reunification rules concerning, for instance, the withdrawal of residence right in case of divorce, enhance precariousness within migrant couples, thus aggravating tensions between partners (see also Bhuyan & Bragg, 2021). Other academics have focused instead on the uncertain and unstable legal, economic and social status of migrant women to explain why they ultimately find it more difficult to access protection when suffering violence from their partners (see, e.g., Erez et al., 2009; Menjívar & Salcido, 2002).

Like the aforementioned studies, this work focuses on those structural factors that shape the intimate lives of migrants in their 'country of destination'. Deflecting the attention – and guilt – placed on migrant women and their co-ethnic migrant communities, allows to look for other determinants of violence, including for the effects of migration policies operating on migrants since they decide to emigrate.

From a post-structural perspective, such analytical shift is motivated by the will to somewhat decolonise scholarly analyses of conjugal violence in the context of migration (see, e.g., Bhabha, 1994; Gikandi, 2004). As for other domains of migration research and migration studies more broadly, 'focusing on individuals as bearers of a supposed ethnic background . . . risks . . . drawing culturalising conclusions [which] essentialis[e] certain groups of migrant[s]' (Dahinden et al., 2021, p. 8). This is particularly relevant since it is only for specific – and racialised – groups of migrants that culture – or ethnicity – is systematically mobilised in scholarly studies and policy reports (see, e.g., Mayblin & Turner, 2021; Tudor, 2022). This explains why here we do not just concentrate on the policy and thus legal environment within which migrants (try to) settle down in Belgium. In fact, for this chapter we give centrality to the lived experiences of migrants (Thambinathan & Kinsella, 2021).

The ground-level functioning of migration policies constitutes, for some, one key risk factor and a source of insecurity for migrants (see, e.g., Orsini, 2016; Lazaridis, 2011). From such a perspective we thus suggest that, to enhance the protection of victims of domestic violence, policymakers must also intervene on the increasingly restrictive policies and regulations governing migration (Tallis, 2022). This seems to be even more the case since integration and acculturation policies have proven to be only scarcely effective for challenging patriarchal mores of living (see, e.g., Scheibelhofer, 2014; Riaño, 2013).

From this perspective, this chapter examines whether and how the Belgian family reunification regime may facilitate the occurrence of violence within migrant families. Moreover, this contribution aims to show how increasingly restrictive laws and regulations can hinder migrants' ability to denounce their abusers and access protection. Importantly, for this chapter we rely on Kelly and Westmorland's (2016) definition of domestic violence, understood as an ongoing process, rather than an occasional event, which goes beyond extreme acts of psychological or physical abuse. In short, we see domestic violence as a recurrent, everyday reality in which much of the abused person's behaviour is micro-managed by the abuser.

3. Researching domestic violence with persons in an (extremely) vulnerable situation: a heterogenous dataset

This study is part of the interdisciplinary project Personal Aspirations and Processes of Adaptation: How the Legal Framework Impacts on Migrants' Agency (LIMA).[1] By combining insights from law, sociology and demography, this interdisciplinary investigation sought to untangle how legal frameworks regulating migration to and in Belgium (i.e., national and EU law) influence third-country nationals' migration, family and professional trajectories, aspirations and plans.

This chapter is based on three different types of primary data, collected by Orsini in the framework of this project: life-history interviews with migrants, semi-structured interviews with specialists and observations in a Belgian family court. Life-history interviews were conducted with eight women of different non-EU nationalities who were contacted through diverse associations and NGOs engaged in the protection of migrants suffering domestic violence. Importantly, all the interviewed migrants had experienced domestic violence after their arrival in Belgium: a country which they entered via family reunification after 2011 – which is the year when the last major restrictive reform of Belgian regulations concerning family reunification was introduced. While we tried to involve in this study also migrant men who had suffered violence from their partner, no contact was shared with us. If most gatekeepers admitted that, in recent years, they had witnessed increasing numbers of migrant men asking for protection, they also made clear that none of them was willing to talk about their experiences (for further elaborations see, e.g., Depraetere et al., 2020; Keygnaert & Guieu, 2015).

It is important to outline that three of the partners of the eight migrant interviewees were Belgian nationals. The others came from several countries outside the European Union. As for the research participants, they came from seven different countries in Africa, Asia or the Americas. Given the difficulties of finding battered migrants willing to speak to us – and thus recall their traumatic experiences in an interview (Williamson et al., 2020) – we had little room to select research participants based on their nationality. Yet, we found such heterogenous sampling extremely valuable to methodologically challenge culturalised perspectives on domestic violence within the context of migration. In fact, the mechanisms by which the perpetrators of violence inflicted psychological or physical suffering on their partners are very similar. All of them have, at some point, exploited the policy-induced precarious legal, but also economic and social status of their partner.

1 Five-year project funded since October 2015 by an ARC grant from the Brussels-Wallonia Federation and supervised by professors Sylvie Sarolea, Bruno Schoumaker, Laura Merla and Jacques Marquet.

The semi-structured interviews involved ten specialists, including lawyers specialised in family and migration law, a judge of a family court as well as civil servants, practitioners and activists. Importantly, these two types of interview data were complemented by field notes which were collected during twenty hours of observations in a Belgian family court. The specific court was chosen because it dealt with several cases involving non-EU migrants, and Orsini was granted access to it. During this fieldwork, Giacomo attended divorce hearings that involved at least one third-country national and included accusations of domestic violence.

The expert interviews focused on their professional experience in assisting and caring for foreign victims of domestic violence in Belgium. Most of these interviews dealt with the direct and indirect consequences that family reunification laws, and in particular those relative to the 2011 reform, had on their work. With migrant women, we chronologically explored their love and migration trajectories before and after their arrival in Belgium, their experience of domestic violence and the support they did (not) receive from institutional and non-institutional actors present on the field. Finally, data drawn from the observation of court hearings combines fieldnotes and follow-up meetings and discussions with the judge in charge of the observed cases and her staff.[2]

We then triangulated among these three different sets of information (see, e.g., Flick, 2004). In fact, data were not collected sequentially but simultaneously so that the different types of materials (and testimonies) could complement and feed into each other. Similarly, data analysis was conducted during and after the collection of data, in a continuous and cumulative movement that consisted in combining these heterogeneous sets of information by developing our analysis across the macro, meso and micro layers of sociological enquiry.

The sensitivity of the issues discussed and the extreme policy-induced vulnerability (Clibborn & Wright, 2020) of the migrant women involved in the research made this fieldwork very challenging, concerning both the search for respondents willing to engage with the research and the many ethical issues arising from conducting interviews on such traumatic experiences. One of the main factors that makes research on domestic violence difficult is the very limited access to potential respondents (Sumiya, 2018). This explains the relatively small number of migrant women we were able to recruit for the research. Their profiles are also specific since, to reach out to the research participants, we had to rely on civil society organisations. Unavoidably, this restricted the recruitment to people who already enjoyed a certain level of protection in Belgium, as all the participants had already ended their abusive relations at the time of the interview. Consequently, we were unable to grasp the experiences of more 'extreme' cases, somewhat reducing the scope of the investigation.

Moreover, collecting such account of traumatic events implies a series of major ethical questions relative, for instance, to the risk of re-traumatising participants

2 In order to preserve the anonymity of the interviewees quoted in this book, the personal data are fictitious.

for the sake of data extraction (Papadakaki et al., 2021). To reduce such dangers, we often reminded participants of the possibility for them to stop or leave the interview at any time and/or to avoid addressing specific questions. Likewise, we also provided them with support on several personal issues – e.g., pointing at known lawyers for legal assistance, counselling for dealing with specific administrative procedures or giving support in public initiatives.

4. An increasingly restrictive policy environment: the securitisation of (family) migration in Belgium

The Belgian immigration policy has undergone profound changes since the mid-twentieth century. In the aftermath of WWII, Belgian authorities signed a series of so-called guest-worker agreements with Southern European countries Morocco and Turkey to import migrant workers. To increase its attractiveness, Belgium had a relatively inclusive family immigration policy that allowed labour immigrants to come with their relatives. These proactive programmes combined with frequent regularisations and a general *laissez-faire* with respect to migrants' irregular entries, stays and employment in the country (Martinello & Rea, 2013).

These evolutions of Belgian policies concerned with migration resembled those recorded in other European countries. For instance, also France and Germany implemented since the fifties similar programmes to the Belgian ones for the recruitment of foreign labour (Djajic, 2014). In general, until about the seventies and eighties, most European countries favoured family reunification or simply turned a blind eye on the presence of so-called irregular migrants on their territories (Stalker, 2002).

However, as the Belgian economy slowed down in the seventies, labour immigration was severely limited. While, over the following decades, the normative framework regulating migration turned increasingly restrictive, legal migration continued through family reunification and asylum. As for most of Europe, the post-9/11 period has in turn been characterised by the increasing securitisation of migration (see, e.g., Orsini et al., 2022; Gsir et al., 2016). Since immigration became a top national security issue, successive Belgian governments introduced new legislation to control and limit foreigners' access to and presence on the national territory (De Cleen et al., 2017). This trend has been continuing and translated into successive reforms, which turned legal frameworks concerned with migration more restrictive and selective but also increasingly complex – also due to the adoption of securitised EU directives and legislations (Maneri & Quassoli, 2016).

Laws regulating migrants' access to family reunification in Belgium are no exception. They de facto establish a differentiated legal regime for migrant families as compared to national ones (Sarolea & Merla, 2021). For instance, nationals who are not from the EEA or Switzerland as well as (so-called static) Belgians[3]

3 See also Corradi and Desmet (this volume).

living in the country and willing to reunify with their relatives abroad must demonstrate sufficient and stable means of subsistence for the whole family. What is more, adequate housing is also required to accommodate the whole family, as well as sickness insurance. Such restrictions, which are in place in other countries as well, make access to family reunification increasingly difficult (Kofman, 2018). In a similar vein, within the broader frame of actions put in place to tackle fraudulent applications for family reunification and marriages of convenience, the length of the probational period following family reunification – that is, the time reunified migrants 'must remain registered in the address of their partner' (Orsini et al., 2022, p. 162) – was extended from three to five years in 2011.

In sum, over a few decades in Belgium, as well as elsewhere in Europe, new policies dramatically transformed the normative environment regulating migrants' lives. Through the process, family and love migration became one of the main targets of new and increasingly restrictive legislations and administrative procedures (see, e.g., Puschmann et al., 2019; Ruffer, 2011). We explore some of these policy tools in the following pages, where we concentrate on the consequences these restrictions produce on some of the more intimate aspects of migrant family and love life in Belgium.

5. Before violence begins: the (un)desired consequences of restricting access to family reunification

The decision to focus on how Belgian family reunification law contributes to the (re)production of domestic violence in a migratory context came about inductively. When Orsini started fieldwork, our initial aim was to explore how laws impact migrants' access to divorce. Yet, during the hearings at the family court, we noticed that almost all the cases which were dealt with each day involved at least one third-country national, and in many of these cases, one of the partners accused the other of domestic violence.

When asked about whether this was a frequent scenario, the judge and several of the experts contacted for this study confirmed that this was a fairly consolidated trend. As most informants indicated, since the reform of family reunification in 2011 there was an increase in the cases of migrant women who entered Belgium through family reunification and decided to divorce. As we were told, many of them explain that domestic violence was among the reasons, if not the main reason, for divorcing.

Increasingly restrictive rules governing family reunification in the country must be understood as a further institutional attempt to repress the arrival and stay of unwanted foreigners to Belgium. As highlighted by Mascia (2020), this legislative change was introduced by policymakers due to growing concerns about the integration of migrants, and because of the (alleged) upsurge of fraudulent marriages for migration purposes. As a tool of migration control (Bonizzoni, 2016), family reunification laws are thus developing in continuity with other restrictive measures characterising the contemporary (and securitised) governance of migration in Europe (Menjívar, 2014).

For this reason, the effects of measures regulating family life in the so-called country of destination must be analysed in relation to other European and Belgian migration policies. For example, the reduction in the number of visas available to third-country nationals for entering and residing in the EU (Van Houtum, 2010) interacts with the rules on family reunification. Indeed, increasingly restrictive visa requirements have reduced the availability of legal channels for migration, prompting people to seek alternative ways to pursue their migratory, love and family plans (Mai & King, 2009). In other words, fraudulent marriages could also be seen as resulting from the narrowing of legal alternatives to emigration (see, e.g., Scheel & Gutekunst, 2019; Alpes, 2017).

As for the eight migrant participants to this study, four of them admitted to having rushed their decision to marry in order to legally join their partner in Belgium. This is the case, for instance, of a thirty-year-old migrant from Mali who entered Belgium in 2012. She joined her husband, who had the chance of doing his doctoral studies at a Belgian university:

> We had been together for several years before he got this opportunity [to do his PhD in Belgium]. Even though we had known each other since we were teenagers, before he [was offered the job], we didn't really intend to get married, or to emigrate. [Well,] at least [for me to get married] was not the plan. . . . I had my own job as an accountant in the capital. . . . I wanted to keep my independence. . . . Marriage was not on my agenda. [However,] once we decided that he couldn't miss this opportunity, [we realised that] to leave all the doors open [and make sure] that I could join him in Belgium, . . . it was better to get married.

What this migrant told us was also confirmed by other women we interviewed. This is the case, for example, of an Iranian migrant who was in her thirties at the time of the interview. She went through a very similar decision-making process, although she decided to get married only once in Belgium:

> I came [to Belgium] on a tourist visa to see my sister who had migrated [to the country] years before. Once here, she introduced me to my future husband. He is also from our country, but he had arrived in Belgium years before [so that he had] a good job [and] a permanent residence permit. . . . We started seeing each other, but my [tourist visa] was expiring. I was a bit careless, but I thought I was in love with him. When he asked me to marry him, I accepted! . . . Everything happened very quickly.

Of course, rushing the decision to marry does not tell much about the authenticity of these unions. However, we can expect this to lead to less stable and more conflictual marriages – a precondition for domestic violence (Erez et al., 2009; Enriquez, 2020).

There are, however, more direct ways in which the legal provisions included in Belgian family reunification regimes contribute to destabilising migrant marriages.

Under the current laws, the sponsor must prove that they have sufficient and stable means of subsistence for the family members reunifying with them. Thus, as for most other European countries (Sarolea & Merla, 2021), access to family reunification in Belgium is granted depending on individual income. Clearly, this situation increases, and possibly exacerbates, the dependence of the reunified member of the couple on their partner. This is particularly the case considering that only the income of the sponsor is included in the calculation.

As already highlighted, this tends to aggravate tensions within families. On the one hand, the sponsor of family reunification will be burdened with additional responsibilities towards their partner and children. On the other hand, these requirements increase the precariousness experienced by the reunified member of the family: as for when the application for family reunification is filed, if these standards are not met also at the time of the renewal of the residence permit this may indeed be revoked (Sarolea & Hardy, 2017). Here is the testimony of a Tunisian migrant in her forties. She arrived in Belgium in 2013 to join her husband, who came from the same village but had already obtained the Belgian nationality:

> Of course, he had to show all the necessary proof that he had a job, and a certain salary, a house which was big enough, a health insurance. . . . When we talked via Skype, he was always very worried about this. . . . Even more since I came here. . . . He was always stressed about it, and always reminded that to me!

Moreover, depending on their partner's residence permit, foreigners who come to Belgium through family reunification might not have automatic or full access to the national labour market.[4] This can lead to their professional and socio-economic devaluation. More importantly, however, such restriction increases the dependence on the sponsor, as recalled by this Malian migrant whom we quoted also earlier:

> When I arrived, I was not allowed to work [because my husband only had a student visa], which was extremely frustrating. [He] left for university in the morning and came back . . . in the evening. I was at home alone for so long! This feeling became almost unbearable when [my husband] started to blame me for not doing anything since I arrived. . . . I was very independent, and [all of a sudden] I found myself 'begging' my husband . . . for everything, even for shopping groceries. It was humiliating.

The inability to access a (good) job can impact power relations within the couple, as one partner loses economic independence and needs to rely on the other. Un- and under-employment often also results in isolation and hinders the ability of

4 Sponsored family members of labour migrants (e.g., single permit holders) can work automatically, yet family members of students are still not allowed to work (see Sarolea & Hardy, 2017).

individuals to accumulate economic and social capital[5]. Un- and under-employed migrant women are therefore more likely to be victims of domestic violence, which is often invisible to the outside world (see, e.g., Anderberg, 2016 or Chiu, 2017).

Restrictive family reunification regimes operating within securitised migration governance systems have a profound impact on the intimate lives of migrant couples. This can be the case even before partners and families decide to leave their home country – as seen, for instance, with reference to the rushed-up marriages narrated at the beginning of this section. By establishing new and often unbalanced power relations between partners, policies can end up deteriorating romantic relationships. Having to ensure a significant income and housing for the partner and/or the whole family can turn into a source of stress which negatively impacts one's love life. Likewise, quick shifts in power relations within a couple can significantly affect one or both partners' feelings with respect to their love relationships. Whether directly or indirectly, restrictive migration and family reunification regimes may thus contribute to the (re)production of violence within migrant families.

Moreover, as the following section shows, laws, regulation and procedures applying to migrants both within and outside the framework of family reunification can also contribute to hindering the ability of foreigners to access protection after they start experiencing domestic violence. These policies often come to operate as more or less tangible boundaries (Yuval-Davis et al., 2018) which impede denouncing the violent partner and/or finding and accessing shelter and support.

6. After violence begins: formal v. actual protection

Many authors focus on migrant women's poor language skills and their substantial lack of social capital in the destination country to explain their inability to access protection services in cases of abuse or violence (see, e.g., Block, 2021; de Hart, 2017; Williams, 2010). After joining their partners, newcomers may indeed need some time to master the local language. This means that, for months or years, they have only limited or no access at all to information about institutional or non-institutional initiatives in place to protect those suffering domestic violence. Arguably, due to the same reasons, these women might also find it more difficult to report their violent spouse to the authorities if no interpretation service is available in police stations (Menjívar & Salcido, 2002; Erez, 2002).

Furthermore, newly arrived foreigners often find themselves with little or no social capital at hand. This can be explained not only by the geographical distance and the more limited contacts they have with family and friends back home, but also by the absence of a local support network (friends or others) apart from their partner (Smit, 2021), especially during the first weeks after arrival. Clearly, such

5 Social capital is a concept used to study the functioning of social groups by focusing on interpersonal relationships, a common sense of identity, shared norms and values, cooperation and reciprocity. It is a measure of the value of tangible and intangible resources and the impact of relationships on the distribution of these resources (see, e.g., Putnam, 1993).

isolation implies major difficulties for accessing support and protection in case of domestic violence (Odasso, 2019).

Language barriers and the general lack of social capital on arrival were mentioned by all interviewees among the most important obstacles they had to overcome in order to access protection in Belgium. This is even more the case when the violent partner is a 'native' – as reported by this woman from Peru:

> Who do you think the police were listening to? Me, a young [twenty-year-old] unemployed Latin American artist . . . who didn't speak a word of Flemish and only a little French . . . or . . . my husband who was a politician and grew up [in the same] neighbourhood where we lived? The authorities never really took me seriously [, and they also informed] my partner [since he] always knew if and when I reported him. . . . [In those instances, when I returned home, he] beat me even stronger. . . . I simply [stopped going] to the police, and I had nowhere else to go for finding support.

The isolation produced by poor language skills and the lack of social capital is certainly reinforced by the long probational period imposed on migrants entering Belgium through family reunification. In 2011, this period was expanded from three to five years. This legal provision imposes long-term affective relationships on persons entering Belgium in the context of family reunification (Sarolea & Merla, 2021).

The fact that the residence right of one of the partners depends on the quality of the relationship with their spouse or partner has profound and pervasive effects on the experience of family and love life abroad. For example, this precariousness can lead one partner to 'use [the other's] legal status as a form of blackmail' (Menjívar & Salcido, 2002, p. 908). Such blackmailing can discourage battered migrants from denouncing their violent partners. This is confirmed in the following extract obtained during an interview with a thirty-year-old Argentinian woman who arrived in Belgium at the end of 2012 to join her Belgian husband:

> I had never thought about this [probational] period before I came. [You're busy with] all the bureaucracy and [the last thing you think about] is whether [it] will be a problem. . . . However, since [my husband] started being violent with me, he never missed an opportunity to make me understand that I had to go back to [my home country] if I wanted to divorce him. . . . I held back so many times from leaving the house, [even though he was at] work for [most of] the day. I was also afraid because of our son, because I didn't know if he [would eventually come with me or if he should] stay here. [At that time, I didn't really know] anyone other than my husband [here in Belgium].

One of the most immediate consequences of this legal provision is that people who experience domestic violence are pushed not to report it to the authorities. The fear of losing their residence permit (Jacques, 2015) leads many to wait before approaching the police or social services, even when they have the help of their relatives in Belgium. The (extreme) experience of this thirty-year-old Iranian woman is illustrative:

> I went to the lawyer with my sister . . . because I had just started my French course, and I preferred to have her with me. It is then when I realised that, if I left [me and my husband's] house, I would have lost my residence permit. So, I decided to resist and, after five years, I received my permanent residence permit and divorced from him. . . . I never saw him again!

The implementation of the probational period conflicts with the state's obligation to protect all victims of domestic violence. For this reason, in Belgium, like in other countries, the revocation of the residence permit can be blocked if the family member can prove to have suffered domestic violence from the partner who sponsored their migration (Hennebry et al., 2019).

According to a social worker in charge of coordinating the activities of non-profit organisations in Flanders, however, this firewall protection is often ineffective. At the time of the interview, this practitioner had been working for more than twenty years with migrants suffering from domestic violence. She explains:

> Domestic violence is always difficult to prove for several reasons. [In general,] the cases are hardly ever accompanied by solid evidence, and it seems to me that migrant women have to face additional difficulties. [When we assist them], our clients and their lawyers tell us that judges often doubt the veracity of their allegations. . . . They think that these women just want to get rid of their husbands and [keep the right to] stay in the country!

The concern expressed by the social worker was confirmed by the interviewed migrants, as well as in the observations made at the Belgian family court. Indeed, there seems to be a conflict between restrictive family reunification policies and the protection of migrants suffering domestic violence. Within such tension, the Belgian judicial system may privilege one logic – migration control – at the expense of the other – the protection of those suffering domestic violence. These tensions are reinforced by the fact that, even if a judge determines that domestic violence has occurred, the decision on whether to grant a new residence permit rests with the Immigration Office, a federal administrative body (Mascia, 2020).

More generally, for migrants who have entered Belgium through family reunification, the right to protection of the integrity of their family life is somehow subordinated to the suspicions of the authorities, whose priority is the fight against marriages of convenience (Sarolea & Merla, 2021). A discussion with the judge that Giacomo had after one of the hearings at the family court shows in an interesting way how these security priorities can impact on judicial decisions.

The exchange with the judge focused on a divorce case between a man of African nationality and his (much older) Belgian wife. The judge explained that she was convinced that it was a 'grey marriage'.[6] As she explained, she found it difficult to assess cases involving non-Europeans. First of all, as she said, judges often do not have enough evidence in hand to make their decision. She pointed out that it is indeed often difficult for litigants of, as she said, 'certain nationalities' to collect authentic official documents. This substantial lack of evidence led her to make a number of assumptions which, as shown from other works (see, e.g., Charsley & Benson, 2012; Infantino, 2014), all depart from a normative understanding of what a 'true/genuine' marriage should be.

For example, she made it clear that 'white marriages [are quite] popular [and] frequent . . . among sub-Saharan Africans'. She mentioned the existence of a local illegal industry dedicated to organising white marriages between Belgian citizens of African origin and migrant African women. She therefore believes that she is usually confronted with a fraudulent marriage when she sees a Belgian man marrying a much younger immigrant woman from Africa or Asia. According to her, grey marriages are more frequent when an African or Latin American man is married to a much older Belgian woman.

In short, as seen in the case of this judge and her family tribunal, security concerns may lead the Belgian judicial system to make decisions on the basis of a constellation of assumptions and stereotypes (racist and/or sexist) that can hamper the ability of migrants to access justice and effective protection. Repressive measures regulating family reunification are at odds with the effective protection of migrants' most fundamental rights.

7. Beyond culture: securitising migration versus the protection of migrants' fundamental rights

The legal provisions in/directly governing family reunification in Belgium have important effects on the intimate lives of migrants. In very general terms, restrictions complicate their love and family life insofar as they reshape power relations between partners (D'Aoust, 2013). As we have seen throughout this chapter, this is the case at different points in the migration trajectory, before and after marriage, and before as well as after violence begins to occur.

The consequences that security-centred migration policies have on the daily love lives of migrants are profound. While they may contribute to the (re)production of domestic violence, they also reduce the ability of victims to access adequate protection and to report their violent partners.

Despite the relatively limited scope of this study, the rules and restrictions on family reunification seem to have produced very similar effects for all interviewees. The cultural background of the perpetrator or the victim of violence seemed to

6 A 'grey marriage' refers to a situation where one partner marries a person in order to obtain a legal residence permit without informing that person – who thus becomes a victim of a fraudulent marriage application. This type of marriage is to be distinguished from 'white marriages', which occur when both partners agree to marry in order for one of them to obtain a new residence permit.

play little role. This appears even more obvious if we consider the different nationalities of the migrant participants.

As we gave centrality to the voices of battered migrants, they described the violence they had been subjected to as the result of the very strict legal conditions imposed on foreigners wishing to settle and live in Belgium. Nevertheless, despite their precariousness, all of them resisted and ultimately overcame this violence by demonstrating an exceptional ability to move forward in an often-hostile Belgian protection system.

The biographies of our migrant research participants counter common views on the (lack of) agency of battered migrants. Especially migrant women are often (re) produced in public discourses and by policies – but also within the academia – as powerless victims of their violent partners (Dutton & Nicholls, 2005). However, the few stories we collected show that, against all the hurdles, these migrants retained their ability to navigate across exceptionally tough life conditions by resisting the violence of both their partners and the institutions (Rajah & Osborn, 2022).

As in other areas of migration governance in Europe – such as border management (see, e.g., Orsini, 2016 or Vollmer, 2019) – securitised policies often result in an experience of insecurity for migrants. In sum, there seems to be an irreconcilable tension between controlling migrants as threats and dangers to the destination society, and effectively protecting migrants' safety and their fundamental rights.

References

Alpes, M. J. (2017). Marriage at the Embassy: Securing the EurAfrican Border in Cameroon. In P. Gaibazzi, S. Dünnwald, & A. Bellagamba (Eds.), *EurAfrican Borders and Migration Management: Political Cultures, Contested Spaces, and Ordinary Lives* (pp. 181–195). Palgrave Macmillan. https://doi.org/10.1057/978-1-349-94972-4_8

Anderberg, D., Rainer, H., Wadsworth, J., & Wilson, T. (2016). Unemployment and domestic violence: Theory and evidence. *The Economic Journal*, *126*(597), 1947–1979. https://doi.org/10.1111/ecoj.12246

Bhabha, H. K. (1994). *The Location of Culture*. Routledge.

Bhuyan, R., & Bragg, B. (2021). Epistemologies of bordering: Domestic violence advocacy with marriage migrants in the shadow of deportation. *Migration Studies*, *9*(2), 159–178. https://doi.org/10.1093/migration/mnz025

Block, L. (2021). "(Im-)proper" members with "(im-)proper" families? Framing spousal migration policies in Germany. *Journal of Ethnic and Migration Studies*, *47*(2), 379–396. https://doi.org/10.1080/1369183X.2019.1625132

Bonizzoni, P. (2016). Policing the Intimate Borders of the Nation: A Review of Recent Trends in Family-Related Forms of Immigration Control. In J. Mulholland, N. Montagna, & E. Sanders-McDonagh (Eds.), *Gendering Nationalism: Intersections of Nation, Gender and Sexuality in the 21st Century* (pp. 223–239). Palgrave Macmillan. https://doi.org/10.1007/978-3-319-76699-7_12

Bui, H. N., & Morash, M. (1999). Domestic violence in the Vietnamese immigrant community: An exploratory study. *Violence Against Women*, *5*(7), 769–795. https://doi.org/10.1177/10778019922181473

Charsley, K., & Benson, M. (2012). Marriages of convenience, and inconvenient marriages: Regulating spousal migration to Britain. *Journal of Immigration, Asylum and Nationality Law*, *26*(1), 10–26.

Chiu, T. Y. (2017). Marriage migration as a multifaceted system: The intersectionality of intimate partner violence in cross-border marriages. *Violence Against Women, 23*(11), 1293–1313. https://doi.org/10.1177/1077801216659940

Clibborn, S., & Wright, C. F. (2020). COVID-19 and the policy-induced vulnerabilities of temporary migrant workers in Australia. *Journal of Australian Political Economy, 85*, 62–70.

Dahinden, J., Fischer, C., & Menet, J. (2021). Knowledge production, reflexivity, and the use of categories in migration studies: Tackling challenges in the field. *Ethnic and Racial Studies, 44*(4), 535–554. https://doi.org/10.1080/01419870.2020.1752926

D'Aoust, A. M. (2013). In the name of love: Marriage migration, governmentality, and technologies of love. *International Political Sociology, 7*(3), 258–274. https://doi.org/10.1111/ips.12022

De Cleen, B., Zienkowski, J., Smets, K., Dekie, A., & Vandevoordt, R. (2017). Constructing the "Refugee Crisis" in Flanders: Continuities and Adaptations of Discourses on Asylum and Migration. In M. Barlai, B. Fähnrich, C. Griessler, & M. Rhomberg (Eds.), *The Migrant Crisis: European Perspectives and National Discourses* (pp. 59–78). LIT Verlag.

de Hart, B. (2017). The Europeanization of love: The marriage of convenience in European migration law. *European Journal of Migration and Law, 19*(3), 281–306. https://doi.org/10.1163/15718166-12340010

Depraetere, J., Vandeviver, C., Vander Beken, T., & Keygnaert, I. (2020). Big boys don't cry: A critical interpretive synthesis of male sexual victimization. *Trauma, Violence, & Abuse, 21*(5), 991–1010. https://doi.org/10.1177/1524838018816979

De Schrijver, L., Vander Beken, T., Krahé, B., & Keygnaert, I. (2018). Prevalence of sexual violence in migrants, applicants for international protection, and refugees in Europe: A critical interpretive synthesis of the evidence. *International Journal of Environmental Research and Public Health, 15*(9), 1979–1996. https://doi.org/10.3390/ijerph15091979

Djajic, S. (2014). Guest-worker programs. *CESifo DICE Report, 12*(2), 16–19.

Dutton, D. G., & Nicholls, T. L. (2005). The gender paradigm in domestic violence research and theory: Part 1 – the conflict of theory and data. *Aggression and Violent Behavior, 10*(6), 680–714. https://doi.org/10.1016/j.avb.2005.02.001

Enriquez, L. E. (2020). *Of Love and Papers: How Immigration Policy Affects Romance and Family*. University of California Press. https://doi.org/10.1525/luminos.88

Erez, E. (2002). Migration/immigration, domestic violence and the justice system. *International Journal of Comparative and Applied Criminal Justice, 26*(2), 277–299. https://doi.org/10.1080/01924036.2002.9678692

Erez, E., Adelman, M., & Gregory, C. (2009). Intersections of immigration and domestic violence: Voices of battered immigrant women. *Feminist Criminology, 4*(1), 32–56. https://doi.org/10.1177/1557085108325413

Flick, U. (2004). Triangulation in Qualitative Research. In U. Flick, E. von Kardoff, & I. Steinke (Eds.), *A Companion to Qualitative Research* (pp. 178–183). Sage. https://doi.org/10.4135/9781529716634

Gikandi, S. (2004). Poststructuralism and Postcolonial Discourse. In N. Lazarus (Ed.), *The Cambridge Companion to Postcolonial Literary Studies* (pp. 97–119). Cambridge University Press. https://doi.org/10.1017/CCOL0521826942.006

Goldman, M. (1999). The violence against women act: Meeting its goals in protecting battered immigrant women. *Family and Conciliation Courts Review, 37*, 375–392. https://doi.org/10.1111/j.174-1617.1999.tb01311.x

Gsir, S., Lafleur, J. M., & Stanek, M. (2016). Migration policy reforms in the context of economic and political crises: The case of Belgium. *Journal of Ethnic and Migration Studies, 42*(10), 1651–1669. https://doi.org/10.1080/1369183X.2016.1162352

Hennebry, J. L., & Petrozziello, A. J. (2019). Closing the gap? Gender and the global compacts for migration and refugees. *International Migration, 57*(6), 115–138. https://doi.org/10.1111/imig.12640

Infantino, F. (2014). Bordering "fake" marriages? The everyday practices of control at the consulates of Belgium, France and Italy in Casablanca. *Etnografia e ricerca qualitativa, 7*(1), 27–48. https://doi.org/10.3240/76246

Jacques, J. P. (2015). La double victimisation des personnes étrangères victimes de violence conjugale en Belgique. *Revue de l'Institut de Sociologie, 85*, 69–84.

Kelly, L., & Westmorland, N. (2016). Naming and defining "domestic violence": Lessons from research with violent men. *Feminist Review, 112*(1), 113–127. https://doi.org/10.1057/fr.2015.52

Keygnaert, I., & Guieu, A. (2015). What the eye does not see: A critical interpretive synthesis of European Union policies addressing sexual violence in vulnerable migrants. *Reproductive Health Matters, 23*(46), 45–55. https://doi.org/10.1016/j.rhm.2015.11.002

Kofman, E. (2018). Family migration as a class matter. *International Migration, 56*(4), 33–46. https://doi.org/10.1111/imig.12433

Lazaridis, G. (2011). *Security, Insecurity and Migration in Europe*. Routledge. https://doi.org/10.4324/9781315608150

Mai, N., & King, R. (2009). Love, sexuality and migration: Mapping the issue(s). *Mobilities, 4*(3), 295–307. https://doi.org/10.1080/17450100903195318

Maneri, M., & Quassoli, F. (2016). Humanity and security under siege. European discursive politics on immigration and asylum. *Dijalog, 1–2*(1), 69–81. https://doi.org/10.5644/DIJALOG.2016.1-2.06

Martinello, M., & Rea, A. (2013). *Une brève histoire de l'immigration en Belgique*. Fédération Wallonie-Bruxelles.

Mascia, C. (2020). How bureaucracies shape access to rights: The implementation of family reunification in Belgium. *Journal of Ethnic and Migration Studies, 47*(9), 2127–2143. https://doi.org/10.1080/1369183X.2020.1726734

Mayblin, L., & Turner, J. (2021). *Migration Studies and Colonialism*. Polity Press.

Md Said, M. H. B., & Emmanuel Kaka, G. (2023). Domestic violence in cross-border marriages: A systematic review. *Trauma, Violence Abuse, 24*(3), 1483–1502. https://doi.org/10.1177/15248380221074321

Menjívar, C. (2014). Immigration law beyond borders: Externalizing and internalizing border controls in an era of securitization. *Annual Review of Law and Social Science, 10*, 353–369. https://doi.org/10.1146/annurev-lawsocsci-110413-030842

Menjívar, C., & Salcido, O. (2002). Immigrant women and domestic violence: Common experiences in different countries. *Gender & Society, 16*(6), 898–920. https://doi.org/10.1177/089124302237894

Narayan, U. (1995). "Male order" bribes: Immigrant women domestic violence and immigration law. *Hypatia, 10*(1), 104–119. https://doi.org/10.1111/j.1527-2001.1995.tb01355.x

Odasso, L. (2019). Des «mariages noirs» Les violences conjugales et le contrôle de la migration familiale en Belgique. *Recherches Familiales*, (1), 87–101. https://doi.org/10.3917/rf.016.0087

Orsini, G. (2016). Securitization as a source of insecurity: A ground-level look at the functioning of Europe's external border in Lampedusa. *Studies in Ethnicity and Nationalism, 16*(1), 135–147. https://doi.org/10.1111/sena.12170

Orsini, G., Smit, S., Farcy, J.-B., & Merla, L. (2022). Institutional racism within the securitization of migration: The case of family reunification in Belgium. *Ethnic and Racial Studies, 45*(1), 153–172. https://doi.org/10.1080/01419870.2021.1878249

Ozcurumez, S., Akyuz, S., & Bradby, H. (2021). The conceptualization problem in research and responses to sexual and gender-based violence in forced migration. *Journal of Gender Studies, 30*(1), 66–78. https://doi.org/10.1080/09589236.2020.1730163

Papadakaki, M., Ratsika, N., Pelekidou, L., Halbmayr, B., Kouta, C., Lainpelto, K., Solinc, M., Apostolidou, Z., Christodoulou, J., Kohont, A., Lainpelto, J., Pithara, C., Zobnina, A., & Chliaoutakis, J. (2021). Migrant domestic workers' experiences of sexual harassment: A qualitative study in four EU countries. *Sexes, 2*(3), 272–292. https://doi.org/10.3390/sexes2030022

Puschmann, P., Sundin, E., De Coninck, D., & d'Haenens, L. (2019). Migration and Integration Policy in Europe: Comparing Belgium and Sweden. In L. d'Haenens, J. Willem, & F. Heinderyckx (Eds.), *Images of Immigrants and Refugees in Western Europe: Media Representations, Public Opinion and Refugees' Experiences* (pp. 21–36). Leuven University Press.

Putnam, R. D. (1993). The prosperous community: Social capital and public life. *American Prospects*, *4*(13), 35–42.

Rai, A., & Choi, Y. J. (2018). Socio-cultural risk factors impacting domestic violence among South Asian immigrant women: A scoping review. *Aggression and Violent Behavior*, *38*, 76–85. https://doi.org/10.1016/j.avb.2017.12.001

Raj, A., & Silverman, J. (2002). Violence against immigrant women – the roles of culture, context, and legal immigrant status on intimate partner violence. *Violence Against Women*, *8*(2), 67–98. https://doi.org/10.1177/10778010222183107

Rajah, V., & Osborn, M. (2022). Understanding women's resistance to intimate partner violence: A scoping review. *Trauma, Violence Abuse*, *23*(5), 1373–1387. https://doi.org/10.1177/1524838019897345

Razack, S. (1998). *Looking White People in the Eyes*. Toronto University Press.

Riaño, Y. (2013). "He's the Swiss Citizen, I'm the Foreign Spouse": Binational Marriages and the Impact of Family-Related Migration Policies on Gender Relations. In A. Kraler, E. Kofman, M. Kohli, & C. Scholl (Eds.), *Gender, Generations and the Family in International Migration* (pp. 265–283). Amsterdam University Press. https://doi.org/10.1515/9789048513611

Romero, M. (2008). Crossing the immigration and race border: A critical race theory approach to immigration studies. *Contemporary Justice Review*, *11*(1), 23–37. https://doi.org/10.1080/10282580701850371

Ruffer, G. B. (2011). Pushed beyond recognition? The liberality of family reunification policies in the EU. *Journal of Ethnic and Migration Studies*, *37*(6), 935–951. https://doi.org/10.1080/1369183X.2011.576196

Sarolea, S., & Hardy, J. (2017). *Family Reunification with Third Country National Sponsors in Belgium*. EMN Belgium.

Sarolea, S., & Merla, L. (2021). Migrantes et sédentaires: Des familles ontologiquement différentes? In L. Merla, S. Sarolea, & B. Schoumaker (Eds.), *Composer avec les normes: Trajectoires de vie et agentivité des migrants face au cadre légal* (pp. 259–292). Academia-L'Harmattan S. A.

Scheel, S., & Gutekunst, M. (2019). Studying marriage migration to Europe from below: Informal practices of government, border struggles and multiple entanglements. *Gender, Place & Culture*, *26*(6), 847–867. https://doi.org/10.1080/0966369X.2018.1489375

Scheibelhofer, P. (2014). Integrating the Patriarch? Constructs of Migrant Masculinity in Times of Managing Migration and Integration. In F. Anthias & M. Pajnik (Eds.), *Contesting Integration, Engendering Migration* (pp. 185–201). Palgrave Macmillan. https://doi.org/10.1057/9781137294005_10

Smit, S. (2021). (Re)construire sa carrière professionnelle et trouver sa place dans le pays de destination: Expériences de femmes migrantes "dépendantes " et qualifiées en Belgique. In L. Merla, S. Sarolea, & B. Schoumaker (Eds.), *Composer avec les normes: Trajectoires de vie et agentivité des migrants face au cadre légal* (pp. 201–220). Academia-L'Harmattan S. A.

Stalker, P. (2002). Migration trends and migration policy in Europe. *International Migration*, *40*(5), 151–179. https://doi.org/10.1111/1468-2435.00215

Stoyanova, V. (2019). On the bride's side? Victims of domestic violence and their residence rights under EU and Council of Europe law. *Netherlands Quarterly of Human Rights*, *37*(4), 311–335. https://doi.org/10.1177/0924051919884756

Sumiya, F. M. (2018). Origin culture and domestic violence against Bangladeshi immigrant women in Southern California. *Migration and Development*, *7*(2), 282–297. https://doi.org/10.1080/21632324.2017.1373445

Tallis, B. (2022). Operationalising the borderscape: Making sense of proliferating (in) securities and (im)mobilities. *International Politics*, *59*(3), 410–427. https://doi.org/10.1057/s41311-021-00280-w

Thambinathan, V., & Kinsella, E. A. (2021). Decolonizing methodologies in qualitative research: Creating spaces for transformative praxis. *International Journal of Qualitative Methods*, *20*, 1–9. https://doi.org/10.1177/16094069211014766

Tudor, A. (2022). Ascriptions of migration: Racism, migratism and Brexit. *European Journal of Cultural Studies*, 1–9. https://doi.org/10.1177/13675494221101642

Van Houtum, H. (2010). Human blacklisting: The global apartheid of the EU's external border regime. *Environment and Planning D: Society and Space*, *28*(6), 957–976. https://doi.org/10.1068/d1909

Vollmer, B. A. (2019). The paradox of border security – an example from the UK. *Political Geography*, *71*, 1–9. https://doi.org/10.1016/j.polgeo.2019.01.016

Williams, L. (2010). *Global Marriage: Cross-Border Marriage Migration in Global Context*. Palgrave Macmillan. https://doi.org/10.1057/9780230283022_5

Williamson, E., Gregory, A., Abrahams, H., Aghtaie, N., Walker, S. J., & Hester, M. (2020). Secondary trauma: Emotional safety in sensitive research. *Journal of Academic Ethics*, *18*, 55–70. https://doi.org/10.1007/s10805-019-09348-y

Yick, A. G. (2007). Role of culture and context: Ethical issues in research with Asian Americans and immigrants in intimate violence. *Journal of Family Violence*, *22*(5), 277–285. https://doi.org/10.1007/s10896-007-9079-x

Yuval-Davis, N., Wemyss, G., & Cassidy, K. (2018). Everyday bordering, belonging and the reorientation of British immigration legislation. *Sociology*, *52*(2), 228–244. https://doi.org/10.1177/0038038517702599

Index

Page numbers in *italics* indicate figures; page numbers in **bold** indicate tables.

For Product Safety Concerns and Information please contact our EU
representative GPSR@taylorandfrancis.com
Taylor & Francis Verlag GmbH, Kaufingerstraße 24, 80331 München, Germany

www.ingramcontent.com/pod-product-compliance
Ingram Content Group UK Ltd.
Pitfield, Milton Keynes, MK11 3LW, UK
UKHW020155200926
475702UK00016B/2715
* 9 7 8 1 0 3 2 8 3 6 4 4 7 *